Arabic for

Nerds one

Fill The Gaps

270 Questions About
Arabic Grammar

Expanded and Revised
First Edition

by
Gerald Drißner

Gerald Drißner (Drissner),

born 1977 in a mountain village in Austria, is an economist and award-winning journalist. He has been living in the Middle East and North Africa for ten years, where he has intensively studied Arabic.

He is the author of *Islam for Nerds* (500 Questions and Answers) and *Arabic for Nerds 2* (450 Questions and Answers).

IMPRINT/IMPRESSUM – Arabic for Nerds 1

1st edition (expanded and revised); October 2015 (250922)

Copyright © 2015 by Gerald Drißner (Drissner)

Cover design, layout: © 2015 by Gerald Drißner

Publisher:	pochemuchka (Gerald Drißner)
Internet:	https://pochemuchka-books.com
E-Mail:	comment@pochemuchka-books.com
Address:	Postfach 35 03 30, D-10212 Berlin, Germany
ISBN-13:	978-3-9819848-7-3 (Paperback)
ISBN-13:	978-3-9819848-2-8 (Hardcover)

For my love
who hates grammar

ARABIC FOR NERDS ONE

Acknowledgements

This book consumed huge amount of work, research and dedication. I would like to express my gratitude to the many people who saw me through this book; to all those who taught me Arabic and allowed me to quote their remarks.

I would like to thank

Michael Guggenheimer
for his numerous comments which I am going to miss.

Judith Zepter, in Hamburg,
for her profound and helpful remarks.

Badrul Aini Sha'ari, in Kuala Lumpur,
for his valuable comments.

Kenan Kalajdzic, in Sarajevo,
for his thorough reading and insightful suggestions.

Above all, I want to thank
my wife
who supported and encouraged me
in spite of all the time it took me away from her.

Introduction

A: كَيْفَ الْحال؟

B: دائِمًا مَنْصُوب !

(A joke shared among Arabic grammar nerds.)

The cover picture was taken when I started to fall in love with Arabic. It happened in 2009 in Egypt after my first lesson with مصطفى حميدة, a highly esteemed professor at the University of Alexandria. When I showed it to my friends at home in Austria, they thought of mathematics or physics – as there are a lot of arrows and arithmetic signs.

This is what Arabic is all about, patterns and structures. If you want to feel the beauty and strength of the Arabic language, you have to understand its inner logic. I used to play chess at a young age and master players told me that I have to study pawn structures and patterns – and not opening moves. I guess it is quite the same with Arabic.

I have been collecting interesting facts about grammar, vocabulary and expressions, hints and traps for almost ten years. Now, I have compiled them to a book: *Arabic for Nerds*.

This book should fill a gap. There are plenty of books about Arabic for beginners and some for intermediate students but it is difficult to find good material on the advanced level.

Which leads us to the question: What is advanced?

If your mother tongue is English, it is said that you need 700 hours (of instruction) to become fluent in French, German, Spanish, Danish or Swahili. You need 1400 hours for Greek, Hindi, Russian or Urdu. And you need 2800 hours if you want to reach the level *advanced high* in Japanese, Korean, Chinese – and Arabic.

This book is suitable for you if you have been studying Arabic intensively for at least two years. You have a sound knowledge of vocabulary (around 3000 words) and know about tenses, verb moods and plurals.

During my studies in the Middle East and North Africa, I met students from Europe and the USA. They all shared a similar experience: They studied Arabic the same way they had learned German, English, French or Spanish – by using the grammar terms and syntax they knew from their native language. This only works in some cases. However, it will definitely make it difficult to achieve an advanced level in Arabic – because you won't get the feeling how this fascinating Semitic language works.

When I decided to study Arabic, I wanted to study it the Arab way. I realized that Arabic grammar is actually much easier than German grammar – but only if you use the Arabic terms. If you read German books on Arabic grammar, you need a Latin dictionary and eventually get frustrated.

I was happy to find an old Arabic teacher who couldn't speak English. I avoided translating words. English has a word for nearly everything. In Arabic, a single word can mean dozens of things depending on the context. Arabic is a poetic language but have you ever felt its poetic core?

Let us look at the word دُنْيا: It is translated in books as *world*. The meaning is correct but if you have a closer look, you will understand that it is not a good idea to focus on translations too much (see *question #147*).

This book doesn't teach you vocabulary, nor are there exercises. This book explains how Arabic works and gives you hints in using and understanding the language better. Since most of the Arabic words are given in translation, you should be able to read this book without a dictionary.

I used تَشْكِيلٌ, diacritical marks, for the correct pronunciation wherever it is necessary – especially when dealing with cases and moods. Before the feminine ending ة ـ, I do not write the short vowel "a" because by definition it must be either the vowel "a" (فَتْحَة) or Aleph (ا), a so-called أَلِفٌ ساكِنة, like in the words فَتاة (*young girl*), مُجاراة (*conformity*) or قُضاة (*judges*). I also mix English and Arabic. I hope you don't mind the strange combination sometimes.

Many Arabic grammar terms can't be translated precisely. For this reason, I use as many options as possible now and then. Sometimes I use the definite, sometimes the indefinite Arabic grammar term, though I may use different forms in the English text.

Since there are already a lot of points in the Arabic alphabet I sometimes don't follow the correct English punctuation (e.g., full stops or commas) to make it easier for the reader.

This book isn't scientific, nor academic. I consider this book a working paper which will constantly be updated, expanded, and revised. I am sure there are inaccuracies as I have a mere practical view.

If you spot mistakes, have ideas or corrections, please kindly let me know by e-mail: *comment@pochemuchka-books.com*

Berlin, October 2015

1. What is the secret of Arabic vowels?

Even if you don't have a clue about the meaning of a word, you can get a hunch – simply by looking at its final vowel.

Arabic is like a mathematical game. You take the root of a word, which normally consists of three letters, and you start playing. Your tools are pre- and suffixes, three vowels, and a marker of silence (anti-vowel).

The vowels at the end of words are essential for understanding the inner meaning and logic of Arabic. If you think about the pronunciation and how this influences the rhythm, you will improve your understanding of a sentence. You will also get a better feeling for الْإِعْرابُ, i.e., case and mood markers.

Let's examine the **main (final) sounds** in Arabic. Note that we use the term *mood* for verbs and *case* for nouns.

u	ضَمّةٌ	The regular ending. Endings in *"u"* mark normal situations and **essential things**. Words ending in ضَمّةٌ are independent and not influenced by other words. In grammar, we use the term مَرْفُوعٌ. It comes from the root-verb رَفَعَ which denotes: *to raise; to place; to take off/to start; to pronounce the final consonant with "u"*. It appears in **nouns** (إِسْمٌ) and **verbs** (فِعْلٌ). Closest meaning in English grammar: *nominative* (nouns) or *indicative* (verbs).
a	فَتْحةٌ	The term فَتْحةٌ comes from the root *to open*. The vowel *"a"* is an open vowel and used for situations of installing, setting up; also for appointing things (نَصْبٌ). In grammar, we use the term مَنْصُوبٌ which literally means *set up, installed*. The فَتْحةٌ at the end of a **noun** enriches a sentence with **additional information**; it

		unfolds the action. It is like a supplement of information (e.g., the object of a verb). The مَنْصُوبٌ-**mood** indicates that a **verb** is used in the context of intention, permission, purpose, expectation, necessity, or possibility. Technically (semantically) speaking, you need the مَنْصُوبٌ-mood after particles such as أَنْ (indicating an action not yet realized) or لَنْ (= *will not*). It occurs in **nouns** and **verbs**. Closest meaning in English: *accusative* (nouns) or *subjunctive* (verbs).
i	كَسْرَةٌ	The vowel "*i*" requires the lips to be stretched way out to the sides. At the end of a noun it marks situations of reduction, dragging, and causing (جَرٌّ) and sets up a dependency in meaning; e.g., after a preposition or the second part of a إِضَافَةٌ-construction. We use the term مَجْرُورٌ which means *dragged* or *pulled*. We can say that the كَسْرَةٌ specifies and coordinates information. You can <u>only</u> find it at the end of **nouns** (اِسْمٌ). Closest English term: *genitive*.
-	سُكُونٌ	Quiescence: mark of silence or anti-vowel (سُكُونٌ). It is an indication that you don't deal with a standard situation – but with a **command, an interdiction, or a conditional meaning**. This mood marker is only used with **verbs**. You mark this mood by cutting the verb's ending (جَزْمٌ). If the last root letter is weak (حَرْفُ الْعِلّةِ), i.e., و or ي, the weak letter will drop if you have to put a سُكُونٌ at the end. In grammar, we use the term مَجْزُومٌ. It literally means *cut short; clipped*. In English, you may use the term *jussive mood* (verbs) or *apocopate*. The term *jussive* relates to the Latin word *jubeō: to order, to command*. It occurs in **verbs** <u>only</u>.

Some remarks: I strongly recommend using the Arabic grammar terms. In this book, I occasionally use Latin terms just to give readers (who aren't familiar with the Arabic terms) a hint. There is one big advantage. Most people have no clue what the Latin grammar terms actually mean. Arabic grammar terms, however, are Arabic words with a meaning (see *question #154*).

Therefore, always try to translate grammar term literally.

It will help you to remember the terms. You will also develop a better idea of the grammar concept. If you use the Arabic terms, Arabic grammar will eventually become a lot easier. For example, verbs or nouns can be مَنْصُوبٌ in Arabic.

- If a **noun** has the مَنْصُوبٌ-ending "*a*", then it might be the *direct object.* Thus, the noun takes the *accusative case.* See example 1 in the table below.

- If a verb has the مَنْصُوبٌ-ending, we may deal with an interpreted infinitive (مَصْدَرٌ مُؤَوَّلٌ) molded by أَنْ plus verb. The Latin grammar term for this situation is *subjunctive mood.* See example 2.

Forget these complicated Latin terms! There is a reason why Arabic uses the same term (مَنْصُوبٌ) for both ideas (verbs and nouns).

A فَتْحةٌ at the end of a word enriches a sentence with **additional information, it unfolds the action.**

I want a book. (*A book* is what **I want.**)	أُرِيدُ كِتابًا.	1
I want to read a book. (*To read a book* is what **I want.**)	أُرِيدُ أَنْ أَقْرَأَ كِتابًا.	2

2. How many roots does the Arabic language have?

Mathematically: 21,952 roots. Practically, you get 6,332 roots.

There are many Arabic dictionaries. *Hans Wehr's Arabisches Wörterbuch für die Schriftsprache der Gegenwart* (named after a German scholar, published in 1952) is the most complete dictionary of **Standard Arabic** ever published in the West. It contains **2967** roots (جِذْرٌ) with 3 letters and 362 with 4 letters.

The most famous dictionary of **Classical Arabic** is *Lisān al-'Arab* (لِسان الْعَرَب), compiled by Ibn Manzūr (ابْن مَنْظُور) in the early 14th century (711 AH). It contains around 80,000 entries and in total **9273** roots (including foreign words).

Since the Arabic alphabet consists of 28 letters (consonant phonemes) there are **21,952** theoretical combinations (= 28^3) of roots with <u>three</u> radicals. However, certain combinations are considered to be impossible (with few exceptions):

- There is <u>no</u> Arabic root which consists of **three identical** consonants.

- There are <u>no</u> Arabic roots with **identical** consonants in the **first** and **second** position.

- There are (almost) <u>no</u> Arabic roots with identical consonants in the **first** and **third** position. An exception would be قَلِقَ which means *to be troubled*.

- However, there <u>are</u> roots whose **second** and **third** letters are **identical**, for example, *to pass* (م-ر-ر).

Taking into account all possible restrictions, the theoretical number of all possible combinations of roots (morphemes) with three letters is **6332**[1].

---

[1] *Gustav Herdan* (1962): "The Patterning of Semitic Verbal Roots Subjected to Combinatory Analysis"

Remark: What are the most common root letters?

In *Hans Wehr*, the most common root letter is ر (722 times). The ظ is the least common, only 42 times (1.4 %). The ن is the most common first radical (235 times).

3. Which letters can you add to a root?

There are only ten.

Almost every Arabic word (except proper nouns and foreign words) has a root that consists of three or four letters, so-called radicals. In Arabic, a radical is called حَرْفٌ أَصْلِيٌّ. The word أَصْلِيّ means *original* or *authentic*.

It is easy to identify a root (جِذْر) as there are **only ten letters** in Arabic which can be added to a root. These letters are called حُرُوفُ الزِّيادةِ:

Hamza (ء-أ-ئ-ؤ), *Mīm* (م), *Aleph* (ا-ى), *Nūn* (ن),
Wāw (و), *Tā'* (ت), *Sīn* (س), *Hā'* (ـه), *Yā'* (ي), *Lām* (ل)

Talking about **verbs**, you can only add **five** extra letters:

أ - ت - س - ن - ا

You can remember them easily because they can be summed up in phrases. For example:

- سَأَلْتُمُونِيهَا – literally: *you (pl.) asked me it (that).*
- أمانٌ وتَسْهيلٌ – *safety and convenience*

Remark: سَأَلْتُمُونِيهَا is a weird phrase. Let's do a quick analysis:

سَأَلْتُم	و	ن	ي	ها
Verb; past tense	This is a وَاوُ لِلإِشْـبَاع (*Wāw of satiation*) ; it helps to lengthen the ضَمّةٌ ("*u*") to become و. Such extra و is added to كُم or تُم when they are followed by another pronoun, resulting in تُمُو.	*Guarding or preventive Nūn* (النُّونُ لِلْوقاية); it prevents the final vowel of the verb from being absorbed by the long vowel "*ee/ii*".	1ˢᵗ direct object (مَفْعُولٌ بِهِ أَوَّلٌ)	2ⁿᵈ direct object (مَفْعُولٌ بِهِ ثانٍ)

4. Letters without dots - Does it work?

It did, a long time ago.

In the beginning of the Arabic language, Arabic was written without vowel signs above or under letters.

Furthermore, letters were written **without dots** which makes reading pretty difficult. The letters ف and ق as well as the letters ب and ن and ي might look the same in certain situations. Try to read the following sentence without the dots:

فىل اں فىل فىل فىل فىل الـهر

This sentence can denote several meanings. It depends on where and how you add the dots, e.g., the first word can mean:

killed	قَتَلَ		before	قَبْلَ		elephant	فِيل

This is how you could read the sentence:

| It was said that the elephant killed an elephant in front of the river. | قيل إن فيل قتل فيل قبل النهر. |
| This is the sentence with all the vowels. | قِيلَ إِنَّ فِيلًا قَتَلَ فِيلًا قَبْلَ النَّهْرِ. |

5. Who was the first Arabic grammar expert?

The first Arabic grammar expert was Abū al-'Aswad al-Du'alī (أَبُو الْأَسْوَد الدُّؤَلِيّ; *603 – 688).*

He converted to Islam during the time of the Islamic prophet Muhammad and later migrated to Basra (which is in present-day Iraq) where a mosque is named after him. When more and more people converted to Islam, many of them couldn't read the Qur'an without making mistakes which led to a misunderstanding of words. The use of pronounced endings (إِعْرَابٌ) had died out by around 600 from spoken Arabic.

Muslim tradition credits Abū al-'Aswad al-Du'alī with the first efforts to codify Arabic in an attempt to stop the corruption of speech. Although many of the anecdotes about him are legendary, he is said to be the inventor of the first vowel signs and markers of nunation (تَنْوِينٌ). He used dots.

Remark: In the 8th century, a grammarian from present-day Oman invented a writing system which we basically use in Standard Arabic until today. His name was al-Khalīl ibn 'Ahmad al-Farāhīdī (الْخَلِيل بِن أَحْمَد الْفَرَاهِيدِيّ).It is said that he started using a small س for the شَدَّةٌ (*Shadda*): ّ

He also compiled the first Arabic dictionary (كِتَابُ الْعَيْنِ).

6. What does the word نَحْوٌ mean?

*It has many meanings: direction; way; manner, fashion; corresponding to; similar to; like – but also: **grammar**!*

The English term *grammar* is derived from Greek γραμματική τέχνη (grammatikē technē), which means *art of letters*. The Arabic term نَحْوٌ follows a different idea. In old grammar books, نَحْوٌ was used to show people a *way* or *manner* (of how people speak). In his famous book الْكِتَابُ, the pioneer of Arabic grammar, Sībawayhi (سيبويه), used to term نَحْوٌ 1118 times. Later, it also acquired the meaning of *for example*. Hence, what we call *grammar* (syntax) was in ancient times just a way to show people how Arabic works.

نَحْوٌ is a tricky word. It is the مَصْدَرٌ of the I-verb نَحَا / يَنْحُو (*to move toward*); therefore, it is a **noun** (اِسْمٌ) and can be used in several ways. Some examples:

A	adverbial accusative of place	ظَرْفُ الْمَكَانِ

Now it is getting complicated. In Arabic, we don't have the word **type** "adverb". Words can only have the **function** of an adverb. In Arabic, an adverb of place is an <u>object</u> (مَفْعُولٌ فِيهِ). This is the reason for the accusative marker "a" (فَتْحَةٌ). So we arrive at نَحْوَ. It only gets one فَتْحَةٌ because it serves as the first part of a إِضَافَةٌ. The second part gets the genitive case (مَجْرُورٌ) and tells you the actual place. نَحْوَ conveys the meaning of *towards, in the direction of*. Note that نَحْوَ is often synonymous with صَوْبَ.

B	placed after a preposition

If you connect نَحْو with a **true preposition** (حَرْفُ الْجَرِّ), then نَحْو is treated as a normal, <u>declinable noun</u> (اِسْمٌ). In other words, نَحْو gets regular case endings. Since it is placed after a preposition, نَحْو gets the genitive case (مَجْرُورٌ). For example: بِنَحْوِ

C	used with numbers; then it conveys the meaning of *about, approximately.* It is the first part of a إِضافة ; the case marker depends on the position in the sentence.

He came to (towards) us.	أَتَى نَحْوَنا.	A

نَحْوَ is in the position of a ظَرْفٌ (*adverb of place*). It gives us information about the direction that is related to the action of *to come.*

around five o'clock...	... فِي نَحْوِ السَّاعةِ الْخامِسةِ	B
in this way...	... عَلَى هذا النَّحْوِ	

We have prepositions (فِي, عَلَى) involved. نَحْو gets the usual treatment of a noun (اِسْمٌ) in such positions. It is dragged into the genitive (مَجْرُورٌ) by the preposition as you can see by the "*i*" (كَسْرةٌ).

approximately eleven years...	... نَحْوُ أَحَدَ عَشَرَ عامًا	C
about four thousand men...	... نَحْوُ أَرْبَعةِ آلافِ رَجُلٍ	
I read about ten books.	قَرَأْتُ نَحْوَ عَشَرةِ كُتُبٍ.	

In the last example, نَحْوَ is the **direct** object (مَفْعُولٌ بِه) of *to read.*

7. How many vowels does Arabic know?

The number of vowels varies with the different forms of dialects.

A vowel is a sound that is made without constriction of the air flow from the lungs. In English, the letters A, E, I, O, and U are called vowels. They can be pronounced in different ways; English is considered to have at least 14 vowel *sounds.*

Standard Arabic contains **three short vowels** (a, i, u) which are marked **by signs** and not by letters. They are interpreted as vowel *sounds*. Whether a ضَمَّةٌ sounds more like *"u"* or *"o"* depends on how dominant the consonant (which carries the vowel sign) is. Letters like ط or ص are dominant and may make a vowel sound deeper and more voluminous.

What about **long vowels**? In Arabic, they are called *extended letters* (حُرُوفُ الْمَدِّ). Therefore, a long vowel is, in fact, just a lengthening of the preceding sound, i.e., *"a"*, *"i"*, or *"u"*. Long vowels can only be produced by و and ي which both are treated as **(semi-)consonants** or semivowels. The letter ا (Aleph) is a special – see *question #9*.

For example, the long vowel ī is composed of a كَسْرةٌ (*"i"*) under the preceding letter plus ي with سُكُونٌ which all together results in the lengthening or prolongation of the preceding sound. This is what we are talking about:

long A	أَلِفُ مَدٍّ	a + a = "aa"	ـَـا
long I	ياءُ مَدٍّ	i + y = "ii"	ـِيْ
long U	واوُ مَدٍّ	u + w = "uu"	ـُوْ

8. Can an Arabic word start with a vowel?

No, it can't.

There is a golden rule in Arabic:

> Every Arabic utterance or sentence has to
> **start** with a **consonant** followed by a **vowel**.

Standard Arabic forbids initial consonant clusters and more than two consecutive consonants in other positions. **If you see**

- the definite article الـ like in the word الْكِتابُ
- an imperative like اُكْتُبْ (*write!*)
- the Arabic word for *son* (اِبْنٌ) or *name* (اِسْمٌ)

… at the beginning of an utterance or in isolation, then the first sound coming out of your mouth has to be a هَمْزةٌ, a so-called glottal stop.

The glottal stop exists in English or German too, but it is not written. It is phonetically a catch in the throat by holding one's breath and suddenly releasing it. The word *little* is an example in colloquial English. If you don't pronounce the *"tt"*, it will sound like *"li'le"*. *Spiegel-Ei* is an example of a German word with a glottal stop (which is pronounced where the dash is).

9. Why is the letter ا (Aleph) special?

Because it can never be part of the root.

There are three letters in Arabic that often cause difficulties:

1	ي	2	و	3	ا

These three letters are called *weak* letters (حُرُوفُ الْعِلّةِ). The word عِلّةٌ means *defect, illness*. Especially the Aleph (أَلِفٌ) is tricky. Three rules will help us to deal with it.

RULE I: An Aleph can never be part of the root.

If you see an Aleph (ا), you can be sure that it is not a root letter. It was originally و or ي which changed its form to ا.

If you want to identify the root of a verb, you should check the present tense (اَلْمُضَارِعُ). For example: to call (دَعَا / يَدْعُو ←) the root is د-ع-و. At the end of a past tense verb, the Aleph is usually written as ى like in to throw (رَمَى / يَرْمِي). You only write ا when the third root letter is و like in the example above.

Watch out: Notice the difference between the ا (long vowel) and the Hamza (هَمْزَةٌ), the glottal stop, in the shape of an Aleph (أ). Let's take, for example, the verb to point at: أَدَّى إِلَى. Here, the Aleph is a real هَمْزَةٌ, only written in the shape of an Aleph with a small هَمْزَةٌ on top. The root is ء - د - و.

RULE II: The special letter آ is called اَلْمَدّةُ. It denotes the sign over Aleph that indicates a Hamza followed by long "aa".

First of all, don't mix it up with the Aleph that works as a long vowel "aa" (أَلِفُ مَدٍّ) and which is written as ا + ◌َ

آ is a **combination of two letters**. One of them is هَمْزَةٌ, the other is Aleph. Since we want to avoid two ا ا in a row, we use the letter آ. There are several positions in which it may occur:

meaning	example		construction	
traces, effects	آثَارٌ	أَاثَارٌ	ا + أ	1
rewards	مُكافآتٌ	مُكافأَةٌ	ا + أ	2
Qur'an	قُرْآنٌ	قُرْأَانٌ	ا + أ	3
to believe	آمَنَ	أَأْمَنَ	أ + أ	4
This is form IV (أَفْعَلَ) of the ا-verb أَمُنَ (to be faithful; reliable). Watch out: The ا-verb (أَمِنَ) with كَسْرَةٌ means to be safe.				

- In #1, two letters were merged (أ plus إ). This is the standard situation as آ usually occurs at the **beginning**.
- In #2, we produced آ as we moved from **singular** to a sound feminine **plural** (جَمْعٌ مُؤَنَّثٌ سالِمٌ). So أ+ا+تٌ = آتٌ
- In #3, we can see that آ may occur in the **middle of a word**.
- In #4, **two Hamzas** collided.

What about the **pronunciation** of آ? You have to pronounce the letter آ (all together) as a **glottal stop plus long "aa"**. And the correct pronunciation matters! Notice the difference in the following two examples:

meaning	explanation	root	
tragedies	This is the plural of مَأْساةٌ (*tragedy*).	ء - س - و	مآسٍ
diamonds	This is a collective noun (إسْمُ جِنْسٍ جَمْعِيٌّ), a *quasi-plural*.	proper noun	ماسٌّ
To express *a single diamond* (unit noun), you add a ة resulting in ماسَةٌ. This is similar to *apples* (تُفّاحٌ) and *one apple* (تُفّاحَةٌ).			

RULE III: An Aleph can't start an utterance.

If you see an ا at the beginning of a word, you need to watch out. You only pronounce it as a glottal stop if it marks the beginning of a sentence or utterance. Otherwise, it is just there to facilitate the pronunciation. In other word, you need to decide whether it is ا or أ.

هَمْزَةُ الْوَصْلِ	هَمْزَةُ الْقَطْعِ
Hamza of liaison; connecting Hamza	*Hamza of rupture; cutting Hamza*

Written as ٱ or أ or إ. Although it looks like an Aleph, it is in fact a هَمْزَةٌ.	Always written with a small هَمْزَة on top = أ. It is cemented.
Only treated as a **consonant** (هَمْزَة) when it marks the **beginning** of an utterance.	Always treated as a **consonant**.
Only pronounced as a glottal stop if it marks the **beginning** of an utterance. Otherwise, it is **not pronounced**. However, you need a **helping vowel** in the preceding word in order to ignore the هَمْزَةُ الْوَصْلِ.	**Always** pronounced as a **glottal stop**.

Examples

هَمْزَةُ الْوَصْلِ		هَمْزَةُ الْقَطْعِ	
He got in touch. Past tense of the VIII-verb	اتَّصَلَ	*I write.* أ occurs in the first person singular ("I") at the beginning of a present tense verb.	أَكْتُبُ
		bigger/biggest; comparative or superlative form (elative)	أَكْبَر
definite article	ال	personal pronoun *you*	أَنْتَ
son	إبْنٌ	مَصْدَرٌ-pattern of a IV-verb. E.g: (إرْسالٌ) *sending* ← يُرْسِلُ / أَرْسَلَ	إفْعالٌ

The هَمْزَةُ الْوَصْلِ is a *joining* or *elidable* Aleph. It is inserted to avoid a cluster of two consonants. The ٱ precedes the initial double consonant and becomes an essential component of the word like in إبْنٌ as you can't pronounce بْنٌ (bnun).

The ٱ is a silent sign that is written as ٱ. The tiny symbol resembles a ص which stands for صِلَة, literally: *connection*.

The following verb patterns in the *imperative* (أَمْرٌ), *past tense* (مَاضٍ) as well as their respective *infinitives* (مَصْدَرٌ) start with a هَمْزَةُ الْوَصْلِ. Depending on the position of the word in a sentence, the ا is pronounced as a glottal stop or not at all.

verb form	مَصْدَر	past tense
VII	اِنْفِعالٌ	اِنْفَعَلَ
VIII	اِفْتِعالٌ	اِفْتَعَلَ
IX	اِفْعِلالٌ	اِفْعَلَّ
X	اِسْتِفْعالٌ	اِسْتَفْعَلَ

If the هَمْزَةُ الْوَصْلِ is preceded by وَ or فَ, you don't pronounce the letter ا at all. Let's take the verb *to get away* (اِنْصَرَفَ) and insert وَ or فَ. How do you pronounce it then? You say: *"wansarafa"* (وَاْنْصَرَفَ) and *"fansarafa"* (فَاْنْصَرَفَ).

10. What is a weak letter?

The letters ي, و, and ا which may get dropped or transformed.

Both و and ي, if part of a root, are called *weak* or *defective* letters (حَرْفُ الْعِلّةِ). We call them defective because **both letters accept to be changed** in certain situations. All other Arabic letters are cemented. Practically speaking, و and ي complicate Arabic grammar as they sometimes have to be deleted or changed into a different letter.

A verb containing a weak letter is called فِعْلٌ مُعْتَلٌّ (*defective* verb). There are several types of weak verbs:

1	**Quasi-sound verb:** و or ي as the first root letter.	فِعْلٌ مِثالٌ

Often translated as *assimilated verb*. Two things are important:

1. Initial ي – you apply the **standard** rules. ي stays in the present tense (الْمُضارِعُ). *to give up all hope:* يَئِسَ → يَيْئِسُ or يَيْأَسُ

2. Initial و – the و **drops**. *to bury alive:* وَأَدَ → يَئِدُ

verb	passive p.	active p.	مَصْدَرٌ	مَنْصُوبٌ	مَجْزُومٌ	present	past t.
to arrive	مَوْصُولٌ	واصِلٌ	وُصُولٌ	يَصِلَ	يَصِلْ	يَصِلُ	وَصَلَ
to be sure	مَيْقُونٌ	ياقِن	يَقْنٌ	يَيْقَنَ	يَيْقَنْ	يَيْقَنُ	يَقِنَ

2	**Hollow verb:** و or ي as second root letter (middle).	فِعْلٌ أَجْوَفُ

to say	مَقُولٌ	قائِلٌ	قَوْلٌ	يَقُولَ	يَقُلْ	يَقُولُ	قالَ

3	**Defective verb:** و or a ي as last root letter.	فِعْلٌ ناقِصٌ

Note: The term فِعْلٌ ناقِصٌ may also denote a verb that needs a predicate to express a complete meaning. For example: *to be* (كانَ).

to call	مَدْعُوٌّ	داعٍ	دُعاءٌ	يَدْعُوَ	يَدْعُ	يَدْعُو	دَعا

4	**Doubly weak verb:** Two weak letters in the root.	فِعْلٌ لَفِيفٌ

to grill	مَشْوِيٌّ	شاوٍ	شَيٌّ	يَشْوِيَ	يَشْوِ	يَشْوِي	شَوَى
to fulfill	مَوْفِيٌّ	وافٍ	وَفاءٌ	يَفِيَ	يَفِ	يَفِي	وَفَى
to shelter	مَأْوِيٌّ	آوٍ	أَوِيٌّ	يَأْوِيَ	يَأْوِ	يَأْوِي	أَوَى
	Very tricky: two weak root letters plus هَمْزَةٌ.						

11. When does ‍ا or ى or ي cause massive trouble?

When they appear at the end of a word.

Arabic is a language that follows simple rules - unless you see one of the following three endings:

اء	ي	ا or ى (Aleph)

Once again, it's the weak letters (حَرْفُ عِلَّةٍ) that cause trouble.

Let's examine the three troublemakers in Arabic nouns.

اِسْمٌ مَمْدُودٌ		اِسْمٌ مَنْقُوصٌ		اِسْمٌ مَقْصُورٌ	
final اء		final ي-		final ا or ى	
the extended		*the incomplete*		*the shortened (Aleph)*	
Noun with **extended** ending		Noun with **curtailed** ending; ends in mandatory ي		Noun with **shortened** ending "a"; ends in mandatory Aleph	
desert	صَحْراءُ	*the judge*	الْقَاضِي	*stick*	عَصًا
red	حَمْراءُ	*the club*	النَّادِي	*young man*	فَتًى

In all three groups, we deal with **nouns** (اِسْمٌ). This has nothing to do with verbs (قَضَى - *to perform*) or prepositions (إِلَى).

These endings play a big role when you...

- ...want to إِعْرابٌ words (put case and mood endings according to the position of words in the sentence);

- ...need to form the <u>dual</u> (الْمُثَنَّى) or <u>plural</u> (الْجَمْعُ).

   Note: We will examine that in the following *questions*.

12. How do you say *his colleagues*? زُمَلاءه or زُمَلاؤُه, زُمَلائه؟

All of them are correct.

How is that possible? Well, it depends on the function and position of the word in the sentence, in short: on the necessary **case ending**. We have to deal with a noun with an extended ending (اِسْمٌ مَمْدُودٌ). What is it made of?

pronoun			plural	col-leagues	←	singular	colleague
ه	his	+	زُمَلاءُ			زَمِيلٌ	

Now, let's check all three possibilities:

1	*his colleagues*	زُمَلاؤُهُ
	subject (مُبْتَدَأٌ or فاعِلٌ)	nominative (مَرْفُوعٌ)
	His colleagues came.	جاءَ زُمَلاؤُهُ.

2	*his colleagues*	زُمَلاءَهُ
	direct object (مَفْعُولٌ بِهِ)	accusative (مَنْصُوبٌ)
	I met his colleagues.	قابَلْتُ زُمَلاءَهُ.

3	*his colleagues*	زُمَلائِهِ
	After a preposition (a) or placed as the 2nd part of a إضافةٌ-construction (b).	genitive (مَجْرُورٌ)

a	I took the books from his colleagues.	أَخَذْتُ الْكُتُبَ مِن زُمَلائِهِ.
b	his colleagues' house (the house of his colleagues)	بَيْتُ زُمَلائِهِ

13. أَلِفٌ مَقْصُورَةٌ - What is so special about this Aleph?

It is an Aleph in the shape of ى producing a long "aa".

Many Arabic words, which have a final Aleph, are written with this **hybrid Aleph,** e.g., *to come* (أَتَى). The أَلِفٌ مَقْصُورَةٌ looks like a dotless ي → ى . This device isn't a letter of the Arabic alphabet. It only occurs at the end of a word and is always preceded by فَتْحةٌ, i.e., the short vowel "a".

What's the idea? مَقْصُورٌ means *limited; shortened.* Such ى serves to complete the preceding vowel فَتْحةٌ at the **end** of a word. It may appear as a substitute for the extension letter ا, however, the أَلِفٌ مَقْصُورَةٌ terminates the word. As a result, **no further letter can be added after ى** which is why it is sometimes pronounced shorter than a long "aa" in the middle of a word. For more details, see *Arabic for Nerds 2, #40.* Some examples:

until	حَتَّى	*to come*	أَتَى	*hospital*	مُسْتَشْفًى
upon	عَلَى	*boy*	فَتًى	*to finish*	إنْتَهَى

- ى is only used at the end of words; never at the beginning, nor in the middle.
- ى is also found in names: عِيسَى (*Jesus*), مُوسَى (*Moses*), لَيْلَى (*Laila*).
- If you add a suffix after ى, a regular Aleph (ا) will take its place. E.g.: مُوسِيقَى (*music*) becomes مُوسِيقاهُ (*his music*).
- Verbs with ى in the past-tense (sing., masc.) will generally take ي (with dots!) for the same person in the present tense: غَنَّى (*he sang*) and يُغَنِّي (*he sings*).
- The opposite happens with ي in the past tense (sing., m.). Such verbs get ى in the present: نَسِيَ (*he forgot*) and يَنْسَى (*he forgets*) or بَقِيَ (*he stayed*) and يَبْقَى (*he stays*).

- When a verb ending with ى gets a suffix, it will turn into ا similar to nouns. E.g.: to protect (حَمَى). May Allah protect you (حَمَاكَ اللَّهُ). However, in prepositions (حَرْفُ الْجَرِّ) like إِلَى and عَلَى, the ى becomes ي. E.g.: to him (إِلَيْهِ). Why? Because a حَرْف never changes its shape! It is **fossilized**.

How do we know when to write ى in **verbs**? Such ى is called a *permanent Aleph* (أَلِفٌ لَازِمَةٌ) because it belongs to the root. Wait! But the Aleph can't be part of the root! Yes, that's true. What we mean is that the Aleph is **not additional**; it disguises its real character. The **3rd root letter** determines the shape:

final Aleph		3rd root letter	root	example	
أَلِفٌ مَقْصُورَةٌ	ى ←	ي	ر-م-ي يَرْمِي	رَمَى	to throw
أَلِفٌ طَوِيلَةٌ	ا	و	د-ع-و يَدْعُو	دَعَا	to call

- Not every Aleph is the same! Sometimes the Aleph is just a **case marker** and <u>not</u> part of the root.

I met Abu Bakr.	قَابَلْتُ أَبَا بَكْرٍ.
In the example, the Aleph of أَبَا is **not part of the root**. It marks the مَنْصُوبٌ-case (direct object, accusative case) of *father* (أَبٌ).	

- When ي and ى collide, ى becomes a standard ا. We run into this situation in the **feminine** form of the **comparative/superlative** (اسْمُ التَّفْضِيلِ) and some **plural** patterns.

		plural	singular
higher	عُلْيَى	عُلَى	عُلْيَا
world	دُنْيَى	دُنَى	دُنْيَا
gifts	هَدَايَى	هَدَايَا	هَدِيَّةٌ

with "instead of" between the two tables.

Since particles and prepositions (حَرْفٌ) never change, let's focus on the interesting stuff: the أَلِفٌ مَقْصُورَةٌ which is found in **nouns** (اِسْمٌ). We will see that sometimes ى changes into ا.

أَلِفٌ at the **third** position?		sound feminine plural (جَمْعُ الْمُؤَنَّثِ السّالِمُ)	dual (الْمُثَنَّى)	word	root
yes	**و** is part of the root. The أَلِف changes into **و**.	عَصَواتٌ sticks	عَصَوانِ two sticks	عَصًا *asan* stick	ع-ص-و
		Note: The feminine plural is a common option for the plural of عَصًا. But there are other plural forms too: عِصِيٌّ or أَعْصٍ or عُصِيٌّ.			
yes	**ى** is part of the root.	فَتَياتٌ girls	فَتَيانِ two boys	فَتًى *fatan* boy	ف-ت-ي
		فَتَياتٌ is the plural of *girl* (فَتاةٌ).			
no	---	كُبْرَياتٌ bigger things	كُبْرَيانِ *two bigger*	كُبْرَى *kubrā* bigger	ك-ب-ر
		Note: If not part of the root, the ى usually marks the feminine form (أَلِفُ التَّأْنِيثِ الْمَقْصُورَةُ).			

What happened? In the <u>dual</u>, the ى changes into its original form (i.e., ي or و). In the <u>sound feminine plural</u>, the ى becomes ي before the suffix ات-

Question: In our examples, would it be possible that the Aleph is an *extended Aleph* (أَلِفٌ مَمْدُودَةٌ)? No!

An *extended Aleph* is **extra** (أَلِفٌ زَائِدَةٌ) and **never belongs** to the root. It is followed by a Hamza (هَمْزَةٌ). The أَلِفٌ مَقْصُورَةٌ, however, is usually part of the root (unless it marks the feminine form). Let's take the Arabic word for *friends*: أَصْدِقَاءُ. The root is ص-د-ق, the Aleph is extra and not part of the root!

Extended, **long** Aleph	أَلِفٌ مَمْدُودَةٌ
Shortened, confined Aleph	أَلِفٌ مَقْصُورَةٌ

Regarding case endings, a اِسْمٌ مَقْصُورٌ gets **virtual** (estimated, assumed) **case markers**. We call that الْإِعْرَابُ الْمُقَدَّرُ. We **cannot** put the usual **visual case endings** on the ى. The root ق-ص-ر means *to be or become short*; but it may also convey *to lock up; to confine* like in قَصْرٌ which means *castle*. Some scholars, e.g., Ibn Mālik (ابْن مالِك), suggested that this may be a reason for the grammar term. Due to their **inner confinement**, words with أَلِفٌ مَقْصُورَةٌ cannot get case endings (لِأَنَّهُ مَحْبُوسٌ عَنِ الْمَدِّ أَوْ عَنْ ظُهورِ الْإِعْرابِ).

Now let's move to the **sound masculine plural** (جَمْعُ الْمُذَكَّرِ السَّالِمُ). For our analysis we use the word أَعْلَى. It is a comparative/superlative (اِسْمُ التَّفْضِيلِ) and means *higher (highest)*.

explanation	masculine plural	root	
You have to delete the أَلِفٌ and add سُكُونٌ on top of و.	أَعْلَوْنَ	ع-ل-و	أَعْلَى
What is the correct pronunciation of أَعْلَوْنَ? It is *'a3lawna* and not: *'a3lūna*.	أَعْلَيْنَ → genitive (مَجْرُورٌ) or accusative (مَنْصُوبٌ)		

What about the تَنْوِينٌ (*nunation*)? In other words, which case markers should we use if the word is **indefinite** (نَكِرَةٌ)? **Nothing changes in any case!** In the following examples the case marker in الْفَتَى is not shown. We say that we use a *hidden, es-*

timated marker, also called *presumptive marker* (مُقَدَّرة). Therefore, the word ends in ى (or let's say: it stays the same) **in all three cases!** Furthermore, the pronunciation doesn't change either. It is *"al-Fata"* in all three cases. This is because the last letter is actually Aleph (أَلِفٌ) and not ي!

The young boy came.	جاءَ الْفَتَى.	1
I met the young boy.	قابَلْتُ الْفَتَى.	2
I greeted the young boy.	سَلَّمْتُ عَلَى الْفَتَى.	3

Subject (فاعِلٌ) of the verbal sentence. Thus, it gets the nominative case (مَرْفُوعٌ). However, we can only mark it by a virtual, assumed case marker (مَرْفُوعٌ بِضَمَّةٍ مُقَدَّرةٍ).	1	
Direct object (مَفْعُولٌ بِهِ) of the verb *to meet*. It would need the marker of the accusative case (مَنْصُوبٌ). But we can't put the appropriate marker. We can only use virtual markers (مَنْصُوبٌ بِفَتْحةٍ مُقَدَّرةٍ).	2	الْفَتَى
Prepositional phrase (الْجارُّ وَالْمَجْرُورُ). The preposition drags الْفَتَى into the genitive (مَجْرُورٌ). Regarding its place value, this is correct. Visually, however, we cannot mark it as such – we use virtual markers (مَجْرُور بِكَسْرةٍ مُقَدَّرةٍ).	3	

14. رَأْي and الْقاضِي - Same ending, same problem?

No, we have to deal with different grammatical problems.

رَأْيٌ denotes *(an) opinion;* الْقاضِي expresses *the judge.*

As a general rule, always watch out if you see the letter ي (the original ي with two dots) at the end of a word. It may affect three things: case ending (تَنْوِينٌ), dual, and plural form.

Before we start our analysis, let's focus on an important grammar term: إِسْمٌ مَنْقُوصٌ. We could translate it as *noun with curtailed ending*. The word مَنْقُوصٌ denotes *reduced; deficient; insufficient* and is the passive participle (إِسْمُ الْمَفْعُولِ) of of the I-verb نَقَصَ / يَنْقُصُ (*to curtail; to lack*).

How can we identify the إِسْمٌ مَنْقُوصٌ? It is easy.

> A إِسْمٌ مَنْقُوصٌ ends in a permanent ي - preceded by the vowel "i" (كَسْرَةٌ). For example: الْقَاضِي
>
> In Arabic, we would say: يُخْتَمُ بِياءٍ لازِمةٍ قَبْلُها كَسْرَة

But that doesn't mean that every word ending in ي is a إِسْمٌ مَنْقُوصٌ. **Let us sum up the conditions for a إِسْمٌ مَنْقُوصٌ:**

1. The word must be capable of getting visible **case endings.** We say that it is a *declinable* noun (إِسْمٌ مُعْرَبٌ). Therefore, words like الَّذِي (relative pronoun meaning *which*) cannot be a إِسْمٌ مَنْقُوصٌ. Words like الَّذِي are *indeclinable/cemented* (مَبْنِيٌّ).

2. The ي must be **part of the root** (ياءٌ لازمةٌ).

3. There is **no** شَدّةٌ above the ي.

4. The **vowel** before the ي has to be كَسْرَةٌ - not سُكُونٌ.

The numbers in the table indicate which condition is violated.

	grammar term; explanation	إِسْمٌ مَنْقُوصٌ؟	example, meaning	
4	It is a regular noun (إِسْمٌ). The ي is not preceded by كَسْرَةٌ.	NO	*opinion*	رَأْي
3; 2	*Nisba* adjective (نِسْبةٌ)	NO	*Egyptian*	مِصْرِيٌّ

> Note: Any Arabic noun (اِسْمٌ) can be turned into an adjective (صِفَةٌ) by adding the ي of relation. Grammarians call such words اِسْمٌ مَنْسُوبٌ (relative noun) or نِسْبَة. Notice the شَدَّة on ي! A Nisba is used to indicate the affiliation to a noun.

Here we go! This is a اِسْمٌ مَنْقُوصٌ.	**YES**	*the judge*	الْقَاضِي

| 3 | The passive participle (اِسـمُ الْمَفْعُولِ) of I-verb بَنَى / يَبْنِي. | NO | *built* | مَبْنِيٌّ |

So far, so good. But what's the problem with the اِسْمٌ مَنْقُوصٌ؟ Answer: It is not always necessary to write ي! Let us see why and check all possible situations.

1. **Keep** the ي → in the <u>dual</u> and the <u>feminine</u> plural.

a messenger; delivery boy	ساعٍ	indefinite
the messenger; the delivery boy	السَّاعِي	definite
the two delivery boys	السَّاعِيانِ السَّاعِيَيْنِ	**dual**
the delivery boys	السَّاعِياتُ	**feminine plural**

2. **Delete** the ي → if it is a sound <u>masculine</u> plural.

a lawyer	مُحامٍ	indefinite
the lawyer	الْمُحامِي	definite
the lawyers	الْمُحامُونَ الْمُحامِينَ	**masculine plural**

Notice the difference between the pronunciation of the last letter in the dual and the masculine plural: السَّاعِيانِ ("*i*"; dual) and الْمُحامُونَ ("*a*"; plural). Now comes the exciting part. What about the case endings?

A. The word functions as the **subject** (فاعِلٌ or مُبْتَدَأٌ). This means that it needs to be in the nominative case (مَرْفُوعٌ).

explanation	case marker	example	
The judge came.	We can't put the standard case marker. We can only assign virtual case endings (مَرْفُوعٌ بِضَمَّةٍ مُقَدَّرةٍ).	جاءَ الْقاضِي.	1
The judge of the city came.		جاءَ قاضِي الْمَدِينةِ.	
A judge came.	Since we can't put a visible ضَمّةٌ on قاضٍ, we say that it is in the nominative case by a virtual ضَمّةٌ.	جاءَ قاضٍ.	2

Fine, but on which letter? On the <u>deleted</u> ي! In Arabic, we say: ضَمّةٌ مُقَدَّرةٌ عَلَى الْياءِ الْمَحْذُوفةِ. Acoustically, you say what is written under ضٍ (="*in*"). According to its **place and function**, قاضٍ is in the location of a **nominative case** although you cannot see that.

B. The word functions as the **direct object** (مَفْعُولٌ بِهِ). This means that it needs to be in the accusative case (مَنْصُوبٌ). In this situation, it is business as usual: the **standard rules** apply.

explanation	case marker	example	
I met **the** judge.	Here you <u>can</u> put the appropriate case marker (مَنْصُوبٌ بِفَتْحةٍ ظاهِرةٍ).	قابَلْتُ الْقاضِيَ.	1
I met **the** judge of the city.		قابَلْتُ قاضِيَ الْمَدِينةِ.	

If you mark the word according to its position in the sentence, you put the ending "a" (فَتْحَةٌ). This is possible here. That is why *the judge* is pronounced with final "a" ("-ya").	

I met a judge.	If the word in the accusative case is **indefinite** (نَكِرَةٌ), you also apply the regular case markers (مَنْصُوبٌ بِفَتْحَةٍ ظاهِرَةٍ): "an".	قابَلْتُ قاضِيًا.	2

C. The word comes **after a preposition** (حَرْفُ جَرٍّ). This means that it needs to be in the genitive case (مَجْرُورٌ).

explanation	case marker	example	
I greeted **the** judge.	We can't use regular case markers. We have to apply virtual case endings for the genitive case (مَجْـرُورٌ بِكَسْرِةٍ مُقَدَّرِةٍ).	سَلَّمْتُ عَلَى الْقاضِيْ.	1
I greeted **the** judge of the city.		سَلَّمْتُ عَلَى قاضِي الْمَدِينِةِ.	

How do you pronounce الْقاضِي? You say what is written: "i". Watch out: The ي has no case marker! (no كَسْرَةٌ under ي).	

I greeted **a** judge.	Same as above: We use virtual case markers for the genitive case (مَجْرُورٌ بِكَسْرِةٍ مُقَدَّرِةٍ).	سَلَّمْتُ عَلَى قاضٍ.	2

Stop! Why do we use virtual markers when we pronounce the ending as "-in" which looks like the usual ending for an indefinite word in the genitive case? Well, the ending is pronounced "in" – but this is **not the real** and **actual case marker**! Don't be confused. Yes, there are two كَسْرَة-signs which looks like nunation (تَنْوِينٌ). But don't forget that the ي was deleted! Thus, the ending cannot be under the last letter. Instead, we have to say that we used a virtual case marker under the deleted letter ي!

Note: For a detailed discussion about the nature of the اِسْمٌ مَنْقُوصٌ, why you can't use certain case markers, and why the ي may get dropped, see *Arabic for Nerds 2*, question #40.

To sum it all up:

You only pronounce the real and appropriate case marker...

... if the اِسْمٌ مَنْقُوصٌ is in the accusative case (مَنْصُوبٌ)!

indefinite, مَنْصُوبٌ	"qaadiyan"	قَاضِيًا
definite, مَنْصُوبٌ	"qaadiya"	الْقَاضِيَ

15. Are there words that look the same in all cases?

Yes, there are.

Let us take a word that is based on a tricky root. Roots that have a weak letter (و or ي) in the third position are always good for a headache. For example:

meaning	plural	singular	root
meaning	مَعَانٍ	مَعْنًى	ع-ن-ي
effort	مَسَاعٍ	مَسْعًى	س-ع-ي

Words like مَعْنًى or مَسْعًى are a اِسْمٌ مَقْصُورٌ. They are unique in one thing. They look the same in all three cases!

case	indefinite	definite
nominative (مَرْفُوعٌ)	مَعْنًى	الْمَعْنَى
genitive (مَجْرُورٌ)	مَعْنًى	الْمَعْنَى
accusative (مَنْصُوبٌ)	مَعْنًى	الْمَعْنَى

Other examples:

meaning	example	root	
level; (indefinite)	مُسْتَوًى	*to be equal*	س-و-ي
villages (plural)	قُرًى	*to receive hospitably*	ق-ر-ي
given; passive participle (اِسْمُ الْمَفْعُولِ) of أَعْطَى	مُعْطًى	to give; IV-verb أَعْطَى	ع-ط-و

Some people say that مَعْنًى is indeclinable as it does not receive case endings. If we only look at what we see and hear,
you may come to this conclusion.

Grammatically, however, this is not correct. مَعْنًى is a **declinable noun** (اِسْمٌ مُعْرَبٌ) and as every noun, it gets case
endings. However, the shape of مَعْنًى **prevents the appearance
of any signs** of declension (case markers) on the last letter because they could not be pronounced (التَّعَذُّرُ). That's why we
need to use virtual case endings. For example, we may say that
مَعْنًى is nominative by virtual markers on the Aleph (مَرْفُوعٌ
بِالضَّمَّةِ الْمُقَدَّرَةِ عَلَى الْأَلِفِ).

Excursus: What is the pattern of مَعْنًى? The regular infinitive (الْمَصْدَرُ الْأَصْلِيُّ) is عَنْيٌ or عِنَايَةٌ. The word مَعْنًى follows
the pattern مَفْعَلٌ. This is a multipurpose pattern in Arabic and
used to form the noun of place (اِسْمُ الْمَكَانِ) or time (اِسْمُ

الزَّمانِ) to denote the place or time when the action occurs. But that is not what we have here. The pattern مَفْعَلٌ is also used for a special type of the مَصْدَر, the so-called مَصْدَرٌ مِيمِيٌّ. For more details see question #76.

16. سَماءٌ - How did the هَمْزَة get into this word?

It has to do with the last root letter: the و.

سَماءٌ means *sky*. In dictionaries, it is listed under the root و-م-س. It is an ancient Semitic root that is found in Aramaic, Ugaritic, and Hebrew and finally also entered Arabic. Its original meaning is probably *high place, the uppermost*.

Some scholars assume that the verb was deducted from the noun, as the noun came before the verbal meaning which is *to be high, elevated; to be above*. In grammar, we call them *denominal verbs* – verbs derived from nouns (*see question #42*).

Let's start our discussion by applying the root letters to our word. If we do that, we will get سَمَاوٌ. Such a word would be difficult to pronounce. For that reason, و turned into ء resulting in سَماءٌ. We call such ء a *converted Hamza* (هَمْزَةٌ مَقْلُوبَةٌ). But the Hamza is the exception.

- In the *Nisba*-form (نِسْبةٌ), which is used to form adjectives (صِفةٌ), the و appears: سَماوِيٌّ. It means *heavenly*.

- This is also true in the plural which will be dealt in *#17*.

What we said here applies to many roots whose last root letter is weak (ي or و). Some examples:

- بِناءٌ (plural: أَبْنِيَةٌ) means *building*. Root: ب-ن-ي. Hence, it should be بِنايٌ . But this would be hard to pronounce.

- لِقَاءٌ (plural: لِقَاءاتٌ) means *meeting*. Root: ل-ق-ي.

Watch out: It isn't always like that. There are many Arabic words that do not use ء instead of و or ي after an Aleph – despite a difficult pronunciation. For ex.: مُتَساوٍ (*equal, similar*).

Remark: What about the **gender** of سَماءٌ? Both genders, masculine and feminine, are possible. However, most scholars treat سَماءٌ as feminine (مُؤَنَّثٌ).

17. What is the plural of the word sky (سَماءٌ)?

You have two options: سَماءاتٌ *and* سَماوَاتٌ.

We should take a step back and have a look at the singular form because this is where the key to understanding these plural forms lies. The singular form is سَماءٌ which has a tricky ending: اء. This consists of an *extended Aleph* (أَلِفٌ مَمْدُودةٌ), indicating that we need to talk about the إِسْمٌ مَمْدُودٌ.

The term مَمْدُودٌ literally means *lengthened* or *extended*. We can safely say that Arabic words ending in اء are usually a إِسْمٌ مَمْدُودٌ. We have to analyze three different situations.

Situation 1: The Hamza (ء) is part of the root (هَمْزةٌ أَصْلِيّةٌ). In this situation, the ء remains.

meaning	masculine plural*	feminine plural	dual*	root	word
construction	---	إِنْشاءاتٌ	إِنْشاءَانِ إِنْشاءَيْنِ	ن-ش-ء	إِنْشاءٌ

meaning	masculine plural	feminine plural	dual	root	word
somebody who reads a lot	قَرّاءُونَ قَرّائِينَ	---	قَرّاءَانِ قَرّاءَيْنِ	ق-ر-ء	قَرّاءٌ

* nominative (مَرْفُوعٌ) and accusative (مَنْصُوبٌ)/genitive (مَجْرُورٌ).

Situation 2: The ء is extra (هَمْزَةٌ زَائِدَةٌ).

- There is <u>no masculine</u> plural.
- All words of this pattern are **feminine**.
- The ء turns into و.

meaning	feminine plural	dual*	root	word
desert	صَحْراوَاتٌ	صَحْراوَانِ صَحْراوَيْنِ	ص-ح-ر	صَحْراءُ

* nominative (مَرْفُوعٌ) and accusative (مَنْصُوبٌ)/genitive (مَجْرُورٌ).

Note: صَحْراءُ is a *diptote* (مَمْنُوعٌ مِنَ الصَّرْفِ) and therefore, it doesn't get *nunation* (تَنْوِينٌ) → You only put one ضَمّةٌ; "u" instead of "-un".

Situation 3: The ء was originally و or ي. Then, ء **remains** or, alternatively, **turns into و.** The latter is used in the Qur'an more often.

meaning	masculine plural*	feminine plural	dual*	root	word
building	---	بِناءَاتٌ	بِناءَانِ بِناءَيْنِ	ب-ن-ي	بِناءٌ
	---	بِناوَاتٌ	بِناوَانِ بِناوَيْنِ		
runner	عَدّاءُونَ	---	عَدّاءَانِ	ع-د-و	عَدّاءٌ

	عَدّاءِينَ		عَدّاءَيْنِ		
	عَدّاوُونَ عَدّاوِينَ	---	عَدّاوَانِ عَدّاوَيْنِ		

* nominative (مَرْفُوعٌ) and accusative (مَنْصُوبٌ)/genitive (مَجْرُورٌ).

Notice the spelling of ء in the dual when عَدّاءَيْنِ takes the مَجْرُورٌ- or مَنْصُوبٌ-case. Since there is a سُكُونٌ on the letter ي of the dual ending (ـيْنِ), you should write a **separate** ء and not ئ (which is, by the way, also called *yā' chair*).

Let' see some action.

The tallest building was built in front of the club.	أُقِيمَ الْبِنَاءُ الْأَعْلَى أَمامَ النَّادِي.
The (two) tallest buildings were built in front of the (two) clubs.	أُقِيمَ الْبِنَاءَانِ = الْبِنَاوَانِ الْأَعْلَيَانِ أَمامَ النَّادِيَيْنِ.

Remark: In the Qur'an and ancient texts, the letter آ ,the مَدَّةٌ, is used to mark the sequence long vowel plus Hamza.

سُوئِلَ	أَصْدِقَاؤُهُ	يَجِيءُ	جَاءَ	سَمَاءٌ
he was asked	*his friends*	*he comes*	*he came*	*sky*

18. حَرْفُ عَطْفٍ - **What is so special about it?**

Such devices "copy" the case of the preceding word and pass it on.

عَطْفٌ literally means *sympathy; affection*. In grammar, it denotes a *letter of attraction* (حَرْفُ عَطْفٍ); a device between two words, which have the same grammatical case. In English, we'd use the term *conjunction*. I call them coordinating devices or "coupler". The most famous example is *and* (وَ). Arabic knows **ten** words that fall into that category:

but	لٰكِنْ	6	*and*	وَ	1
but rather; in fact	بَلْ	7	*even*	حَتَّى	2
or	أَمْ	8	*or*	أَوْ	3
then, thereupon	ثُمَّ	9	*so, and*	فَ	4
not	لا	10	*except*	إلّا	5

Let's now analyze a sentence to understand the finesses.

Zayd didn't come, it was rather Khālid.	مَا جَاءَ زَيْدٌ بَلْ خَالِدٌ.	7

Both زَيْدٌ and خَالِدٌ take the same case: **nominative** (مَرْفُوعٌ). *Zayd* is the **subject** (فَاعِلٌ) of the verbal sentence. بَلْ is a *conjunction* (حَرْفُ عَطْفٍ) which means that it will pass on the case of the preceding word. Therefore, the word *Khalid* is the so-called *attracted* (مَعْطُوفٌ) in the grammatical analysis. In Arabic, we would say: مَعْطُوفٌ عَلَى "خَالِد" تَابِعٌ لَهُ فِي الرَّفْعِ.

I ate all the fish, even its head.	أَكَلْتُ السَّمَكَةَ حَتَّى رَأْسَها.	2

Fish is the direct object (مَفْعُولٌ بِهِ); so it takes the **accusative case** (مَنْصُوبٌ). Since *head* has the same case, we know that in our example حَتَّى is not working as a preposition (حَرْفُ الْجَرِّ) denoting *until* because then *head* would get the genitive (مَجْرُورٌ).

Watch out for the difference!

Even with شَدّة on ن, this word expresses *but*. So what's the difference? You have to use لٰكِنَّ when a full sentence follows. This sentence has to follow the rules of إنَّ:	لٰكِنَّ

- The "subject" (اِسْمُ إِنَّ) is in the accusative case (مَنْصُوبٌ).
- The predicate (خَبَرُ إِنَّ) takes the nominative case (مَرْفُوعٌ).

In the following example, *Mustafā* starts a new sentence.

My two sisters are dark skinned, but **Mustafā's** two sisters are fair skinned.	أُخْتَايَ سَمْرَاوَانِ وَلٰكِنَّ أُخْتَيْ مُصْطَفَى شَقْرَاوَانِ.

- The pronunciation of أُخْتَايَ is *ukhtāya*. It is the dual of *sister* (أُخْتٌ) plus the possessive pronoun *my*. We have a إِضَافَةٌ-construction. When a dual serves as the first part of a إِضَافَةٌ, the dual loses the final ن of أُخْتَانِ. In the nominative, we need to keep the ا. In the two other cases, an assimilation happens: ـيْ merges with suffix ـي resulting in يَّ. For ex.: *the table of my two friends* (مَائِدَةُ صَدِيقَيَّ)
- After لٰكِنَّ the pronunciation of أُخْتَيْ is *ukhtay*. The Aleph is gone because. Why? أُخْتَيْ is the "subject" after a *sister of* إِنَّ and thus gets the accusative case (مَنْصُوبٌ).
- Remark: When a dual is the first part of a ضَافَةٌ and the second part has the article الْ, you need a helping vowel on ي. This helping vowel is always كَسْرَةٌ. For example: *I saw the two sisters of the student* (رَأَيْتُ أُخْتَيِ الطَّالِبِ).

19. شُؤُونٌ or شُئُونٌ - What is correct?

Both are correct.

Both words are the plural (جَمْعٌ) of شَأْنٌ which denotes *affair* or *matter*. In Egypt, شُئُونٌ is more common whereas in most other parts of the Arab world, شُؤُونٌ - with ء over و - is more used. ؤُو is the original form (الْأَصْلُ). So, what is the idea behind ئُو? People want to avoid two وو in a row!

20. What is the definite article ٱل made of?

It is not entirely clear.

The Arabic grammarians call the definite article أَلْ the *instrument of definition* (أَداةُ التَّعْرِيفِ). It consists of:

- The **letter** ا. This prefixed letter is a helping device, mainly to facilitate the pronunciation. It does not make a word definite. Most grammarians treat it is a *Hamza of liaison* (هَمْزةُ وَصْلٍ) – see #9. If ٱل starts an utterance or sentence, it is pronounced as a Hamza (glottal stop) resulting in أَلْ. Otherwise, the ا is neglected – see *#21*.

- The **letter** لام. Grammarians call this لـ a *Lām of definition* or *determination* (لامُ التَّعْرِيفِ). It is this device which makes a word definite. This type of لـ is not a preposition. It is the kind of لـ that is also found in ٱلَّذِي. In fact, it is the demonstrative letter لـ. It is a device that shows which person or thing is being referred to.

The resulting definite article is treated as one entity and is always joined with a following word. Though it has become *determinative* (making the expression definite), it was originally denoting a direction (*demonstrative*). Such characteristic still appears in words like ٱلْيَوْمَ, expressing *to-day* (more like *this* day and not *the* day), having the accusative case (مَنْصُوبٌ) as it is usually placed as an adverb of time (ظَرْفُ زَمانٍ).

Remark: Some scholars regard the Aleph as an integral part of the definite article. They suggest that it was originally أَلْ, with a pronounced Hamza (أَلِفُ الْقَطِعِ), similar to words such as هَلْ or بَلْ. Over time, it was gradually weakened to ٱل.

21. Why does the definite article sometimes have a ribbon?

It indicates that the ا in ٱل is not pronounced.

The first part of ٱل, the *Hamza of liaison* (هَمْزَةُ وَصْلٍ), is a tricky letter. You only hear it, when it marks the beginning of a sentence or utterance and when it must be pronounced as a **glottal stop**. However, if there is anything before ٱل, the ا is not pronounced, and the ribbon comes into the game.

This Hamza is treated as if it wasn't there. The sign of connection (وَصْلٌ) looks like a ribbon above ا.	ٱ
It indicates the fall of the Hamza by pronunciation. The sign probably reflects the letter ص which is included in صِلَةٌ which means *link; connection*. It is rarely used in books or newspapers.	

Let us examine it.

the book	ʾal-kitābu	أَلْكِتابُ
The هَمْزَةُ وَصْلٍ becomes a *(cutting) Hamza of rupture* (هَمْزَةُ قَطْعٍ) if it marks the beginning of a sentence. Then, you write it as أ and pronounce a glottal stop! The ل is pronounced as ل if there is a so-called moon letter (حَرْفٌ قَمَرِيٌّ) after ل.		

this book	Hādha-l-kitābu	هٰذا ٱلْكِتابُ
You don't pronounce a glottal stop! Instead, you use the preceding vowel *"a"* of هٰذا and connect it with the ل.		

Remark: Purist grammarians never write the definite article as أَلْ with هَمْزَةُ قَطْعٍ. Instead, they prefer the writing of a simple dash (plain Aleph: ا) with a vowel on the top or at the bottom of the letter – even at the beginning of a sentence or in isolation when it has to be pronounced as هَمْزَةٌ.

Excursus: **sun letters** and **moon/lunar letters**

In Arabic, there are two different kinds of consonants: *sun letters* (حَرْفٌ شَمْسِيٌّ) and *moon letters* (حَرْفٌ قَمَرِيٌّ).

- **Sun letters** take the attention and make the ل of the definite article **disappearing**. In other words, sun letters assimilate the ل in a definite article which eventually results in doubling the sun letter (شَدّةٌ).

- **Moon letters** keep the pronunciation of ل in الـ as it is.

The names are no coincidence. The Arabic word for *the sun* is الشَّمْسُ and pronounced *ash-shams* → the ل is digested. However, *the moon*, الْقَمَرُ, is pronounced *al-Qamar* – with *"l"*.

The sun letters are:

ت	ث	د	ذ	ر	ز	س	ش	ص	ض	ط	ظ	ل	ن
t	th	d	dh	r	z	s	sh	ṣ	ḍ	ṭ	ẓ	l	n

The moon letters are:

ء	ب	ج	ح	خ	ع	غ	ف	ق	ك	م	و	ي	ه
ʾ	b	j	ḥ	kh	ʿ	gh	f	q	k	m	w	y	h

22. The word *but* - How do you spell it?

You use a dagger Aleph resulting in لٰكِنْ.

It is an ancient spelling of the letter ا when it functions as a long vowel *aa*. Even until today, some Arabic words are written in this old fashion, and one of them is the word لٰكِنْ which equals لاكِنْ. Such Aleph is called *dagger Aleph* (أَلِفٌ خَنْجَرِيّةٌ) as خَنْجَرٌ means *dagger*. The dagger Aleph is a vowel sign which means that in unvowelled texts, it is usually not written – with the unpleasant effect that Arabic students read a short vowel instead of a long *a*.

If you have a look at the first sura of the Qur'an, *The Opening* or *Opener* (الْفاتِحةُ), you will see that the word الْعالَمِين in the second verse has no Aleph which is also true for مالك in the fourth verse. Instead, they have *daggers*.

translation	Sura الْفاتِحةُ	
Praise belongs to God, Lord of the Worlds,	الْحَمْدُ لِلّٰهِ رَبِّ الْعُلَمِينَ.	2
the Lord of Mercy, the Giver of Mercy,	الرَّحْمٰنِ الرَّحِيمِ	3
Master of the Day of Judgment.	مٰلِكِ يَوْمِ الْدِينِ.	4

Today the dagger Aleph is rare. However, some of the most common words still carry it, for example, *Allah* (اللّٰهُ). Such words are often spelled with فَتْحَةٌ (e.g., هَذا) instead of the dagger since many fonts cannot display it correctly. Strictly speaking, فَتْحَةٌ is a mistake as it marks a short and not a long vowel.

this	هٰذا	*but*	لٰكِنْ	*the merciful*	الرَّحْمٰن	*Allah*	اللّٰه

23. *This* and *that* – Why are they extraordinary in Arabic?

Both words are a combination of words.

This and *that* are *demonstratives* (اِسْمُ إشارةٍ); we use them to point to people and things. In Arabic, they are nouns (اِسْمٌ).

هٰذا (hādhā) means *this* and ذٰلِكَ (dhālika) *that*. Both are written with a dagger Aleph (see #22). So how come we have a long vowel *ā* after the first consonant? Both words consist of two parts. Let's take them apart and focus on the **main body which is the <u>demonstrative</u> part.**

feminine singular (various options)	ذِى, ذِه تا, تَه
feminine dual	تان
feminine plural	أُولاءِ

<->

masculine singular	ذا
masculine dual	ذان
masculine plural	أُولاءِ
for places	هُنا

If you talk about **something close**, you'll have to combine the above words with a *device of attention* (حَرْفُ تَنْبِيهٍ), the ها لِلتَّنْبِيهِ, which consists of the letter ه plus Aleph = ها. The word تَنْبِيهٌ means *warning; notification*. ها conveys *look!* or *there!* and is an amplifier and indicator of distance. Some examples:

Look, there he is!	ها هُوَ !
Hey, you!	ها أَنْتُمْ !
Here I am! (Note that the final Aleph of أنا is omitted.)	ها أَنَذا !

Let's continue with the expression *this*. It is used when the speaker points to something <u>**near**</u> (أَسْماءُ الْإِشارَةِ إِلَى الْقَرِيبِ). Hint: Since you talk about something **close** to you, you place the amplifier ها right at the **beginning**.

feminine singular	هٰذِهِ
*feminine dual;	هَاتانِ

masc. singular	هٰذا
masculine, dual;	هٰذانِ

these two	
fem. plural; *these*	هُؤُلاءِ

<->

these two	
masc. plural; *these*	هُؤُلاءِ
*for (near) places	هاهُنا or هَهُنا

* If the consonant after **ها** is **ت** or **ه**, you don't use *dagger Aleph* (see *question #22*). This is just a convention. The pronunciation is the same.

How do we express that something or someone is **far** from the speaker (أَسْماءُ الْإِشارَةِ إِلَى الْبَعِيدِ)? How do we say *that* in Arabic? We need a different *amplifier* and an *indicator of distance*.

A hint: Since you talk about something that is **far** from you, you place the amplifier and indicator at the **end**! What would be a suitable device? There are two possibilities:

- You use a *K of allocution* (كافُ الْخِطابِ): **ك**

- You use a *L of distance* (لامُ الْبُعْدِ) plus a *K of allocution*: **لك**

feminine singular	تِلْكَ
feminine dual	تانِكَ or تَيْنِكَ
feminine plural	أُولَئِكَ

<->

masculine singular; *that*	ذاكَ or ذَلِكَ
masc. dual; *those two; both of those*	ذانِكَ or ذَيْنِكَ
masculine plural; *those*	أُولَئِكَ
for places	هُناكَ or هُنالَكَ

Some remarks:

- The **ل** is a long-distance indicator and usually signals that something is *far away*; it is called لامُ الْبُعْدِ.

- Regarding the كَ: It agrees in case, number, and gender with the addressee! (see *question #178*)

masculine plural	كُمْ
feminine plural	كُنَّ

singular	كِ or كَ
dual	كُما

- If there is لَكَ or لِكَ after اذ, the long Aleph is written as a dagger Aleph (vertical dash). After the letter تـ, the long Aleph is omitted.

- You can never use both ها and ل together because ها denotes nearness and ل remoteness.

Let's do some combinations.

explanation	construction	
ذا is the إِسْمُ الْإِشارةِ. It is combined with the word ما. See *question #24*.	*what*	ذا + ما = ماذا	1
ها is used to give attention; to give notice to the addressed. Watch out: Only اذ is the demonstrative (إِسْمُ الْإِشارةِ).	*this*	ها + ذا = هذا	2
For things that are further away.	*that*	ذا + ل + ك = ذلِكَ	3
Combined with a personal pronoun, it expresses: *that one; look at that one!*		هُوَ ذا هِيَ ذي	4

Let's dissect a sentence. If there is a **definite noun after the demonstrative device**, the analysis is tricky!

This student is diligent.	هذا الطَّالِبُ مُجْتَهِدٌ.

Demonstrative (اِسْمُ الْإِشارَةِ) which is placed as the **subject** (مُبْتَدَأٌ) of the nominal sentence (جُمْلَةٌ اِسْمِيَّةٌ). Since it is the مُبْتَدَأ, it would need the nominative case; however, هـٰذا has an **indeclinable**, cemented shape (مَبْنِيٌّ عَلَى السُّكُونِ) and therefore, we can't put case markers. We can only **assign a place value** and say that هٰذا is located in the **position (place) of a nominative case** (فِي مَحَلِّ رَفْعٍ).	هٰذا
The student is the expression to which the demonstrative *this* **points to** (الْمُشارُ إِلَيْهِ). If we look at its function, it is an **apposition** (بَدَلٌ لِاسْمِ الْإِشارَةِ) for the subject (*this*). In grammar, an apposition describes the situation when you have two words next to each other which refer to the same person/thing. For example, *my friend Peter...* In Arabic, an apposition is a *follower* (تابِعٌ) and gets the same case as the word to which it refers. Therefore, *the student* is also in the nominative case (مَرْفُوعٌ بِالضَّمَّةِ). See *question #209 for more information about the apposition.*	الطّالِبُ
Predicate (خَبَرٌ); in the nominative case (مَرْفُوعٌ بِالضَّمَّةِ).	مُجْتَهِدٌ

24. ذا - Does it only mean *this*?

No, it doesn't. It may also indicate possession – in one case.

Let's put ذا on the operating table and see what it's all about.

- ذا is a *demonstrative* (اِسْمُ إِشارَةٍ) for masculine singular.
- ذا basically denotes *this (one)*; in combinations also: *that*.
- The feminine form of ذا is ذِي (also written as ذِهِ).
- The plural of ذا is أُولاءِ.

So, how is it possible that ذا denotes possession?

We need to look at another word to get the answer, ذُو, which means *master of; owner of*. It is a so-called *five* (sometimes: *six*) *nouns* (الْأَسْماءُ الْخَمْسةُ); for example: *father* (أَبٌ). In such nouns the third letter was eliminated leaving them with two letters (*see #29*). These nouns get و in the nominative (مَرْفُوعٌ), ي in the genitive (مَجْرُورٌ), and ا in the accusative case (مَنْصُوبٌ).

→ ذُو in the accusative case (مَنْصُوبٌ) becomes ذا and in the genitive case (مَجْرُورٌ), it will turn into ذِي.

nominative case (مَرْفُوعٌ)	
The man with a hat...	الرَّجُلُ ذُو قُبْعةٍ...
The possessor of money came.	جاءَ ذُو الْمالِ.

genitive case (مَجْرُورٌ)	
Next to the man with the hat...	إِلَى جِوارِ الرَّجُلِ ذِي الْقُبْعةِ...
I passed by the possessor of money.	مَرَرْتُ بِذِي الْمالِ.

accusative case (مَنْصُوبٌ)	
I saw a man with a hat.	رَأَيْتُ رَجُلًا ذا قُبْعةٍ.
I saw the possessor of money.	رَأَيْتُ ذا الْمالِ.

25. ماذا and ما ذا (with space) – What is the difference?

The meaning is the same – the grammatical analysis different.

In both **ماذا** and **ما ذا** we find **ذا**. In general, you will encounter **ماذا** (without space) in **verbal** sentences (جُمْلَةٌ فِعْلِيّةٌ).

So, is there a difference in meaning? Not really. It is slightly about emphasis. But regarding the grammar, the difference is huge. We have three options for the إِعْرابٌ, and all are correct.

APPROACH A: ما and ذا are written separately (space).

1 **ذا** is treated as a **demonstrative device** (اِسْمُ إِشارةٍ).

meaning	example	
What is this book?	= ما هذا الْكِتابُ؟	ما ذا الْكِتابُ؟

- **ما**: *subject* (مُبْتَدَأٌ) of the nominal sentence (جُمْلَةٌ اِسْمِيّةٌ);
- **ذا**: *predicate* (خَبَرٌ); in the location of a nominative case;

2 **ذا** is treated as a **relative pronoun** (اِسْمٌ مَوْصُولٌ), having the meaning of الَّذِي (*which, that*).

meaning	example	
What brings you here?	= ما الَّذِي أَتَى بِكَ؟	ما ذا أَتَى بِكَ هُنا؟

- **ما**: *subject* (مُبْتَدَأٌ) of the nominal sentence (جُمْلَةٌ اِسْمِيّةٌ);
- **ذا**: *predicate* (خَبَرٌ); in the location of a nominative;

APPROACH B: ما and ذا are written together (no space).

3 **ذا** merges with **ما**; it is a compound (one entity; a single word). **ماذا** is treated as a question word (اِسْمُ اِسْتِفْهامٍ).

What did you write?	ماذا كَتَبْتَ؟

ماذا is the fronted direct object (مَفْعُولٌ بِهِ مُقَدَّمٌ).

Why did you come?	لِماذا جِئْتَ؟

ماذا is an indeclinable interrogative noun (اِسْمُ اِسْتِفْهامٍ مَبْنِيٌّ), located in the spot of a genitive case (فِي مَحَلِّ جَرٍّ) as it is preceded by a preposition (حَرْفُ جَرٍّ). → it is a prepositional phrase (جارٌّ وَمَجْرُورٌ).

Watch out for the difference:

What does he exactly want?	ماذا يُرِيدُ بِالضَّبْطِ؟	1
What is it **that** he wants?	ما ذا يُرِيدُ بِالضَّبْطِ؟	
	= ما الَّذِي يُرِيدُ بِالضَّبْطِ؟	
Who is **this** in the office?	مَنْ ذا فِي الْمَكْتَبِ؟	2
Who is **this who** is in the office?	مَنْ ذا الَّذِي فِي الْمَكْتَبِ؟	

Some remarks:

1. The question word ماذا (without space): *what?*

- ماذا is normally used in verbal sentences (جُمْلَةٌ فِعْلِيّةٌ);
- ماذا can serve as a subject (فاعِلٌ) or object (مَفْعُولٌ بِهِ);

subject	**What** happened after that?	ماذا حَدَثَ بَعْدَ ذلِكَ؟
object	**What** do you want?	ماذا تُرِيدُ؟

2. ما ذا (with space; ذا used as a **relative pronoun**)

What can you place after a relative pronoun? There are quite some options.

verbal sentence (جُمْلةٌ فِعْلِيّةٌ)	1
I read the book that you bought.	قَرَأْتُ الْكِتابَ الَّذِي اشْتَرَيْتَهُ.

nominal sentence (جُمْلةٌ اِسْمِيّةٌ)	2
Those who are my friends came.	حَضَرَ الَّذِينَ هُمْ أَصْدِقائِي.

quasi sentence (شِبْهُ جُمْلةٍ): prepositional (جارٌّ وَمَجْرُورٌ) or adverbial phrase (ظَرْفُ مَكانٍ)	3
Give me the pen that is in the office. (prepositional phrase)	أَعْطِنِي الْقَلَمَ الَّذِي فِي الْمَكْتَبِ.
Give me the pen that is in front of you. (adverbial phrase)	أَعْطِنِي الْقَلَمَ الَّذِي أَمامَكَ.

26. Are there biliteral roots (only two letters) in Arabic?

Yes, very few Arabic roots consist of two consonants only.

Scholars have tried to count the biliteral Arabic roots. *Theodor Nöldeke* from Germany (1836 - 1930) as well as Andrzej Zaborski from Poland suggested that there are **37 Arabic roots with only two radicals**.

Most of these roots go back to the early beginnings of the Semitic languages (ca. 3800 to 2400 BC). Words with only two radicals are part of the very basic vocabulary which people needed in ancient times to survive. Some examples:

water	ماءٌ	father-in-law	حَمٌ	hand	يَدٌّ
father	أَبٌ	blood	دَمٌ	mouth	فَمٌ
				vulva	حِرٌ

Most grammarians agree that the following words too consist of only two root letters:

son	اِبْنٌ	tongue	لِسانٌ	name	اِسْمٌ
root	ب-ن	(with lexicalized suffix)		root	س-م

Note: The Aleph اِسْمٌ and اِبْنٌ is **not** part of the root. It disappears in speech. Such Aleph *is a connecting Hamza or Hamza of liaison* (هَمْزَة الْوَصْلِ). Western grammarians call it *prothetic Aleph "i-"*.

How do you find a biliteral root in the dictionary? Usually you find them as a triliteral root which is based on the plural:

root	plural	word
ف-و-ه	أَفْواهٌ	فَمٌ
ب-ن-و	أَبْناءٌ	اِبْنٌ
ل-س-ن	أَلْسُنٌ	لِسانٌ
ح-م-و	أَحْماءٌ	حَمٌ

root	plural	word
د-م-و	دِماءٌ	دَمٌ
م-و-ه	مِياهٌ	ماءٌ
س-م-ي	أَسْماءٌ	اِسْمٌ
ء-ب-و	آباءٌ	أَبٌ
ح-ر-ح	أَحْراحٌ	حِرٌ
حِرٌ is an exception to the rule. The origin is probably حِرْحٌ.		

What about roots with four consonants? They are rare. Many of them are artificially built by the reduplication of original root consonants, for ex., *to shake, to upset* (خَضْخَضَ). In the Qur'an, only 15 roots with four consonants are found against 1160 roots with three consonants.

27. Are there Arabic roots which are related to each other?

Yes, there are.

Georges Bohas (University of Paris) has done quite some research about this subject. He basically says that Arabic roots are derived from what he calls *etymons* – a combination of two letters to which a third letter is added. The third letter can appear in any position: beginning, middle, or as a final letter.

It is fascinating how roots containing two of three of the same consonants can be related in meaning. For ex., ح-م-د and ح-د-م and د-ج-م. They all share two root letters: م and د. Although they occur in different positions, interestingly, they express similar things:

- حَمِدَ / يَحْمَدُ basically means *to praise* in the meaning of *to thank*. It is mainly used with the word *Allah*.

- مَدَحَ / يَمْدَحُ also means *to praise* – but more in the sense of *to commend, to say good things*.

- مَجَدَ / يَمْجُدُ conveys *to be glorious, exalted, praised*.

But don't take such relationships for granted. Many verbs have the same root letters in different positions, but express different things: نَقَشَ (*to paint*) vs. شَنَقَ (*to hang; to execute*).

Let's take a look at some roots that start with the very same two root letters: قط – most of them are related in meaning.

to cut	يَقْطَعُ	قَطَعَ
to cut off	يَقْطِلُ	قَطَلَ
to cut off; to break off	يَقْطِمُ	قَطَمَ
to concentrate at one point; to frown	يَقْطِبُ	قَطَبَ
to skim off; to harvest (to cut off a fruit)	يَقْطِفُ	قَطَفَ
to trim; to sharpen	يَقُطُّ	قَطَّ
to trickle; to drip; to drag	يَقْطُرُ	قَطَرَ

28. Does the word order matter in Arabic?

Not really.

In Arabic, the word order usually doesn't change the meaning of a sentence. However, changing the position of a word can be used as a stylistic device: to convey emphasis.

The standard word order in **English** is **subject + verb + object**. Let's quickly brush up on the terms.

subject	Usually a noun or pronoun (a person, thing or place).
verb	The action. It tells you what the subject actually does.
object	Any word that is influenced by the verb. *I read **a book**.*

In English, since there are no case markers, your options of playing with the word order are limited.

For example: *The dog crossed the street*. If you change the sequence, the result will be rubbish: *The street crossed the dog*.

In Arabic, this is different – mainly thanks to case markers. Arabic has a relatively free word order. The standard word order depends on the type of sentence:

verbal sentence (جُمْلةٌ فِعْلِيّةٌ)

(1) verb (فِعْلٌ) + (2) subject (فاعِلٌ) + (3) object (مَفْعُولٌ بِهِ)

nominal sentence (جُمْلةٌ اِسْمِيّةٌ)

(1) subject (مُبْتَدَأٌ) + (2) predicate (خَبَرٌ)

Inversion happens when we reverse the standard word order of a sentence. In grammar, we have two terms to describe that we changed the usual word order. We may **forward** (تَقْدِيمٌ) or **delay** (تَأْخِيرٌ) a word.

The following sentences roughly mean the same: *The students read the books.* However, by changing the position of words, we may produce some emphasis (تَأْكِيدٌ).

read (past) + *the students* + *the books*	قَرَأَ الطُّلّابُ الْكُتُبَ.	1
read (past) + *the books* + *the students*	قَرَأَ الْكُتُبَ الطُّلّابُ.	2
the books + *read* (past) + *the students*	الْكُتُبَ قَرَأَ الطُّلّابُ.	3
the students + *read* (past tense, 3rd person plural = they) + *the books*	الطُّلّابُ قَرَؤُوا الْكُتُبَ.	4

Sentence 4 is a nominal sentence (جُمْلةٌ اِسْمِيّةٌ)! If you put the subject before the verb, there are two effects:

- the **subject** gets more **emphasis**;
- the **object** is <u>unstressed</u>;

the books (nominative case!) - *to read* (them) - *the students*	الْكُتُبُ قَرَأَها الطُّلّابُ.	5
Here, the natural subject (the last word: *students*) is <u>un</u>stressed.		

In general, we can say that the dominant thing or person stands at the beginning of the sentence. Eventually, it will also depend on the intonation. If your native language is English, it may be difficult to feel the nuances. Let's look at an example. Both of the following sentences mean: *Zayd hit.*

verbal sentence	Here we assume that the action has happened. Of course, we want to know **who** has performed the action – therefore, the logical emphasis is on **Zayd**.	ضَرَبَ زَيْدٌ.
nominal sentence	Here we know that Zayd did something – so, we want to know **what** he did. The sentence answers the question of what Zayd has done. Since it was the action of *to hit*, the logical emphasis is on the **verb**. A nominal sentence may also help to start a new paragraph and present a new event or idea.	زَيْدٌ ضَرَبَ.

Remark: If you want to convey emphasis, there is a trick called *anacoluthon*. You isolate the natural subject with the effect that you emphasize the subject. How can you do that? By a personal pronoun suffix or a separate personal pronoun.

The income of Karīm is big.	دَخْلُ كَرِيمٍ كَبِيرٌ.
Karīm's income is big.	كَرِيمٌ دَخْلُهُ كَبِيرٌ.
Here, we isolate the word كَرِمٌ.	

Zayd, I killed him.	زَيْدٌ قَتَلْتُهُ.
Zayd, his father died.	زَيْدٌ ماتَ أَبُوهُ.
In both examples, we have isolated the word زَيْدٌ. Instead of زَيْدٌ, you could use the expression: ...إِنَّ زَيْدًا	

For a deep analysis of this construction, see *Arabic for Nerds 2*, question #112, #113, #216, and #222.

29. What is special about the Arabic word for *son* (اِبْنٌ)?

It is the first letter ا which sometimes vanishes.

The Arabic word for *son* is اِبْنٌ. It is one of the so-called *five nouns* (أَسْماءٌ خَمْسةٌ) which we examine in *question #220*.

But اِبْنٌ belongs to another **special group of words** which are characterized by two features:

- Some of them have only **two root** letters.

- All of them **start** with the letter ا.

two, masculine	إِثْنانِ		*son*	اِبْنٌ
two, feminine	إِثْنَتانِ		*daughter*	اِبنةٌ
name	اِسْمٌ		*man*	اِمْرُؤٌ
I swear by God	اَيْمُ اللهِ			

The letter ا in the above words is a *connecting Hamza*, also called *Hamza of liaison* (هَمْزةُ وَصْلٍ). What is its purpose here? Classical Arabic does not know the **occurrence of two conso-**

nants at the beginning of a word which means that no Arabic word can begin with سُكُونٌ on top, like the original word for *son*: بْن. But there's good news. We fix that with a هَمْزَةُ وَصْلٍ.

Now, what happens if we start the utterance or sentence with اِبْن؟ Then the Aleph is pronounced as a هَمْزَةٌ because an Arabic sentence/utterance cannot start with a vowel either. **We need a consonant followed by a vowel.** → You pronounce a هَمْزَةٌ and a كَسْرَةٌ resulting in: *'ibn*.

The first letter ا brings along more complications regarding the pronunciation. If ا in words like اِبْنٌ or اِسْمٌ is **not the first** letter of the utterance, you have to <u>neglect it</u>! We mark that with *Wasla* (وَصْلةٌ; *see #21*) → The correct spelling is اُبْنٌ then.

meaning	pronunciation	expression
And his name	*wasmuhu*	وَاسْمُهُ
O son of a dog!	*yabnalkalb(i)*	يا اِبْنَ الْكَلْبِ!
	Note: This expression is an insult (شَتِيمةٌ).	
What's your name?	*masmuka?*	ما اسْمُكَ؟

There are three special situations:

1. The *Basmalah* (بَسْمَلةٌ): the expression بِسْمِ اللهِ. It literally means *in the name of God/Allah*. In this special sentence, the هَمْزَةُ وَصْلٍ is not written.

2. If you start a question with the device أ (similar to هَلْ), the هَمْزَةُ وَصْلٍ will be deleted. For example: *Is your son present?* In Arabic, you write: أَبْنُكَ مَوْجُودٌ؟

3. If you add لِ or لَ before the definite article الْ, the letter ا drops. For example: لِلْبَيْتِ and not: لِالْبَيْتِ

30. Osama *bin* Laden or Osama *ibn* Laden - What is correct?

Even if you try hard, you will never get "bin" in Arabic.

In English, you will hear and read the name *Osama bin Laden*. He was the former head of the terrorist organization *al-Qāʿida*. His name is the transliterated form of بنُ أسامةُ لادِن, *Osama, son of Laden*. The second part of the name – *son of Laden* – stands in apposition to the first name, i.e., *Osama*.

In Hebrew, the word for *son* is *ben* (בֶּן). In ancient times, when the Semitic languages emerged, the word only consisted of these two letters. In Arabic, however, the word for *son* has another type of skeleton. A third letter comes into the game: the letter ا, a so-called *Hamza of liaison* (هَمْزةُ وَصلٍ); *see #29*.

The letter ا makes it impossible to arrive at *bin* in Arabic. Why? In Classical Arabic, when the word does not start an utterance, the letter ا is neglected. Therefore, we have to deal with the letter-combination بن. It is pronounced as follows:

The sequence is: "u/a/i" plus "bn" plus "u/a/i".

Let me explain this:

- Since ابْن is not the first word but follows a word, you need a vowel bridge to connect it: **a case ending, a mood marker,** or a **helping vowel.**

- This has the effect that the ا of ابْن is neglected.

- What do we have then? If the preceding word is in the nominative case (مَرْفُوعٌ), we will get *ubn*. If it needs the accusative case (مَنْصوبٌ), we will have *abn*.

- ابْن gets a **case marker** as well which depends on the position and function in the sentence. Therefore, we could theoretically get *bnu, bna,* or *bni*.

The son of Karīm came.	جاءَ ابْنُ كَرِيمٍ.
Pronunciation: *jā'abnukarīm*.	

Arabic newspapers often write the name *Bin Laden* with quotation marks: "بن لادن". So what is the **correct spelling** of اِبْن؟

The spelling rules regarding اِبْن

- Usually you write ابْنٌ with هَمْزةُ وَصْلٍ if it marks the beginning of a sentence or utterance.

- In genealogical citations, however, you don't write the هَمْزةُ وَصْلٍ in the words for *son* (اِبْنٌ) and *daughter* (اِبْنةٌ) - if they stand in apposition (بَدَلٌ) to the first word. What does that mean? For example:

Muhammad, son of Abdallah (= his father).	مُحَمَّدُ بْنُ عَبْدِ اللهِ

The pronunciation of this sequence is *muhammadubnu 'abdi...* Why? Well, personal names that get the standard case endings (*triptotes*) **lose the sign of indefiniteness** (*nunation*) in **genealogical citations** before the word بن (*son of*)!

If you use nunation, the sentence would mean: Muhammad **is** the son of Abdallah (مُحَمَّدٌ اِبْنُ عَبْدِ اللهِ). That is why I highlighted the comma in the translation.

Let's see the difference:

1	Khālid **is** the son of Muhammad.	خالِدٌ اِبْنُ مُحَمَّدٍ.

Here, the part *son of Muhammad* is the **predicate** (خَبَرٌ) of the subject (مُبْتَدَأ), i.e., Khālid. You have to write the هَمْزةُ وَصْلٍ! You can't write بن.

2	Khālid, son of Muhammad	خالِدُ بنُ مُحَمَّدٍ

Here, the part *son of Muhammad* (إضافة-construction) stands in **apposition** (بَدَلٌ) to *Khālid*. This is <u>not</u> a complete sentence. In this situation, the هَمْزةُ وَصْلٍ is <u>not</u> written.

Note: *Arabic for Nerds 2, qu. #102,* discusses the word اِبْن in depth.

In a nutshell:

- If you express *Bin Laden* in Arabic, you should pronounce the هَمْزةُ وَصْلٍ at the beginning and write: اِبْنُ لادِن

- If you cite his entire name, you should say and write: أُسامةُ بْنُ لادِن

Remark: If you are wondering why there is the feminine ending ة although Osama was a man, go to *#57.* Note that **masculine proper names** ending in ة are *diptotes* (مَمْنُوعٌ مِن الصَّرْفِ).

31. How are family names constructed in Arabic?

The system is completely different from that in the West.

In Europe or the USA we have a first name (given name), maybe a middle name, and a surname (family name). How is it in the Arab world?

Arab(ic) names are a string of names listing ancestors on the father's side. Usually, you will see the first name the person's own), the father's name, and the paternal grandfather's name. Since only the person's first name is really his or hers, it is the most important name which his used together with a title (e.g. Mr., Doctor, Professor). Strangely, in Egypt, the name of former ruler Muhammad Husnī Mubārak (مُحَمَّد حُسْنِي مُبارَك) was used in the Western media to an extent that the Egyptian people adopted it and spoke of *President Mubarak*.

Since names reflect only the father's side, women have masculine names after their first name! The word ابن between ancestral names is especially common in the Arabian Peninsula. But that is not the end of the story. Let us examine the name:

Muhammad al-Farūq 'Ibn Khālid al-Baghdādīy

('Abū Karīm)

مُحَمَّد الْفارُوق ابن خالِد الْبَغْدادِيّ

(أَبُو كَرِيمٍ)

In general, Arabic names consist of **five parts** which don't necessarily have to follow a particular system.

1 إسْمٌ	2 لَقَبٌ	3 نَسَبٌ	4 نِسْبةٌ	5 كُنْيةٌ

(Ibn... Ibn... Ibn...)

(First) name	مُحَمَّدٌ	إسْمٌ 1

This could be a traditional Arab name that is found in the Qur'an, a (nice) attribute, a foreign name, or a compound with the most common prefix عَبْد which means *servant of* and is followed by one of the 99 names (attributes) of Allah.

Epithet	الْفارُوقُ	لَقَبٌ 2

The لَقَبٌ is defined as an epithet, usually a religious, honorific, or descriptive title. The لَقَبٌ can precede the إسْمٌ and sometimes comes to replace it. There are mainly three possibilities:

• physical qualities: الطَّوِيلُ - *the tall*

- virtues: الْفَارُوقُ - *he who distinguishes truth from falsehood* or الرَّاشِدُ - *the rightly guided.*

- compounds with الدِّينِ (*religion*): *light of the religion* (نُورُ الذِّينِ)

Genealogy (family origin): son of... son of... son of...	إِبْنُ خَالِدٍ	نَسَبٌ	3

The نَسَبٌ is the patronymic. It is more or less a list of ancestors, each introduced with *son of* (إِبْن) or *daughter of* (بِنْت).

It often relates back to two or three generations. That's why Arabic names can be very long: أَبَىُّ بْنُ عَبَّاسِ بْنِ سَهْلِ بْنِ سَعْدٍ

In this example, 'Abbās is the father and Sahl the grandfather and Sa'd the grand-grandfather.

Indication of origin. The *Nisba* is usually preceded by the definite article الْ.	الْبَغْدَادِيٌّ	نِسْبَةٌ	4

The نِسْبَةٌ is similar to what people in the West may call the surname. It is rarely used in Egypt and in Lebanon where the لَقَبٌ incorporates its meaning. A person may have several نِسْبَةٌ

It is usually an adjective (نِسْبَةٌ) derived from:

- the place of birth, origin: الْبَغْدَادِيٌّ (*from Baghdad*);

- the name of a religious sect or tribe or family: التَّمِيمِيٌّ (*belonging to the Tamīm tribe*);

- a profession: الْعَطَّارِيٌّ (*the perfume vendor*);

Honorific name (street name) – to identify a person by his first-born child.	أَبُو كَرِيم	كُنْيَةٌ	5

Name under which people call somebody on the street; mostly named after the first child: *father of; mother of.*

The كُنْيَةٌ is a **honorific name.** It is <u>not part of a person's formal</u>

name and is usually not printed in documents. The كُنْية is very important in Arabic culture – even a person who has no child might have a كُنْية which makes him (or her) symbolically the parent of a special quality, such as *father of good deeds*.

Watch out: In the Arab world women don't take their husband's surname when they get married. They keep their names they were given at birth. Children, however, do take their father's name which is expressed in the نَسَب: *daughter of* (name of the father).

32. الْبَرادِعِيُّ - What is the meaning of this name?

It denotes a person who makes a piece of cloth for saddles.

Mohamed ElBaradei (مُحَمَّد الْبَرادِعِيُّ), Egyptian Nobel Peace Prize winner and one-time presidential-hopeful, has quite an unusual name. He uses a نِسْبة as his (Western) last name.

الْبَرادِعِيُّ relates to بَرْدَعة (alternative spelling: بَرْذَعة) which denotes a piece of cloth which is put under the saddle of a donkey, mule, or camel (رَحْل). The plural form of is بَرادِعُ (alternative spelling: بَرَاذِعُ), a diptote.

If we form a *noun of relation* (نِسْبة) of the plural, we first put a كَسْرة under the last letter, then add the letter ي plus شَدّة. We can say that el-Baradei's name denotes a person who makes pieces of cloth for the saddle. Arab names sometimes relate to professions and are expressed by a نِسْبة or a *form of exaggeration* (صيغة الْمُبالَغة) - see *questions #51 and #86*. Some examples:

weaver	نَسّاج	*tiler*	بَلّاط	*perfume vendor*	عَطّار

33. Are there pet names in Arabic?

Yes, they are very common.

The term for *pet name* is اِسْمُ الدَّلْعِ. The root د-ل-ع means *to loll; to let the tongue hang out.* There are many pet names in Arabic and you will hear them quite often. Some of them have tricky endings. Although the person is masculine, the nickname may look feminine.

pet name	meaning of the name	proper name	
حَمادة	'Ahmad (lit.: *more praiseworthy*) can be used as a synonym for Muhammad (lit.: *praised*).	'Ahmad, Muhammad	أَحْمَدُ مُحَمَّدٌ
دَرْش	*Chosen; selected; the chosen one;* Mustafā is also a synonym for Muhammad.	Mustafā	مُصْطَفَى
	دَرْش means *black leather*. But that is not the origin of the pet name. Legend has it that دَرْش relates to an Ottoman Sultan called Mustafa, who became a *Dervish* (دَرْوِيشٌ). Over time, دَرْوِيشٌ was reduced to دَرْش.		
زَنُّوبة	*an aromatic tree*	Zaynab	زَيْنَبُ

You also find pet names that are less formal:

pet name	meaning of the name	proper name	
أَبُو تُوت	Lit.: *success* (granted by God), *happy outcome; adjustment.*	Tawfīq	تَوْفِيقٌ
سُوسُو	Name of a prophet.	Ismā'īl	إِسْماعِيلُ
كَوْكَبُ الشَّرْقِ	كُلْثُومٌ denotes fullness of the	'Umm	أُمُّ كُلْثُومٍ

| | face (round cheeks); elephant | **Kulthūm** | |

كَوْكَبُ الشَّرْقِ means *star of the East/Orient* is the pet name of the famous Egyptian singer 'Umm Kulthūm. Note that the third daughter of the Islamic prophet Muhammad was also named 'Umm Kulthūm.

34. What are the main plural forms in Arabic?

In Arabic there are sound (intact) and broken plural forms.

The plural form in Arabic is a noun indicating **more** than **two** units. **Sound plural forms** are mostly used for human beings. Let's have a look at the three major types:

Sound **masculine** plural (جَمْعُ الْمُذَكَّرِ السّالِمُ) - *regular*
It is formed by adding ونَ in the nominative case (مَرْفُوعٌ); for the genitive (مَجْرُورٌ) and accusative (مَنْصُوبٌ) case, you add ينَ. Important: The final letter ن always takes فَتْحةٌ, i.e, the vowel *a*.

translation	plural; gen. (مَجْرُورٌ) and acc. (مَنْصُوبٌ)	plural; nominative (مَرْفُوعٌ)	singular
engineer/s (m)	مُهَنْدِسِينَ	مُهَنْدِسُونَ	مُهَنْدِسٌ

Sound **feminine** plural (جَمْعُ الْمُؤَنَّثِ السّالِمُ) - *regular*
It is formed by adding اتٌ in the nominative case (مَرْفُوعٌ). For the genitive (مَجْرُورٌ) and accusative (مَنْصُوبٌ) case, add or اتٍ.
Watch out: A singular noun can be of masculine gender, but the plural is built like a sound feminine plural. مُسْتَشْفَى is a *noun of place* (اسْمُ الْمكانِ) and means *hospital*. Let's see how the plural be-

haves: *I saw big hospitals* - شاهَدْتُ مُسْتَشْفَياتٍ كَبِيرةً

translation	plural; gen. (مَجرُورٌ) and acc. (مَنْصُوبٌ)	plural; nomina- tive (مَرْفُوعٌ)	singular
engineer/s (f)	مُهَنْدِساتٍ	مُهَنْدِساتٌ	مُهَنْدِسةٌ

GOLDEN RULE #1

In **sound <u>feminine</u> plurals**, you **<u>never</u>** use a فَتْحةٌ ("*a*") on the final letter ت!

Whether they are definite or indefinite, sound feminine plurals use **only two markers** for the three cases: ضَمّةٌ and كَسْرةٌ.

Broken plural (جَمْعُ التَّكْسِيرِ) - *irregular*

If you ask Arabic students what is the most difficult thing about Arabic, you often hear the broken plural. Indeed, there are many patterns and, to accelerate the headache even more, some of them produce *diptotes* (مَمْنُوعٌ مِن الصَّرْفِ).

translation	plural; gen. (مَجرُورٌ) and acc. (مَنْصُوبٌ)	plural; nomina- tive (مَرْفُوعٌ)	singular
man/men	رِجالٍ - رِجالًا	رِجالٌ	رَجُلٌ
book/books	كُتُبٍ - كُتُبًا	كُتُبٌ	كِتابٌ

The broken plural brings us to another very important principle in Arabic. The main rule of agreement.

GOLDEN RULE #2

A word that has to grammatically **agree** with a <u>**non-human plural**</u> will always be **feminine singular**!

In other words, we treat non-human plural nouns as grammatically <u>feminine singular</u>! This is important for the correct agreement. An adjective or verb that goes along with such a noun has to be in the feminine singular!

I saw beautiful cars in many places.	رَأَيْتُ سَيَّارَاتٍ جَمِيلَةً فِي أَمَاكِنَ كَثِيرَةٍ.

broken plural	Direct object (مَفْعُولٌ بِهِ), indefinite; it should get two فَتْحَةٌ (nunation: -an) in the **accusative** case. However, since this is a **sound feminine plural**, it is مَنْصُوبٌ by كَسْرَةٌ (nunation: -in).	سَيَّارَاتٍ
adjective (صِفَةٌ)	Adjective for the direct object *cars*. It has to agree with the noun to which it refers (*cars*); thus, it gets the accusative case (مَنْصُوبٌ), the regular مَنْصُوبٌ-ending -an. All words that are in agreement with a feminine sound plural need to be in the **singular** (feminine) form!	جَمِيلَةً
broken plural	Noun in the genitive case (مَجْرُورٌ) as it follows the preposition فِي. Since it is indefinite, it should nunation (كَسْرَةٌ) resulting in -in. The **broken plural** of singular مَكَانٌ produces a diptote (مَمْنُوعٌ مِن الصَّرْفِ), a pattern that does <u>not</u> get nunation and instead takes one فَتْحَة to mark the genitive case. *See question #240.*	أَمَاكِنَ
adjective (صِفَةٌ)	Adjective for *places* (أَمَاكِنَ), which is grammatically (but not visibly) in the genitive case. Thus, كَثِيرَةٍ gets nunation: two كَسْرَةٌ. It has to be feminine, singular!	كَثِيرَةٍ

35. What is a preposition in Arabic?

One of only 17 words in total.

Prepositions in English are words like *in, at, on, above, with*. In Arabic, we only call the following words *prepositions* (حَرْفُ جَرٍّ). Note that even a one-letter-word can be a preposition.

مُنْذُ	13	عَنْ	7	ب	1
مُذْ	14	فِي	8	ت	2
عَدَا	15	عَلَى	9	ل	3
حاشا	16	مِن	10	ك	4
خَلا	17	إِلَى	11	تاءُ الْقَسَم	5
		حَتَّى	12	واوُ الْقَسَم	6

A حَرْفٌ never changes its shape and cannot receive any sign of declension; it never gets case markers. It is cemented.

What about بَعْدَ (*after*) or تَحْتَ (*under*) which are prepositions in English? In Arabic, they are **nouns** (اسْمٌ) and get case markers. They are **circumstantials of time** (ظَرْفُ زَمانٍ) or **place** (ظَرْفُ مَكانٍ); ظَرْفٌ means *circumstance; container*. In the analysis (الْإِعْرابُ), when we determine the function of words in a sentence, we call them *local* or *temporal objects* (مَفْعُولٌ فِيه). It is just another way of saying *adverbs of time* or *place*.

adverb of time	ظَرْفُ الزَّمانِ	1
You traveled on the day off.	سافَرْتَ يَومَ الْعُطلةِ.	

adverb of place	ظَرْفُ الْمَكانِ	2
The bee sat on the tree.	جَلَسَتْ النَّحْلةُ فَوْقَ الشَّجَرةِ.	

→ Notice the فَتْحَةٌ on يَوْمَ and فَوْقَ!

Since they are treated as **objects**, we get an idea why they receive a فَتْحَةٌ (remember that an object in Arabic gets the accusative case). Technically speaking, they usually serve as the **first part** of a إِضافَةٌ. If they are **not followed** by another word, they get **nunation**.

preposition in English	I came **before** sunset.	جِئْتُ قَبْلَ الْمَغْرِبِ.
adverb in English	I came **before**.	جِئْتُ قَبْلًا.
		Also: جِئْتُ قَبْلُ = جِئْتُ مِنْ قَبْلُ

Let's see some **circumstantials of place**. In English, most of them are called prepositions. In Arabic, they are nouns (اِسْمٌ), usually doing the job of a ظَرْفٌ.

above	فَوْقَ	towards	ناحِيةَ
under	تَحْتَ	during; through	خِلالَ
behind	خَلْفَ	beside	جانِبَ
near	قُرْبَ	right	يَمِينَ
around	حَوْلَ	left	يَسارَ
towards	تُجاهَ	north	شَمالَ
in front of	أَمامَ	south	جَنُوبَ
between; among	بَيْنَ	east	شَرْقَ
middle; among(st)	وَسْطَ	west	غَرْبَ

36. Is مَع (with) a noun (إِسْمٌ) or a preposition (حَرْفُ جَرٍّ)؟

Most grammarians say that مَع is a noun (إِسْمٌ) in Arabic.

It is still a debate but the majority of the grammarians suggest that مَعَ, which denotes *with*, is a إِسْمٌ and not a حَرْفٌ. But why is the word *with* rather a noun than a preposition (which it is in English grammar)?

The answer has to do with one of the main features of an Arabic noun: مَع sometimes receives **nunation** (تَنْوِينٌ).

They came together.	جاؤُوا مَعًا.

This is crucial. Any حَرْفٌ is by definition *indeclinable* (مَبْنِيٌّ). It has a permanent structure and always stays the same – no matter what the position in the sentence may be. It has a **cemented shape**. For example, the Arabic word for *in* (فِي).

What jobs could the word مَع take on in a sentence? Basically, there are three possibilities.

Adverb of time/place (ظَرْفُ زَمانٍ / مَكانٍ)	You played with the children.	لَعِبْتَ مَعَ الأَطْفالِ.	1
مَعَ is fixed on the vowel "a" (فَتْحةٌ) and has a cemented form as it serves as a circumstantial object (مَفْعُولٌ فِيهِ) to define place or time. It is the first part of a إِضافة; treated as a **noun** (إِسْمٌ).				

Declined noun (إِسْمٌ مُعْرَبٌ), after a preposition.	I went together with him.	ذَهَبْتُ مِنْ مَعِهِ.	2
Here, مَع receives case endings. مَع in the expression *with him* مَعِهِ has the vowel "i" under ع. Why? Because the preceding preposition مِنْ drags مَع into the genitive case (مَجْرُورٌ).				

| 3 | جاؤُوا مَعًا. | They came together. | Circumstantial description (حالٌ). مَعًا is in the accusative case (مَنْصُوبٌ). |

What is a حالٌ؟ It describes the aspect of a certain noun during the occurrence of the action of the verb. For example: *he came, smiling*. (جاءَ مُبْتَسِمًا). *Smiling* is a حالٌ – see #245 and #246.

We say that مَعًا is an **inert noun** (not derived from a root or another word), but interpreted as if it were derived (إِسْمٌ جامِدٌ مُؤَوَّلٌ بِمُشْتَقٍّ). Thus, it gets nunation.

So, why do some people say that مَع is a preposition?

Mostly because it is placed as the first part of a إِضافةٌ. This brings along that the second part (مُضافٌ إِلَيْهِ) – the annexed noun – has to be in the genitive case (مَجْرُورٌ).

If we only looked at the result, we could assume that the genitive case was not induced by the إِضافةٌ, but by a preposition. Let us look at two examples:

| | جَلَسَ كَرِيمٌ مَعَ مُحَمَّدٍ. | Karīm **sat** with Muhammad. |

| مَعَ | Adverb of **place** (ظَرْفُ مَكانٍ), because the action of *to sit* is more associated with a place and not with time. It also works as the first part of the إِضافةٌ-construction. |

| | جاءَ كَرِيمٌ مَعَ مُحَمَّدٍ. | Karīm **came** with Muhammad. |

| مَعَ | Adverb of **time** (ظَرْفُ زَمانٍ), because the action of *to come* is more associated with time. First part of the إِضافةٌ. |

What about the word *Muhammad* in both examples?

| مُحَمَّدٍ | إِضافةٌ؛ 2nd part of the (مُضافٌ إِلَيْهِ مَجْرُورٌ بِالْكَسْرةِ). genitive |

37. Why is it important to count syllables in Arabic?

It will give you some hints for the correct word stress.

Arabic has two kinds of syllables (C=consonant; V=vowel):

1. **Open syllables:** CV and CVV (VV = long vowel)

2. **Closed syllables:** CVC

Arabic has some special features.

- **Every syllable begins with a consonant** and never with a vowel! Note that the Hamza (e.g., اِ) is a consonant.

- The سُكُونٌ is the sign of **quiescence**. It is the anti-vowel. It tells us that a consonant does not have a vowel. The word literally means *tranquility* or *quietude.*

- The سُكُونٌ is the absence of sound and **cuts the word into syllables.** There are light and heavy syllables.

light syllable	C V	open
heavy syllable	C V V	open
	C V C	closed

What about verbs such as ظَنَّ (*to think*)? They actually follow the sequence ظَنْنَ. The first ن takes سُكُونٌ. Hence, we count two syllables (**C V C - C V**), although they are usually not pronounced as such (نَ + ظَنْ).

So, how can we find the right stress? In general, *word stress* (German: *Betonung*) means that one syllable in a word is more prominent than other syllables. Word stress in Arabic does not really matter, it is not distinctive in Arabic. In other words, word stress in Arabic does not change the meaning of words.

The first Arabic grammarians did not cover the topic. Only when the readings of the Qur'an were developed, people started to think about accentuation. However, most of these rules are based on stress patterns of modern dialects. Many scholars have tried to set up rules for the correct accentuation of Classical Arabic.

Before we go into the details, two hints:

- The ultimate (last) syllable is <u>never</u> stressed.

- The stress <u>can't be</u> put on the definite article ال, a preposition, or conjunction.

Let's analyze the three main rules for Classical Arabic and Modern Standard Arabic.

RULE 1: **Stress a <u>super-heavy</u> last syllable** - but only, if you use the pausal form which means that you don't pronounce the last vowel (case or mood marker).

ya-**qūl**	light-→super-heavy	he says	يَقُول

RULE 2: **Stress the rightmost <u>non</u>-final <u>heavy</u> syllable.**

mu-dar-ri-**sū**-na	light-heavy-light-→heavy-light	teachers	مُدَرِّسُونَ
mas-ʾa-la-tu-ha	→heavy-light-light-light-light	her problem	مَسْأَلَتُها

RULE 3: Otherwise, **stress the <u>antepenult</u>** (=the <u>third-to-last</u> syllable of a word).

This rule applies also to the standard I-verb, for example, *he wrote/to write* (كَتَبَ).

| **ka**-ta-ba | ➜light-light-light | he wrote | كَتَبَ |
| ka-**ta**-ba-tā | light-➜light-light-heavy | they both wrote (fem. dual) | كَتَبَتا |

In modern Arabic dialects, stress is important because it is one of the distinguishing features and ingredients of the sounds and melody of a dialect.

In **Egyptian Arabic**, the stress is put on the penultimate syllable (= <u>second</u> from end). This is different to **Eastern Arabic** dialects where we stress the <u>third</u> from the end like in formal Arabic. Regarding word stress, Classical Arabic and the dialects of Palestine and Damascus follow almost the same rules.

Eastern dialects	Egyptian Arabic	syllable structure	example/ meaning
mad-ra-sa	mad-**ra**-sa	CV - CV - CV	مَدْرَسة
➜light-light-light	light-➜light-light	light-light-light	*school*
mu-**dar**-ri-sa	mu-dar-**ri**-sa	CV - CVC - CV - CV	مُدَرِّسة
light-➜light-light-light	light-light-➜light-light	light-light-light-light	*teacher (f.)*

38. Why do you need helping vowels?

You need helping vowels to avoid consonant clusters.

In Arabic, most words end with a vowel (case marker, mood marker for verbs, hidden/implied pronoun, etc.). We use this vowel as a connector.

You are the teacher.	أَنْتَ الْمُدَرِّسُ.

explanation	pronunciation
This is, precisely speaking, wrong. Beginners who are still reading sentences word by word are likely to pronounce it like this – with a pause after the word أَنْتَ.	*'anta 'al-Mudarrisu*
This is how a native speaker would pronounce the sentence. The sentence is pronounced as if it was only one entity; without a pause.	*'anta-l-mudarrisu*

The هَمْزَةُ وَصْلٍ of the definite article ال is not pronounced; it basically disappears. It would only remain if it would be the first letter of an utterance or sentence – in such a situation, you have to pronounce the أ of أَلْ as a glottal stop.

But what happens if the preceding word ends with سُكُونْ? What should we do if the preceding word is, for e.g., مِنْ, هَلْ, or مَنْ? For this, we transform our sentence into a question.

Is the teacher present?	هَلْ الْمُدَرِّسُ مَوْجُودٌ؟

You can't pronounce this sentence because two consonants would collide: the لْ of هَلْ and the لْ of the definite article. We have to get rid of the first سُكُونْ and replace it with a helping vowel.

In most situations, we use the vowel "*i*" (كَسْرَة) as a helping vowel. This is how the above sentence would be pronounced then: هَلِ الْمُدَرِّسُ مَوْجُودٌ؟

The particle هَلْ, which originally ends in سُكُونٌ, is now connected to the following word by the vowel "i". We basically added a vowel.	halilmudarrisu mawjūdun?

But there are exceptions:

- The preposition مِن often gets فَتْحةٌ as a helping vowel. Strictly speaking, the helping vowel of مِن is فَتْحةٌ **only** if مِن is followed by the definite article: مِنَ الـ. Otherwise, it is كَسْرةٌ. For example: مِن امْتِحان.

- Only some **pronouns** and **pronominal endings** use ضَمّةٌ ("u") as a helping vowel. This happens, for example, in قابَلَكُمُ الْمُدَرِّسُ. E.g.: هُم، كُم، تُم (The teacher met you all.)

- In all other set ups, the helping vowel is كَسْرةٌ - even if the preceding syllable contains "u": For ex.: لَمْ يَعُدِ الرَّجُل

39. فَ plus اِسْمَعُوا - How do you pronounce that?

You say: "fasma'ū!"

The sentence فَاسْمَعُوا means: *and listen*.

- If you say the entire expression, you should not stop after فَ. This brings along that you should ignore the letter ا, i.e., the *Hamza of liaison* (هَمْزةُ وَصلٍ).

- Therefore, you say *fasma'ū* and <u>not</u> *fa 'isma'ū*, because you don't pronounce the letter ا.

- Without فَ, however, when اِسْمَعُوا is the start of your utterance, you say *'isma'ū!* – with a glottal stop and "i".

40. Can you study Arabic grammar in verses?

Yes, you can.

If you want to study Arabic in the most cultivated way, there is a book for you: *ʾAlfīya* (أَلْفِيّة). It contains most of the Arabic grammar – in **1000 verses**.

The famous grammarian Ibn Mālik (ابْن مالِك), an Andalusian scholar who lived in the 13th century, summarized almost the entire Arabic grammar in this book. It contains the essential things about نَحْوٌ (*grammar*) and صَرْفٌ (*morphology*).

But it is not for the faint of heart and only for proficient readers. Ibn Mālik died in Damascus in 1274 (672هـ).

41. What is essential to know about verb forms?

*Many Arabs don't know what a I-verb or X-verb is. They only know **patterns**.*

Grammarians use the term وَزْنٌ (or plural أَوْزانٌ) which literally means *measure; weight* to describe a **model**.

The word *weight* is a good description for what we actually do in Arabic. Imagine a pair of scales and weights in form of vowels and extra letters. On the left side, we place what we want to get: the pattern. On the right side, we only throw in the root letters, In order to keep the balance, we have to add weights (vowels and/or extra letters) to the root.

The Roman numerals which are widely used in the West to describe the different verb forms were invented by Western scholars. If you want to increase your understanding of Arabic, it is important to switch from numbers to patterns as this will automatically give you a better feeling for the language.

Theoretically, each triliteral Arabic root could be transformed into one of **15 possible (and documented) verb forms.** Forms 11 through 15 (as well as 9) are very rare.

There are basically two groups of verbs:

unaugmented – the **pure** root The verb consists only of its three or four root letters.	مُجَرَّدٌ	1
augmented – **enhanced** root Used for the verb-patterns from II to X.	مَزِيدٌ	2

Grammarians use the term مُجَرَّدٌ ثُلاثِيٌّ if a verb consists of its 3 root letters only and مُجَرَّدٌ رُباعِيٌّ if it is based on 4 root letters. If you see the term ثُلاثِيٌّ in this book, you know that we talk about a form I-verb. All other forms are called مَزِيدٌ.

Let's now go on a short journey through the most important patterns. The capital letters next to the examples refer to the capital letters in the list.

Only <u>**one**</u> Arabic letter is added to the root: A) تَضْعِيفٌ (doubling of a letter) B) an *Aleph* (أَلِفٌ) C) a "real" Hamza (you pronounce it) D) the letter ت	مَزِيدٌ بِحَرْفٍ	2.1

root has 3 radicals	to teach	عَلَّم - يُعَلِّمُ	II	فَعَّلَ	A
	to meet	قابَلَ - يُقابِلُ	III	فاعَلَ	B

	to take out	أَخْرَجَ - يُخْرِجُ	IV	أَفْعَلَ	C
root has 4 radicals	*to quake*	تَزَلْزَلَ - يَتَزَلْزَلُ	II	تَفَعْلَلَ	D

	2.2

Two Arabic letters are added to the root:
  A) ت plus تَضْعِيفٌ
  B) ت plus أَلِفٌ
  C) *Hamza of liaison* (هَمْزَةُ وَصْلٍ) plus ن
  D) *Hamza of liaison* (هَمْزَةُ وَصْلٍ) plus ت
  E) *Hamza of liaison* plus تَضْعِيفٌ
	مَزِيدٌ بِحَرْفَيْنِ

root has 3 radicals	*to study*	تَعَلَّمَ - يَتَعَلَّمُ	V	تَفَعَّلَ	A
	to cooperate	تَعاوَنَ - يَتَعاوَنُ	VI	تَفاعَلَ	B
	to be broken	إِنْكَسَرَ - يَنْكَسِرُ	VII	إِنْفَعَلَ	C
	to take part in	إِشْتَرَكَ - يَشْتَرِكُ	VIII	إِفْتَعَلَ	D
	to become green	إِخْضَرَّ - يَخْضَرُّ	IX	إِفْعَلَّ	E
root has 4 radicals	*to be reassured*	إِطْمَأَنَّ - يَطْمَئِنُّ	IV	إِفْعَلَلَّ	E

	2.3
Three letters are added to the root.	مَزِيدٌ بِثَلاثَةِ أَحْرُفٍ

This is a combination of three ingredients:
  1) a *Hamza of liaison* (هَمْزَةُ وَصْلٍ)
  2) The letter س
  3) The letter ت	

root has 3 radicals	*to import*	إِسْتَوْرَدَ - يَسْتَوْرِدُ	X	إِسْتَفْعَلَ

42. Does every verb pattern convey a different meaning?

In principle, yes, but there are exceptions.

Even if you don't know a verb, you may be able to derive an idea just by looking at its pattern; form (أَوْزانٌ). This is due to the fact that the respective verb patterns express a specific underlying meaning. In the following tables, the capital letters next to the examples refer to the capital letters in the list.

يُفَعِّلُ	فَعَّلَ	fa"ala	II - 2

A) Can strengthen the meaning of a I-verb (often an **intensive version** of the I-verb).

B) Can make a I-verb **transitive** (فِعْلٌ مُتَعَدٍّ). Transitive verbs can have a direct object.

C) Can make a I-verb **causative**. Causative verbs are verbs that show the reason that something happened. Usually they express the following events: to make (someone) doing (something); to let (someone) doing (something).

<table>
<tr><td colspan="3" align="center">II-verb</td><td></td><td colspan="3" align="center">I-verb</td></tr>
<tr><td>A</td><td>to teach</td><td>دَرَّسَ</td><td></td><td>to study</td><td>دَرَسَ</td></tr>
<tr><td>B</td><td>to clean something</td><td>ظَهَّرَ</td><td>◄</td><td>to be clean</td><td>ظَهَرَ</td></tr>
<tr><td>C</td><td>to remind somebody</td><td>ذَكَّرَ</td><td></td><td>to remember</td><td>ذَكَرَ</td></tr>
</table>

يُفاعِلُ	فاعَلَ	fā'ala	III - 3

A) Shows the **attempt** to do something – *try to...*

B) *To do to* (someone); **to involve someone**. Describes someone doing the action in question to or with someone else.

Watch out: I-verbs need a preposition in Arabic to connect the action with the other part – <u>III-verbs don't</u>. In Arabic, III-verbs go along with a direct object (مَفْعُولٌ بِهِ). In English, however, the meaning of III-verbs is often translated with an **indirect object** – so you will need the English words *with* or *against* to produce a meaningful sentence.

	III-verb			I-verb	
A	*to try to kill (to fight)*	قاتَلَ		*to kill*	قَتَلَ
B	*to do business with*	عامَلَ	◄	*to work*	عَمِلَ
B	*to correspond*	كاتَبَ		*to write*	كَتَبَ

to dance	رَقَصَ - يَرْقُصُ	فَعَلَ	I-verb
*to dance **with***	راقَصَ - يُراقِصُ	فاعَلَ	III-verb

He danced at the party.	رَقَصَ فِي الْحَفْلةِ.	I
He danced **with her** at the party.	راقَصَها فِي الْحَفْلةِ.	III

In Arabic, III-verbs often take a direct object (مَفْعُولٌ بِهِ). They are **transitive** (فِعْلٌ مُتَعَدٍّ). In English, the meaning of Arabic III-verbs are often **intransitive** (فِعْلٌ لازِمٌ) which means that they are translated with a preposition.

يُفْعِلُ	أَفْعَلَ	'af'ala	IV - 4

A) Makes a I-verb **transitive** (having a direct object);

B) Makes a I-verb **causative** – *to make* or *cause someone or something to do or be*. This is the pattern's most common application. Form IV-has the strongest causative meaning.

C) It can **strengthen** the meaning of a I-verb.

IV-verb

A	to make happy	أَسْعَدَ
B	to inform somebody	أَعْلَمَ
C	to lock	أَغْلَقَ

I-verb

to be happy	سَعِدَ
to know	عَلِمَ
to close	غَلَقَ

◄

يَتَفَعَّلُ	تَفَعَّلَ	tafaʿʿala	V - 5

A) **Reflexive meaning** of the II-verb (فَعَّلَ). It may also convey a light passive meaning. What does reflexive mean? Reflexive verbs show that the person who does the action is also the person who is affected by it.

B) Sometimes it is an **intensive** version of a I-verb.

C) Occasionally, it has the meaning of **pretending something**.

V-verb

A	to be separated	تَفَرَّقَ
A	to be frightened	تَرَوَّعَ
B	to track	تَتَبَّعَ
B	to congregate	تَجَمَّعَ
C	to pretend/claim to be a prophet; to foretell	تَنَبَّأَ بِ
C	to force oneself; to take upon over something	تَكَلَّفَ بِ

I- or II-verb

to separate	فَرَّقَ
to scare	رَوَّعَ
to follow	تَبِعَ
to gather; join	جَمَعَ
to inform, to tell	نَبَّأَ بِ
to charge, to assign	كَلَّفَ بِ

◄

يَتَفَاعَلُ	تَفَاعَلَ	tafāʻla	VI -6

A) **Reflexive** form of a **III-verb** (فَاعَلَ). It often has a **reciprocal** meaning: *to do something together; to do something between or among each other.* A reciprocal verb expresses the idea of an action that is done by two or more people or things to each other.

B) May convey (similar to stem V) the meaning of **pretending**.

	VI-verb		**I- or III-verb**	
A	to share with one another	تَشَارَكَ	to share	شَارَكَ
A	to reveal (secrets, thoughts, feelings) to each other	تَكَاشَفَ	to reveal	كَاشَفَ بِ
B	to feign sleep; to pretend to be asleep	تَنَاوَمَ	to sleep	نَامَ

يَنْفَعِلُ	إِنْفَعَلَ	ʼinfaʻala	VII - 7

A) **Passive** meaning of the **I-verb** (the basic stem). Watch out: This form is not the real passive voice. Why? If we use a VII-verb, the action happens to the subject (فَاعِلٌ) without knowing the actual doer of the action (agent). In the passive of a I-verb, we usually know the doer but hide him by the passive.

B) **Reflexive meaning** – showing that the person, who does the action, is the one who is targeted/affected by it. However, in most situations, a VII-verb indicates both: passive and reflexive meaning.

VII-verb   I-verb

	VII-verb			I-verb	
A	to be/become broken	إِنْكَسَرَ		to break sth.	كَسَرَ
A	to be wrung out	إِنْعَصَرَ		to squeeze	عَصَرَ
B	to be uncovered	إِنْكَشَفَ	◄	to uncover	كَشَفَ
B	to be put to flight	إِنْهَزَمَ		to put to flight	هَزَمَ

يَفْتَعِلُ	إِفْتَعَلَ	'ifta'ala	VIII - 8

A) **Reflexive** or **passive** meaning of a **I-verb** (similar to VII).

B) It may express the meaning of: *to do something for oneself.*

C) It may express: *to do something with someone else.*

VIII-verb   I-verb

	VIII-verb			I-verb	
A	to take fire; to be burned	إِحْتَرَقَ		to burn sth.	حَرَقَ
A	to be occupied (with)	إِشْتَغَلَ بِ		to occupy	شَغَلَ
B	to be far from homeland	إِغْتَرَبَ	◄	to go away	غَرَبَ
B	to take for oneself; take up	إِتَّخَذَ		to take	أَخَذَ
C	to be associated (with)	إِقْتَرَنَ		to associate	قَرَنَ

يَفْعَلُّ	إِفْعَلَّ	'if'alla	IX - 9

A) **Reflexive** meaning of a II-verb (referring to colors or physical deficiencies).

XI-verb				II-verb	
A	to blush; to become red	اِحْمَرَّ		to make red	حَمَّرَ
A	to be crooked	اِعْوَجَّ	◄	to bend, crook sth.	عَوَّجَ

يَسْتَفْعِلُ	اِسْتَفْعَلَ	ʾistafʿala	X - 10

A) It expresses **to regard/find/consider** something as...

B) Derived verbal meaning of a noun (اِسْمٌ) - *denominal verbs*.

C) Expresses a **wish or a desire** (*to let sb. do sth. for you; to demand sth. for yourself*) → *to seek, ask for, require an action*.

D) **Reflexive** meaning of أَفْعَلَ (form IV).

E) X-verbs may make **I-verbs causative**.

	X-verb			I- or IV-verb; noun	
A	to find ugly	اِسْتَقْبَحَ		to be ugly	قَبُحَ
C	to ask for permission	اِسْتَأْذَنَ		to allow	أَذِنَ
B	to invest; to profit	اِسْتَثْمَرَ		fruit (noun)	ثَمَرٌ
B	to adopt oriental manners; to study the Orient	اِسْتَشْرَقَ	◄	the Orient	شَرْقٌ
C	to inquire	اِسْتَعْلَمَ		to know	عَلِمَ
D	to prepare oneself	اِسْتَعَدَّ		to prepare	أَعَدَّ
D	to consider oneself great	اِسْتَكْبَرَ		to deem great	أَكْبَرَ
E	to cause to serve; to use	اِسْتَخْدَمَ		to serve	خَدَمَ
E	to cause (call) to witness	اِسْتَشْهَدَ		to witness	شَهِدَ

Remark: Form X is not the only pattern that produces *denominal verbs*. The root of such verbs is based on a **concrete noun** (اِسْمٌ), especially, when the noun is one of the very first and essential words used by people.

Many verb forms II (فَعَّلَ), IV (أَفْعَلَ), and X (اِسْتَفْعَلَ) have such roots. Some examples:

meaning	stem	verb	meaning	noun
to shine; to blossom	IV - 4	أَزْهَرَ	*blossoms*	زَهْرٌ
to greet	II – 2	سَلَّمَ	*greeting, peace*	سَلامٌ
to appoint as successor	X – 10	اِسْتَخْلَفَ	*successor*	خَلَفٌ

43. How do you say *both* in Arabic?

You use the dual form of a special word.

In Arabic, there is a special way to express the English word *both*. Two words are essential to express the idea in Arabic:

both; masc. sing.	Both are exclusively used in a إضافةٌ- construction and thus lost their final نٌ. Originally they were كِلانِ and كِلْتانِ.	كِلا	1
both; fem. sing.		كِلْتا	2

They both express the dual (مُثَنَّى) – grammatically, however, they are **singular** (مُفْرَدٌ)! The only difference between كِلا and كِلْتا is the gender. كِلا is masculine; كِلْتا is feminine.

So far, so good – but where should we put them in a sentence?

There are two possibilities.

First part of the **إِضافةٌ**.	*both men*	كِلَا الرَّجُلَيْنِ	1
The second part must be a <u>definite</u>, <u>dual</u> noun.	*both times*	كِلْتا الْمَرَّتَيْنِ	

In this application, both **كِلَا** and **كِلْتا** are so-called **proper nouns** of genus (**إِسْمُ عَلَمٍ جِنْسِيٌّ**).

Apposition (**بَدَلٌ**).	*both men*	الرَّجُلانِ كِلاهُما	2
Placed after a dual noun. You must add a <u>dual</u> pronoun suffix (**ضَمِيرٌ الْمُؤَكَّدِ**) to **كِلَا** and **كِلْتا** respectively.	*both times*	الْمَرَّتانِ كِلْتاهُما	

In this application, we treat **كِلَا** and **كِلْتا** as *followers* (**تابِعٌ**). They convey **emphasis** (**أَلْفاظُ التَّوْكِيدِ الْمَعْنَوِيِّ لِلشُّمُولِ**).

Although the literal translation is slightly different, both options express the same meaning.

Your **both** (two) sisters have traveled.	سافَرَتْ كِلْتا أُخْتَيْكَ.	1
Your two sisters have traveled, **both of them**.	سافَرَتْ أُخْتاكَ كِلتاهُما.	2

How can we understand the grammar behind it? Both words must agree in gender with the noun or pronoun they refer to. So we match **كِلْتا** and **كِلَا** either with...

- Option 1: the gender of the second part of the **إِضافةٌ**-construction (i.e., **مُضافٌ إِلَيْهِ**);
- Option 2: the gender of the word to which **كِلَا** or **كِلْتا** refer. It is the word before them, i.e., **مُبْدَلٌ مِنْهُ**.

What you need to keep in mind in option 1 – the إضافةٌ:

كِلَا and كِلْتا agree in gender with the noun they modify – but **not** in case! What does that practically mean? Well, ...

- When they serve as the first part of the إضافةٌ-construction and when they are followed by an *evident, apparent, visible noun* (اِسْمٌ ظاهِرٌ), then they are <u>not</u> inflected.

- However, when they are followed by a pronoun suffix in the إضافةٌ-construction, they do get <u>inflected</u>!

- كِلَا and كِلْتا are grammatically treated as singular. Thus, a verb, adjective, or noun that relates to them is either masculine or feminine <u>singular</u>.

What you need to keep in mind in option 2 – apposition:

- When كِلَا or كِلْتا are combined with a pronoun suffix, you have to mark the <u>case</u> visibly. In the nominative (مَرْفوعٌ), they stay as they are. In the accusative (مَنْصوبٌ) or genitive case (مَجْرورٌ), however, they will get a visible marker. How can we do that? We change the ا into ي.

- This is similar to the dual of nouns or verbs which also have ا in the nominative (مَرْفوعٌ) and ي in the مَنْصوبٌ- and مَجْرورٌ-case.

- Eventually, we get كِلَيْهِما (kilayhima) and كِلْتَيْهِما (kiltay-hima). The ضَمَّةٌ of the suffix هُما or هُمْ or هُنَّ is changed into كَسْرةٌ after ـِ or ـِي or ـَيْ resulting in هِما or هِمْ.

Let's put all this stuff into sentences. We start with **option 1 – the إضافةٌ-construction.**

| Both of them are teachers. | كِلَاهُما مُدَرِّسٌ. |

Both were nice.	كانَ كِلاهُما لَطيفًا.

Since كِلا is the "subject" (إسْمُ كانَ) and needs the **nominative** case (مَرْفُوعٌ), the Aleph stays.

Both men saw her.	كِلا الرَّجُلَيْنِ رَآها.

The verb is used in the third person, masculine, **singular** – and not in the dual form although we are referring to a dual.

I saw both young men.	رَأَيْتُ كِلا الْفَتَيَيْنِ.

Since كِلا is followed by a noun (and not a pronoun!), it does not undergo visible changes – although it is in the position of an accusative case! The same is true for the genitive case; for example: *I passed by two young men* (مَرَرْتُ بِكِلا الْفَتَيَيْنِ).

In both times...	في كِلْتا الْمَرَّتَيْنِ

Although كِلْتا is preceded by a preposition, it is not inflected for case. Why? Because it is the **first part** of a إضافةٌ.

with both of us	بِكِلَيْنا

Since it is not connected to a إسْمٌ but to a personal pronoun, we have to use the مَجْرُورٌ-case! → The Aleph turns into ي.

Everything that happened to both of us...	كُلُّ ما حَدَثَ لِكِلَيْنا.

Let's continue with **option 2** – the apposition.

It belongs to both of you (plural).	هُوَ لَكُما كِلَيْكُما. هِيَ لَكُما كِلْتَيْكُما.

These are tricky sentences. The expressions كِلَيْكُمَا and كِلْتَيْكُمَا are placed as appositions. They have to agree in case and gender with the words to which they refer.

The لِ in the expression لَكُمَا is a preposition (حَرْفُ جَرٍّ) which drags the suffix كُمْ into the genitive case (مَجْرُورٌ). However, the suffix is indeclinable and cannot get case markers – we can only assign a place value. Since the apposition gets the same case as the word to which it refers, كِلَيْكُمَا has to be in the genitive (مَجْرُورٌ) too.

I saw young men, both of them.	رَأَيْتُ الْفَتَيَيْنِ كِلَيْهِما.

Young men is the **direct object** (مَفْعُولٌ بِهِ) and has to be in the accusative case (مَنْصُوبٌ) – and so does the apposition.

44. My two colleagues - How do you say that?

Answer: زَمِيلايَ *(nominative) and* زَمِيلَيَّ *(genitive/accusative).*

My two colleagues in Arabic – sounds easy, but it is actually a quite complicated task. We need to solve **three things**:

1. We need to form the dual (مُثَنَّى) of *colleague*. It is زَمِيلانِ in the nominative (مَرْفُوعٌ) and زَمِيلَيْنِ in the other cases;

2. We need the correct possessive marker for the first person (*my*): ي;

3. We have to solve how to add that pronoun because the possessive pronoun is the second part of a إِضَافَةٌ-construction.

Here is a step-by-step-guide:

1. First form the dual: زَمِيلَيْنِ or زَمِيلانِ.

2. Delete the ن of the dual. → We get زَميلا and زَميلَي.

3. Add the possessive pronoun ي. → We get زَميلَاي and زَميلَيْنِ which merges to زَميلَيّ.

4. Add فَتْحةٌ on top of the last letter ي. Why? By definition, the possessive suffix ي needs the vowel *"i"* (كَسرةٌ) before. When the preceding letter can't carry كَسرةٌ, because it is already occupied with a vowel, then we fix and cement the last letter ي on a vowel, i.e., the *"a"* (مَبْنِيٌّ عَلَى الْفَتْحِ). This is done to harmonize the sounds and is exactly the situation if we have a dual.

5. Eventually, we get زَميلاي and زَميلَيّ.

case	pronuncia-tion	*my two colleagues*	*two colleagues*	*(one) col-league*
مَرْفوعٌ	zamīlā-ya	زَميلاي	زَميلانِ	زَميلٌ
مَجْرُورٌ / مَنْصُوبٌ	zamīlayya	زَميلَيّ	زَميلَيْنِ	

For a detailed discussion, see *Arabic for Nerds 2, question #105*

45. وَالِدَيَّ - How would you translate that?

It means: my (two) parents – in the accusative or genitive case.

Let us first check the pronunciation of وَالِدَيّ. It is *wālidayya*.

The challenging part is the last letter and its vocalization, the يّ. Its shape indicates that we deal with a dual in the accu-sative (مَنْصُوبٌ) or genitive (مَجْرُورٌ) case. If you are not sure why, have a look at the previous *question #44*.

Let's put our hands on the word.

translation	remarks	word
father		وَالِدٌ
(two) parents	Nominative case (مَرْفُوعٌ); you use this form, for example, if the word serves as the subject (مُبْتَدَأٌ or فَاعِلٌ).	وَالِدانِ
(two) parents	Accusative (مَنْصُوبٌ) or genitive (مَجْرُورٌ).	وَالِدَيْنِ
my (two) parents	Nominative (مَرْفُوعٌ). Notice: There is **no** شَدّة at the end!	وَالِدايَ
my (two) parents	Accusative (مَنْصُوبٌ) or genitive (مَجْرُورٌ). Notice the شَدّة!	وَالِدَيَّ

Let's check another example.

translation	remarks	word
brother		أَخٌ
my two brothers	Nominative (مَرْفُوعٌ) → no شَدّة!	أَخَوايَ
my two brothers	Accusative (مَنْصُوبٌ) or genitive (مَجْرُورٌ) → with شَدّة!	أَخَوَيَّ

Some remarks:

- The ن of the dual is omitted in a إضافةٌ-construction or if a possessive pronoun is added (which is a إضافةٌ).
- If we add the possessive pronoun *my* to a dual, and if this expression needs to take the genitive (مَجْرُورٌ) or accusative (مَنْصُوبٌ) case, we need some fixing. Why? Because we have two colliding letters at the end: ي+ئ. This is expressed by a شَدّة over the ي.

- Last step: We need to add فَتْحَةٌ on top of the ـيّ. For the reasons, see *question #44*.

Excursus: Brother or stepbrother?

The common Arabic word for *brother* is أَخٌ (plural: إِخْوَةٌ or إِخْوانٌ). But there is another word which bears a fine difference.

شَقِيقٌ (plural: أَشِقَّةٌ or أَشِقّاءُ) describes that you have the same mother and father as your brother (الْأَخُ مِن الْأَبِ وَالْأُمّ); i.e., he is a brother on the paternal and maternal side. أَخٌ, on the other hand, can also be used if either the mother or father is different or if you want to use *brother* figuratively. The same is true for شَقِيقةٌ (*full sister*).

شَقِيقٌ is based on the root ش-ق-ق which means *to split; to divide it lengthwise*. شِقٌّ denotes *the half of a thing of any kind*. When a thing is divided in halves, each of the halves is called the شَقِيقٌ. Hence, the *counterpart* of a person or thing.

Both شَقِيقٌ and شَقِيقةٌ (plural: شَقِيقاتٌ or شَقائِقُ) are used by politicians when talking about Arab nations. Both may be used to denote *brother-, sister-*. In such application, they are placed after a noun and work as adjectives (نَعْتٌ) or may precede the noun functioning as an apposition (بَدَلٌ).

half-brother; stepbrother	أَخٌ غَيْرُ شَقِيقٍ
the brother country	الْقُطْرُ الشَّقِيقُ
the Arab sister states	الدُّوَلُ الْعَرَبِيّةُ الشَّقِيقةُ
two sister nations	شَعْبانِ شَقِيقانِ
the sister-country Iraq	الشَّقِيقةُ الْعِراقُ

46. *This car is mine* - How do you express that in Arabic?

We need a trick, because there is no word for "mine".

Arabic has no words for *mine; yours; his* or *hers*. In English, these words are a form of the possessive case of the pronoun *I* used as a predicate adjective. It mainly depends on the intended meaning and context to find a good Arabic translation.

To express *mine* in Arabic, there are a few auxiliary constructions. Here is an easy option:

1. **Repeat** the thing that is possessed.

2. Add the appropriate **possessive marker**, a pronoun suffix.

This car is **mine**.	هٰذِهِ السَّيّارةُ سَيّارَتي.
The book is **hers**.	الْكِتابُ كِتابُها.
Is this book **yours** or **mine**?	أَهٰذا كِتابُكَ أَمْ كِتابي؟

Another solution – with the expression لي (lit.: *to me*).

The red gloves are mine.	القُفّازاتُ الحَمراءُ لي.
He is an old friend of mine (lit.: for a long time).	إنَّه صَديقٌ لي مُنْذُ أَمَدٍ طَويلٍ.
It's not mine.	لَيْسَ لي.

47. شِبْهُ الْجُمْلةِ - What is that?

It is an adjunct: a prepositional or adverbial phrase which cannot stand alone as it does not provide a full meaning.

شِبْهٌ means *like; semi-; quasi; almost.* جُمْلةٌ means *sentence.* The literal translation is something like *semi sentence.*

To understand the logic behind such phrases, we should first understand the idea of a normal sentence. We call that a جُمْلةٌ مُفيدةٌ, a *meaningful* sentence. In Arabic, it is either a nominal sentence (جُمْلةٌ اِسْميّةٌ), which starts with a noun, or a verbal sentence (جُمْلةٌ فِعْليّةٌ), which starts with a verb.

In contrast, a شِبْهُ الْجُمْلةِ cannot stand alone and only gives you junks of information that cannot be understood without the main part: it has optional elements that are not the subject, verb or object. It usually gives you additional information related to the verb. There are two possibilities:

Adverb of time or **place** plus **noun** (in the genitive case) → إضافة-construction.	ظَرْفٌ + مُضافٌ إلَيْهِ	1
above the tree	فَوْقَ الشَّجَرةِ	
afternoon	بَعْدَ الظُّهرِ	

Preposition plus **noun** (genitive case).	حَرْفُ الْجَرِّ plus مَجْرُورٌ	2
in the house	في الْبَيْتِ	
on the desk	عَلَى الْمَكْتَبِ	

48. How many types of words are there in Arabic?

Three.

The grammar terms we use in English, e.g., adverb, adjective, preposition, pronoun, etc., don't really work in the Arabic universe. This has to do with the core of the language body. In Arabic, there are **only three main types of words:**

اِسْمٌ • فِعْلٌ • حَرْفٌ

- A اِسْمٌ (*noun*) refers to a place, time, person, thing, condition, adverb, adjective, etc. It is <u>not</u> affected by time. Crucial: Only a اِسْمٌ can get **case markers** (nunation).

- A فِعْلٌ (*verb*) is a word that is stuck in time. It indicates an action or occurrence. Arabic tenses don't really express time, but rather an aspect. In other words, an action is either finished/complete (الْماضِي) or it is ongoing/incomplete (الْمُضارِعُ). Complete here means *perfect* (→ aspect); *past* (→ tense). Incomplete means *imperfect* (→ aspect); *present* (→ tense). Don't forget: Only verbs can get **mood markers**: jussive (مَجْزُومٌ), subjunctive (مَنْصُوبٌ) mood. See also *Arabic for Nerds 2, #24, #61.*

- A حَرْفٌ (*particle*) is a word that (usually) does <u>not</u> convey a meaning on its own. It needs to be connected to other words. A حَرْفٌ **never** gets case or mood endings. It has an **indeclinable, cemented** (مَبْنِيٌّ) shape and always stays the same. Watch out: حَرْفٌ can also denote a single letter.

In **English**, every word or phrase can be classified as one of the **nine parts of speech** depending on its function. Part of speech refers to one the nine word categories. English has four major word classes: nouns, verbs, adjectives, and adverbs. The others are prepositions, pronouns, determiners, conjunctions, and interjections.

In Arabic, a اِسْمٌ can serve in different **functions** and carry various jobs depending on the position in the sentence. This varies from sentence to sentence. It may be placed in the **position** of a *subject* (فاعِلٌ or مُبْتَدَأٌ), an *adjective* (نَعْتٌ or صِفةٌ), or an *adverb* (ظَرْفٌ), but it always remains a اِسْمٌ. In Arabic, we name the function in the sentence – but not the type.

Here is a list of common types of حَرْفٌ:

	grammatical term	translation
فِي	حَرْفُ جَرٍّ	preposition; particle of subordination
لا, لَمْ	حَرْفُ نَفْي	negation particle
بَلْ	حَرْفُ إِضْرابٍ	particle of digression, retraction
وَ	حَرْفُ عَطْفٍ	conjunction; copulative particle
هَلْ	حَرْفُ اِسْتِفْهامٍ	interrogative particle
لَوْ	حَرْفُ شَرْطٍ	conditional particle

49. How do you recognize a اِسْمٌ in a text?

There are three features that only nouns (اِسْمٌ) have.

To understand the skeleton of an Arabic sentence, it is helpful to identify the nouns. This is a fairly simple task, because there are three features that are only found with nouns (اِسْمٌ).

One characteristic alone is enough to be sure that the word in question is a noun. Let's use the word كِتابٌ (*book*).

	feature	explanation	example
1	nunation (تَنْوِينٌ)	In Arabic, only a noun (اِسْمٌ) can get nunation. Nunation tells us that the noun is indefinite (نَكِرَةٌ).	هٰذا كِتابٌ. *This is a book.*

2	definite article (تَعْرِيفٌ بِأل)	Only a اِسْمٌ can have the definite article.	قَرَأْتُ الْكِتابَ.
			*I read **the** book.*
3	annexation (إِضافةٌ)	Only a اِسْمٌ can serve as the first part of a إِضافةٌ-construction. The second part is normally a noun too; however, a sentence may occur in this position as well.	قَرَأْتُ كِتابَ النَّحوِ.
			*I read the book **of** the grammar (grammar book).*

50. What can be used as adjectives in Arabic?

You have mainly four options.

In English, the word *beautiful* is an adjective. In Arabic, the corresponding word جَمِيلٌ is a noun (اِسْمٌ) that may have the **function** of an adjective (صِفةٌ or نَعْتٌ).

This is confusing for native speakers of English because Arabic doesn't know a specific word *class* called *adjective*. If we use the term adjective in Arabic, we only denote a function and not a type or class.

But that is the only difference.

Like in English, an adjective in Arabic is a word (or phrase) that describes or clarifies a noun or pronoun. Adjectives tell us more about size, shape, age, color, origin, or material of a person, thing, a place, or time.

In Arabic, adjectives are called صِفةٌ or نَعْتٌ. Both terms denote *description, characterization*.

What are the main forms that can serve as adjectives or attributes in Arabic?

4	3	2	1
صِيغةُ الْمُبالَغةِ	الصِّفةُ الْمُشَبَّهةُ	إِسْمُ الْمَفْعُولِ	إِسْمُ الْفاعِلِ
form of exaggeration	adjectives similar to active (and passive) participles	passive participle	active participle

Let us check them in detail:

1. The **active participle** (إِسْمُ الْفاعِلِ) is a description of an action (صِفةٌ بالْحَدَثِ). This is pretty much the same in English. The active participle for *to go* is *going*.

2. The **passive participle** (إِسْمُ الْمَفْعُولِ) refers to something having undergone the action of the verb. *to break → broken.*

3. The **quasi participle** (الصِّفةُ الْمُشَبَّهةُ), literal meaning: *similar quality,* is a noun that indicates a meaning of firmness. It indicates persistence and permanence. It usually denotes a quality inherent in people or thing. This explains why the root of a صِفةٌ مُشَبَّهةٌ cannot build an active participle (إِسْمُ فاعِلٍ). A صِفةٌ مُشَبَّهةٌ like *noble* (كَرِيمٌ) denotes not something that happens on one occasion only but something that is inherent in the character. We could say that the الصِّفةُ الْمُشَبَّهةُ is a representative or substitute for the non-existent إِسْمُ الْفاعِلِ.

Regarding its form, it is a derived noun (إِسْمٌ مُشْتَقٌّ) of the root. Purist grammarians, by the way, say that you should use the مَصْدَرٌ for analyzing and forming derived nouns – and not the past tense verb.

The exact and complete term is الصِّفةُ الْمُشَبَّهةُ بِاسْمِ الْفاعِلِ which could be translated as: a *quality similar to the active participle (agent-noun).* مُشَبَّهٌ is the passive participle of the II-verb شَبَّهَ / يُشَبِّهُ denoting *o make it to be like* or *to resemble.*

4. The **form of exaggeration** (صِيغَةُ الْمُبالَغةِ) is derived from a root that is capable of forming the active participle (إِسْمُ الْفاعِلِ.) Now, can every verb build an active participle? As we have seen above, the الصِّفةُ الْمُشَبَّهةُ is not capable of that; so the answer is **no**! We will analyze that in *question #143*.

The صِيغةُ الْمُبالَغةِ is actually just a way to say that someone is performing the active participle (i.e., an action) often, many times, or intensively (يَحْدُثُ كَثيرًا لَهُ إِسْمُ الْفاعِلِ).

Watch out: In order to <u>qualify</u> as an adjective in Arabic, the above mentioned forms need to be in **agreement** with the word to which they relate.

Hence, they have to "mirror" the following grammatical features: **number** (singular, dual, plural), **gender** (masculine or feminine), **determination** (definite or indefinite), and **case** (nominative/مَرْفُوعٌ, genitive/مَجْرُورٌ, accusative/مَنْصوبٌ).

→ If you want to know more about the difference between the terms صِفةٌ and نَعْتٌ, check out *Arabic for Nerds 2, question #171.*

51. Why do adjectives need agreement?

Full agreement is necessary to charge a word with the function of an adjective (نَعْتٌ). Otherwise, it may be the predicate (خَبَرٌ).

You will often hear that an adjective has to agree with a noun. But what does *agreement* (الْمُطابَقةُ) mean?

If you encounter this term, you know that a word needs to share **four grammatical features** with another one:

1. Gender: masculine or feminine (التَّذْكيرُ وَالتَّأْنيثُ)

2. Definiteness or indefiniteness (التَّعْرِيفُ وَالتَّنْكِيرُ)

3. Number: singular, dual, or plural (الْإِفْرَادُ وَالتَّثْنِيَةُ وَالْجَمْعُ)

4. Case (الْإِعْرَابُ)

Don't forget that the adjective is placed **after** the noun which it further describes (مَنْعُوتٌ)! Let's see an example:

The sincere man came.	جاءَ الرَّجُلُ الْفاضِلُ.

We say that *sincere; kind-hearted; honest* (الْفاضِلُ) is a *true description* (نَعْتٌ حَقِيقِيٌّ); a *real attributive adjective*. This is because the adjective grammatically (fully) agrees with the preceding إِسْمٌ, i.e., *the man* (الرَّجُلُ).

But what happens, if we have to deal with a plural?

	form of the noun to which the adjective refers	translation	example
1	singular; masculine	*a new student*	طالِبٌ جَدِيدٌ
	singular; feminine	*a new student*	طالِبَةٌ جَدِيدَةٌ
2	dual; masculine	*two new students*	طالِبانِ جَدِيدانِ
	dual; feminine	*two new students*	طالِبَتانِ جَدِيدَتانِ

When we talk about **human** beings in the plural, then, the adjective has to be in the **plural** too.

3	sound plural; human; masculine	*new teachers*	مُدَرِّسُونَ جُدُدٌ
		Arab journalists	صِحافِيُّونَ عَرَبِيُّونَ

4	sound plural; human; feminine	*new students*	طالِباتٌ جَدِيداتٌ
		Arab customers	زَبُوناتٌ عَرَبِيّاتٌ

5	broken plural; human; masculine *Remark: nouns referring to female humans usually take a feminine sound plural.*	*new students*	طُلّابٌ جُدُدٌ
		military rulers	حُكّامٌ عَسْكَرِيُّونَ
		respected neighbors	جِيرانٌ مُحْتَرَمُونَ
		unwanted guests	ضُيُوفٌ ثِقالٌ

When we refer to something in the plural that is **non-human**, then, the adjective has to be **singular; feminine**.

6	broken plural; non-human; masculine	*new books*	كُتُبٌ جَدِيدةٌ
		black crows (Note: سُوداءُ is the feminine form of أَسْوَدُ)	غِرْبانٌ سُوداءُ
		long days	أَيّامٌ طَوِيلةٌ

7	sound plural; non-human; feminine *(Note: In such situations we almost always get a fem. sound plural.)*	*new cars*	سَيّاراتٌ جَدِيدةٌ
		marvelous animals	حَيَوَاناتٌ رائِعةٌ
		the United States of America	الْوِلَايَاتُ الْمُتَّحِدَةُ الأَمْرِيكِيّةُ
		small companies	شَرِكاتٌ صَغِيرةٌ

- The easy part: If the adjective refers to a **non-human** plural, the adjective will be <u>**singular, feminine**</u>.

- The tough task: If the adjective refers to a **human plural**, the adjective needs to be in the **plural** as well. With masculine adjectives, the result is often a **broken plural form** like *new* (جُدُدٌ). This can be challenging. In Arabic, there are 29 patterns of broken plurals for words derived from triliteral roots.

Excursus: Can only a single noun work as an adjective? No, that's not the end of the story.

1	noun (إِسْمٌ ظاهِرٌ)
Cairo is a great city.	الْقاهِرةُ مَدِينةٌ عَظِيمةٌ.
adjective (نَعْتٌ)	عَظِيمةٌ

2	semi sentence (شِبْهُ الْجُمْلةِ): adverb (ظَرْفٌ) or preposition (حَرْفُ جَرٍّ)
I listened to a professor on the platform.	إِسْتَمَعْتُ إِلَى أُسْتاذٍ فَوْقَ الْمِنْبَرِ.

Is فَوْقَ الْمِنْبَرِ an adjective for *professor*? This is a debate. Some say yes. Others say that the prepositional phrase is not an adjective – but linked to a deleted predicate (خَبَرٌ مَحْذُوفٌ) which could be, e.g., the word *found* (مَوْجُودٌ). See *Arabic for Nerds 2, #140*, to know more about the nature of such sentences.

3.1	nominal sentence (جُمْلةٌ إِسْمِيّةٌ)
A very cold day passed.	مَضَى يَوْمٌ بَرْدُهُ قارِصٌ.

> The entire nominal sentence بَرْدُهُ قارِصٌ is placed as an adjective for *day* (نَعْتٌ لِيَوْم).

3.2	verbal sentence (جُمْلَةٌ فِعْلِيّةٌ)

This is a work which is useful. (meaning: This is a useful work.)	هذا عَمَلٌ يُفيدُ.

> The verb يُفيدُ is placed as an adjective for *work* (نَعْتٌ لِعَمَل). Instead of the verb you could also use مُفيدٌ, which is the active particle (اِسْمُ فاعِلٍ) of the IV-verb يُفيدُ / أَفادَ (*to be of use*).

Watch out: If you want to place an entire sentence (3.1 & 3.2) as an adjective, the مَنْعُوتٌ has to be be __in__definite (نَكِرَةٌ). Otherwise, you may produce a حالٌ! See #246.

Remark: Did you know that there is a so-called *causative description* (نَعْتٌ سَبَبِيٌّ)? If not, jump to *question #144.*

52. How do you say *would* in Arabic?

In Arabic, there is no simple equivalent to English "would".

What is the nature of the English word *would*? Technically, *would* is the past tense of *will*. It is an *auxiliary modal verb* that is used to form tenses, questions, or the passive voice.

The past tense can express time but also an idea (e.g., the conditional mood). When a sentence makes a statement, it is in the indicative mood (فِعْلٌ مَرْفُوعٌ) - the standard situation and mood. When it indicates possibility, a verb is in the **conditional** mood – this is what we talk about.

We should now briefly talk about *modal verbs*. We use such verbs to indicate that you believe something is certain, probable, or possible (or not). In English, devices can help us to make sentences conditional – for example, by adding a word like *may, should, could, would*, or *must*. → Do not use modal verbs for things which happen definitely.

In English, we use *would* all the time – mainly, because we want to be polite or express a hypothetical situation. In Arabic, we don't have a word for *would*. Instead, you need to learn some phrases which can be used in certain situations. Let's check some workarounds.

A. You use the **future tense** in Arabic; however by looking at the circumstances, it becomes evident that the meaning is conditional. Usually, a past tense verb is involved earlier in the sentence – which helps to clarify the meaning. We usually encounter this situation in the **reported, indirect speech!**

They said the weather would be clear.	قالُوا إِنَّ الْجَوَّ سَيَكُونُ صافِيًا.
He promised he would go.	وَعَدَ بِأَنَّهُ سَيَذْهَبُ.
I thought you would like it.	اعْتَقَدْتُ أَنَّكَ سَتُحِبُّهُ

B. You can use كان plus a verb in the present tense (الْمُضارِعُ). This is typical for conditional statements.

he would have done it	كانَ سَيَفْعَلُ
he would not have done it	لَمْ يَكُنْ سَيَفْعَلُ

Who would have thought that?	تُرَى مَنْ كانَ يُمْكِنُ أَن يَتَصَوَّرَ ذلِكَ؟

Who would have believed it?	مَنْ كانَ سَيُصَدِّقُ هذا؟
I wondered if you would come.	تَساءَلْتُ عَمّا إذا كُنْتَ سَتَجيءُ.
I would have found out sooner or later.	كُنْتُ سَأَكْتَشِفُ ذلِكَ عاجِلًا أو آجِلًا

C. You use *would* to express a wish, command, or suggestion.

You can use I-verb يَوَدُّ / يُريدُ / أرادَ (*to want*) or I-verb يَوَدُّ / وَدَّ (*to want/would like*) or any other polite expression. Note that it doesn't sound rude to say *"I want"* - but don't forget to add an appropriate form of address, for example, حَضْرَتُكَ.

I wish I could spend the summer in the mountains.	وَدِدْتُ لَوْ أَقْضي الصَّيْفَ في الْجَبَلِ
I said I would do it. Note: مُسْتَعِدٌّ لِ means *to be ready for.*	قُلْتُ إنّني مُسْتَعِدٌّ لِعَمَلِهِ.
Would you be so kind to tell him? Note: The V-verb يَتَفَضَّلُ / تَفَضَّلَ means *to be kind enough to.*	هَلا تَفَضَّلْتَ بِإخْبارِهِ؟
Would you mind closing the door? Note: مانِعٌ literally means *obstacle, something preventing.*	هَلْ لَدَيْكَ مانِعٌ مِن غَلْقِ الْبابِ؟
You would! (Literally: *This is what was expected of you!*)	هذا ما كانَ مُتَوَقَّعًا مِن أمْثالِكَ!
Would you be interested in buying one?	هَلْ تَوَدُّ أَنْ تَشْتَرِيَ واحِدًا؟

D. You use a conditional construction (جُمْلةُ الشَّرْطِ) to express a hypothetical situation.

You achieve that by the device لَوْ plus past tense verb in the first part (الشَّرْطُ - *apodosis*) and by adding the device لَ at the beginning of the second part (جَوابُ الشَّرْطِ - *protasis*).

I would do it if I were you. Note: لَوْ كُنْتُ مَكانَكَ is a common expression for *If I were you...*	لَوْ كُنْتُ مَكانَكَ لَفَعَلْتُ... = لو كُنْتُ مَكانَكَ لَما فَعَلْتُ ذلِكَ.
I wouldn't do it if not...	ما كُنْتُ لِأَفْعَلَ لَوْ لا...
I would call her in case she isn't at home.	لو كُنْتُ مَكانَكَ لَاتَّصَلْتُ بِها فِي حالِ ما لَمْ تَكُنْ فِي البَيْتِ.

53. Do all English tenses exist in Arabic?

No, they don't.

Tenses are among the most difficult things in most languages – but not in Arabic.

In French, for example, there are five past tense forms: *l'imparfait, le passé simple, le passé composé, le plus-que-parfait, le passé antérieur.* And in Arabic?

We need to introduce two linguistic terms in order to understand the concept of tenses in Arabic:

- **Tense:** a form of the verb which shows the *time* at which an action happened – in relation to the speaker.

- **Aspect:** deals with the degree of *completeness* of an action or state. Is the action completed, ongoing, or yet to happen?

Arabic does not have accurate time-points as English or French. The *imparfait* in French, for example, is used for incomplete actions; it explains what was happening, with no indication of when or even if it ended. If you want to translate an Arabic sentence, you have to understand the situation of an event and context to find an appropriate English translation.

I also use the term *tense* in this book because I don't want to confuse readers. In Arabic, there are two main "tenses":

- The **past tense** or perfect tense (الْماضِي). It denotes that the action is completed at the time to which reference is being made.

- The **present tense** or imperfect (الْمُضارِعُ). It is used for incomplete or yet to happen actions.

Now, what should we do if we want to express the past perfect tense, a verb tense which is used to talk about actions that were completed before some point in the past?

We use a combination of verbs or devices to express the idea. Here is a list of the most important English tenses and how they may be expressed in Arabic. Watch out for the mood markers! Note that there are other solutions as well.

1. Present tense (الْمُضارِعُ الْبَسِيطُ)

he does	يَفْعَلُ
he does indeed	لَيَفْعَلَنَّ
he doesn't	لا يَفْعَلُ
he doesn't; rarely used	ما يَفْعَلُ

2. Present progressive tense (اَلْمُضَارِعُ الْمُسْتَمِرُّ). In English: *to be* plus *-ing*. The present continuous is used to talk about something that is happening at the time of speaking. In most situations, you can use an *active participle* (اِسْمُ فَاعِلٍ). Sometimes, the *simple present tense* (اَلْمُضَارِعُ) would do the job as well plus an *adverb of time*, e.g., *now* (الْآنَ).

She is studying now.	إِنَّها تُذاكِرُ الْآنَ.
He is coming.	هُوَ قَادِمٌ.
I am not studying now.	لا أَدْرُسُ الْآنَ.

3. Past tense (الْماضِي الْبَسِيطُ). To make sure that you are talking about an event in the past, you could add an adverb of time like *yesterday* (أَمْسِ). The negation is done with the particle لَمْ plus verb in the jussive mood (مَجْزُومٌ).

he did/he has done	فَعَلَ
he has already done; he had done	قَدْ فَعَلَ
he (indeed) did; he (indeed) has done	لَقَدْ فَعَلَ

he did not do; he has not done	لَمْ يَفْعَلْ
he did not do; he has not done	ما فَعَلَ
he has not done yet	لَمْ يَفْعَلْ بَعْدُ

4. Past tense progressive (الْماضِي الْمُسْتَمِرُّ). In English: *was* or *were* plus *-ing*. It is used to express an action that was going on during a certain time in the past or when another action took place.

he was doing	كانَ يَفْعَلُ
he was (still) doing	ظَلَّ يَفْعَلُ

he was not doing* (negation of فَعَلَ)	كانَ لا يَفْعَلُ
he was not doing (negation of كانَ)	لَمْ يَكُنْ يَفْعَلُ

* The negation of فَعَلَ is more common than the negation of كانَ.

He was traveling.	كانَ مُسافِرًا.
I was going to say that...	كُنْتُ سَأَقُولُ إنَّ...
I was writing the letter when the telephone rang.	كُنْتُ أَكْتُبُ الْخِطابَ عِنْدَما دَقَّ جَرَسُ التِّلِيفُون.
While I was walking, I fell down.	بَيْنَما كُنْتُ أَسِيرُ وَقَعْتُ عَلَى الْأَرْضِ.

5. Past perfect tense; pluperfect (صِيغَةُ الْماضِي التَّامِّ or just الْماضِي الْبَعِيدُ). This tense is not common in Arabic. It is used to express two actions: one has happened before the other. You have several options to express this idea in Arabic:

- You use قَدْ كانَ in the first event and عِنْدَما before the second event.
- You connect both actions with *after* (بَعْدَ ما + past tense verb; also بَعْدَ أَنْ + **past** to paraphrase the pluperfect).
- It may be even enough to just use the simple past tense since the notion of time is understood from the context.

he had done it	كانَ قَدْ فَعَلَ

he had not done it* (negation of كانَ)	ما كانَ قَدْ فَعَلَ
	لَمْ يَكُنْ قَدْ فَعَلَ
he had not done it (negation of فَعَلَ)	كانَ ما فَعَلَ
	كانَ لَمْ يَفْعَلْ

* The negation of كانَ is more common than the negation of فَعَلَ.

After I had studied my lesson, I played soccer.	بَعْدَ ما ذاكَرْتُ دَرْسِي لَعِبْتُ كُرَةَ الْقَدَمِ.
After we had left we realized that...	بَعْدَ ما غادَرْنا أَدْرَكْنا أَنَّ...
They didn't call the police after you explained the situation.	لَمْ يَتَّصِلُوا بِالشُّرْطِةِ بَعْدَ ما شَرَحْتَ الْمَوْقِفَ.
She had told him.	كانَتْ قَدْ أَبْلَغَتْهُ.

6. Past perfect continuous (الْماضِي التّامُّ الْمُسْتَمِرُّ). In English: *had* + *been* + participle. This tense is used to express the duration of an action up to a certain time in the past. In Arabic, you can just use the past tense progressive (4). The notion of time is usually understood from the context.

Su'ād told me that she had been trying to get me on the phone three times.	أَخْبَرَتْنِي سُعادُ أَنَّها حاوَلَتْ أَنْ تَتَّصِلَ بِي ثَلاثَ مَرّاتٍ بِالتِّلِيفُون.

7. Future tense I (الْمُسْتَقْبَلُ). You use the future particle سَ for the near future and سَوْفَ for the distant future plus a verb in the present tense indicative (الْمُضارِعُ). The negation is done with the particle لَنْ plus verb in the subjunctive (مَنْصُوبٌ).

he will do (in near future)	سَيَفْعَلُ
he will do (distant future)	سَوْفَ يَفْعَلُ

he will not do (near future)	لَنْ يَفْعَلَ
he will not do (distant future)	سَوْفَ لا يَفْعَلُ

Remark: In English, the *immediate future* is expressed by the present progressive (*to be* + *-ing*). In Arabic, we use the simple future tense with the prefix س.

She is coming here next month.	إِنَّها سَتَأْتِي هُنا الشَّهْرَ الْقادِمَ.
We are going out at five.	سَنَخْرُجُ السَّاعَةَ الْخامِسَةَ.

8. Future tense progressive (الْمُسْتَقْبَلُ الْمُسْتَمِرُّ)

he will be doing	سَيَظَلُّ يَفْعَلُ
	active participle + يَكُونُ
	يَكُونُ + فِي + ال + مَصْدَرٌ

Okay, I will be waiting.	حَسَنًا, سَأَكُونُ فِي الْانْتِظارِ.
He will be traveling.	يَكُونُ مُسافِرًا.

In English, you often express the *definite future* with the future continuous tense. In Arabic, you just use the simple future (7). It is understood from the context.

Hurry up! The bus will be leaving in a few minutes!	إِسْرَعْ! سَيَرْحَلُ الْأُوتُوبِيسُ خِلالَ بَعْضِ دَقائِقَ.

9. Future perfect/future II (الْمُسْتَقْبَلُ التَّامُّ). This is very rare in Arabic.

he will have done it	كانَ سَوْفَ يَفْعَلُ
he will have done it	سَيَكُونُ (قَدْ) فَعَلَ

he will not have done it* (negation of كانَ)	سَوْفَ لا يَكُونُ (قَدْ) فَعَلَ
	لَنْ يَكُونَ (قَدْ) فَعَلَ
he will not have done it (negation of فَعَلَ)	كانَ سَوْفَ لا يَفْعَلُ
	كانَ لَنْ يَفْعَلَ

* The negation of كانَ is more common than the negation of فَعَلَ.

He will have contacted us tomorrow.	سَيَكُونُ قَدْ اِتَّصَلَ بِنا غَدًا.
She will have finished the job.	تَكُونَ قَدْ اِنْتَهَت الْعَمَلَ.

Watch out: You may use قَدْ plus past tense verb (الْماضِي) to distinguish the future perfect (*will have done it*) from the subjunctive (*would have done it*).

10. The German *Konjunktiv I.* In German, it is mainly used for reporting indirect speech and old-fashioned or polite commands and requests (*er möge bitte warten*). There is no real equivalent to that in Arabic. Besides, you don't need that mood form if you convert a direct speech into the reported speech – see *Arabic for Nerds 2, quest. #267.*

11. Past subjunctive (Konjunktiv II) - *should, would, could.*

The past subjunctive mood of *I want* is *I would*; of *I can* is *I could*. In English, this mood is used for hypothetical situations and to express doubt or wishes; for situations when the standard mood (indicative) - *I want* - would sound rude or boring.

In many situations, you use a conditional sentence (جُمْلةُ الشَّرْطِ). If you want to express something impossible, you usually have two ingredients: لَوْ and لَ – see #126 and #253. You have many options regarding the appropriate tense as the meaning mostly depends on the context. For *would* see #52.

12. Imperative (الْأَمْرُ). The imperative is derived from the present tense of the verb with some modifications. It always receives the jussive mood ending (مَجْزُومٌ).

	sing. m.	sing. f.	dual m./f.	plural m.	plural f.
do!	إِفْعَلْ	إِفْعَلِي	إِفْعَلا	إِفْعَلُوا	إِفْعَلْنَ
don't do!	لا تَفْعَلْ	لا تَفْعَلِي	لا تَفْعَلا	لا تَفْعَلُوا	لا تَفْعَلْنَ

For details about the construction of the imperative, see quest. #60.

54. *Prayer is better than sleep* - Is it really *better*?

Yes, at least regarding the grammar.

In Sunni Islam, the Muezzin uses a special phrase to call people to come and pray during dawn (الْفَجْرُ). It goes like this:

الصَّلاةُ خَيْرٌ مِن النَّوْمِ.

Prayer is better than sleep.

This is an interesting grammatical construction. We do not use the regular *comparative form* (اِسْمُ التَّفْضِيلِ) here, following the pattern أَفْعَلُ. **So why do we translate خَيْرٌ as better?**

خَيْرٌ is usually translated as *good*, which is correct. But it also can convey another meaning – that of a اِسْمُ تَفْضِيلٍ.

The word خَيْر has pretty much the same meaning as أَحْسَنُ which means *better*. Let us check some examples:

Prayer is **better** than sleep.	الصَّلاةُ خَيْرٌ مِن النَّوْمِ.
Work is **better** than laziness.	الْعَمَلُ خَيْرٌ مِن الْكَسَلِ.
He is **better** than...	هُوَ خَيْرٌ مِنْ...
I am not **better** than the student.	لَسْتُ خَيْرًا مِن الطَّالِبِ.
couldn't be **better**	عَلَى خَيْرِ ما يُرامُ
better luck next time	خَيْرُها بِغَيْرِها

The word for *better* was originally أَخْيَر and later became خَيْر. This happened a long time ago. In the Qur'an, خَيْر is already used in the meaning of *better*.

Good to know: If you use خَيْرٌ or شَرٌّ in a إِضافةٌ-construction, they will have the meaning of the **superlative**.

(the) best student	خَيْرُ طالِبٍ

In Arabic you don't use the definite article although it has a definite meaning in English. Since خَيْر is the first part in a إِضافةٌ-construction, it doesn't get nunation.

Watch out when you have to form the plural.

meaning	plural	singular	
good; excellent/better; best	خِيارٌ or أَخْيارٌ	خَيْرٌ	1
blessing; good thing	خُيُورٌ	خَيْرٌ	2

There are other words which behave like خَيْرٌ, for example, شَرٌّ (*bad, evil;* or: *worse*), but it is less common.

She is **worse** than...	هِيَ شَرٌّ مِنْ...
Note that there is no feminine form of شَرٌّ.	

Remark: What kind of noun is صَلاةٌ (plural: صَلَواتٌ)? It is a so-called *noun of origin* (اِسْمُ مَصْدَرٍ). It conveys almost the same meaning as the standard infinitive (الْمَصْدَرُ الْقِيَاسِيُّ), but usually misses some letters which are not compensated for. In a nutshell: The اِسْمُ مَصْدَرٍ often points to the **result**, whereas the regular مَصْدَر more to the **process/action**. See #165, #204.

The مَصْدَرٌ of II-verb يُصَلِّي / صَلَّى (*to pray*) would be تَصْلِيةٌ - but this word is not used by Muslims. The root ص-ل-و is almost only used for pattern II (فَعَّلَ). This may indicate that the verbal root is actually derived from a noun. Note: The old spelling of صَلَاةٌ is صَلَوةٌ. → If you want to know more about the اِسْمُ مَصْدَرٍ, see *Arabic for Nerds 2*, question #110.

55. What does the name *Husayn* (حُسَيْنٍ) mean?

It literally means: little beauty.

Husayn (or *Hussein*) is a male Muslim name (اِسْمٌ شَخْصِيٌّ). It is a diminutive of the name Hasan (حَسَنٌ) which means *good, handsome,* or *beautiful*. The meaning of حُسَيْنٌ, however, is different. By its form, حُسَيْن is a diminutive (تَصْغِيرٌ) which means that it denotes something small – a *young/little beauty*. Diminutives are often difficult to translate because you don't find them in dictionaries. You have to know the patterns!

Let's see some common patterns of diminutives.

		فُعَيْلٌ
1	Derived from a إسْمٌ consisting of **three letters**. → Not 3 root letters, but the total number of letters.	

door	بابٌ		small door	بُوَيْبٌ
child	وَلَدٌ	→	little child	وُلَيْدٌ
river	نَهْرٌ		small river	نُهَيْرٌ

Watch out: Also *adverbs of place/time* (ظَرْفٌ) use this pattern: قَبْلَ - قُبَيْلَ (*shortly before*) or بَعْدَ - بُعَيْدَ (*shortly after*).

		فُعَيْلِلٌ
2	The original noun consists of **four letters** in total. Again, we don't mean 4 root letters!	

friend	صاحِبٌ	→	little friend	صُوَيْحِبٌ

		فُعَيْلِلٌ
3	**Feminine nouns**. They end in ة and follow the rules of option 2. Note: If the original noun is feminine but does not end in ة, the diminutive will nonetheless get ة. For example, سُوقٌ (*market*) is treated as feminine.	

tree	شَجَرَةٌ		bush	شُجَيْرَةٌ
drop	نُقْطَةٌ	→	droplet	نُقَيْطَةٌ

market	سُوقٌ		small market	سُوَيْقةٌ

4	Used when the **second** letter of the اِسْم, serving as the basis, is followed by a **long vowel**.	فُعَيِّلٌ

book	كِتابٌ		small book; booklet	كُتَيِّبٌ
small	صَغِيرٌ	→	tiny	صُغَيِّرٌ

56. Is حَرْبٌ (*war*) masculine or feminine?

Strangely, the word for war (حَرْبٌ) is feminine in Arabic.

This may not be so surprising. In French *la guerre* is, oddly enough, also feminine. The problem in Arabic is that you cannot see the gender because unlike French, the definite article is the same for masculine (مُذَكَّر) and feminine (مُؤَنَّثٌ) words.

Before we dive into the mysteries of the Arabic noun, let's quickly look at the regular feminine endings In Arabic, there are **three indicators** to define the feminine gender:

Tā' of feminization (تاءُ تَأْنِيثٍ)		Aleph of feminization (أَلِفُ تَأْنِيثٍ)			
		extended (مَمْدُودَةٌ)		shortened (مَقْصُورَةٌ)	
1	ة	**2**	اء	**3**	يَا or ى
طالِبةٌ (*a female student*)		صَحْراءُ (*desert*), سَوْداءُ (*black, fem.*)		عُلْيا (*higher/highest*), كُبْرَى (*bigger/biggest*) – feminine comparative/superlative; ذِكْرَى (*memory*)	

Some remarks about the Aleph of feminization (2 and 3):

- The ending اء is also part of the pattern for colors and physical deficiencies (صِفَةٌ) in the singular feminine form.

- The letter ى is the pattern used for the feminine form of a comparative (اِسْمُ تَفْضِيلٍ).

What about حَرْبٌ? It doesn't look feminine – but it is! In Arabic there are words that look masculine by shape but are treated as feminine. Here is a list of common exceptions:

war	حَرْبٌ	fire	نارٌ	sun	شَمْسٌ
land	أَرْضٌ	house	دارٌ	wind	رِيحٌ
soul	نَفْسٌ	cup	كَأْسٌ	paradise	الْفِرْدَوْسُ
market	سُوقٌ	well	بِئْرٌ	Ghoul; ghost	غُولٌ

Now, if you want to add an **adjective** (صِفَةٌ), which form should you take? You need the feminine form!

a central market	سُوقٌ مَرْكَزِيَّةٌ

Watch out if you deal with body parts!

- When there are <u>two parts</u> of one (mostly pairs), then these words are treated as <u>feminine</u>. *Leg* (رِجْلٌ), *eye* (عَيْنٌ), *ear* (أُذْنٌ / أُذُنٌ), *tooth* (سِنٌّ), or *hand* (يَدٌ)

- By contrast, *nose* (أَنْفٌ), *mouth* (فَمٌ), etc. are <u>masculine</u> in Arabic as you only have one!

- Some parts of the body can either be masculine or feminine: *head* (رَأْسٌ), *liver* (كَبِدٌ), *upper arm* (عَضُدٌ).

But that's not all. Also feminine are:

- Names of newspapers and magazines: *al-Ahram* (الأَهْرامُ);

- Names of countries, cities, and towns – except for: *Morocco* (الْمَغْرِبُ), *Jordan* (الأُرْدُنُ), *Lebanon* (لُبْنانُ), *Iraq* (الْعِراقُ) and *Sudan* (السُّدانُ).

Finally, some words which break with the stringent logic of Arabic because they can be treated as masculine **or** feminine:

country	بَلَدٌ	*way*	سَبِيلٌ	*wine*	خَمْرٌ
situation	حالٌ	*road*	طَرِيقٌ	*salt*	مِلْحٌ
sky	سَماءٌ	*alley*	زُقاقٌ	*gold*	ذَهَبٌ
soul	رُوحٌ	*hell(fire)*	جَحِيمٌ		

57. Why does the Arabic word for caliph (خَلِيفةٌ) end in ة?

Perhaps to intensify the meaning.

There are Arabic words that end in ة but refer to masculine human beings. This is found primarily in words usually denoting an excess (صِيغةُ الْمُبالَغة) of a certain feature in a male person (*see question #86*). The most important are:

successor, Caliph	خَلِيفةٌ	*tyrant*	طاغِيةٌ
explorer; a widely traveled man	رَحّالةٌ	*Mu'āwiya* (name of a Caliph)	مُعاوِيةٌ
very learned man	عَلّامةٌ	*Hamuda* (man's name)*	حَمُودةٌ

eminent scholar	بَحّاثةٌ	Osama/'Usāma*; male given name; originally it denoted a species name for *lion* (عَلَمٌ لِلأَسَدِ).	أُسامةُ
distinguished man	نابِغةٌ		

Now, what happens if we want to use an adjective? The **adjective** (صِفةٌ) has to be **masculine**!

a just caliph	خَلِيفةٌ عادِلٌ
a great explorer	رَحّالةٌ عَظيمٌ
the great scholar	العَلّامةُ الكَبيرُ

How can we explain the feminine ending ة in خَلِيفةٌ؟ Early Arab grammarians realized that the feminine gender, grammatically speaking, is more complex than the masculine. **They named three types of feminine nouns:**

1. *The "real" feminine* (مُؤَنَّثٌ حَقيقيٌّ): biological females; marked or unmarked with a feminine ending.

2. *Figuratively feminine* (مُؤَنَّثٌ مَجازيٌّ): inanimate nouns with <u>or</u> without a feminine ending.

3. *Implicitly, semantically feminine* (مُؤَنَّثٌ مَعْنويٌّ): words with no visible sign of feminization which are **understood as feminine**. Mainly proper names for women which look masculine.

4. *Morphologically feminine* (مُؤَنَّثٌ لَفْظيٌّ): these are **masculine** *nouns* that have a feminine ending. Many of these nouns were common proper names for men in the pre- and early Islamic time. Some are still used. Grammatically they are always masculine!

1	mother	f	أُمٌّ	4	Caliph	m	خَلِيفَةٌ
	lioness	f	لَبُؤَةٌ		Moses*	m	مُوسَى
2	heaven	f	جَنّةٌ		Talha*	m	طَلْحَةُ
	sun	f	شَمْسٌ		Zacharias*	m	زَكَرِيّاءُ
3	Suad*	f	سُعادُ		'Uqba*	m	عُقْبةُ
	Mary*	f	مَرْيَمُ		'Ubada*	m	عُبادةُ

* Watch out! Proper names (masculine or feminine) ending in ة are diptotes (مَمْنُوعٌ مِن الصَّرْفِ) as well as feminine proper names with more than four letters.

Excursus: What can a feminine ending indicate in Arabic?

- Scholars suggested that the ة in خَلِيفَةٌ intensifies the signi-fication (لِلْمُبَالَغَةِ) and expresses some kind of emphasis. خَلِيفَةٌ is masculine because it (only) applies to males!

- Furthermore, the feminine suffix ة is used to build collec-tives, abstract nouns, diminutives, intensives, and single items of collectives. For example: flowers (وَرْدٌ) - singular masculine; a flower (وَرْدَةٌ) - singular feminine.

- Interestingly, it is also to do more or less the opposite: to derive collective nouns out of active participles. For ex-ample: unbeliever (كافِرٌ); unbelievers (كَفَرةٌ)

Excursus: What is the original idea of the تاءُ الْمَرْبُوطَةِ?

The suffix ة was at the very beginning perhaps not a marker of the feminine gender (of persons or things), but rather a de-vice to indicate that something is inferior or less important.

Originally, Semitic languages relied on size and importance to distinguish between words. Words denoting small, insignificant objects (diminutives, abstract nouns, collectives) were marked with suffixes of the feminine gender. Thus, the feminine ending started out to indicate a diminutive or to downgrade a thing or person.

58. Can you use a masculine adjective for a feminine noun?

Yes, this is possible.

In Arabic, when you say that a woman is *pregnant*, you use the حامِلٌ. It is the active participle (اِسْمُ الْفاعِلِ) of the I-verb حَمَلَ / يَحْمِلُ which means *to carry*.

a pregnant woman	إِمْرَأَةٌ حامِلٌ

But why on earth do we use the masculine form to express that a woman is pregnant? When we talk about things, states, or events that can only happen to women – like being *pregnant* –, then we don't have to write ة at the end. Some of these words are not exclusively attributed to women – but maybe were in ancient times.

pregnant	حامِلٌ		*divorced woman*	طالِقٌ
menstruating	حائِضٌ		*barren, sterile*	عاقِرٌ
unmarried and of middle age	عانِسٌ		*unveiled*	حاسِرٌ

Notice the difference!

She is pregnant.	هِيَ حامِلٌ.
She is carrying luggage.	هِيَ حامِلةٌ مَتاعًا.

However, sometimes these special adjectives (صِفةٌ) can be used for men and women:

an old woman	إِمْرَأَةٌ عجُوزٌ
an old man	رَجُلٌ عَجُوزٌ = شَيْخٌ

59. أَمْسِ - Does it always stay the same as *yesterday*?

No, it doesn't.

The Arabic word for *yesterday* (أَمْسِ) can be difficult to handle. Usually, you encounter it with a fixed, cemented shape based on the ending in "*i*" (مَبْنِيٌّ عَلَى الْكَسْرِ).

However, it may change its character, meaning and ending depending on the function in a sentence. **Rule of thumb:** If it has the definite article ال or is the first part of a إِضافةٌ, it denotes *past days* (الْأَيّامُ الْمَاضِيَةُ); *days ago* – and not only that: it loses its cemented form.

I came yesterday.	جِئْتُ أَمْسِ	1
Adverb of time (ظَرْفُ زَمانٍ); fixed shape (مَبْنِيٌّ عَلَى الْكَسْرِ).		

I came yesterday (days ago).	جِئْتُ أَمْسًا.	2
Adverb of time; **vague** meaning in the sense of *past days* (ظَرْفٌ زَمانٍ مُعْرَبٌ مُبْهَمٌ). It is stripped of the second part of the إِضافةٌ		

which is the reason for the ending "an" (مُعْرَبٌ مَنْصُوبٌ). It indicates *the past days*.	

Yesterday passed.	مَضَى الْأَمْسُ.	3
Yesterday was Friday.	كَانَ الْأَمْسُ يَوْمَ الْجُمْعَةِ.	
Declined noun; subject (الْفَاعِلُ); nominative case (مَرْفُوعٌ), visibly marked. It indicates *the past days* (**vague** meaning).		

Yesterday passed.	مَضَى أَمْسِ.	4
Noun with a fixed shape; subject (الْفَاعِلُ). We can only apply virtual case markers (فِي مَحَلِّ رَفْعٍ).		

Remark: The grammarians have different ideas about the character of أَمْسِ and its grammatical analysis (الْإِعْرَابُ). Some say it is a **diptote** (مَمْنُوعٌ مِنَ الصَّرْفِ) because it is definite by nature.

60. Why is there a و in the proper name عَمْرٌو (Amr)?

It is an old way of spelling the proper name Amr.

By adding the letter و, people can visually distinguish between *Amr* and the proper name *Omar* which is written in the same way: عُمَرُ.

Note that *Amr* takes *nunation* (تَنْوِينٌ), but *Omar* not. *Omar* is a diptote (مَمْنُوعٌ مِنَ الصَّرْفِ). It doesn't take *nunation* like all proper names which follow the pattern فُعَلُ. For example, Omar (عُمَرُ), Zuhal (زُحَلُ), Hubal (هُبَلُ), Juha (جُحَا).

Let's see how *Amr* and *Omar* behave:

accusative (مَنْصُوبٌ)	genitive (مَجْرُورٌ)	nominative (مَرْفُوعٌ)	
عَمْرًا	عَمْرٍو	عَمْرٌو	Amr
عُمَرَ		عُمَرُ	Omar

Amr gets *nunation* (تَنْوِينٌ); rarely, you see it spelled with و. In إِضافة-constructions, و is usually written.	*I saw Amr.*	رَأَيْتُ عَمْرًا.
No Aleph, no nunation – it is a diptote.	*I saw Omar.*	رَأَيْتُ عُمَرَ.

61. How do you build the imperative of قَالَ in the dual?

To express "you both say", you use قُولا.

Admittedly, this is a very rare form that you will rarely encounter, as the dual (الْمُثَنَّى) is pretty much not used in colloquial Arabic anymore.

Instead, in spoken Arabic, you use the plural of the imperative (أَمْرٌ) to express the dual.

Let us recall how we build the imperative in Arabic:

1. Form the present tense. For example: *you write* (تَكْتُبُ)

2. Put the verb into the jussive mood (مَجْزُومٌ) → you delete the last vowel and add سُكُونٌ resulting in: تَكْتُبْ

3. Delete the prefix – which is the ت. → we get: كْتُبْ

4. If you now have a word that has a vowel on the first consonant, you are already done. This would be the situation in all verb forms other than form I (فَعَلَ). For example V-verb *you speak* (تَتَكَلَّمُ ← تَتَكَلَّمْ ➔ تَكَلَّمْ) (*speak!*)

5. If you end up with a word starting with consonant plus سُكُونٌ, you need to add a helping device (prefix) based on the stem vowel. This is our situation: كْتُبْ

6. If the stem vowel is "*u*" (ضَمَّةٌ), the prefix is أُ. This is what we have in يَكْتُبُ / كَتَبَ. The final result is أُكْتُبْ (*write!*)

7. If the stem vowel is "*a*" (فَتْحةٌ) or "*i*" (كَسْرةٌ), the prefix is إِ. For example: يَجْلِسُ / جَلَسَ (*to sit*). We get اِجْلِسْ (*sit!*)

This is the normal situation without spoilers. As soon as a weak letter (حَرْفُ عِلَّةٍ) appears, a و or ي, we have to adjust our recipe. The verb *to say* (قَالَ) has و as the second root letter. Let's follow our steps to form the imperative. Note that we can stop after the first three steps!

step 1		step 2		step 3 = imperative
تَقُولُ	→	تَقُلْ	→	قُلْ !

But what about the other imperative forms? What happens if we have to add a suffix after قُلْ?

say!	قُلْ!	you; masculine	أَنْتَ
	قُولِي!	you; feminine	أَنْتِ
	قُولا	you (both); dual	أَنْتُما
	قُولُوا!	you; masculine, plural	أَنْتُمْ
	قُلْنَ!	you; feminine, plural	أَنْتُنَّ

We see that the vowel on the last root letter ل is crucial for the form of the imperative. Let's dig deeper.

impact	vowel on ل	imperative
the weak letter **disappears**	no vowel (سُكُونٌ)	قُلْ ؛ قُلْنَ
the weak letter is **written**	"i" (كَسْرَةٌ) or "u" (ضَمَّةٌ)	قُولِي ؛ قُولُوا

A key principle of Arabic is responsible for whether you see the weak letter or not:

- It is impossible to have two consecutive سُكُونٌ. For example: قُوْلْ or قُوْلْنَ – thus, the weak letter is omitted!

This explains, why we have و in قُوْلَا (*say!* - dual).

meaning	dual	present tense	past tense verb
(you both) say!	قُوْلَا	يَقُولُ	قَالَ
(you both) be!	كُونَا	يَكُونُ	كَانَ

The imperative often causes difficulties for learners of Arabic. Although the imperative is used frequently in everyday life, it is used rather little in class. Let's see how all the verb forms (with or without weak letters) work in the imperative.

meaning	imp. dual	imperative - sing. masculine & fem.	verb	
write!	اُكْتُبا	اُكْتُبْ, اُكْتُبِي	كَتَبَ - يَكْتُبُ	I
stop!	قِفا	قِفْ, قِفِي	وَقَفَ - يَقِفُ	
laugh!	إِضْحَكا	إِضْحَكْ, إِضْحَكِي	ضَحِكَ - يَضْحَكُ	

want!	وَدَّا	وَدَّ، وَدِّي *	وَدَّ - يَوَدُّ	
follow!	لِيَا	لِ، لِي	وَلِيَ - يَلِي	II
agree!	وَافِقَا	وَافِقْ، وَافِقِي	وَافَقَ - يُوَافِقُ	III
arrest!	أَوْقِفَا	أَوْقِفْ، أَوْقِفِي	أَوْقَفَ - يُوقِفُ	IV
stop!	تَوَقَّفَا	تَوَقَّفْ، تَوَقَّفِي	تَوَقَّفَ - يَتَوَقَّفُ	V
be humble!	تَوَاضَعَا	تَوَاضَعْ، تَوَاضَعِي	تَوَاضَعَ - يَتَوَاضَعُ	VI
leave!	إنْطَلِقَا	إنْطَلِقْ، إنْطَلِقِي	إنْطَلَقَ - يَنْطَلِقُ	VII
connect!	إتَّصِلا	إتَّصِلْ، إتَّصِلِي	إتَّصَلَ - يَتَّصِلُ	VIII
blush!	إحْمَرَّا	إحْمَرِرْ، إحْمَرِّي *	إحْمَرَّ - يَحْمَرُّ	IX
stop (sb.)!	إسْتَوْقِفَا	إسْتَوْقِفْ، إسْتَوْقِفِي	إسْتَوْقَفَ - يَسْتَوْقِفُ	X

* Note that وَدَّ is the contracted form of اِوْدَدْ and إحْمَرَّ is the contracted form of إحْمَرِرْ. How is that? The jussive (مَجْزُومٌ) is يَوْدَدْ or يَوَدَّ which is the same in the subjunctive (مَنْصُوبٌ) mood as well. Regarding إحْمَرَّ, the jussive is يَحْمَرِرْ or يَحْمَرَّ (which is also the subjunctive).

62. إِزْدَحَمَ - What is the root of this word?

The root is ز-ح-م. The verb means "to be crowded".

إِزْدَحَمَ / يَزْدَحِمُ is a VIII-verb following the pattern اِفْتَعَلَ.

Arabic is often described as a language that sounds harsh. Interestingly, just the opposite is true. Arabic takes great care that sounds fit together. The root of إِزْدَحَمَ is ز-ح-م. So what on earth is the letter د doing here?

Well, د has replaced ت in the pattern إِفْتَعَلَ to facilitate the pronunciation! ت in VIII-verbs always turns into د if the first root letter is ز. Hence, the pattern إِفْتَعَلَ changes into إِفْدَعَلَ.

meaning	root	present tense	past tense
to be crowded	ز-ح-م	يَزْدَحِمُ	إِزْدَحَمَ
to swallow; to gulp	ز-ر-د	يَزْدَرِدُ	اِزْدَرَدَ
to increase	ز-ي-د	يَزْدَادُ	إِزْدَادَ

63. Are there abbreviations in Arabic?

Yes, there are.

Germans love abbreviations, and they are also widely used in English. In Arabic, however, they are rare contemporaries. Actually, they are almost only used for religious purposes.

translation and meaning	full text	abbr.
Peace be upon him (PBUH).	عَلَيْهِ السَّلَامُ	عم
Muslims add this phrase when they mention the name of the Islamic prophet Muhammad. Meaning: *Allah bless him and grant him salvation* (i.e., eulogy for Muhammad).	صَلَّى اللهُ عَلَيْهِ وَسَلَّمَ	صلعم صَلَّى اللهِ عَلَيْهِ وَسَلَّمَ
Muslims add this to the name of companions (الصَّحابةُ) of Muhammad. Literal meaning: *May Allah be pleased with him.*	رَضِيَ اللهُ عَنْهُ	رضه
Said if a person died (eulogy for the dead). Lit.: *May Allah have mercy upon him.*	رَحِمَهُ اللهُ	رحه

et cetera (etc.) Used at the end of a list to indicate that further, similar items are included. Literal meaning in Arabic: *to its end*.	إِلَى آخِرِهِ	الخ

64. The letter ء - How do you spell it correctly?

You need to know which vowels are stronger than others.

Spelling is not really an issue in Arabic, as one wrong letter usually changes the meaning completely. Errors only occur in two areas, when a weak letter or the letter Hamza is involved.

The glottal stop, the هَمْزَة, has various shapes: أ or ء or ئ or ؤ. The secret behind it is quickly revealed. **The three Arabic vowels have different strengths.**

- The stronger vowel decides which letter becomes the bearer of the هَمْزَة. The letters ا, و, and ى serve as carriers or seats of the Hamza. In some situations they do not work and we must rely on ء, the pure version with no seat.
- The vowel "*i*" is stronger than "*u*".
- The vowel "*u*" is stronger than "*a*".

In short: i → u → a

Let's process this information.

Note that we check the **diacritical mark (vowel)** on the letter **before** Hamza and **on Hamza**.

explanation	spelling of ء	vowel before
1 كَسْرَةٌ is the strongest vowel. If there is كَسْرَةٌ **before** or **after** Hamza (ء), it becomes ئ.	ئ ←	ِ
You also use this spelling if Hamza is preceded by ي. The letter ي (with سُكُونٌ) is considered to be as strong as كَسْرَةٌ.	ؤ or ـئـ	ي
Note: The ي loses its diacritical marks (the two dots underneath) when it serves as a seat for the Hamza.		
2 The second strongest vowel is ضَمَّةٌ. If there is **no** كَسْرَةٌ before or after Hamza, but if there is ضَمَّةٌ, the Hamza will be spelled like ؤ.	ؤ	ُ
3 The weakest vowel is فَتْحةٌ. If there is no other vowel involved but only "a", ء becomes أ.	أ	َ
4 As a **first** letter, Hamza (ء) is written in the shape of Aleph – no matter what the vowel is.	اُ - أ - إ	
5 At the **end of the word,** after a long vowel or after سُكُونٌ (end of syllable), it is written in its pure form: ء.	ء	
The سُكُونٌ is not a vowel and therefore does not have a related letter. It marks the absence of a vowel. It is treated as the weakest of all sounds, except for the situation in which it goes along with ي resulting in ئ (see no. 1).		ْ

Let us look at some examples. Note that the numbers on the left correspond to the numbers in the table above.

	explanation	meaning	e.g.	spelling of ء
1	We have سُكُونٌ on top of ي which has the same value of strength as the كَسْرةٌ → so, the "a" afterwards doesn't count.	environ-ment	بِيْئَةٌ	ـُٔ (ئ)
5	Hamza is the final letter of the word. We have a preceding سُكُونٌ, how-ever, it is not written on ي but on ز → we use the pure version.	portion	جُزْءًا	ء
5	This is different to the first example. We have سُكُونٌ before, followed by the vowel "a". However, the سُكُونٌ is not on the letter ي but on ا, so we need to the pure version of ء.	two buildings (nomi-native)	بِنَاءَانِ	ء
4	The Hamza is at the beginning.	daughter	أُخْتٌ	أ
4		fee	أُجْرةٌ	أ
3	There is no كَسْرةٌ and neither ضَمّةٌ before – but the vowel "a".	head	رَأْسٌ	أ
3		to ask	سَأَلَ	أ
2	ضَمّةٌ is stronger than فَتْحةٌ. Remark: The singular form is رَئِيسٌ.	presi-dents	رُؤَساءُ	ؤ
1	كَسْرةٌ is stronger than فَتْحةٌ.	presi-dency	رِئَاسةٌ	ـِٔ (ئ)
1		to be thirsty	ظَمِئَ	ئ
5	As a final letter after سُكُون, it is ء.		شَيْءٌ	ء
1	Here, we have شَيْءٌ in the accusative	thing	شَيْئًا	ـٔ (ئ)

	case (مَنْصُوبٌ). It is written in this form because it follows ي.			
5	As a final letter after a long vowel, it gets its pure, standalone form: ء.	sky	سَماءٌ	ء

Watch out: In the **middle of a word** – after سُكُونٌ or a long vowel – هَمْزَةٌ (in Classical Arabic) used to be written as ء.

meaning	Modern Standard Arabic	Classical Arabic
issue, matter	مَسْألَةٌ or مَسْئَلَةٌ	مَسْءَلةٌ

Good to know: How do you write the *nunation* (تَنْوِينٌ) on top of a final Hamza (الْهَمْزةُ الْمُنَوَّنةُ)? As often, it depends on the vowel/letter before. These are our options:

example		result		What letter / vowel is before Hamza?
thing	شَيْئًا	ـئًـ		ي
sky	سَماءً	ءً		ا
subject	مُبْتَدَأً			فَتْحةٌ
part	جُزْءًا	ءً +	سُكُونٌ any other letter than ي
pearl	لُؤْلُؤًا	ءًا		ضَمّةٌ
alike	مُتَكافِئًا			كَسْرةٌ

65. What is syntax, what is form?

Two linguistic concepts we apply to understand a sentence.

If you have to translate a sentence, you should check every word from two perspectives:

1. Examine the shape and form of a word: صَرْفٌ.
2. Examine the position & function in the sentence: إِعْرَابٌ.

In the following three sentences the word *reader* (الْقَارِئ) is charged with different grammatical functions.

The reader sat in the library.	جَلَسَ الْقَارِئُ فِي الْمَكْتَبَةِ.	1
I saw the reader.	شَاهَدْتُ الْقَارِئَ.	2
I greeted the reader.	سَلَّمْتُ عَلَى الْقَارِئِ.	3

If we take a closer look at الْقَارِئ, something stands out: it looks visually the same everywhere. الْقَارِئ is the *active participle* (اِسْمُ الْفَاعِلِ) of the I-verb يَقْرَأُ / قَرَأَ (*to read*). An active participle is a noun expressing that someone is carrying out the action of a verb (*to read → the reader*).

- If we want to analyze the <u>form</u> (صِيغَةٌ) of word, we have to isolate it and enter the area of *morphology* (صَرْفٌ).

- In order to identify the function of the word *reader*, we have to identify its <u>position</u> in the sentence.

The function of the اِسْمُ الْفَاعِلِ in the examples is different.

- **Sentence 1:** *reader* is the **subject** (فَاعِلٌ) of the verbal sentence. Note that فَاعِلٌ is the active participle (اِسْمُ فَاعِلٍ) of the verb *to do* (فَعَلَ), as the grammatical term *subject* describes *the do-er*.

- **Sentence 2:** *reader* is the **direct object** (مَفْعُولٌ بِهِ). Note that مَفْعُولٌ is the passive participle (اِسْمُ مَفْعُولٍ) of *to do*, so the direct object can never describe the person or thing which is doing the action – but the one to whom or which the action is being done.

- **Sentence 3:** *reader* takes the *genitive* (مَجْرُورٌ) case. The word مَجْرُورٌ literally means *drawn* or *dragged*. Grammatically speaking, it describes a word which is *governed* by a preposition or by the first part of a إِضافةٌ-construction. The second part, the مُضافٌ إِلَيْهِ, has to be genitive.

Watch out: In the third example, *reader* would be the direct object in English (*I saw him*). But since the Arabic verb for *to greet* demands a preposition (سَلَّمَ عَلَى), it can't be the direct object (مَفْعُولٌ بِهِ) because the direct object always follows the verb without a preposition. Remark: There are verbs in Arabic that can have two or three direct objects! See #109 and #110.

Excursus: What does a إِضافةٌ-construction consist of?

First part of the إِضافةٌ	*the possessed thing*. It **never** has the **definite article**. It can take all case endings depending on the function and position in the sentence – but never *nunation* (تَنْوِينٌ). The case markers are only *"u", "a", or "i"* (and never: *"-un", "-an", or "-in"*).	الْمُضافُ
A mnemonic: The term consists of <u>one</u> word (one = first).		

Second part of the إِضافةٌ	*the possessor*. Definite or indefinite. Always in the **genitive** case (مَجْرُورٌ).	الْمُضافُ إِلَيْهِ
A mnemonic: The term consists of <u>two</u> words (two = second).		

Don't forget: It is all or nothing!

The last part of a إِضافةٌ defines if we treat the entire construction as definite or indefinite:

> If the last part is <u>definite</u> (مَعْرِفةٌ), the entire construction is definite (every word of it): *the house of the teacher = the teacher's house* (بَيْتُ الْمُدَرِّسِ).

> If the last part is <u>indefinite</u> (نَكِرةٌ), the entire construction is indefinite: *A house of a teacher = a teacher's house* (بَيْتُ مُدَرِّسٍ).

See *Arabic for Nerds 2*, #105, for how to express: *a house of **the** teacher*.

66. Do we always need a second part in the إِضافةٌ?

No, we don't!

In Arabic, there are four special types of nouns:

a) Nouns that can <u>never</u> serve as the first part of a إِضافةٌ – such as the pronouns أنا or the demonstrative هٰذا.

b) Nouns that can <u>never stand alone</u> (ما يَلْزَمُ الْإِضافةَ لَفْظًا وَمَعْنًى) but must be followed by an annexed word (the 2nd part of the إِضافةٌ) – like the word *at* (عِنْدَ). Why? Because such words can't express a meaning by themselves.

c) Nouns that usually serve as the first part of a إِضافةٌ but <u>may do without it</u> (ما يَلْزَمُ الْإِضافةَ مَعْنًى دُونَ لَفْظٍ) – such as the word *all* (كُلّ) or *some* (بَعْض). You can use them also as single, unconnected word (بِلا إِضافةٍ). They get the case according to their position in the sentence.

Everybody is laughing.	كلّ ضاحِكٌ. ‏1

We say that the إضافة-construction is understood by meaning, but without pronouncing it, because the second part of the إضافةٌ is deleted (الْمُضَافُ إِلَيْهِ مَحْذُوفٌ). We are allowed to use the word كُلّ as a singular noun (مُفْرَدٌ). We compensate the deleted part by using nunation (تَنْوِينٌ) for كُلٌّ.

| All of the students are laughing. | كلُّ الطُّلّابِ ضاحِكٌ. | 2 |

The standard situation: We use كُلّ in a إضافةٌ which means that it gets followed by a second part (مُضافٌ إلَيْهِ). Why did we use the singular form ضاحِكٌ although we talk about students? Because students is not the subject – it is كُلّ, which is singular. But you could use the **logical subject** and use ضاحِكُونَ – see q. #259.

d) Words like قَبْل or بَعْد or غَيْر or أَوَّل or دُون may be used as the 1ˢᵗ part of a إضافةٌ → In such a situation, they get the case marker (إعْرابٌ) according to the function and position. However, they may do without a إضافةٌ and stand alone. → Then they get fixed on the vowel "u" (عَلَى). مَبْنِيٌّ الضَّمّ). Although we delete the second part, we assume that the meaning still survives. See *question #221*.

67. الدَّرْسُ مَفْهُومٌ and فُهِمَ الدَّرْسُ - **Any difference?**

Both mean: The lesson is understood. But there is a finesse.

Let us look deeper into the structure of both sentences:

| جُمْلة فِعْلِيّة | verbal sentence | فُهِمَ الدَّرْسُ. |

فُهِمَ is a **verb** in the passive voice! Every verb contains three things:
- an indicator of time
- a هَدَفٌ (*goal*; what are you actually doing = the action)
- the actor (subject - فاعِلٌ)

Any verb will automatically give us some hints about the time of the action; when it happened – **now, in the future,** or in the **past.**

Since the past tense in Arabic does not necessarily tell us much about the time but rather whether the action has been completed or not, we do get a feeling that in this sentence, **the action/event has already happened.**

جُمْلةٌ اِسْمِيّةٌ	nominal sentence	.الدَّرْسُ مَفْهُومٌ

There is no verb! We use a passive participle (اِسْمُ مَفْعُولٍ), which is a **noun** in Arabic. Although the English translation is the same, we have less information than in the verbal sentence. In the passive participle, there is **no indicator of time** included at all. We **can't tell, when** the actual event of *understanding* happened: now, in the past, or in the future.

68. Can a verbal sentence serve as the predicate (خَبَرٌ)?

Yes, it can.

Even if you often do not notice it – it happens very often that the *predicate* (خَبَرٌ) of a *nominal sentence* (جُمْلةٌ اِسْمِيّةٌ) consists of a *verbal sentence* (جُمْلةٌ فِعْلِيّةٌ). Let us look at two sentences which both mean the same:

The child sits.	يَجْلِسُ الْوَلَدُ.	verbal sentence	1
	الْوَلَدُ يَجْلِسُ.	nominal sentence	2

The first sentence is a جُمْلةٌ فِعْلِيّةٌ since the sentence starts with a verb. A verbal sentence consists of a verb (فِعْلٌ) and a subject (فاعِلٌ). It may include a direct object (مَفْعُولٌ بِه) as well as other additional information, all governed by the verb.

The second sentence is a جُمْلَةٌ إِسْمِيّةٌ. A nominal sentence consists of a subject (مُبْتَدَأٌ) and a predicate (خَبَرٌ). In our example, الْوَلَدُ is the subject and يَجْلِسُ is the predicate.

But do the different terms make a difference?

Although a nominal sentence may do a better job to start a new idea or paragraph, there is no real difference in meaning. Nevertheless, the internal structure is very different. In fact, sentence 2, the nominal sentence, has quite a complicated building. The predicate يَجْلِسُ itself is a verbal **sentence** (جُمْلَةٌ فِعْلِيّةٌ).

The verb يَجْلِسُ has a hidden/implied pronoun (*he*). If we only look at the verb, it means: *he sits* – which is an entire sentence. Thus, the sentence 1 literally means:

The child, he sits.	الْوَلَدُ يَجْلِسُ.
This is why we say that the predicate (خَبَرٌ) is a complete verbal sentence (جُمْلَةٌ فِعْلِيّةٌ).	

يَجْلِسُ		الْوَلَدُ	
predicate (خَبَرٌ)	+	subject (مُبْتَدَأٌ)	**First layer:** nominal sentence
Verb in the present tense, indicative mood (فِعْلٌ مُضارِعٌ مَرْفُوعٌ). Subject (فاعِلٌ) is an implied personal pronoun (ضَمِيرٌ مُسْتَتِرٌ), present but not visible, expressing *he* (هُوَ).			**Second layer:** verbal sentence

Remark: See *Arabic for Nerds 2, question #56,* if you want to know whether there is a difference between a nominal and verbal sentence.

69. أَوْ or أَمْ – What is the correct word for *or*?

It depends on the question.

In English, there is only one word to express doubt or equalization (in your preference) – the word *or*. In Arabic, we have two words: أَمْ and أَوْ.

The word أَوْ

	Used if there is doubt.	الشَّكُّ
1	Muhammad may come in the evening **or** at night.	قَدْ يَصِلُ مُحَمَّدٌ مَسَاءً أَوْ لَيْلًا.

	Letting choose	التَّخْيِيرُ
2	I advise you to join the literature faculty **or** law faculty.	أَنْصَحُكَ بِأَنْ تَلْتَحِقَ بِكُلِّيَّةِ الْآدَابِ أَوْ كُلِّيَّةِ الْحُقُوقِ.

The word أَمْ → it corresponds more closely to *either … or*.

	Used to separate a single pair of choice → you have to choose one.	طَلَبُ تَعْيِينِ أَحَدِ الشَّيْئَيْنِ
1	أَمْ is often used after the non-translated question word أ which is similar to the French *est-ce que*.	
	Do you want coffee **or** tea?	أَقَهْوَةً تُرِيدُ أَمْ شَايًا؟
	Did Zayd **or** Khalid come?	أَزَيْدٌ جَاءَ أَمْ خَالِدٌ؟
	Important: The device أ is needed before introducing the two possibilities. Notice the word order!	

2	Equalization	التَّسْوِيَةُ

regardless of whether it is right **or** wrong	سَواءٌ \ سَواءٌ أَكانَ صَحِيحًا أَمْ خَطَأً
It doesn't make any difference to me if you travel **or** stay here.	سَواءٌ عَلَيَّ أَسافَرْتَ أَمْ بَقِيْتَ هُنا.
You could use أَوْ **or** here; if you do so, you must delete أ before سافَرْتَ.	= سَواءٌ عَلَيَّ سافَرْتَ أَوْ بَقِيْتَ هُنا.

Note: Both أَمْ and أَوْ are *conjunctions* (حَرْفُ عَطْفٍ). The word which comes <u>after</u> *or* takes the same case as the word <u>before</u>.

70. Why is *lesson* (دِراسةٌ) a مَصْدَرٌ but *river* (نَهْرٌ) not?

Because river is not linked to any action.

The word دِراسةٌ means *lesson*. The word نَهْرٌ *river*.

A مَصْدَرٌ is the *noun of the event*. Any مَصْدَرٌ in Arabic is a إِسْمُ مَعْنًى: an **abstract noun**; something that has no color, no size, something that is not connected to the five senses – but to an action. For example, *writing, swimming*. Such words don't give us information about the actor/doer and don't provide any indication of time → they only tells us about the action.

All other nouns are called إِسْمُ ذاتٍ: *concrete nouns*. They are tangible things and can be recognized with your senses – you can see, smell, taste, or hear them.

That is why نَهْرٌ (river), جَبَلٌ (mountain), or كُرْسِيٌّ (chair) cannot be a مَصْدَرٌ. A مَصْدَرٌ doesn't have a body; it doesn't have a concrete shape or form. For example, how would you describe the word *reading*? You can't say it is big, blue, or loud.

Note: Every مَصْدَرٌ - like every verb – needs a **goal** (هَدَفٌ) and you can only grasp it with your mind.

71. How do you build the مَصْدَرٌ of a verb?

Except for I-verbs, this is easy – because there are patterns.

Arabic is an almost mathematical language. A few formulas are enough to generate a mountain of vocabulary.

Unfortunately, the مَصْدَرٌ (*original noun*) of the primary I-verb (فَعَلَ) follows no real logic; there are many exceptions. You have to learn them by heart.

Let's check the **verb pattern II to X**:

example		verb	مَصْدَرٌ	PATTERN	
training	تَدْرِيبًا	دَرَّبَ	تَفْعِيلٌ		
congratulations	تَهْنِئَةً	هَنَّأَ	تَفْعِلةٌ	فَعَّلَ	II
Pattern تَفْعِلةٌ is used if the last letter is weak (و or ي) or Hamza (ء).					
struggle	جِهادًا	جاهَدَ	فِعالٌ	فاعَلَ	III
observation	مُشاهَدةً	شاهَدَ	مُفاعَلةٌ		
transmission	إِرْسالًا	أَرْسَلَ	إِفْعالٌ	أَفْعَلَ	IV
coming forward	تَقَدُّمًا	تَقَدَّمَ	تَفَعُّلٌ	تَفَعَّلَ	V
cooperation	تَعاوُنًا	تَعاوَنَ	تَفاعُلٌ	تَفاعَلَ	VI
discontinuation	إِنْقِطاعًا	إِنْقَطَعَ	إِنْفِعالٌ	إِنْفَعَلَ	VII
gathering	إِجْتِماعًا	إِجْتَمَعَ	إِفْتِعالٌ	إِفْتَعَلَ	VIII

yellowing	إِصْفِرارًا	إِصْفَرَّ	اِفْعِلالٌ	اِفْعَلَّ	IX
plea for pardon	اِسْتِغْفارًا	اِسْتَغْفَرَ	اِسْتَفْعالٌ	اِسْتَفْعَلَ	X

- The مَصْدَر of a IV-verb always starts with a إ = ء.

- The Aleph in the other verb forms is only pronounced as هَمْزَة, if the مَصْدَر is the beginning of an utterance/sentence. See *question #8*.

- When you look up a مَصْدَر in a dictionary, it is often presented it in the accusative case (مَنْصُوبٌ). What you see is the form of the *absolute infinitive* – to **emphasize the idea of the verb in the abstract**, i.e., it speaks of an action (or state) without any regard to the agent (subject; doer of the action) or to the circumstances of time and mood under which it takes place. This idea is found in the *absolute object* (مَفْعُولٌ مُطْلَقٌ); see *question #122*.

72. How do you express *already*?

You need to be creative – Arabic has no word for already.

Already is a tricky word even in English. In Arabic, there is no word for it which always works, similar to *still*. In colloquial Arabic, especially people from the upper class use foreign words to express the idea.

- In Algeria, the French *déja* is used;
- in Saudi-Arabia, you hear أَصْلًا (*originally*);
- in Egypt, you hear *already* (the English word itself), خَلاص or لِسّا;
- in Palestine and Lebanon, you hear صار (*to become*).

How can we express the idea in formal Arabic?

already (by now): مُنْذُ الْآنَ	
You can already see the house.	تَسْتَطِيعُ أَنْ تَرَى الْبَيْتَ مُنْذُ الْآنَ.

already (previously; before): سَبَقَ لَهُ or سابِقًا or مِنْ قَبْلُ by	
I have already been to Cairo. (Literally: I visited Cairo before.)	زُرْتُ الْقاهِرةَ سابِقًا.
He had already done it before.	لَقَدْ سَبَقَ لَهُ أَنْ فَعَلَهُ.
Note: After أَنْ we use the past tense here – in order to paraphrase the pluperfect! See *question #108*.	
He had met him before.	سَبَقَ لَهُ أَنْ قابَلَهُ.
We have already said that...	سَبَقَ لَنا الْقَوْلُ بِأَنَّ...
I have already talked to him.	سَبَقَ أَنْ تَحَدَّثْتُ مَعَهُ

already (by that time) – expressed by a device of emphasis: قَدْ or إِنَّ	
She was already there when I arrived.	إِنَّها كانَتْ مَوْجُودةً عِنْدَما وَصَلْتُ.
Have you eaten your dinner already?	هَلْ قَدْ تَناوَلْتَ عَشاءَكَ؟

already – expressed by VIII-verb إِبْتَدَأَ (to begin, to start) in the past	
I am already doing it.	قَدْ إِبْتَدَأْتُ فِي ذَلِكَ.

73. What is an implied (hidden) pronoun?

A pronoun which is apparently not there (unwritten, not pro-nounced) – but implicitly understood.

Arabic is a particularly economical language. The verb can carry the subject along without needing a separate word – un-like English, where you need a separate personal pronoun.

For example: *He goes.* (يَذْهَبُ). The conjugated verb in-cludes the pronoun, symbolized by letters. We call this phe-nomenon ضَمِيرٌ مُسْتَتِرٌ which can be translated as *implied, un-derstood, implied, inferred pronoun.*

In Arabic, the implied pronoun is only possible for the sub-ject, i.e., a pronoun in the nominative (ضَمِيرُ الرَّفْعِ). Let's take the past tense verbs كَتَبَ (*he wrote*) and كَتَبَتْ (*she wrote*). In the third person singular, we say that the subject of the verb is a *hidden, implied pronoun.* It has the virtual, estimated mean-ing of *he* (هُوَ) or *she* (هِيَ). What's the logic behind it?

In Arabic, there are two kinds of personal pronouns: *appar-ent pronouns* (بَارِزٌ) such as *I* (أَنَا), *we* (نَحْنُ) and *hidden, implied* (مُسْتَتِرٌ) pronouns which you can't see nor hear. For example:

The girl wrote the lesson.	كَتَبَتْ الْبِنْتُ الدَّرْسَ.	1
Here, the position of the subject (فَاعِلٌ) is filled by an *apparent noun* (اِسْمٌ ظَاهِرٌ). This is only possible if we have a verb in the third person singular. We don't necessarily need a hidden pro-noun here since we have a given subject in the sentence.		
She wrote the lesson.	كَتَبَتْ [هِيَ] الدَّرْسَ.	2
Here, we need to find a subject for the verb كَتَبَتْ. Why? The تْ here is <u>not</u> a pronoun – but simply a marker for femininity! Thus, we say that the subject (فَاعِلٌ) is a *hidden pronoun* (ضَمِيرٌ مُسْتَتِرٌ) having the virtual, estimated meaning of *she* (هِيَ).		

In Arabic, we can only use the singular form of a verb to start a sentence. Only if we use the **verb** in the **third person singular** (*he; she* - الْغَائِبُ), we can use a *visible noun* (اِسْمٌ ظَاهِرٌ) as the subject (فَاعِلٌ) in the nominative case (example 1). That is why we say that we may hide the pronoun (ضَمِيرٌ مُسْتَتِرٌ جَوازًا). In all the other forms, we cannot do that (مُسْتَتِرٌ وُجُوبًا). Let's check some examples to illustrate the issue.

Scenario 1: If we used a **separate personal pronoun** (ضَمِيرٌ مُنْفَصِلٌ), we'd change the meaning – and produce **emphasis**.

I am happy.	أَفْرَحُ.	1
It's me who is happy.	أَفْرَحُ أَنا.	2
This sentence has a **different meaning**! The word أَنا here serves as an *amplifier* (تَأْكِيدٌ) and emphasizes the subject (which is the implied pronoun included in the verb). Thus, if we want to express *I am happy* (أَفْرَحُ), we need to hide the pronoun.		
I am happy. Literal meaning: *I, I am happy.*	أَنا أَفْرَحُ.	3
That is a different story. We have changed the DNA of the sentence. Now, we have a **nominal sentence** (جُمْلَةٌ اِسْمِيَّةٌ). The entire verbal sentence – which has an implied subject (فَاعِلٌ with virtual meaning of أَنا) – serves as the predicate (خَبَرٌ).		

Scenario 2: If we used a **visible noun** (اِسْمٌ ظَاهِرٌ), the sentence **wouldn't make sense** anymore – except for the third person singular (*he, she*).

I write.	أَكْتُبُ.	1
??? (The sentence doesn't make sense.)	أَكْتُبُ مُحَمَّدٌ.	2
The combination *I write* plus *Muhammad* as the subject of the		

verb – that's a mismatch. We can't place an apparent noun after the verb as the subject (فَاعِلٌ) instead of the implied pronoun.

All this is sophisticated and part of the core of Arabic grammar. Let's dig deeper and examine what is actually happening inside verbal sentences.

meaning	example	
The river overflows.	يَتَدَفَّقُ النَّهْرُ.	1

This is a verbal sentence (جُمْلَةٌ فِعْلِيَّةٌ). We place a clearly visible noun as the subject (النَّهْرُ) after the verb which is possible since we have the verb in the third person singular.

meaning	example	
The river overflows. Lit. meaning: *The river, [he/it] overflows.*	النَّهْرُ يَتَدَفَّقُ [هُوَ].	2

Here, we have **two sentences** (a compound): A primary nominal sentence (جُمْلَةٌ اِسْمِيَّةٌ) starting with النَّهْرُ which functions as the **subject** (مُبْتَدَأٌ). And there is a verbal sentence (جُمْلَةٌ فِعْلِيَّةٌ) consisting of يَتَدَفَّقُ which serves as the predicate (خَبَرٌ).

There is something invisible here that is theoretically needed in order for the sentence to work. You need to **connect both sentences**. The virtual pronoun هُوَ is already contained in the verb which is why we call it *implied pronoun* (ضَمِيرٌ مُسْتَتِرٌ). This **hidden pronoun** takes the place of the noun which stands before the verb. We can say that it falls back upon it, that it is referential.

meaning	example	
The river's water is overflowing. Literal meaning: *The river, his water is overflowing.*	النَّهْرُ يَتَدَفَّقُ مَاؤُهُ.	3

Such sentences are called *topic-comment sentences* by Western grammarians. Usually, they cannot be rendered into English in their original word order. مَاءٌ is the subject (فَاعِلٌ) of the verb يَتَدَفَّقُ. Therefore, it gets the nominative case (مَرْفُوعٌ). What about the **pronoun** at the very end? Such pronoun is called *binder* or *connector* (رابِطٌ) and are typical for this structure. It represents (falls back upon) the noun at the very beginning (مُبْتَدَأٌ), in our example, the word النَّهْرُ.

Remark: In rare situations, if the sense is pretty clear, you may go without a *binder*. For example: *The one who I like arrived* (جاءَتْ الَّتِي أُحِبُّ). The syntactical (virtual) meaning is: جاءَتْ الَّتِي أُحِبُّها.

Note: If you want to know how the subject is expressed in the past and present tense verbs, see *Arabic for Nerds 2, question #36.*

Excursus: What types of personal pronouns does Arabic know? Let's check the two main forms.

A. The separated, detached personal pronoun (ضَمِيرٌ مُنْفَصِلٌ)

It is a separate noun with a fixed shape (اِسْمٌ مَبْنِيٌّ). It comes in two versions: **a)** for the nominative case (when it functions as the subject – *I, he, she*); **b)** for the accusative case (when it functions as the object – *me, him, her*).

pronoun is found in the (gram.) position of a...		
...accusative case (فِي مَحَلِّ نَصْبٍ)	...nominative case (فِي مَحَلِّ رَفْعٍ)	
إِيّاهُ، إِيّاهُما، إِيّاهُمْ، إِيّاها، إِيّاهُما، إِيّاهُنَّ	هُوَ، هُما، هُمْ، هِيَ، هُما، هُنَّ	3rd person (غائِبٌ - *absent*)
إِيّاكَ، إِيّاكُما، إِيّاكُمْ، إِيّاكِ، إِيّاكُما، إِيّاكُنَّ	أَنْتَ، أَنْتُما، أَنْتُمْ، أَنْتِ، أَنْتُما، أَنْتُنَّ	2nd person (مُخاطَبٌ - *spoken-to*)
إِيّايَ، إِيّانا	أَنا، نَحْنُ	1st person (مُتَكَلِّمٌ - *speaker*)

B. The attached pronoun (ضَمِيرٌ مُتَّصِلٌ)

It only occurs at the end of words. When do you use it?

- Attached to the **past tense verb** and serving as the **subject**. For example: *I wrote* (كَتَبْتُ) - the تُ is the pronoun.
- Attached to a **verb** – then it is the **direct object** (مَفْعُولٌ بِهِ). For example: *He wrote it* (كَتَبَهُ).
- Serving as the **second part** of a إِضافةٌ-construction – we may call it *possessive pronoun* (my, yours, hers). For example: *his book* (كِتابُهُ).
- After a **preposition**. For example: *on us* (عَلَيْنا).

accusative (نَصْبٌ) / genitive (جَرٌّ)					nominative (رَفْعٌ)		
his book	كِتابُهُ	he promised *him*	وَعَدَهُ	هُ	-	-	هُوَ
their (b.) book	كِتابُهُما	he promised *them* (b.)	وَعَدَهُما	هُما	*they* (b.) do	يَفْعَلانِ	انِ	هُما
their book	كِتابُهُمْ	he promised *them*	وَعَدَهُمْ	هُمْ	*they* do	يَفْعَلُونَ	ونَ	هُمْ
her book	كِتابُها	he promised *her*	وَعَدَها	ها	-	-	هِيَ
their (b.) book	كِتابُهُما	he promised *them* (b.)	وَعَدَهُما	هُما	*they* (b.) do	تَفْعَلانِ	انِ	هُما
their (f. pl.) book	كِتابُهُنَّ	he promised *them* (f. pl.)	وَعَدَهُنَّ	هُنَّ	*they* (f. pl.) do	يَفْعَلْنَ	نَ	هُنَّ
your (m.) book	كِتابُكَ	he promised *you*	وَعَدَكَ	كَ	*you* did	فَعَلْتَ	تَ	أَنْتَ
your (b.) book	كِتابُكُما	he promised *you* (both)	وَعَدكُما	كُما	*you* (b.) did	فَعَلْتُما	تُما	أَنْتُما
your	كِتابُكُمْ	he promised	وَعَدَكُمْ	كُمْ	*you*	فَعَلْتُمْ	تُمْ	أَنْتُمْ

book		you (pl.)			(pl.) did			
your (f.) book	كِتابُكِ	he promised you (f.)	وَعَدَكِ	كِ	do! (f.)	افْعَلِي	ي	أَنْتِ
your (b.) book	كِتابُكُما	he promised you (both)	وَعَدَكُما	كُما	do! (dual)	افْعَلا	ا	أَنْتُما
your (f. pl.) book	كِتابُكُنَّ	he promised you (f. pl.)	وَعَدَكُنَّ	كُنَّ	do! (f. pl.)	افْعَلْنَ	نَ	أَنْتُنَّ
my book	كِتابِي	he promised me	وَعَدَني	ي ني	I did	فَعَلْتُ	ـتُ	أَنا
our book	كِتابُنا	he promised us	وَعَدَنا	نا	we did	فَعَلْنا	نا	نَحْنُ

A ضَمِيرٌ مُتَّصِلٌ can never stand alone. It would be wrong to use a space (فاصِلٌ).

Can I use a separate pronoun instead of an object pronoun?

If you need emphasis and specification, yes. But otherwise – you shouldn't. Arabic likes brevity which is the main reason for the object pronoun! See *question #105*.

correct & best	ضَمِيرٌ مُتَّصِلٌ	I honored you.	أَكْرَمْتُكَ.
	ضَمِيرٌ مُنْفَصِلٌ	I honored, it is you.	أَكْرَمْتُ إِيّاكَ.

74. Can you use an active participle (اِسْمُ فاعِلٍ) instead of a verb (فِعْلٌ)؟

Yes, the meaning is basically the same.

The **active participle** is not a verb. It is a noun (اِسْمٌ) as its name says already: اِسْمُ الْفاعِلِ.

Since it is a اِسْمٌ, it gets case endings depending on the function in a sentence.

The **verb** (فِعْلٌ) is a multi-pack. It already contains quite a bit of information. You know about the subject (فَاعِلٌ). It is also capable of forming tenses, telling us about the circumstances of the action, when it happened or if it is already over. A verb does not take case endings. It can only express *moods*.

However, both can express more or less the same meaning. But not only that: The اِسْمُ الْفَاعِلِ has the power of a verb to guard other words and induce cases. In Arabic, we say it can work as a governor (عَامِلٌ). This explains why there may be a direct object in the accusative case after an active participle.

In both sentences, *the lesson* (الدَّرْسَ) is the direct object (مَفْعُولٌ بِهِ) and gets the accusative case (مَنْصُوبٌ).	We use the active participle instead of the verb.	كُنْتُ فَاهِمًا الدَّرْسَ.
		I understood the lesson.
	We use the verb.	كُنْتُ أَفْهَمُ الدَّرْسَ.
		I understood the lesson.

I turned on the lamp to light up the room.	أَنْوَرْتُ الْمِصْباحَ مُنيرًا الْغُرْفةَ.
Room is the **direct object** (مَفْعُولٌ بِهِ), but of which verb? Well, not a verb. The active participle مُنيرًا works as a regent/governor (عَامِلٌ).	

75. Is every noun (اِسْمٌ) derived from a root?

No, it is not.

Arabic nouns are of two natures: one has a solid foundation and others are abstract, artificially constructed. Precisely speaking, a اِسْمٌ can occur in **two forms**:

1   Static, aplastic, inert noun (اِسْمٌ جَامِدٌ)

جَامِدٌ literally means *frozen* or *in a solid state*. Such nouns are <u>not</u> taken from another word. It is initially laid down in its actual form. It is the ground floor. Such words describe the **core meaning of the root** (الْمَصْدَرُ الْمُجَرَّدُ) or describe things which you can grasp with your **five senses** like *mountain* (جَبَلٌ), *man* (رَجُلٌ), or *Egypt* (مِصْرُ). Remember, a مَصْدَرٌ is a word which...

- describes the action without giving you information about the one who is performing the action;
- does not give you information about the time.

For example, شُرْبٌ (*drinking*). This word describes the action, but we don't have information about the person who drinks and when this event happened.

2   Derived noun (اِسْمٌ مُشْتَقٌّ)

مُشْتَقٌّ means *derived*. Such nouns are taken from another word; unlike the type above they are not level 0. They are closely related to the meaning of the root and include the root letters. Derived nouns are a peculiarity that makes Arabic (and Semitic languages) unique. With a مُشْتَقٌّ, you can express the place or time of the action, frequency, strength of the action, an item to perform the action, the person performing it, etc.

Most grammarians agree that such nouns are built from the core past tense verb (الْماضِي الْمُجَرَّدُ) which in turn is built from the bare original noun (مَصْدَرٌ مُجَرَّدٌ) we covered above.

How do we produce a مُشْتَقٌّ? Practically, we take the root, e.g., *to write* (ك-ت-ب). If we want to create a word which denotes the place where the process of *writing* is done - *the desk* -, we use a pattern and eventually get مَكْتَبٌ (*desk* or *office*). It is the place where the action of *to write* is done.

The most common مُشْتَقَّاتٌ are:

example		FORMULA	type	
a liar	كاذِبٌ	رَجُلٌ + كَذَبَ person + verb	إِسْمُ فاعِلٍ agent-noun; active participle	1

The active participle may describe:

- a state of being: *understanding* (فاهِمٌ);
- what a person is doing right now: *sleeping* (نائِمٌ);
- that someone/something is in a state of having done something: *having put something somewhere* (حاطِطٌ).

somebody who lies a lot	كَذَّابٌ	رَجُلٌ + كَذَبَ كَثِيرًا person + verb	صِيغَةُ الْمُبالَغةِ noun of excess	2

Such a form doesn't exist in English. It is a noun of exaggeration or superlative. It denotes that a person is doing the action many times. It is similar to the active participle (اِسْمُ فاعِلٍ), but emphasizes the intensity of the action.

factory	مَصْنَعٌ	مَكانٌ + صِناعةٌ place + مَصْدَرٌ	اِسْمُ مَكانٍ noun of place	3

A اِسْمُ مَكانٍ denotes the place where the action takes place. Since the person is not important for the place, the مَصْدَرٌ is the under-lying basis and not the verb itself (as the verb always gives you in-formation about the subject/the doer).

appointment	مَوْعِدٌ	زَمانٌ + وَعَدَ time + مَصْدَرٌ	إِسْمُ زَمانٍ noun of time	4

Denoting the moment of the action. Since the person is not impor-tant for the time of the action, the مَصْدَر provides the underlying plot and not the verb.

known	مَعْرُوفٌ	رَجُلٌ + مَعْرِفةٌ person + مَصْدَرٌ	إِسْمُ مَفْعُولٍ passive participle	5

The action was done but the word doesn't give us information who had done it. As the person isn't important in the passive, we relate to the مَصْدَر and not the verb.

stronger	أَقْوَى	رَجُلٌ + قُوّةٌ + أَكْثَرُ person + مَصْدَرٌ + comparison	إِسْمُ تَفْضِيلٍ noun of preference	6

Comparative or superlative (elative) of an adjective.

great	عَظِيمٌ	رَجُلٌ + عُظمةٌ person + مَصْدَرٌ	صِفةٌ مُشَبّهةٌ quasi partici-ple; adjective	7

A صِفةٌ مُشَبّهةٌ denotes a meaning of firmness, the absolute exis-tence of a characteristic in the possessor. We create a noun with a quality similar to the active participle. Such words often have the meaning of English adjectives; *see #50*. The مَصْدَر we use has an abstract meaning which is not always easy to translate.

key	مِفْتاحٌ	أَداةٌ + فَتْحٌ tool/thing + مَصْدَرٌ	إِسْمُ آلةٍ noun of instrument	8

It denotes the tool of the action. There are several patterns which are used to build words for tools and instruments. *See quest. #175.*

76. A مَصْدَرٌ can never be indefinite – Is that true?

Yes, this is true – but only in the nominative case (مَرْفُوعٌ).

Any مَصْدَرٌ has to be definite, either by the article الـ or by serving in a إِضافةٌ-construction – if it serves in a position that demands the **nominative** case (مَرْفُوعٌ).

This can help you to identify a مَصْدَرٌ in a sentence, especially if you don't understand the structure or meaning.

77. Why is there a مَصْدَرٌ مِيمِيٌّ in Arabic?

The مَصْدَرٌ مِيمِيٌّ is a special form of a مَصْدَرٌ. It is called مِيمِيٌّ because it always starts with the additional letter مـ.

A مَصْدَرٌ مِيمِيٌّ basically means the same as the standard مَصْدَرٌ. So, what is it good for? Well, the poets needed it. The extra مـ changes the length of the word. It has more rhythm and melody as the original مَصْدَرٌ. But that's not all. Sometimes, a مَصْدَرٌ مِيمِيٌّ may convey some emphasis (تَأْكِيدٌ) and firmness regarding the meaning (*see question #77*).

How do we build a مَصْدَرٌ مِيمِيٌّ؟

A. The standard I-verb (الثُّلاثِيُّ)

You use the patterns of the إِسْمُ الزَّمانِ and the إِسْمُ الْمَكانِ:

- مَفْعَلٌ
- مَفْعِلٌ - especially for verbs starting with و. For example, the verb *to promise* (وَعَدَ) → مَوْعِدٌ
- مَفْعَلةٌ - making the word feminine by the تاءُ التَّأْنِيثِ

B. Verb forms II to X (غَيْرُ الثُّلاثِيِّ) → They are already words with more than three letters; you rarely see the مَصْدَرٌ مِيمِيٌّ

You use the pattern for the إِسْمُ الْمَفْعُولِ. Some examples:

translation	الْمَصْدَرُ الْمِيمِيُّ singular and plural		original infinitive (الْمَصْدَرُ الْأَصْلِيُّ)	verb
question	مَسائِلُ	مَسْأَلةٌ	سُؤالٌ	سَأَلَ
existence, life	مَعايِشُ	مَعِيشةٌ	عِيشةٌ or عِيشٌ	عاشَ
benefit, utility	مَنافِعُ	مَنْفَعةٌ	نَفْعٌ	نَفَعَ
demand, request	مَطالِبُ	مَطْلَبٌ	طَلَبٌ	طَلَبَ
killing, murder	مَقاتِلُ	مَقْتَلٌ	قَتْلٌ	قَتَلَ
food	مَآكِلُ	مَأْكَلٌ	أَكْلٌ	أَكَلَ
drink	مَشارِبُ	مَشْرَبٌ	شُرْبٌ	شَرِبَ
descent, decline	مُنْحَدَراتٌ	مُنْحَدَرٌ	إِنْحِدارٌ	إِنْحَدَرَ

Finally, there is another reason for the مَصْدَرٌ مِيمِيٌّ. The **plural form** is usually easier to build because you can often avoid broken plural forms and diptotes (مَمْنُوعٌ مِن الصَّرْفِ) – if you follow the pattern of a sound feminine plural.

Let's see why.

plural	الْمَصْدَرُ الْمِيمِيُّ	plural	الْمَصْدَرُ الأَصْلِيُّ	meaning	root
مَضَرَّاتٌ or مَضارُّ	مَضَرَّةٌ	أَضْرارٌ	ضَرَرٌ	damage	ض-ر-ر
مَنْفَعاتٌ or مَنافِعُ	مَنْفَعةٌ	نَوافِعُ	نَفْعٌ	benefit	ن-ف-ع

Watch out if you have to identify a مَصْدَرٌ مِيمِيٌّ. In the following table, the word مُسْتَخْرَج occurs in every sentence.

But does it have the same meaning and function? Not at all!

translation	example	type
The well is the place of extraction for petroleum.	الْبِئْرُ مُسْتَخْرَجُ النَّفْطِ.	إسْمُ الْمَكانِ
Petroleum is extracted from the well.	النَّفْطُ مُسْتَخْرَجٌ مِن الْبِئْرِ.	إسْمُ الْمَفْعُولِ
The extraction of the oil is in the morning.	مُسْتَخْرَجُ النَّفْطِ صَباحًا.	إسْمُ الزَّمانِ
I extracted petroleum quickly.	إسْتَخْرَجْتُ النَّفْطَ مُسْتَخْرَجًا عَجِيلًا.	الْمَصْدَرُ الْمِيمِيُّ

78. Do سُؤَالٌ and مَسْأَلَةٌ both mean the same?

Basically, yes. Both mean "question".

This is an area where Arabic becomes melodic and conveys things through single letters that cannot be grasped in English with one word.

- سُؤَالٌ is the original infinitive noun (الْمَصْدَرُ الْأَصْلِيُّ) of the I-verb سَأَلَ / يَسْأَلُ;
- مَسْأَلَةٌ is an augmented infinitive, a الْمَصْدَرُ الْمِيمِيُّ;

The مَصْدَرٌ مِيمِيٌّ is easier and smoother to pronounce. It may also indicate a stronger meaning and reinforce the original مَصْدَرٌ. If you find a ة at the end of a مَصْدَرٌ مِيمِيٌّ, it may signal a slight exaggeration or widening of the action or a special focus on the abundance/frequency of the action.

So it is no surprise that مَسْأَلَةٌ does not only mean *question*. It also denotes *issue, problem; matter, affair*.

79. *Freedom* (حُرِّيَّةٌ) - What kind of word is that in Arabic?

It is an artificial infinitive noun (مَصْدَرٌ صِناعِيٌّ).

Let's pick out the suffix يّ of حُرِّيَّةٌ and think for a moment where else it appears. In Arabic, we call it *Nisba* (نِسْبةٌ or اِسْمٌ مَنْسُوبٌ). You add يّ to any اِسْمٌ and get a word that can be used as an *adjective* (صِفةٌ), often to denote that someone is from a certain country or has a special profession. For example, *Egyptian* (مِصْرِيٌّ/مِصْرِيّةٌ).

Now, if we add a ة to a *Nisba* resulting in يّة, it becomes a **noun** indicating an **abstract meaning** which it did not have before this augmentation. We produced a so-called *artificial infinitive noun* (مَصْدَرٌ صِناعِيٌّ). Many of such words describe political, economic, or scientific terms (chemistry, biology).

meaning	مَصْدَرٌ صِناعِيٌّ		source	
humanity	إِنْسانِيَّةٌ		human	إِنْسانٌ
progressiveness	تَقَدُّمِيَّةٌ		progression	تَقَدُّمٌ
socialism	إِشْتِراكِيَّةٌ		partnership	إِشْتِراكٌ
freedom	حُرِّيَّةٌ		independent	حُرٌّ
democracy	دِيمُوقْراطِيَّةٌ	◄	---	---
communism	شُيُوعِيَّةٌ		spreading, circulation	شُيُوعٌ
capitalism	رَأْسُمالِيَّةٌ		capital	رَأْسُمالٍ رَأْسُ مالٍ
			Note: The plural of رَأْسُمالٍ is رَساميلُ or رُؤُوسُ الأَمْوالِ	

80. *To raise* (رَبَّى) - What is the مَصْدَر of this verb?

It is تَرْبِيَةٌ *and means: upbringing.*

The II-verb يُرَبِّي / رَبَّى means *to raise; to breed*. There is an issue here which we need to solve. The last root letter is not ي. It is an Aleph spelled as ى!

We said in *question #9* that an Aleph can never be part of the root; it got this shape due to a transformation of either و or ي. To find out the correct letter, we need to go back to the base verb: I-verb رَبَا / يَرْبُو (*to grow*). Through this we learn that the third root letter is و!

Now that we have solved that, we get a new problem. The مَصْدَر of a II-verb is built by using the pattern تَفْعِيلٌ (see #41). However, when the last root letter is weak (حَرْف عِلّةٍ), the pattern is تَفْعِلةٌ. How does و fit into that? It doesn't. The كَسرة under ع doesn't really go along with و; it would be ugly to pronounce تَرْبِوَةٌ. So, we use ي and get تَرْبِيةٌ as the مَصْدَر of رَبَّى.

Watch out: تَرْبِية is often mispronounced. There is no شَدّة on top of ي! The stress is on the first letter ت.

81. *To have* - How can you express that in Arabic?

Unfortunately, there is no universal Arabic verb for to have.

So what should we do? We need a few detours. We can use adverbial expressions, prepositions, or express it by verbs.

عِنْدَ • لِ • لَدَى + pronoun	عِنْدَ and لَـدَى denote *at* or *by*. لِ denotes *for* and is especially used to express ownership.

Very important: The sentence is turned over in English. The direct object in English becomes the subject (مُبْتَدَأٌ) in Arabic and therefore is in the nominative case (مَرْفُوعٌ)!

He has...	عِنْدَهُ [شَيْءٌ] or لَدَيْهِ [شَيْءٌ] or لَهُ [شَيْءٌ]
He doesn't have...	لَيْسَ عِنْدَهُ [شَيْءٌ]
He had...	كانَ عِنْدَهُ [شَيْءٌ]

He didn't have...	عِنْدَهُ [شَيْءٌ]	مَا كَانَ
		لَمْ يَكُنْ
He had no time for...	لَمْ يَكُنْ لَدَيْهِ الْوَقْتُ الْكَافِي لِ	

| The focus is on **belonging**. | لِ |

لِ denotes the strongest notion of owning. It can even be used for abstract or possible actions (e.g.: *a book is reserved for you in the library*). Also for relatives (e.g.: *I have a brother*).

Is it important that we know **where** the thing is now? **No**; we just guess from the context.

| The focus is on **having a thing physically with you**. | عِنْدَ |

عِنْدَ may be used for possessing or owning in general as well. It may be used for temporary possession. E.g.: *You have a book which you borrowed from your friend.*

Do we know **where** the thing is? **Yes**. عِنْدَ usually indicates that you have a thing in your possession at your place – at your office, flat, etc. Do we know who owns the book? We could say **yes**. It implies that the thing belongs **to you/the person** (unless stated differently).

| Indicates having a thing in **possession physically** - which is either at a **certain place** or **with you**. | لَدَى |

Do we know who **owns** it? **Not really**. If you say لَدَيَّ كِتابٌ (*I have a book*), it could also mean that it is the book of someone else. لَدَى and عِنْدَ often denote the same idea and can be used interchangeably. لَدَى is more stylish – but not used in spoken language.

SOME OTHER OPTIONS:

to have something with one	مَعَ

The focus is on having something physically with you. Do we know who owns the thing? No, not really; we can only assume it form the context.

I don't have money with me.	لَيْسَ مَعِي مالٌ.

Watch out: مَعَ and عِنْدَ and لَدَى can **only be used with <u>human</u> beings.** Never use them if the "subject" is an animal, plant, or any kind of inanimate. In such cases, you should use لِ.

meaning of: *to own something*	مَلَكَ - يَمْلِكُ
He has a house.	يَمْلِكُ بَيْتًا.

to have to do	pronoun plus عَلَى
She has to go.	عَلَيْها الذَّهابُ.

English expressions with *to have* that are expressed by special verbs.	
to have fear	خافَ - يَخافُ
to have patience	صَبَرَ - يَصْبِرُ
I got it! (German: *Ich hab's!*)	وَجَدْتُهُ!

to have a cold	يُصابُ بِالْبَرْدِ
to have the chance	تَسْنَحُ لَهُ الْفُرْصَةُ
to have a crush	يَنْجَذِبُ لِ
to have it in mind	(كانَ) ذَلِكَ عَلَى بِلِه
to have a good knowledge of	يَعْرِفُ جَيِّدًا
to have a good time	يُمَتِّعُ نَفْسه
Have a good weekend!	أَتَمَنَّى لَكَ نِهاية أُسْبُوعٍ سَعِيدةٍ
to have a hangover	يُعاني مِن تَأْثِيرِ الْكُحُولِ
to have a hard time doing sth.	يُواجِهُ صُعُوبَةً في
to have a heart attack	يُصابُ بِأَزْمةٍ قَلْبِيّةٍ
to have a look at	يَفْحَصُ
to have a piece of	يَتَشارَكُ في
to have lunch	تَناوَلَ الْغداءَ
to have a baby	أَنْجَبَت طِفْلًا

82. Do أُرِيدُ الذَّهابَ and أُرِيدُ أَنْ أَذْهَبَ mean the same?

Yes, they do! Both mean the same: *I want to go.*

ذَهابٌ is the مَصْدَر of the I-verb يَذْهَبُ / ذَهَبَ (*to go*).

The construction أَنْ plus a verb in the present tense, sub-junctive mood (مَنْصُوبٌ) conveys the same meaning as the pure مَصْدَر. It is even called an *interpreted* مَصْدَر, a مَصْدَر

مُؤَوَّل. The term **مُؤَوَّل** is the passive participle of the II-verb **أَوَّل / يُؤَوِّل** which means *to explain; to interpret*. The original **مَصْدَر** is called **مَصْدَرٌ صَرِيحٌ**.

You usually build the **مَصْدَر مُؤَوَّل** with **أَنْ** or **ما**. They are *particles/devices of the infinitive* (**الحُرُوفُ المَصْدَرِيَّة**); other examples of such devices are **لِ, كَيْ, هَمْزَة**, and **لَوْ**.

أَنْ يَذْهَب	=	ذَهابٌ
الْمَصْدَرُ الْمُؤَوَّل	=	الْمَصْدَرُ الصَّرِيحُ
going; go	=	going; go

Watch out: يَذْهَبَ has فَتْحةٌ because it is preceded by أَنْ. Thus, the verb has to be in the *subjunctive mood* (مَنْصُوبٌ).

We will examine now how to change a **مَصْدَر مُؤَوَّل** into a **مَصْدَرٌ صَرِيحٌ** and vice versa:

type of مَصْدَرٌ	EXAMPLE A	
مَصْدَرٌ مُؤَوَّلٌ	أَنْ تَصُومُوا خَيْرٌ لَكُمْ.	1
مَصْدَرٌ صَرِيحٌ	صِيامُكُمْ خَيْرٌ لَكُمْ.	2
Both sentences mean the same: *(Your) fasting is good for you.*		

grammatical explanation	مَصْدَرٌ	
The interpreted infinitive is the **subject** of the **nominal sentence** and thus in the position of a nominative case (مَصْدَرٌ مُؤَوَّلٌ فِي مَحَلِّ رَفْعٍ مُبْتَدَأً).	أَنْ تَصُومُوا	1
Subject of the **nominal** sentence (مُبْتَدَأً مَرْفُوعٌ).	صِيامُكُمْ	2
In short: The grammatical job of both types is exactly the same – because they are located in the same spot. Therefore, an interpreted		

infinitive can be located as a subject, direct object, etc.

type of مَصْدَرٌ	EXAMPLE B	
مَصْدَرٌ مُؤَوَّلٌ	أَسْعَدَني ما عَمِلْتَ.	1
مَصْدَرٌ صَريحٌ	أَسْعَدَني عَمَلُكَ.	2

The meaning is the same: *Your work (what you did) made me happy.*

grammatical explanation	مَصْدَرٌ	
The interpreted infinitive is located in the position of the **subject** of the **verbal sentence**, thus it is located in the spot of a nominative case (مَصْدَرٌ مُؤَوَّلٌ فِي مَحَلِّ رَفْعِ فاعِلٍ).	ما عَمِلْتَ	1
Subject of the **verbal** sentence (فاعِلٌ مَرْفُوعٌ)	عَمَلُكَ	2

Also here, although you can't see it visibly, the grammatical assessment of both sentences is the same!

83. تَغْنِيَةٌ and غِناءٌ - Do they mean the same?

Not exactly. It is the difference between singing and song.

Both words are related to the II-verb *to sing* (غَنَّى / يُغَنِّي).

The word تَغْنِيَةٌ

The مَصْدَرٌ of a II-verb (فَعَّلَ) uses the pattern تَفْعِيلٌ. For example, *to teach* (دَرَّسَ - يُدَرِّسُ) → *teaching* (تَدْرِيسٌ). This is true for regular verbs. But the pattern looks different if the last root letter is weak (حَرْفُ عِلّةٍ), i.e., و or ي. Then, the pattern changes to تَفْعِلةٌ. This is why the regular مَصْدَرٌ of غَنَّى is تَغْنِيةٌ.

The word غِناءٌ

This word conveys a meaning similar to the مَصْدَر - with a fine difference. The regular مَصْدَر denotes the **occurrence of the action** (= singing), whereas the *noun* of the مَصْدَر, the إِسْمُ مَصْدَرٍ, focuses more on the **result** of process (= song). Nevertheless, it often denotes the same idea as the original مَصْدَرٌ.

In general, a إِسْمُ مَصْدَرٍ is shorter than the original مَصْدَرٌ and **misses (extra) letters**. Watch out: Even if the word is shorter, as soon as you add a letter, it is not a إِسْمُ مَصْدَرٍ anymore. For example, I-verb وَعَدَ (*to promise*). The derived عِدَةٌ (*promise*) is a مَصْدَرٌ and not a إِسْمُ مَصْدَرٍ since ة was added.

For native speakers, the pronunciation of تَغْنِيةٌ is a little hard which explains why this word is used rarely. They prefer غِناءٌ. Let us quickly check the correct pronunciation of غناء:

1	غَناءٌ	غَناءٌ with فَتْحةٌ over غ is the مَصْدَرٌ of the verb غَنِيَ. This is a I-verb and means: *to be rich*. The مَصْدَرٌ can be translated as *wealth*.
2	غِناءٌ	Notice the "*i*"-sound (كَسْرةٌ) at the beginning of the word under غ. It is related to the II-verb غَنَّى as explained above. غِناءٌ means *song* or *singing*.
	Without vowels, you need to understand the context because both words for *song* and *wealth* look exactly the same!

Now let's see some examples of the إِسْمُ مَصْدَرٍ.

verb		pattern		مَصْدَرٌ أَصْلِيٌّ	إِسْمُ مَصْدَرٍ = result of the action	
to sing	غَنَّى	فَعَّلَ	II	تَغْنِيَةٌ	song	غِناءٌ
to make a mistake	أَخْطَأَ	أَفْعَلَ	IV	إِخْطاءٌ	mistake	خَطَأٌ
to travel	سافَرَ	فاعَلَ	V	مُسافَرَةٌ	journey	سَفَرٌ
to buy things	إِشْتَرَى	إِفْتَعَلَ	VIII	إِشْتِراءٌ	purchase	شِراءٌ
to marry	تَزَوَّجَ	تَفَعَّلَ	V	تَزَوُّجٌ	marriage	زَواجٌ
to speak	تَكَلَّمَ	تَفَعَّلَ	V	تَكَلُّمٌ	speech	كَلامٌ
to talk	تَحَدَّثَ	تَفَعَّلَ	V	تَحَدُّثٌ	conversation	حَديثٌ
to pray	صَلَّى	فَعَّلَ	II	تَصْلِيةٌ	prayer	صَلاةٌ

For a special application of the إِسْمُ مَصْدَرٍ see *question #204*.

84. What are the so-called five verbs (أَفْعالٌ خَمْسةٌ)?

They contain information which will tell you more about the mood of the verb.

In the present tense (and future since it is expressed by the suffix سَ or سَوْفَ + verb in the present tense), there are **only three different suffixes** which can be added to the verb with regard to the doer of the verb. **These three suffixes are:**

- plural Wāw (و) for هُمْ and أَنْتُمْ;
- dual Aleph (ا) for هُما and أَنْتُما;
- feminine yā' (ي) for أَنْتِ (second person feminine);

In the regular present tense (الْمُضَارِعُ), indicative mood, the letter ن is added to these suffixes. The three suffixes finally make up <u>five</u> forms which is the reason why Arab grammarians introduced the term *five verbs* (أَفْعَالٌ خَمْسَةٌ).

They (both) go.	يَذْهَبانِ	هُما	1
You (both) go.	تَذْهَبانِ	أَنْتُما	2
They go.	يَذْهَبُونَ	هُمْ	3
You (plural) go.	تَذْهَبُونَ	أَنْتُمْ	4
You (feminine, singular) go.	تَذْهَبينَ	أَنْتِ	5

Things get exciting when we put these five forms into the **jussive** (مَجْزُومٌ) mood. The term *jussive* relates to the Latin word *jubeō: to order*. We use the jussive for the imperative, after particles of the negation (لَمْ), and in conditional sentences. We mark it by putting سُكُونٌ on the last letter of the verb – but not in the *five verbs*! Instead, we let the ن **disappear**!

They (two) did not go.	لَمْ يَذْهَبا	هُما	1
You (two) did not go.	لَمْ تَذْهَبا	أَنْتُما	2
They did not go.	لَمْ يَذْهَبُوا	هُمْ	3
You did not go.	لَمْ تَذْهَبُوا	أَنْتُمْ	4
You (feminine, singular) did not go.	لَمْ تَذْهَبِي	أَنْتِ	5

Some remarks:

- After the negation لَمْ and the *prohibitive* لا (لا النّاهِيَةُ), we have to use the مَجْزُومٌ-mood. The *prohibitive* لا is used to warn or discourage people, usually translated as: *don't...!*

- What we have seen above is also applied to the *subjunctive mood* (مَنْصُوبٌ). This mood weakens the clear meaning of the verb by giving it a touch of intent, hope, ability, necessity, doubt, purpose, or expectation. It is used after the particles أَنْ • لَنْ • حَتَّى.

- → In both moods, we elide the ن to mark the mood.

Let's use this moment to look in detail at the jussive mood. It is characterized by the fact that we **clip** something; مَجْزُومٌ literally means *cut off; clipped* or in the linguistic hemisphere: *vowelless*. We get rid of the last vowel and achieve this by putting سُكُونٌ. Let's look at all the possibilities.

Situation 1: **Regular verb – no weak letter**. If the conjugated verb in the present tense doesn't have an extra letter added, put سُكُونٌ on the last letter. We get this in the verb conjugation of *I* (أنا), *we* (نَحْنُ); *he* (هُوَ), *she* (هِيَ); *you* m./sing. (أَنْتَ).

He did not go.	لَمْ يَذْهَبْ.
I did not write.	لَمْ أَكْتُبْ.
We did not open.	لَمْ نَفْتَحْ.

Situation 2: If you have a conjugated verb ending in long vowel plus ن, then delete the ن to mark the jussive mood. This is true for regular verbs and roots with weak letters. We run into this situation in the verb conjugation of *you f. sing.* (أَنْتِ), *you both* (أَنْتُما), *you m. pl.* (أَنْتُمْ), *they* (هُمْ), *they both* (هُما).

jussive (مَجْزُومٌ)		example; present tense	verb
They did not go.	لَمْ يَذْهَبُوا.	*they go*	يَذْهَبُونَ ذَهَبَ

You did not say.	لَمْ تَقُولِي.	you (f.) say	تَقُولِينَ	قَالَ
You (b.) didn't buy.	لَمْ تَبِيعا.	you both buy	تَبِيعَانِ	بَاعَ
They (b.) didn't call.	لَمْ يَدْعُوَا	they both call	يَدْعُوَانِ	دَعَا
You did not keep.	لَمْ يَفُوا.	you (pl.) keep (a promise)	تَفُونَ	وَفَى

Situation 3: If the verb does not have any suffix in the present tense conjugation, but includes a **weak letter** (حَرْفُ عِلّةٍ), then delete the weak letter to mark the jussive.

- If the weak letter is in the middle, put سُكُونٌ on the final letter.

- Otherwise, just use the third person singular in the present tense and cut the last letter.

jussive (مَجْزُومٌ)		example; present tense		verb
He did not say.	لَمْ يَقُلْ.	he says	يَقُولُ	قَالَ
He did not buy.	لَمْ يَبِعْ.	he buys	يَبِيعُ	بَاعَ
He did not meet.	لَمْ يَلْقَ.	he meets	يَلْقَى	لَقِيَ
He didn't invite.	لَمْ يَدْعُ.	he invites; calls	يَدْعُو	دَعَا
He did not keep.	لَمْ يَفِ.	he keeps (a promise)	يَفِي	وَفَى

However, there are two constellations that are somewhat unusual and connected to the **feminine <u>plural</u> forms** they (هُنَّ) and you (أَنْتُنَّ). The indicative (مَرْفُوعٌ) and jussive (مَجْزُومٌ) as well as the subjunctive (مَنْصُوبٌ) mood **all look the same!**

	jussive	subjunctive	indicative	verb	
You (pl.; f.) didn't write.	لَمْ تَكْتُبْنَ	أَنْ تَكْتُبْنَ	تَكْتُبْنَ	تَكْتُبْنَ - كَتَبْتُنَّ	أَنْتُنَّ
They (pl.; f.) didn't write.	لَمْ يَكْتُبْنَ	أَنْ يَكْتُبْنَ	يَكْتُبْنَ	يَكْتُبْنَ - كَتَبْنَ	هُنَّ

85. سَوْفَ يَذْهَبُ and سَيَذْهَبُ - Do they mean the same?

Almost.

Both denote *I will go* – but with a different notion of time:

سَـ	near future	الْمُسْتَقْبَلُ الْقَرِيبُ	سَيَذْهَبُ غَدًا.
		He will go tomorrow.	
سَوْفَ	far future	الْمُسْتَقْبَلُ الْبَعِيدُ	سَوْفَ يَذْهَبُ بَعْدَ شَهْرَيْنِ.
		He will go in two months.	

How do you **negate** the future? You have two options.

The best is to use the particle لَنْ plus a verb in the subjunctive mood (مَنْصُوبٌ). But you may also use لا after سَوْفَ.

She won't write you a letter.	(هِيَ) لَنْ تَكْتُبَ لَكَ رِسالةً.	1
	(هِيَ) سَوْفَ لا تَكْتُبُ لَكَ رِسالةً.	2

86. If someone died, why do you use the passive voice?

It is related to the omnipotence of God.

In Arabic, there are many ways to express that someone has died. Most often you will encounter one of these two verbs:

I-verb; **active** voice	*to die; to decease*	يَمُوتُ - مَاتَ

He died of cancer.	مَاتَ بِمَرَضِ السَّرَطانِ
He died at the age of twenty	مَاتَ عَنْ عِشْرِينَ سَنةً
He almost died.	كَادَ يَمُوتُ.

V-verb; **passive** voice	*to die; pass away;* literal meaning: *to receive in full; to take one's full share*	يَتَوَفَّى - تُوُفِّيَ

The active voice يَتَوَفَّى / تَوَفَّى denotes **to let die** in the sense of the IV-verb أَماتَ but also *to take* in the meaning of *God has taken his soul* (أَخَذَ رُوحَهُ). The root includes two weak letters: R1=و, R3=ي.

God has taken him unto himself.	تَوَفّاهُ اللّٰهُ.	active voice
God takes the people to Him.	اللّٰهُ يَتَوَفَّى النّاسَ.	active voice
He died in a traffic accident.	تُوُفِّيَ بِحادِثِ سَيْرٍ.	**passive** v.

The **active voice** (مَعْلُومٌ فاعِلُهُ) of تَوَفَّى can only be used if God is the <u>subject</u> (فاعِلٌ). In religious beliefs, only God knows and decides when death will happen. Therefore, you should only use the active voice when God is the subject (the doer).

In all other situations, the verb should be used in the **passive voice** (مَجْهُولٌ فاعِلُهُ) **to express that someone has died**: تُوُفِّيَ. The passive can be translated as *to die; to pass away*.

Professor *xy* has died.	تُوُفِّيَ إِلَى رَحْمَةِ اللهِ تَعالَى الْأُسْتاذُ xy.

What about the word for *the deceased*? You can use الرَّاحِلُ or الْفَقِيدُ or مُتَوَفَّى (plural: مُتَوَفُّونَ) which is the **passive** participle (اِسْمُ مَفْعُولٍ) of the V-verb تَوَفَّى.

87. كَذَّابٌ - What kind of liar is he?

He is a notorious or big liar.

In Arabic, you can distinguish elegantly if somebody *just lied to you once* (كاذِبٌ) or is a *notorious liar* (كَذَّابٌ).

The latter form is called صِيغَةُ الْمُبالَغةِ (*form of exaggeration*) and is a special outgrowth of the active participle (اِسمُ الْفاعِلِ). It conveys the idea of force or repetition which is included in the pattern: *very...* or *notorious...* or *strong...* or *often done*. It expresses a superlative meaning. Such nouns are common in Arabic and used for human qualities, but even for job terms; e.g., a *butcher* (جَزَّارٌ) is someone *who slaughters a lot*.

translation	plural form	صِيغةُ الْمُبالَغةِ	verb		pat-tern
notorious liar	كَذَّابُونَ	كَذَّابٌ	to lie	كَذَبَ يَكْذِبُ	فَعَّالٌ
very grateful	شُكُر	شَكُورٌ	to thanks	شَكَرَ يَشْكُرُ	فَعُولٌ
merciful	رَحِيمُونَ / رُحَماءُ	رَحِيمٌ	to be merciful	رَحِمَ يَرْحَمُ	فَعِيلٌ
courageous	مَقادِيمُ	مِقْدامٌ	to lead	قَدَّمَ	مِفْعالٌ

translation	plural form	صِيغَةُ الْمُبالَغةِ	verb		pat-tern
			the way	يُقَدَّمُ	
cautious, wary	حَذِرُونَ / حَذِراتٌ	حَذِرٌ	*to be cautious*	حَذِرَ يَحْذَرُ	فَعِلٌ

Remark: Pronunciation matters! كُذَّاب (with "*u*" on the first letter) is a plural form of the active participle كاذِبٌ.

Nouns denoting *excess* (الْمُبالَغة) can be built from **I-verbs**. We call them ثُلاثِيٌّ مُجَرَّدٌ which means that no extra letter is added to the root. Many verbs have a preferred pattern (like the examples above), but you could use other patterns as well.

Verb forms II to X are often not capable of forming such nouns. If they do, you have to use pattern مِفْعالٌ. This explains why the صِيغَةُ الْمُبالَغةِ of the **II-verb** قَدَّمَ (*to lead the way; to make precede*) is مِقدامٌ. Another example is the IV-verb أَغارَ (*to invade*) which is مِغْوارٌ (*being notorious aggressive*) in the form of exaggeration. Some remarks:

- The forms فَعّالٌ and فَعُولٌ denote exactly the same.
- For the feminine form, just add ة.
- **Watch out:** The final letter ة of some patterns does not mark the feminine gender but excess (لِلْمُبالَغةِ) and is used for male persons. For example: عَلّامةٌ (*very learned; erudite*); *see question #57.*
- فَعُولٌ and rarely مِفْعالٌ may be used for both genders. However, you can also add ة which is fine.

He is a (notorious) liar.	هُوَ كَذُوبٌ.
She is a (notorious) liar.	هِيَ كَذُوبٌ.

She is a (notorious) liar.	هِيَ كَذُوبَةٌ.
	هِيَ كَذَّابَةٌ.

88. *To respect each other* - How do you say that in Arabic?

There are several ways. It mainly depends on the verb you use.

Each other is indicating reciprocity, actions in which two or more people do the same thing to each other. Arabic offers nifty ways to express this idea.

The most elegant solution is to choose a suitable verb. Let's develop it. We start with the verb pattern فَاعَلَ which is a **III-verb** in Western terms. Such verbs can express that another person is involved in the action. But that is only half the story. We need to solve how we can achieve to express that the action is done on a mutual basis.

This is where the letter ت comes into play: a device to denote reciprocity. If we add ت to فَاعَلَ, we automatically convert a III-verb to a **VI-verb** (تَفَاعَلَ). A VI-verb usually expresses association (مُشَارَكَةٌ). It rarely denotes that you produce something. That's what we need!

to discuss with each other	تَنَاقَشَ يَتَناقَشُ			to discuss	نَاقَشَ يُناقِشُ	
to help one another; to work together	تَعَاوَنَ يَتَعَاوَنُ	VI	◄	to help	عَاوَنَ يُعاوِنُ	III
to fight one another	تَقَاتَلَ يَتَقَاتَلُ			to fight	قَاتَلَ يُقَاتِلُ	
to share with one an-	تَشَارَكَ			to share	شَارَكَ	

other; to be partners	يَتَشارَكُ		يُشارِكُ
to argue with one another; to quarrel	تَجادَلَ يَتَجادَلُ	to argue	جادَلَ يُجادِلُ

But what can we do if the verb is not known in the pattern فاعَلَ? For example, VIII-verb إِحْتَرَمَ which means *to respect*. In such a situation, we cannot build a reflexive verb just by changing the pattern.

We need to add an **expression**: بَعْضُنا بَعْضًا (for *we*) or بَعْضُهُمْ بَعْضًا (for *they*) or بَعْضُها بَعْضًا (*she*; or if it relates to a non-human plural). If you refer to two people: بَعْضُهُما بَعْضًا. It may be rendered as *mutually; each other; one another*. You can use this expression also with any other verb. *See #216.*

We respect each other.	نَحْتَرِمُ بَعْضُنا بَعْضًا.	إِحْتَرَمَ	VIII
We understand each other.	نَفْهَمُ بَعْضُنا بَعْضًا.	فَهِمَ	I
They know each other.	يَعْرِفُ بَعْضُهُمْ بَعْضًا.	عَرَفَ	I
A believer is like a brick for another believer, the one supporting the other. (Hadith; Sahīh Muslim 2585)	الْمُؤْمِنُ لِلْمُؤْمِنِ كَالْبُنْيَانِ يَشُدُّ بَعْضُهُ بَعْضًا.	شَدَّ	I
Business and economic development reinforce one another.	إِنَّ الْأَعْمالَ التِّجارِيَّةَ وَالتَّنْمِيَةَ الْإِقْتِصادِيَّةَ تُعَزِّزُ بَعْضُها بَعْضًا.	تَعَزَّزَ	V

89. How do you express probability with only one word?

You use the particle قَدْ.

In Arabic, there is a fine way of expressing probability.

قَدْ plus a verb in the <u>present</u> tense (الْمُضارِعُ)

It describes an action that might happen (but is not certain).

The liar may tell the truth.	قَدْ يَصْدُقُ الْكَذُوبُ.	قَدْ + **present** tense verb
She might come.	قَدْ تَأْتِي.	
I might not see him.	قَدْ لا أَراهُ.	

In this application قَدْ works as a particle of rarity or uncertainty (حَرْفُ تَقْلِيلٍ) and expresses doubts about whether or not an action will take place. For example, قَدْ تَكْتُبُ can denote:

- *You might write.*
- *Sometimes you write.*
- *It could be that you write.*
- *It happens that you write.*

Watch out: قَدْ plus <u>past</u> tense (الْماضِي) does the opposite! It indicates the termination and confirmation of an action (حَرْفُ تَحْقيقٍ) and emphasizes the definite occurrence of an action.

Regarding the notion of time, it usually indicates that something had happened further in the past → *pluperfect* = **had** + past participle.

He already left.	قَدْ ذَهَبَ.	قَدْ + **past** tense verb
She said that he had (already) done it.	قالَتْ إِنَّهُ قَدْ فَعَلَهُ.	
[Allah] said, "You have been granted your request, O Moses." *(Sura 20:36)*	قالَ قَدْ أُوتِيتَ سُؤْلَكَ يَا مُوسَى.	

90. Can, should, must - Does Arabic have modal verbs?

Yes, there are – but they work differently in Arabic.

In English, *can*, *may*, *might*, *must*, *should*, and *would* are modal verbs. Such verbs are not conjugated or negated in the same way as regular verbs. Modal verbs allow the speaker to express the possibility, ability, necessity, obligation, or certainty of an action (verb). **How do they work in Arabic?**

➤ In Arabic, you conjugate the modal (= first) verb.

➤ Regarding the second verb, you have to options:

1. You use أَنْ with the effect that the second verb takes the subjunctive mood (مَنْصُوبٌ).

2. You use the مَصْدَرٌ instead of the verb. Then, however, you need to identify the grammatical function of the مَصْدَرٌ in order to pick the correct case ending. Is it the subject? The direct object?

He has to pay.	subjunctive mood	يَجِبُ (عَلَيْهِ) أَنْ يَدْفَعَ.	1
	subject (الْفَاعِلُ); nominative	يَجِبُ (عَلَيْهِ) الدَّفْعُ.	2

He wanted to go.	subjunctive mood	أَرَادَ أَنْ يَذْهَبَ.	1
	direct object (الْمَفْعُولُ بِهِ); accusative case (مَنْصُوبٌ);	أَرَادَ الذَّهَابَ.	2

Here is a list of Arabic verbs that can be used as modal verbs. Some are impersonal verbs (e.g.: *it is necessary that…*) and are conjugated in the third person, singular (*he*; occasionally *she*).

English	present tense (الْمُضارِعُ)	past tense (الْماضِي)
1 *want; would*	يُرِيدُ	أَرادَ
2 *can; could*	يَسْتَطِيعُ	إِسْتَطاعَ
	pronoun + يُمْكِنُ	pronoun + أَمْكَنَ

يُمْكِنُ is tricky. You need a pronoun suffix to indicate the person. *He can go with you* (يُمْكِنُهُ أَنْ يَذْهَبَ مَعَكَ = يُمْكِنُهُ الذَهابُ مَعَكَ).

Furthermore, instead of the past tense (أَمْكَنَ), the present tense يُمْكِنُ is used with كانَ instead. In the translation of such a construction, you may use the word *actually*. For example: *He could have gone with you actually* (كانَ يُمْكِنُهُ أَنْ يَذْهَبَ مَعَكَ).

3 *must*	يَجِبُ (عَلَيْهِ)	وَجَبَ (عَلَيْهِ)

This verb is always used in the 3rd person singular (*he*). If you want to express *I must*, you have to add a personal pronoun to the preposition عَلَى. Eventually, we get يَجِبُ عَلَيَّ

4 *should; to be necessary*	يَنْبَغِي (عَلَيْهِ)	إِنْبَغَى (عَلَيْهِ)
	يَلْزَمُ (عَلَيْهِ)	لَزِمَ (عَلَيْهِ)

These two verbs are always used in the 3rd person singular (*he*). If you want to express, for example, *you should*, you have to add a personal pronoun to the preposition عَلَى; so you get: يَنْبَغِي عَلَيْكَ

should	عَلَى الْمَرْءِ أَنْ = يَنْبَغِي عَلَى الْمَرْءِ أَنْ

5 *may; to be allowed*	يَجُوزُ لِ	جازَ لِ

This verb is always used in the 3rd person singular

	English	present tense (الْمُضارِعُ)	past tense (الْماضِي)
		(he). If you want to express, e.g., *you were allowed*, you have to add a personal pronoun to the preposition لـ and will get: جازَ لَكَ	
6	*to like to*	وَدَّ + مَصْدَرٌ مَنْصوبٌ <u>or</u> أَنْ + فِعْلٌ مَنْصوبٌ	
		Remark: This expression is often used to express a wish that can't be fulfilled anymore. In such application, you have to use لَوْ after وَدَّ.	
		She likes to go with him.	تَوَدُّ أَنْ تَذْهَبَ مَعَهُ.
		He *would* like to travel with you.	يَوَدُّ لَوْ يُسافِرُ مَعَكَ.
		He *would* have liked to travel with you.	وَدَّ لَوْ سافَرَ مَعَكَ.

Remark: You may use كانَ plus a present tense verb to express an **unreal situation** (conditional II; Konjunktiv II).

He **would** have wished to see you today.	كانَ يَوَدُّ لِأَنْ يَراكَ الْيَوْمَ.
You **could** have asked him.	كانَ يُمْكِنُكَ أَنْ تَسْأَلَهُ.
You **should** have written her a letter.	كانَ يَنْبَغِي عَلَيْكَ أَنْ تَكْتُبَ لَها رِسالَةً.

91. Can you use a present tense verb to describe the past?

Yes, this is possible.

It is all about the context. It must be evident that you are talking about a situation in the past. In Arabic, it helps to look at the verb from two sides:

TENSE denotes the grammatical category. Tense is marked by the concrete form of the verb → <u>what is written</u>. Frankly, it's nothing but a term because a certain tense may refer to a different time than that expressed by its name. For example, the past tense may express an event in the future.

TIME describes the situation outside the grammatical sphere → <u>what is intended</u>. Time is a concept which is related to the overall context. So always try to put yourself in the narrator's shoes to check what *time* he had in mind.

How can a present tense verb describe the past tense? Usually you use a verb in the <u>past tense</u> at the <u>beginning</u> of the sentence and later switch to the present tense to describe what has happened (despite that the action is already over from the time now). **What you should pay attention to:** The (second) action – expressed by the present tense – occurs at the same time as the (first) action which is expressed by the past tense.

For example:

I thought that the house **was** collapsing.	اِعْتَقَدْتُ أَنَّ الْبَيْتَ يَنْهارُ.
She instructed me what I **had** to do.	شَرَحَتْ لِي ما يَجِبُ أَنْ أَفْعَلَ.

92. Past and future tense together - Does that work?

Yes, it does.

There are sentence constructions in Arabic that look weird, yet are correct. They often occur in conditional sentences if the intended meaning is *would* or *would have*.

إذا + past tense (الْماضِي) + future tense (الْمُسْتَقْبَلُ)
= إذا + كانَ + سَوْفَ + verb in the present tense
This construction expresses the future or conditional II.

إذا كانَ سَوْفَ يَتَنَحَّى...	If he resigned... = if he would resign...

وَقَدْ دَخَلَ الْمُهَنْدِسُونَ الْمَبْنَى فِي الْوَقْتِ الَّذِي انْتَظَرَ فِيهِ سُكّانُ الْبُرْجِ وَسُكّانُ الْمَبانِ ، الْمُحاوِرَةِ، وَهُمْ لا يَعْلَمُونَ ما إذا كانَ سَوْفَ يَتِمُّ السَّماحُ لَهُمْ بِالْعَوْدَةِ لِمَنازِلِهِمْ فِي وَقْتِ الاحْتِفالِ بِعِيدِ الْمِيلادِ.	The engineers entered the building (at a time when) as the residents of the tower and residents of nearby buildings waited, unaware whether they would be allowed to return home at the time of Christmas. *(source: shorouknews.com)*

93. How do you attract someone's attention in Arabic?

In Arabic, you use a letter or short word to address a person.

A *vocative* (الْمُنادَى) is a word which is used to address someone or attract attention. In English, it is usually the personal name or a word of respect (*madam; sir*). In Arabic, we need an extra device (حَرْفُ نِداءٍ) which is placed before the *spoken-to*, مُنادَى, which is the passive participle (اِسْمُ مَفْعُولٍ) of the III-verb *to call out* (يُنادِي - نادَى). Thus, مُنادَى doesn't refer to the helping device, but only to the addressee.

Now, what are these ominous tools to address someone?

| 1 | **Used in literature** | to call a person who is <u>close/near</u> | أَيْ • أَ |

| O little son! | أَيْ بُنَيَّ! | | O Zainab! | أَ زَيْنَبُ! |

| 2 | **Used in literature** | to call a person who is <u>far away</u> | أَيْ ا • هَيَا |

| O Karīm! | أَيا كَرِيمُ! |

| 3 | **Used in general speech and writing** | to call a person who is <u>near or far</u> | يا |

| O Muhammad! | يا مُحَمَّدُ! | | O Aisha! | يا عائِشَةُ! |

Let us focus on the most common particle يا. It is quite challenging to find the correct case ending for the addressee!

OPTION A. Uninflected (don't put the normal case marker). The addressee is fixed on the vowel "u" (مَبْنِيٌّ عَلَى ما يُرْفَعُ بِهِ).

| 1 | Just "u" (ُ) | يا + عَلَم مُفْرَدٌ |

You address a **person with his or her name** (proper noun). In this situation, the proper noun (addressee) is fixed on the last <u>vowel "u"</u> (ضَمّة), which is the original vowel of the word before the vocative came into the game. Why is that?

Grammatically speaking, the addressee is **actually located in the position of an accusative case** (فِي مَحَلِّ نَصْب). Why? Because we assume that it is a direct object of a deleted verb. Just imagine a sentence like: *I call Muhammad* (أُنادِي مُحَمَّدًا).

| O Aisha! | يا عائِشَةُ! | | O Khalid! | يا خالِدُ! |

2	Just "*u*" (ُ)	يا + نَكِرَةٌ مَقْصُودَةٌ

Specifically intended vocative: a particular person is addressed, but **not** by his or her **name**! We have the same situation as in number 1. The person addressed is fixed on the <u>vowel "*u*"</u> (مَبْنِيٌّ عَلَى ما يُرْفَعُ بِهِ). Therefore, it does not get case inflection.

O (female) student!	يا طالِبَةُ!	O man!	يا رَجُلُ!

OPTION B. The addressee is in the accusative (مَنْصُوبٌ).

1	ending: "*a*" (َ)	يا +إِضافةٌ

We have a compound name or expression, formed by a إِضافةٌ. The first part (مُضافٌ) gets the case ending (inflection) according to its position in the sentence – which is the location of a direct object (of the deleted but implicitly understood verb: *I call*). Thus, the addressee has to get the <u>accusative</u> (مَنْصُوبٌ). Watch out: Since it is the first part of the إِضافةٌ, it only takes one فَتْحةٌ.

O employees of the company! (Note: The word was originally مُوَظَّفِينَ. In a genitive construction, the ن disappears!)	يا مُوَظَّفِي الشَّرْكَةِ!
O students of the center!	يا طُلّابَ الْمَرْكَزِ!
O Abdallah (Note that ʿAbdullāhi is a إِضافةٌ literally meaning *servant of Allah*.)	يا عَبْدَ اللهِ!

2	ending: "*-an*" (ً)	يا + شِبْهٌ بالْمُضافِ

A construction **resembling a إِضافةٌ**. The addressee is not a proper name (→A1) nor the first part of a إِضافةٌ (→B1). Instead, it is a word which gets described by additional information.

The word after يا is <u>indefinite</u> (نَكِرةٌ) and has to be مَنْصُوبٌ because according to its location, it is the direct object of a deleted, virtual verb (e.g., أُنادي). Therefore, it gets <u>nunation</u>: "*-an*".

What about the last part? It completes the meaning and is connected to the word before. It may be serving as a subject (فَاعِلٌ), a direct object (مَفْعُولٌ بِهِ), a prepositional (جارٌّ وَمَجْرُورٌ), or adverbial phrase (ظَرْفٌ).

O you, who reads the book!	يا قارِئًا الْكِتابَ!
O you (people), who love reading books!	يا مُحِبِّينَ الْقِراءَةَ!
O you, who are living in this house!	يا مُقيمًا فِي البيتِ!
O you, who are sitting in the car!	يا جالِسًا فِي السَّيّارَةِ!
O you, who drinks the water of the Nile!	يا شارِبًا مِنْ ماءِ النّيلِ!

3	ending: "*-an*" (ً)	يا + نَكِرَةٌ غَيْرُ مَقْصُودةٍ

If you don't address a particular person but want to address a **group** or **people in general** (e.g., in a speech), you use an abstract, <u>indefinite</u> word after the vocative particle, which will be in the accusative case (مَنْصُوبٌ) and take regular nunation (تَنْوينٌ).

O intellectual!	يا مُثَقَّفًا!		O Arab!	يا عَرَبِيًّا!

Remark: If you want to understand the reason and logic behind the case endings, see *Arabic for Nerds 2, question #412 and #413.*

What is the situation if we don't want to address a person by his or her proper name? Or if we want to use a single word to address someone which would mean that we have to use the definite article? Then, we need something in-between:

1. A *demonstrative* (إِسْمُ إِشارةٍ). Actually, this is similar to what we have seen in A1 (proper name).

2. The expression أَيُّها for a male and أَيَّتُها for a female person. That's a different type of construction. For example:

O respected viewers!	يا أَيُّها الْمُشاهِدُونَ الأَعِزّاءُ!

Let us put both options under the microscope.

O (this) girl!	يا هٰذِهِ الْفَتاةُ!	1

Vocative particle (حَرْفُ نِداءٍ)	يا
The *spoken-to, addressee* (مُنادًى). It has a fixed shape (مَبْنِيٌّ) which never changes. However, it is a noun (إِسْمٌ) by its nature. We say that هٰذِهِ is located in the spot of an accusative case (فِي مَحَلِّ نَصْبٍ) - but you cannot mark nor see that.	هٰذِهِ
This word stands in *apposition* (بَدَلٌ) to هٰذِهِ, in other words, it refers to the same person.	الْفَتاةُ

Why is it in the nominative case then? It's complicated. If we used *Muhammad* instead of هٰذِهِ, Muhammad would be fixed on the final vowel "u" resulting in يا مُحَمَّدُ. We assume that hypothetically, the same happened to هٰذِهِ. Since الْفَتاةُ stands in apposition, and since an apposition has to mirror the case ending of the word to which it refers, it also gets "u".

O citizens!	يأَيُّها الْمُواطِنُونَ!	2

The addressee (مُنادًى). Imagine this word as a proper noun! → This is the reason why it has a cemented shape and is set on the vowel "u" (مَبْنِيٌّ عَلَى الضَّمِّ).	أَيُّها

Derived noun (اِسْمُ فاعِلٍ) of the root و-ط-ن.	الْمُواطِنُونَ

Is this information important for the case ending? No, but it matters if we want to identify its position and function! If the word after أَيُّها is ...

- ... a **static noun** (not taken from a root; e.g., رَجُلٌ - *man*), then it is an **apposition** (بَدَلٌ)!
- ... a **derived noun** (اِسْمٌ مُشْتَقٌّ), it takes the position of an **adjective** (نَعْتٌ). Therefore, الْمُواطِنُونَ is a نَعْتٌ.

In grammar, both the بَدَلٌ and the نَعْتٌ are *followers* (تابِعٌ) and mirror the case of the preceding word.

Some additional remarks on أَيُّها and أَيَّتُها (أَيٌّ and أَيَّةٌ):

- Both always take the same vowel: a single ضَمّةٌ.
- The ها is just there to underline the attention.
- They can merge with يا to يأَيُّها but don't have to. It is also possible to write يا أَيُّها – for greater emphasis. E.g.:

O mother!	يا أَيَّتُها الأُمُّ!	O friend!	يا أَيُّها الصَّديقُ!

Watch out: Sometimes you can delete the vocative particle – but even then, it will take the same vowel as if it was there!

O Muhammad, o student! (Notice that Muhammad takes only one ضَمّةٌ.)	مُحَمَّدُ! أَيُّها الطّالِبُ!
O my friend! (It was originally: يا صَديقي. This shortening is called تَرْخيمٌ – *see q. #93*)	صَديقُ!
O Lord!	رَبِّ!

94. يا فاطِمَةُ – **What is correct for: *O Fatima?***

or يا فاطِمَ

Both are correct.

Fatima (فاطِمةُ) is a female given name. If you want to address Fatima, you say يا فاطِمةُ. Interestingly, there is another correct option – يا فاطِمَ

In Arabic, this style is called تَرْخيمٌ which literally means *softening the voice*. Why should we do that? We achieve *euphony*, a pleasant combination of agreeable sounds in spoken words. The result, so the idea, is easier to pronounce and pleasing to the ear. In Arabic, we achieve تَرْخيمٌ in the vocative by **cutting the last letter of the addressed person's name**. It usually happens with feminine proper nouns that have a final letter ة as a sign of feminization; rarely with feminine proper nouns ending in ى (which is also a sign of feminization).

When you delete ة, the name now ends with the vowel that was on top of the letter that preceded ة which is in almost all situations فَتْحةٌ. But you could also add ضَمّةٌ ("*u*") instead as if in the standard vocative. Both are correct.

meaning	التَّرْخيمُ	regular form
O Fatima!	يا فاطِمَ! = يا فاطِمُ!	يا فاطِمَةُ!
O Marwa!	يا مَرْوُ!	يا مَرْوَى!

Even proper nouns without a feminine ending can be shortened in the vocative. This must not work as a first part of a إِضافةٌ and must consist of more than three letters. For تَرْخيمٌ you simply **cut the last letter.**

But this is really very rare.

O Ja'far!	يا جَعْفَ! = يا جَعْفُ!	يا جَعْفَرُ!

O Mālik!	يا مالِ! = يا مالُ!	يا مالِكُ!
O Suʿād!	يا سُعا!	يا سُعادُ!

95. The letter ج - Which pronunciation is correct?

It is not specified. It depends on the country.

ج is the fifth letter of the Arabic alphabet. It is pronounced very differently in Arabic dialects. Occasionally it was even softened to a mere ي. The pronunciation as "g" is probably the original sound (Proto-Semitic) and was gradually softened.

	جِيمٌ قُرَيْشِيّةٌ	جِيمٌ قاهِرِيّةٌ	جِيمٌ شاميّةٌ
Where?	rest of the Arab world	Egypt, Yemen, Oman, Sudan	Palestine, Lebanon, Syria, Jordan; Maghreb
Pronunciation of ج	"t-sha"	"g"	"d-sha"; close to "sh"
English sound	Jennifer	girl	germ; job; Jerry

96. *Immediately after... - How do you express that in Arabic?*

There is an elegant solution with إِثْرَ.

إِثْرَ denotes *immediately after; following; followed by.* It is a noun (اِسْمٌ) which is usually placed as a circumstantial of time (ظَرْف زَمانٍ). This is the reason for the vowel "a" which fixes the shape of the word (مَبْنيٌّ عَلَى الْفَتْح). In such constructions, إِثْرَ serves as the first part of a إِضَافَةٌ; therefore, the word that follows has to be in the genitive case (مَجْرُورٌ).

Now comes the tricky part. إِثْرٌ is a اِسْمٌ. You can also place it after a preposition and get: عَلَى الإِثْرِ. The preposition drags إِثْر into the genitive case which is why we have كَسْرَةٌ.

following two explosions	إِثْرَ وُقُوعِ انْفِجَارَيْنِ
The nuclear plant exploded **after/followed** by an earthquake in Japan.	اِنْفَجَرَتْ مَحَطَّةٌ نَوَوِيَّةٌ إِثْرَ زِلْزَالٍ كَبِيرٍ فِي الْيَابان.
one after the other	واحِدًا إِثْرَ الآخَرِ
immediately after xy; as a result of xy	عَلى إِثْرِهِ xy / فِي إِثْرِهِ xy

Watch out: إِثْرَ can also denote *thereupon, as a result of* as well as consequence: *one after another.*

She began to hand me book after book.	أَخَذَتْ تُعْطِينِي الْكِتابَ إِثْرَ الْكِتابِ.
The students left the university, one after the other (one by one).	اِنْصَرَفَ الطُّلَّابُ مِن الْجامِعةِ واحِدًا إِثْرَ الآخَرِ.

97. The direction *right* - Should you use أَيْمَن or يَمِين؟

It depends on what you want to express: adjective or adverb.

The main difference between an adverb (ظَرْفٌ) and an adjective (صِفَةٌ) is in what they describe: adjectives describe a noun; adverbs usually verbs.

right; right side	**adverb** (German: *rechts*).	ظَرْفُ مَكانٍ	يَمِين	1

	Invariable for gender!			
right; right-hand; on the right	adjective (German: rechte, rechter).		أَيْمَنُ صِفةٌ يُمْنَى	2

In Arabic, a صِفةٌ needs to **agree** with the noun to which it refers (gender, number, definite or indefinite, case).

to the right	إِلَى الْيَمِينِ	1
to your right	إِلَى يَمِينِكَ	1
the right hand (يَدّ is feminine!)	الْيَدُ الْيُمْنَى	2
the right side	الْجانِبُ الْيَمِينُ	2

That was quite simple. Most of the time we need the function as an adverb (يَمِين). There are a few subtleties:

She looked neither right nor left.	لَمْ تَلْتَفِتْ يَمِينًا وَلا يَسارًا.	a
I walked at the right (of the street).	مَشَيْتُ يَمِينًا.	a
I walked at the right of the street.	مَشَيْتُ يَمِينَ الطَّرِيقِ.	b
I walked at the right.	مَشَيْتُ يَمِينُ.	c

In all examples, we used يَمِين, but with different case endings. يَمِين is usually the first part of a إِضافةٌ-construction.

a	If it is cut off from the إِضافة by pronunciation and by meaning, then it gets the ending "-an" (ً).
b	If it serves as the first part of a إِضافة, it gets the usual case ending of an adverb of place (مَفْعُولٌ فِيهِ) which is the **accusative**

	case (مَنْصُوبٌ). "*a*" (ـَ). The second part takes the genitive case.
c	There is an alternative option: You can fix يَمِينُ on the vowel "*u*" (مَبْنِيٌّ عَلَى الضَّمِّ) resulting in ـُ. This happens if it is cut off from the إِضافة by pronunciation, but not by meaning → we delete the second part with the intention of the survival of its meaning. يَمِينُ is located in the spot of an accusative (فِي مَحَلِّ نَصْبٍ), but you can't see that. This is similar to قَبْلُ; *see #221.*

Excursus 1: What about the nature of أَيْمَنُ? It is quite tricky. You can only tell the difference by checking the feminine form.

fem. plural	f. sing.	m. plural	m. sing.	type	
يُمْنَيَاتٌ or أَيْمَانٌ or أَيْمُنٌ	يُمْنَى	أَيامِنُ or أَيْمَانٌ or أَيْمُنٌ	أَيْمَنُ	adjective of pattern أَفْعَلُ	1
يَمْناوَاتٌ	يَمْناءُ	يُمْنٌ		صِفةٌ مُشَبَّهةٌ	2

Some remarks about type 1:

- أَيْمَنُ looks like a *noun of preference* (اِسْمُ تَفْضِيلٍ) like أَكْبَرُ - كُبْرَى (bigger), but it is not! We just use the same pattern.
- أَيْمَنُ is the opposite of يُسْرَى - أَيْسَرُ (f.) which means *left; left-handed.* E.g.: *to write left-handed* (كَتَبَ بِيَدِهِ اليُسْرَى)
- You cannot apply the sound masculine plural form (جَمْعُ الْمُذَكَّرِ السّالِمِ).
- Watch out: أَيْسَرُ which usually denotes *left* could be a real comparative (اِسْمُ تَفْضِيلٍ) which would then denote *easier* in the meaning of أَسْهَلُ.

Some remarks about type 2 (صِفةٌ مُشَبَّهةٌ):

- أَيْمَنُ is the *quasi* active participle (صِفَةٌ مُشَبَّهَةٌ) of the I-verb (يَمُنَ - يَمِنَ) *to be fortunate about*. Thus, أَيْمَنُ denotes *somebody who does or enjoys good things; lucky*. Like type 1, it is also used as an Arabic **adjective** (صِفَةٌ).

- The صِفَةٌ مُشَبَّهَةٌ has many patterns. Among them is أَفْعَلُ for the masculine and فَعْلاءُ for the feminine gender. This pattern is also used for colors (لَوْنٌ) and permanent characteristics (حِلْيَةٌ) like *lame* (أَعْرَجُ) or *stupid* (أَحْمَقُ).

Ayman is a hard-working student.	أَيْمَنُ طَالِبٌ مُجِدٌّ.	male proper name
Yumna is a hard-working student.	يُمْنَى طَالِبَةٌ مُجِدَّةٌ.	female proper name
Zayd is more fortunate than Amr.	زَيْدٌ أَيْمَنُ مِنْ عَمْرٍو.	اِسْمُ التَّفْضِيلِ
Zayd is right-handed.	زَيْدٌ أَيْمَنُ الْيَدِ.	صِفَةٌ مُشَبَّهَةٌ

Note: يَمِينٌ can also denote *oath* and in this application, is treated as a <u>feminine</u> noun. The plural is أَيْمانٌ (which could, theoretically, also denote *right hands*).

Excursus 2: What is the relation between being fortunate and a direction?

This has to do with the Islamic tradition that **right is good and left is bad**. For example: You should eat with your right hand – since you use your left hand in the toilet. In ancient times, *left hand* was expressed by الْيَدُ الشُّؤْمَى. The masculine form of it would be أَشْأَمُ which denotes *more/most unlucky, unfortunate, unprosperous*. It is pretty much the opposite of أَيْمَنُ and يُمْنَى. The word أَشْأَمُ is used in the sense of شُؤْمٌ (*unluckiness*) similar to أَيْمَنُ which is used in the sense of يُمْنٌ

(*prosperity, blessing*). It is also interesting that in English, the word *right* is used to denote both *right* (direction) and *correct*, whereas *left* is used in the sense of *not included; abandoned*.

What about **directions** (of the compass)? For example, the expression شَامًا وَيَمَنًا means *to the north and south (northward and southward)*. In the beginning of Islam, people used the **prayer direction** (قِبْلة) to name directions.

All directions were seen as if one was standing in front of the door of the Kaaba in Mecca. This may explain the meaning of the country name *Yemen* (الْيَمَنُ) because Yemen lies on the right side of the Kaaba in Mecca in Saudi-Arabia (سُمِّيَتْ الْيَمَنَ لِأَنَّهَا عَنْ يَمِينِ الْكَعْبَةِ).

However, other scholars suggested that the name may simply denote the core meaning of the root: *felicity* or *blessing* as much of the country back then was fertile.

a fortunate man (enjoying prosperity and good tidings - ذُو يُمْنٍ وَبَرَكَةٍ)	رَجُلٌ أَيْمَنُ
the guided ones; (lit. *the people of the right-hand-side*); epithet for *the saved*.	أَصْحَابُ الْيَمِينِ
the street on the right side.	الشَّارِعُ الْأَيْمَنُ
right side	الْجِهَةُ الْيُمْنَى
He is right-handed, his brother left-handed.	هُوَ أَيْمَنُ وَأَخُوهُ أَيْسَرُ.
He looked to the right.	نَظَرَ أَيْمَنَ.
We called to him **from the right-hand side** of the mountain... (Sura 19:52)	وَنَادَيْنَاهُ مِن جَانِبِ الطُّورِ الْأَيْمَنِ...

98. Is the predicate of a verb the same as the direct object?

Not exactly, but there is a connection.

Regular verbal sentences (جُمْلةٌ فِعْلِيّةٌ) have a subject (فاعِلٌ) and may have <u>objects</u> which provide us with **additional** information.

Every sister of كانَ or كادَ, for example, has a <u>predicate</u> (خَبَرٌ) which usually gives us more information about the **subject**.

Such verbs are called *incomplete* (كانَ النّاقِصة) because without a predicate, they cannot be understood – *see question #98.*

Though this is not in line with the traditional method, we could interpret a sentence with كانَ also as *agent* (= subject; independent) and *object* (= predicate; dependent) of كانَ which would explain the cases we use:

حارًّا.	الْجَوُّ	كانَ
hot	the weather	was
predicate; the dependent part – which is the reason for the accusative (مَنْصُوبٌ).	**subject**; agent (إسمُ كـانَ); the independent part – which is the reason for the nominative (مَرْفُوعٌ).	Incomplete **verb** that only makes sense with a predicate. "*The weather was*" is not enough.

99. فِعْلٌ ناقِصٌ - What is that?

An incomplete verb.

The term فِعْلٌ ناقِصٌ has two applications: one is used for grammar, one for morphology.

- صَرْفٌ which means **inflection; forming of nouns, con-jugation of verbs**. We look at a word in an isolated way.

- نَحْوٌ which means **grammar**. We analyze the function and application of a word in a sentence.

A	نَحْوٌ	فِعْلٌ ناقِصّ

When we analyze a sentence and use the term *incomplete, defi-cient verb*, we mean the following: A verb which doesn't give you a sufficient, complete (تَامٌّ) meaning if you only use it with the subject. For ex.: *You were* (كُنْتَ). *You become* (تُصْبِحُ).

Therefore, you must add another word – a predicate (خَبَرّ) – to complete the meaning. The standard grammar rules don't work here. You must put the "subject" into the nominative (رَفْعُ الْإِسْم) and the predicate into the **accusative** case (نَصبُ الْخَبَرِ). That's why these verbs are called أَفْعالُ ناسِخةٌ – *abrogators*; the root ن-س-خ means *to abrogate; to revoke*.

There are two main groups:

- كانَ and its sisters
- كادَ and its sisters

What is the idea behind the *sisters*?

- These verbs intervene in the nominal sentence as the grammarians use to say (يَدْخُلُ عَلَى الْجُمْلةِ الْإِسْمِيّةِ).
- These verbs are called ناقِصّ because they **only point to time** (يَدُلُّ عَلَى الزَّمانِ فَقَطْ), but not to an action (لا يَدُلُّ عَلَى الْحَدَثِ) which regular verbs (فِعْلٌ تامٌّ) do. Since they do not point to an action, they don't need a verbal sub-ject (فاعِلٌ). Let us check the difference:

The weather is nice.	الْجَوُّ جَميلٌ.	1
This is a **nominal** sentence (جُمْلةٌ إِسْميّةٌ).		

The weather became nice.	أَصْبَحَ الْجَوُّ جَميلًا.	2
Most scholars say that this is a **verbal** sentence (جُمْلةٌ فِعْليّةٌ).		

Incomplete verb in the past tense (فِعْلٌ ماضٍ ناسِخٌ).	أَصْبَحَ
"Subject" which is called <u>noun</u> of to become (إِسْمُ أَصْبَحَ). It must get the nominative case (مَرْفوعٌ).	الْجَوُّ
This is the <u>predicate</u> of to become (خَبَرُ أَصْبَحَ). It must get the accusative case (مَنْصوبٌ).	جَميلًا

B	صَرْفٌ	فِعْلٌ ناقِصٌ - مُعْتَلٌ

In the area of morphology, a *deficient verb* is a verb whose last root letter is weak (حَرْف الْعِلّةِ). See *question #10*.

Watch out: If you encounter the Arabic term فِعْلٌ ناقِصُ التَّصريفِ, it means that a verb cannot be conjugated in all tenses. For example, the expression *still* (ما زالَ). See *question #100*.

100. *To be* (كانَ) - **What is so tricky about its predicate?**

The predicate (خَبَرُ كانَ) *has to get the accusative case* (مَنْصوبٌ).

The verb *to be* (كانَ) is a special verb in Arabic. It governs its **predicate** (خَبَرُ كانَ) in the **accusative** case (مَنْصوبٌ).

What would be suitable to serve as the predicate of كانَ?

1	The predicate consists of <u>one word</u> (مُفْرَدٌ).
The weather was nice.	كانَ الْجَوُّ جَمِيلًا.

2	The predicate is a <u>verbal sentence</u> (جُمْلَةٌ فِعْلِيّةٌ).
The professor was talking.	كانَ الْأُسْتاذُ يَتَكَلَّمُ.

The predicate is an entire verbal sentence (يَتَكَلَّمُ) with a hidden/implied pronoun! Notice that the verb has ضَمّةٌ on top of the last letter – however, grammatically, the verbal sentence is located in the position of an accusative (فِي مَحَلِّ نَصْبٍ).

3	The predicate is a <u>nominal sentence</u> (جُمْلَةٌ اسْمِيّةٌ).
The story was boring. (Lit.: The events of the story were boring.)	كانَتْ الْقِصَّةُ أَحْداثُها مُمِلَّةً.

There is ضَمّةٌ on *events* (أَحْداثُها - "*u*") and on the predicate of events: *boring* (مُمِلّةٌ - "un"). We say that the entire nominal sentence (أَحْداثُها مُمِلّةٌ) is located in the position of an accusative case (فِي مَحَلِّ نَصْبٍ) because it serves as the predicate of كانَ. What about the pronoun suffix ها in أَحْداث؟ It links the nominal sentence with the "subject" (= *story*).

4	The predicate is a *(a)* <u>prepositional</u> (جارٌّ وَمَجْرُورٌ) or *(b)* <u>adverbial</u> phrase (ظَرْفٌ), a so called شِبْهُ الْجُمْلةِ.	
The car was in its parking lot.	كانَتْ السَّيّارةُ فِي الْمَوْقِفِ.	a
The car was in front of the house.	كانَتْ السَّيّارةُ أَمامَ الْبَيْتِ.	b

101. What are the sisters of كانَ (*to be*)?

There are thirteen verbs.

كانَ (*to be*) is an intriguing verb which is not alone there in the Arabic grammar world. It has thirteen *sisters* (أَخَواتُ كانَ) which all behave grammatically in the same way. **They link a subject with a predicate.**

Like كانَ, also its *sisters* have usually an auxiliary function governing a subordinate verb. These are the sisters of كانَ:

to be (past tense)	I-verb; R2=و	كانَ - يَكونُ

to become; to grow into; to come to be; original: to be in the morning.	IV-verb	أَصْبَحَ يُصْبِحُ

If it is <u>followed</u> by **a present tense verb** (فِعْلٌ مُضارِعٌ), it usually conveys the meaning of *to begin*. Only in the **present tense** (فِعْلٌ مُضارِعٌ), it may have the original meaning of *to begin a new day*; *to wake up in the morning*. For example: If you wish *good night* in Arabic, you literally say: "*Wake up well!*" (تُصْبِحْ عَلَى خِير)

to become; to begin; lit. meaning: between morning and midday, e.g., 9 o'clock in the morning.	IV-verb; R3=و	أَضْحَى يُضْحِي

to become (in the meaning of to remain); to continue; to keep on.	I-verb; R2=R3	ظَلَّ يَظَلُّ

to become; to develop to the point of; come to be. Only in the present tense (فِعْلٌ مُضارِعٌ), it may denote the original meaning of to be in the evening or when it is getting dark.	IV-verb; R3=و	أَمْسَى يُمْسِي

to become (in the meaning of *to remain*); *time of the night*; literal meaning: *to stay overnight (used in Colloquial Arabic).*	I-verb; R2=ي	بَاتَ يَبِيتُ

to become; to come to be; to begin.	I-verb; R2=ي	صَارَ يَصِيرُ

not to be; used to **negate** a nominal sentence (جُمْلَةٌ اِسْمِيّةٌ).	لَيْسَ

still; not to cease to be	Watch out: These verbs are **NEGATED.** Only in the negation, they convey the meaning on the left.	ما زَالَ
still; not to cease; not to stop		ما فَتِئَ
still; not to go away		ما بَرِحَ
still		ما إنْفَكَّ

to continue, to last; as long as	This verb is **not** negated! The ما here is used to produce a circumstantial **interpreted infinitive** (مَصْدَرٌ مُؤَوَّلٌ).	ما دَامَ

Such ما is called ما الْمَصْدَرِيّةُ الظّرْفِيّةُ since it has the power to mold an infinitive. It **replaces** the *adverb of time* (ظَرْفُ الزّمانِ) which was eliminated and was placed as the first part of the إِضافةٌ. For example: *I will fight as long as I live* (سَأُكافِحُ ما دُمْتُ حَيًّا).

I won't go to the market as long as it is still raining. (*raining* is مَنْصُوبٌ.)	لَنْ أَذْهَبَ إِلَى السُّوقِ مادامَ المَطَرُ مُتَساقِطًا.
The weather became nice.	أَضْحَى الْجَوُّ جَمِيلًا.

102. *Almost, just about to* - How do you say that in Arabic?

In Arabic, you use verbs to express "almost"; to be near to doing.

Such verbs are called *verbs of approximation* (فِعْلُ مُقَارَبةٍ). The best-known example is كَادَ - يَكَادُ which may be translated as *to be about to; he (would have) almost*. In principle, these verbs follow the rules of كَانَ **–** but with some differences:

- The **predicate** of a *verb of approximation* is a **verbal sentence** (جُمْلةٌ فِعْلِيّةٌ) in the **present tense** (فِعْلٌ مُضـارِعٌ) which follows <u>directly</u> after the *verb of approximation*.

- Sometimes, however, you may insert the device أَنْ which produces an **interpreted infinitive** (مَصْدَرٌ مُؤَوَّلٌ) following the formula: أَنْ + verb in the present tense <u>subjunctive</u> (فَعْلُ مُضارِعٌ مَنْصُوبٌ).

When should we use أَنْ?

1. أَنْ is **always** used with *verbs of hope* (فِعْلُ رَجاءٍ).

2. أَنْ is used with **some** *verbs of approximation* (فِعْلُ مُقَارَبةٍ).

3. أَنْ is **never** used with *verbs of initiative* (فِعْلُ شُرُوعٍ).

All of these verbs above are called *sisters* of كَادَ (أَخَواتُ كَادَ). Although the predicate consists of a verbal sentence, we need to think about the appropriate case – despite the fact that only nouns in Arabic can take case endings. Thus, we apply a place value and say that the predicate (= the verbal sentence) is located in the position of an accusative case (فِي مَحَلِّ نَصْبٍ).

If this is all too sophisticated, you can't do anything wrong if you just mark the endings by using the standard rules for a regular sentence (although the logic is entirely different).

The following verbs describe a situation or an event that is very likely and that will take place very soon. They all denote *be on the verge of; to be about to.*

usually used	explanation	verb
without أَنْ	The choice of the tense (past or present) depends on the view of the narrator (if he wants to tell something in the past or present).	كادَ - يَكادُ
with أَنْ	to draw near	أَوْشَكَ - يُوشِكُ
(usually) without أَنْ	Only used in literature.	كَرَبَ - يَكْرُبُ

Let us look at two examples:

Soon the winter will be over (just about to end).	كادَ الشِّتاءُ يَنْتَهِي.
The boy was about to go.	أَوْشَكَ الْوَلَدُ أَنْ يَذْهَبَ.
The night was about to end.	كَرَبَ اللَّيْلُ يَنْقَضِي.

Notice the difference in the following sentences. They both mean: *The train will move soon.*

With أَنْ: The second verb (after أَنْ) needs the **subjunctive** mood (مَنْصُوبٌ): "*a*".	أَوْشَكَ الْقِطارُ أَنْ يَتَحَرَّكَ.
Without أَنْ: The second verb takes the standard, **indicative** mood (مَرْفُوعٌ): "*u*".	أَوْشَكَ الْقِطارُ يَتَحَرَّكُ.

Watch out:

- كادَ cannot be used in the imperative (أَمْرٌ).
- The present tense (الْمُضارِعُ) of كادَ is not يَكُودُ. It is كادَ يَكادَ. It uses the same conjugation pattern as *to sleep* (نامَ - يَنامُ) or *to fear* (خافَ - يَخافُ). The reason for the letter ا in the middle of the present tense lies in the **stem vowel** of the present tense of such verbs which is *"a"*.
- If كادَ is negated, it denotes *hardly* or *scarcely*! See q. #125.

103. What are the *verbs of hope* (فِعْلُ رَجاءٍ)?

The name says it all. Verbs which denote that something is hopefully going to happen.

رَجاءٌ means *hope* or *expectation*. Verbs of hope (فِعْلُ رَجاءٍ) are pretty unique in Arabic for one reason. They are almost exclusively **used in the past tense,** but the sentence conveys the meaning of the **present tense** or **future**!

The following verbs can be translated as *to wish; perhaps; it could be that; it is possible that.*

This verb is only used in the past. It is a *static, unipersonal verb* (فِعْلٌ جامِدٌ). Usually, such verbs **can't** be conjugated in the **present tense** (الْمُضارِعُ). Furthermore, they can't be used in the imperative (أَمْرٌ) and sometimes, they don't have a مَصْدَرٌ. The past tense verb عَسَى is usually **not conjugated at all.** Instead, it takes a **pronoun suffix** to express the subject. عَسَى needs أَنْ to be connected to the predicate.	عَسَى
Only used in literature; it goes along with أَنْ to get connected with the predicate.	حَرَى
	إخْلَوْلَقَ

- All three verbs are *sisters* of كادَ.
- They need a **predicate** (خَبَرٌ) which has to be a <u>verb</u> in the **present tense** (فِعْلٌ مُضارِعٌ). You need to use the particle أَنْ producing an interpreted infinitive. Thus, a following verb takes the *subjunctive mood* (مَنْصوبٌ) → ending *"a"*.

Some examples – we don't use the past in the translation!

I wish (that) the exam will be easy.	عَسَى الْإِمْتِحانُ أَنْ يَكُونَ سَهْلًا.
The (fem.) student wishes to see the teacher.	الطالِبَةُ اِخْلَوْلَقَتْ أَنْ تَرَى الْمُدَرِّسَ.
Perhaps you are...?	عَساكَ...؟

104. *To begin something* - How do you express that in Arabic?

There are many verbs in Arabic which can do that job.

Verbs, which express that something *starts, begins,* or *is being started* are called فِعْلُ شُرُوعٍ. The word شُرُوعٌ means *attempt; embarking on; engaging in.* Thus, we can translate the grammar term as *verbs of beginning* or *initiative.*

The following verbs basically all denote the same: *to start, to begin, to undertake* – **when they are used in the <u>past</u> tense!**

قامَ I;R2=و	أَخَذَ I;R1=ء	جَعَلَ I	إِبْتَدَأَ VIII;R3=ء	بَدَأَ I
to rise	to take; start	to create	to begin	

شَرَعَ I	أَقْبَلَ IV	راحَ I; R2=و	إِنْبَرَى VII; R3=ي
to initiate	to approach	to go	to undertake

I	عَلِقَ	IV; R3=ء	أَنْشَأَ	I	هَبَّ	I	طَفِقَ
lit.: to hang		to create		to start moving		to do straightaway	

Six things you should know about these verbs:

1. They are *inert, static verbs* (فِعْلٌ جامِدٌ). We can call them *defective*, because you must use the past tense form if you want them to work as *verbs of beginning*. In other words, only when they are used in the past tense, they convey the meaning of *to begin*. Otherwise, they retain their original meaning – for example, *to take* (يَأْخُذُ).

2. There is one exception. بَدَأَ conveys *to begin* also in the present tense (يَبْدَأُ) - but then, it is a regular, full verb!

3. All other forms and derived nouns are treated as being taken from a complete verb (فِعْلٌ تامٌّ) → with the consequence that the original meaning of the root is expressed.

4. They **must be followed by a verb** in the present tense and **never** by a مَصْدَرٌ.

5. **Never** use أَنْ after these verbs!

6. They are all *sisters of* كادَ which means that the rules for كادَ must be applied. Since they are *sisters of* كادَ, they have a predicate. The predicate (خَبَرٌ) of these verbs is normally a verb in the present tense (الْمُضارِعُ).

Let's check some examples:

She began to cry.	أَخَذَتْ تَبْكِي.	1
She started to laugh.	شَرَعَتْ تَضْحَكُ.	2
He starts walking.	يَبْدَأُ الْمَشْيَ.	3

> Wait! Didn't we say that you can't use a مَصْدَرٌ? Yes, this is true. So, what happened here? Well, we use بَدَأ not as a فِعْلُ شُرُوعٍ but as a regular, complete verb which means we have a direct object (مَفْعُولٌ بِهِ): the مَصْدَرٌ of *to walk* (مَشَى).

105. When do you need to focus on agreement (الْمُطابَقةُ)?

In basically four situations.

When a word has to correspond with a preceding word and copy certain features, we say that it needs agreement (مُطابَقةٌ). Such words are *followers* (تابِعٌ) in Arabic and often help to clarify the meaning of a word.

example		grammar term		
the nice student	الطالِبُ الجَميلُ	adjective	نَعْتٌ	1
the students, both of them	الطّالِبانِ كِلاهُما	emphasis	تَأْكيدٌ	2
these lawyers	هؤُلاءِ المُحامُونَ	apposition	بَدَلٌ	3
Khālid and Muhammad	خالِدٌ وَمُحَمَّدٌ	conjunction	عَطْفٌ	4

Agreement in Arabic means to adjust 4 things:

1	Determination	definite (مَعْرِفةٌ) or indefinite (نَكِرةٌ)
2	Gender	masculine (مُذَكَّرٌ), feminine (مُؤَنَّثٌ)
3	Number	singular (مُفْرَدٌ), dual (مُثَنَّى), or plural (جَمْعٌ)
4	Case	Copy the case of the word to which you refer.

106. How do you express *me* in Arabic?

You use the word إِيَّايَ.

إِيَّايَ is, indeed, a strange looking word. It is the accusative form (مَنْصُوبٌ) of the personal pronoun *I* (أَنَا): *me*.

In Arabic, it is very rare to come across accusative (مَنْصُوبٌ) forms of personal pronouns. Unlike in English, you only use them if you are not allowed to use a pronoun suffix or if you want to throw some **emphasis** into the sentence.

- **Direct object** (مَفْعُولٌ بِهِ): If you forward the direct object which is expressed by a pronoun. → emphasis.

It is You we worship; it is You we ask for help. *Sura 1:5 - The Opening* (الْفَاتِحَة)	إِيَّاكَ نَعْبُدُ وَإِيَّاكَ نَسْتَعِينُ.

Here, إِيَّاكَ is used to show the importance of the word *you* which is the reason why we use a stand-alone form (ضَمِيرٌ بارِزٌ مُنْفَصِلٌ). This style is only used in literature or texts of high quality. Since it precedes the verb, it **emphasizes** *you*. We achieve that by forwarding (تَقْدِيمٌ) the direct object.

- **Follower** of a direct object (تابِعُ الْمَفْعُولِ بِهِ) → emphasis.

It is he who we respect.	نَحْتَرِمُهُ إِيَّاهُ.

- We also encounter this form, for example, after the particle *except* (إِلَّا) in the expression *without me* because we are **not allowed to use a pronoun suffix.**

example		meaning	accusative	nominative
except me	إِلَّا إِيَّايَ	*me*	إِيَّايَ	أَنا

The forms are basically a combination of إِيّا plus the usual pronoun suffix:

remark		مَنْصُوب
Notice the فَتْحَة above the last letter ي	*me*	إِيّايَ
Notice the ضَمّة above the last letter ه	*him*	إِيّاهُ
	you	إِيّاكَ or إِيّاكِ
	us	إِيّانا

Watch out:

- If إِيّا starts a sentence and if a particular person is addressed, it may denote: *Beware of...* or *don't...*

(You!) Don't break the glass!	إِيّاكَ أَلّا تَكْسِرَ الْكُوبَ!
Note that أَلّا is a combination of لا + أَنْ.	

- The particle إِيّا can express *with* if it is connected to و – a so-called *Wāw of concomitance* or *association* (واوُ الْمَعِيّة). This is a type of object! See *Arabic for Nerds 2*, #144, #224, #355.

We go **with** her to the room.	نَذْهَبُ وَإِيّاها إِلَى الْغُرْفةِ.

107. Do you always need أَنْ to connect two verbs?

No, this is not true.

In English, most verbs are connected with *to* (*I want to go*). In English, we would call *to* a conjunction.

In Arabic, you usually apply the particle أَنْ to connect two verbs. When you use أَنْ and add a verb in present tense, subjunctive mood (مَنْصُوبٌ), then you automatically produce the meaning of a مَصْدَرٌ – see *question #81*. However, some Arabic are immediately followed by a second verb.

There are mainly two situations:

- All verbs that may express *to begin* (بَدَأَ), *keep on doing* (ما زالَ), and *to be close to do* (كادَ) don't need أَنْ.

- Sentences with a *circumstantial qualifier* (الْحالُ). Then, the second verb is describing the first verb. There is nothing wrong with using a verbal sentence (جُمْلةٌ فِعْلِيّةٌ) as a حالٌ. Let us examine an example:

She let him go.	تَرَكَتْهُ يَذْهَبُ.

First verb. The subject is a hidden, implied pronoun with the virtual meaning of: *she*.	تَرَكَتْ	1
This personal pronoun (*him*) is attached to the first verb. It is referring to the target person. Remark: If there is no other person involved (if we talk about only one person in the entire sentence), there is no need for a pronoun.	هُ	2
The **second verb** has to be in the present tense, indicative mood (الْمُضارِعُ). It literally means: *he goes*. The second verb has to be conjugated with respect to the preceding pronoun; in our example: third person singular (*he*).	يَذْهَبُ	3

Here are some examples:

1	to leave	تَرَكَ - يَتْرُكُ

	He let him writing.	تَرَكَهُ يَكْتُبُ.

2	to begin – see *question #104*.	بَدَأَ - يَبْدَأُ • إِنْتَدَأَ - يَبْتَدِئُ
	He began to work.	إِبْتَدَأَ يَعْمَلُ.
	He started to laugh.	رَاحَ يَضْحَكُ.
	He started to work.	قَامَ يَعْمَلُ.

3	to continue	إِسْتَمَرَّ - يَسْتَمِرُّ
	He continued to work.	إِسْتَمَرَّ يَعْمَلُ.

4	to hear	سَمِعَ - يَسْمَعُ
	I heard him saying.	سَمِعْتُهُ يَقُولُ.

5	to find	وَجَدَ - يَجِدُ
	I found her sleeping.	وَجَدْتُها تَنامُ.

6	still doing	ما زالَ - لا يَزالُ
	He is still working.	ما زالَ يَعْمَلُ.

7	to do again	عادَ - يَعُودُ
	She is not working again.	ما عادَتْ تَعْمَلُ.

8	to keep doing	بَقِيَ - يَبْقَى
	He kept stopping.	بَقِيَ يَقِفُ.

9	to see	رَأَى - يَرَى
	I saw him coming.	رَأَيْتُهُ يَأْتِي.

10	to watch	شَاهَدَ - يُشاهِدُ
	She watched him going.	شَاهَدَتْهُ يَذْهَبُ.

108. After أَنْ, is it okay to use a verb in the past tense?

Yes, it is. But it is extremely rare.

أَنْ serves as a device to mold an interpreted infinitive (مَصْدَر مُؤَوَّل). What about the verb after أَنْ?

- If you use a verb in the **present tense** after أَنْ, it has to be in the **subjunctive** mood (مَنْصُوبٌ) – which means it gets the final vowel "*a*".

- If you use a **past tense** verb, you don't need a marker – you just use the regular past tense. You simply can't put any marker on a past tense verb because past tense verbs have a **cemented** shape (مَبْنِيٌّ).

You get such a situation with a past tense verb after أَنْ when you paraphrase the **past perfect** (pluperfect; *he had written*).

I was happy that you (had) succeeded.	سَرَّنِي أَنْ نَجَحْتَ. = سَرَّنِي نَجاحُكَ.

Interpreted infinitive (مَصْدَر مُؤَوَّل), produced with the help of a past tense verb.	أَنْ نَجَحْتَ
Original infinitive noun (مَصْدَر صَرِيحٌ).	نَجاحُكَ

109. *He gives it to me* - How do you say that in Arabic?

Sounds easy – but it is not. You need to handle two objects.

The IV-verb أَعْطَى - يُعْطِي (*to give*) can have two objects. In Arabic, the first object is usually the person, the second is the object. In English, this is different! For example: *I gave the student a present = I gave a present **to** the student* (أَعْطَيْتُ الطَّالِبَ هَدِيَّةً). So, but how do we add two pronouns (*it; me*)?

- The **first** pronoun is **attached** to the verb directly. In our example: *me*.

- The **second** pronoun is **detached** from the verb and is used in the accusative form (مَنْصُوبٌ). In our example: *it*.

So, we end up with the **opposite English structure**, which is important to keep in mind if you translate.

- The **indirect** object (German: *Dativ*) of an English sentence is attached <u>directly</u> to the verb.

- The **direct** object of an English sentence is attached to إِيّا.

- This works for all verbs that take two objects – see *#110*.

He gives it (masculine) to me.	يُعْطِينِي إِيَّاهُ.
He gives it (feminine) to me.	يُعْطِينِي إِيَّاها.
You (fem.) give it (e.g., the books) to him.	أَهْدَيْتِهِ إِيَّاها.
You (fem.) give it (e.g., the book) to her.	أَهْدَيْتِها إِيَّاهُ.

110. Which verbs may carry two (direct) objects in Arabic?

Quite many.

In English, sentences can have a direct and an indirect object. An indirect object in English is a noun or pronoun that occurs in addition to a direct object and indicates the person or thing that receives what is being given or done.

In German, you use the dative case to mark the indirect object. In English, you often use a prepositional phrase with *to* or *for* which demands a repositioning of the objects!

I read	her	the letter.
	the letter	**to** her.

In Arabic, you use **two direct objects**! This explains why the translation of verbs with two objects is often tricky, because you will end up with a direct and an indirect object and the indirect object is not marked by a special case marker nor by a preposition. In Arabic, there are **two verb groups** which can carry two objects (فِعْلٌ مُتَعَدٍّ إِلَى مَفْعُولَيْنِ):

GROUP I: The objects were originally the subject and predicate of a nominal sentence (جُمْلةٌ اِسْمِيّةٌ).

1	**verbs of preponderance, superiority** (see #112)	أَفْعالُ الرُّجْحانِ
to think; to suppose	حَسِبَ - يَحْسِبُ خالَ - يَخالُ	ظَنَّ - يَظُنُّ	1
to allege		زَعَمَ - يَزْعُمُ	2

2	**verbs of certainty**	أَفْعالُ الْيَقينِ

to know; to perceive	رَأَى - يَرَى	*to know*	عَلِمَ - يَعْلَمُ
to regard; to consider	عَدَّ - يَعُدُّ	*to find*	وَجَدَ - يَجِدُ

3	transmutative verbs – expressing transfer	أَفْعالُ التَّحْويلِ

to take (on)	إتَّخَذَ - يَتَّخِذُ	to make; to reduce to	جَعَلَ - يَجْعَلُ

Some examples (group I):

The teacher found the students present.	وَجَدَ الْمُدَرِّسُ الطُّلّابَ حاضِرينَ.

1	First object (مَفْعُولٌ بِهِ أوَّلٌ)	الطُّلّابَ
2	Second object (مَفْعُولٌ بِهِ ثانٍ)	حاضِرينَ

The second part was originally a nominal sentence (جُمْلةٌ إسْمِيّةٌ): *The students are present* (الطُّلّابُ حاضِرُونَ.).

The student thinks (that) his colleagues are present.	ظَنَّ الطّالِبُ الزُّمَلاءَ مَوْجُودينَ.
The student alleges that the grammar is difficult.	زَعَمَ الطّالِبُ النَّحْوَ صَعْبًا.
People perceive knowledge as useful.	رَأى النّاسُ الْعِلْمَ نافِعًا.
The man found the door closed.	وَجَدَ الرَّجُلُ الْبابَ مُغْلَقًا.
The professor considered the answer as correct.	عَدَّ الْأُسْتاذُ الإجابةَ صَحيحةً.
The goldsmith made a ring from gold.	جَعَلَ الصّائِغُ الذَّهَبَ خاتَمًا.

GROUP II: The two objects did not (and could not) form a nominal sentence (جُمْلةٌ إسْمِيّةٌ).

to grant; to donate	مَنَحَ - يَمْنَحُ	to dress	أَلْبَسَ - يُلْبِسُ	
to ask for	سَأَلَ - يَسْأَلُ	to give	أَعْطَى - يُعْطِي	IV-verb
to give sustenance	رَزَقَ - يَرْزُقُ	to nourish	أَطْعَمَ - يُطْعَمُ	

Let's look at the DNA of such sentences:

The student gave his colleague a book.	أَعْطَى الطَّالِبُ زَمِيلَهُ كِتابًا.

This sentence fragment wouldn't make sense if it stood alone! → That's different to the verbs in group I.	زَمِيلُهُ كِتابٌ

Some examples (group II):

The director granted the student a prize.	مَنَحَ الْمُدِيرُ الطَّالِبَ جائِزَةً.
The mother dressed her child with his clothes.	أَلْبَسَتْ الأُمُّ طِفْلَها مَلابِسَهُ.
The student asked his colleague for help.	سَأَلَ الطَّالِبُ زَمِيلَهُ الْمُساعَدةَ.

111. Are there verbs which may carry three objects?

Yes, there are.

In Arabic, there are verbs which may carry three (direct) objects (فِعْلٌ مُتَعَدٍّ إِلَى ثَلاثِةِ مَفاعِيـلَ). In English, you would build a subordinate clause (German: *Nebensatz*) which carries the information of the second and third object. Let's analyze the following sentence:

He showed him that the car is nice.	أَرَاهُ السَّيَّارَةَ جَمِيلَةً.

him	**First object** (مَفْعُولٌ أَوَّلٌ). The pronoun has a cemented shape (مَبْنِيٌّ عَلَى الضَّمِّ); thus, we cannot use case markers but can only say that it is located in the position of an accusative case (فِي مَحَلِّ نَصْبٍ) since it is one of the three direct objects.	هُ
the car	**Second object** (مَفْعُولٌ ثانٍ); hence, it takes the accusative case (مَنْصُوبٌ), visibly marked as such.	السَّيَّارَةَ
nice	**Third object** (مَفْعُولٌ ثالِثٌ); also in the accusative case (مَنْصُوبٌ).	جَمِيلَةً

Another example:

She told him that Karīm is lazy.	حَدَّثَتْهُ كَرِيمًا كَسُولًا.

Arabic verbs which carry three objects convey the meaning of *to inform; show; to tell*. They are mainly IV- or II-verbs.

to show	أَرَى - يُرِي	IV
to inform	أَنْبَأَ - يُنْبِئُ	IV
to inform	أَخْبَرَ - يُخْبِرُ	IV

to tell	حَدَّثَ - يُحَدِّثُ	II
to let to know	أَعْلَمَ - يُعْلِمُ	IV

112. *I thought that...* – How do you express that in Arabic?

You should not translate it word by word.

Many verbs in English are followed by the conjunction *that* which introduces a new clause. For example: *I assume that... I think that... I claim that... I believe that... I expect that...*

In Arabic, *verbs of preponderance* (أَفْعالُ الرُّجْحانِ) are not followed by *that* (أَنَّ) in Arabic. Instead, you use **one or two direct objects**.

I thought **that** he is lazy.	زَعَمْتُهُ كَسُولًا.
Did you (f.) think **that** Fatima is his sister?	هَلْ خِلْتِ فاطِمَةَ أُخْتَهُ؟
I thought **that** the guy is present.	ظَنَنْتُ الرَّجُلَ مَوْجُودًا.

Verbs that work like that:

to proclaim	زَعَمَ - يَزْعُمُ		*to assume*	حَسِبَ - يَحْسِبُ
to think	ظَنَّ - يَظُنُّ		*to deem*	حَجا - يَحْجُو
to suppose	خالَ - يَخالُ		*to find*	أَلْفَى - يُلْفِي

113. Can an Arabic sentence start with the object?

Yes, it can. But we need a little fine tuning.

Arabic sentences often resemble building blocks that you can move back and forth. Here is an example:

word order	meaning	example	
verb + subject + object	*The professor wrote the letter.*	كَتَبَ الأُسْتاذُ الرِّسالةَ.	1
object + verb + subject		الرِّسالةُ كَتَبَها الأُسْتاذُ.	2

Let us look at the construction. Note that we use the terms of sentence number 1.

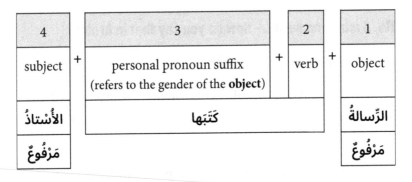

4	3	2	1
subject +	personal pronoun suffix (refers to the gender of the **object**) +	verb +	object
الأُسْتاذُ	كَتَبَها		الرِّسالةُ
مَرْفُوعٌ			مَرْفُوعٌ

If you want to give the listener a hint that the first word is not
the actual subject (but the object!), you may pause after the
object – with the effect that the verb, which comes after it, is
automatically stressed.

Excursus: You also have to add a *referential, referring pro-*
noun to the verb in a *relative clause* (صِلةُ الْمَوْصُول). Since people tend to mix them up, let's go over all forms of الَّذِي again.

	masc.	feminine
singular	الَّذِي	الَّتِي
dual nominative (مُثَنَّى مَرْفُوعٌ)	اللَّذانِ	اللَّتانِ
dual acc. (مَنْصُوبٌ) and genitive (مَجْرُورٌ)	اللَّذَيْنِ	اللَّتَيْنِ
plural (جَمْعٌ)	الَّذِينَ	اللَّواتِي / اللَّاتِي

Now, what about the pronoun?

You need it to link the relative clause with the main word to
which it refers. See *Arabic for Nerds 2, question #74.*

The book that/which I knew...	...الْكِتابُ الَّذِي عَرَفْتُهُ

114. A man who went... - How do you say that in Arabic?

In no case with a relative clause.

Non-native Arabic speakers occasionally translate sentences like *A man who went...* word by word – and fall into a grammatical trap:

> In Arabic, you **can't** link a **relative pronoun** (الَّذي) with an **indefinite** word.

We should take a closer look at that.

NOT possible	Such sentences do not work in Arabic.	رَجُلٌ الَّذي ذَهَبَ...	1
		رَجُلٌ مَنْ ذَهَبَ...	
CORRECT	This sentence works, however, it means: **The** man who went...	الرَّجُلُ الَّذي ذَهَبَ...	2

But then how do you translate: *A man who went...*? Answer: رَجُلٌ ذَهَبَ. But there is a problem.

In Arabic, without knowing the context, such a sentence could express several things. You need to understand the context and may have to adjust things or restate the sentence. Some possible translations:

1	A man went...	رَجُلٌ ذَهَبَ...
	A man, he went...	
2	A man **who/that** went...	

Another example:

| A man, who also went to Austria, called me. | رَجُلٌ ذَهَبَ أَيْضًا إلَى النِّمْسا اتَّصَلَ بي . |

115. *One student* - How do you say that in Arabic?

You only use the number one if you want to stress that you really mean only one.

Otherwise, you use the indefinite article which is expressed in Arabic not by a word but nunation (تَنْوِينٌ). What is the difference between the definite and indefinite article? The difference refers to whether the information in the noun phrase is shared by the speaker and the listener.

If you call your friend and tell him: *Bring **the** book tomorrow*, then you indicate that you want a particular book and that your friend knows which one. If you tell him *Bring **a** book*, your friend could bring any title. If you want to stress that your friend should only bring **one** book or **some book**, you add the number.

In English, the word *one* is a word which always stays the same, no matter what the position or function in the sentence is. In Arabic, we have to words: أَحَدٌ (*one unit*) and واحِدٌ.

- أَحَدٌ (masculine) and إِحْدَى (feminine). They both serve as the first part of a إِضافةٌ-construction. It denotes *a; one of* but also *somebody; someone; anyone*.

- واحِدٌ and واحِدةٌ (f.) are placed as adjectives (صِفةٌ) after the main word. Alternatively, you can use them with مِنْ. Oftentimes they are used if you want to stress the meaning *one* or if want to express *a single one*.

the student	a particular student	الطّالِبُ
a student	It could be any student.	طالِبٌ
one student	أَحَد + definite plural	أَحَدُ الطُّلّابِ
	singular noun + واحِد	طالِبٌ واحِدٌ

one (f.) student	إحْدَى + def. feminine plural	إِحْدَى الطَّالِباتِ
	singular noun + واحِدة	طالِبَةٌ واحِدةٌ
one of the students	واحِدٌ + definite plural form	وَاحِدٌ مِن الطُّلّابِ

Which gender is our reference for أَحَدٌ **or** إِحْدَى **when we have a complex construction?** In other words, when they are placed as the predicate (خَبَرٌ)? It is up to you. You can harmonize them with the subject (مُبْتَدَأٌ) or, alternatively, with the second part of the إِضافةٌ-construction (مُضافٌ إِلَيْهِ).

Money is one of two happi-nesses.	الْمالُ أَحَدُ السَّعادَتَيْنِ.	**Both are**
	الْمالُ إِحْدَى السَّعادَتَيْنِ.	**correct.**

Watch out! *One* can express positive or negative things:

- واحِدٌ may be used in a **negative** or **positive** sense.

- أَحَدٌ, however, if it is used as a single word (*anyone, one, someone*) and not in a إِضافةٌ-construction, is only used to convey a **negative** context. In other words, if there is a negation in the sentence, you use أَحَد. In Arabic literature, أَحَدٌ is <u>hardly ever</u> used in a positive sense – except in the Qur'an with reference to Allah.

Say, He is Allah, [who is] One… (*Sura 112:1*)	قُلْ هُوَ اللهُ أَحَدٌ...

- However, if you place أَحَدٌ as the first part of a إِضافةٌ and add another word, it can be used in a **positive** sense as well. It then conveys *one of...*

one of the travelers	أَحَدُ الْمُسافِرينَ

Some examples:

There is **no one** present.	لَيْسَ أَحَدٌ مَوْجُودًا. 1
There is **nobody** home.	ما مِن أَحَدٍ فِي المَنْزِلِ.
I haven't hit **anyone**.	لَمْ أَضْرَبْ أَحَدًا.
I don't know **anyone**.	لا أَعْرِفُ أَحَدًا.

There is **someone** present.	مَوْجُودٌ واحِدٌ. 2
In don't want **a single** word from you.	لا أُرِيدُ مِنْكَ كَلِمةً واحِدةً.
She's **one** of us.	هِيَ واحِدةٌ مِنّا

- Never **combine** أَحَدٌ and مِنْ. Why? Because both words indicate a vague number. You can only use one of them.

	correct	مِن الْأَسْبابِ 1
one reason		أَحَدُ الْأَسْبابِ 2
	incorrect	مِنْ أَحَدِ الْأَسْبابِ 3

116. Is there a German *man* (one) in Arabic?

Yes, there is.

The German impersonal word *man* (which has nothing to do with the English word *man*) is an indefinite pronoun. It is the 58th most common word in German. It refers to one or more people with an unspecified identity. The translation de-

pends on the context: *one, someone, a person, you, they, people.*
Also the passive voice in English may fit.

In Arabic, there is no particular word which would do this
job perfectly. Instead, you use expressions which convey the
meaning of German *man,* French *on,* or English *one.*

It is said that... (***Man sagt, dass...***)	يُقالُ إنَّ...	1
Here, you use the passive voice of the I-verb قالَ - يَقُولُ.		
As they say... (*Wie **man** sagt...*)	كَما يَقُولُونَ...	2
Here, like in English, you use the third person plural (they).		
One could say... (***Man kann sagen...***)	يُمْكِنُ الْقَوْلُ..	3
Here you use the IV-verb *to be possible* (أَمْكَنَ - يُمْكِنُ).		
It is generally believed that... (***Man ist all-gemein der Meinung, dass...***)	يُجْمِعُ النّاسُ عَلَى...	4
Here you use the word *people* (النّاسُ) with the IV-verb *to agree unanimously* (أَجْمَعَ - يُجْمِعُ).		
One has to... (***Man muss...***)	مِن الْواجِبِ...	5
A common construction. We will examine it in *question #117.*		
Common rumor has it (***Man munkelt, dass...***)	شاعَتْ الشّائِعةُ أنَّ / حَوْلَ	6
Lit. meaning: *the rumor is circulating, spread...*		

However, there is a word which many describe as the closest to
the German *man.* You see it in literature and in the Qur'an.

	fem.	masc.
1	*Men* or *women* (in general). The masculine form corresponds approximately to the English *one* or German *man*.	مَرْأَةٌ الْمَرْأَةُ	مَرْءٌ الْمَرْءُ
	plural form	نِساءٌ	not used (مَرْءُونَ)

2	If you talk about a *man* or a *woman* in particular. Genitive: اِمْرِئٍ; accusative: اِمْرَءًا	اِمْرَأَةٌ	اِمْرُؤٌ
	Notice: If اِمْرُؤٌ starts the sentence, you have to pronounce the first letter as a glottal stop – *Hamza of rupture* (هَمْزَةُ قَطْعٍ). So you actually say إِمْرُؤٌ. The same is true for إِمْرَأَةٌ.		

Some examples:

One cannot…	لا يَسْتَطِيعُ الْمَرْءُ...
One would think….	يَظُنُّ الْمَرْءُ...
One would like to think that they are honest.	يَوَدُّ الْمَرْءُ أَنْ يَعْتَقِدَ أَنَّهُمْ شُرَفاءُ
Know that God comes between a man and his heart, and that you will be gathered to Him. *(Sura 8:24)*	وَاعْلَمُوا أَنَّ اللَّهَ يَحُولُ بَيْنَ الْمَرْءِ وَقَلْبِهِ.
Does every one of them expect to enter a Garden of bliss? *(Sura 70:38)*	أَيَطْمَعُ كُلُّ امْرِئٍ مِّنْهُمْ أَن يُدْخَلَ جَنَّةَ نَعِيمٍ.
I found a woman ruling over them. *(Sura 27:23)*	إِنِّي وَجَدْتُ امْرَأَةً تَمْلِكُهُمْ.

117. *One must... - How do you say that in Arabic?*

There are several ways to express that.

It is peculiar that Arabic has no verbs to express the core meaning of *must*. We have to rely on a few detours and constructions that get us there after all. Let us see how it works:

1	مِن الْواجِبِ (عَلَيْهِ) أَنْ *It is necessary to = one must*

You use the active participle (اِسْمُ فاعِلٍ) of the I-verb وَجَبَ - يَجِبُ عَلَى (R1=و) which means *to be necessary*.

مِن الْواجِبِ عَلَيْكَ أَنْ تَكْتُبَ.   You (one) must write.

2	مِن اللَّازِمِ (عَلَيْهِ) أَنْ *it is someone's duty = one must*

You use the active participle (اِسْمُ فاعِلٍ) of the I-verb لَزِمَ - يَلْزَمُ عَلَى which means *to be someone's duty*.

مِن اللَّازِمِ عَلَيْكَ أَنْ تَكْتُبَ.   You (one) must write.

3	لا بُدَّ (مِن) أَنْ *it is necessary, inescapable, unavoidable that*

- The word بُدّ means *escape* or *way out*.
- The لا is a device used for the *generic negation* or *complete denial* (لا النَّافِيَةُ لِلْجِنْسِ). It intervenes in the nominal sentence and induces the **accusative** case (مَنْصوبٌ) in a following word → so you have to put فَتْحةٌ on بُدّ (see #248).
- Based on this construction, لا بُدَّ expresses the meaning of *definitely, certainly; by all means.*
- لا بُدَّ is followed by a prepositional or adverbial phrase. لا بُدَّ مِنْ has the meaning of: *it is necessary; inevitable.*

- Can you use مِنْ if you have a construction with أَنْ + plus verb in the subjunctive mood? Yes, but it is usually omitted.
- Notice: أَنْ and أَنَّ are sometimes preceded by the conjunction وَ (last example).

You (one) must write to succeed.	لا بُدَّ (مِنْ) أَنْ تَكْتُبَ كَيْ تَنْجَحَ.
The must be a solution.	لا بُدَّ مِنْ وُجودِ حَلٍّ.
He simply must do it.	لا بُدَّ لَهُ مِنْهُ.
One must be alert.	لا بُدَّ مِنَ التَّنْبِيهِ.
She must have told him something.	لَا بُدَّ أَنْ تَكُونَ قَدْ قالَتْ لَهُ شَيْئًا.
No doubt he is here.	لا بُدَّ وَأَنَّهُ مَوْجُودٌ.

to be necessary to (وَجَبَ - يَجِبُ)	يَجِبُ أَنْ	4
You (one) must write.	يَجِبُ عَلَيْكَ أَنْ تَكْتُبَ.	

118. خِدْمة (*service*) - What is the Arabic plural of this word?

The easiest way is a sound feminine plural.

Even the simplest things can sometimes unfold hidden difficulties. The sound feminine plural (جَمْعُ الْمُؤَنَّثِ السّالِمُ) is often described in such a way that you only have to add ات. Is it really that easy? It depends.

If we only go by what we see: yes. If we have to pronounce the word correctly: no. Let's try it.

We have four options: خَدَماتٌ or خِدِماتٌ or خِدَماتٌ or خِدْماتٌ.

If you chose the same as many native Arab speakers, خَدَماتٌ, then you should keep on reading. Let us check all options of **sound feminine plurals**.

Pattern: فَعْلَةٌ	I
• First letter has فَتحةٌ. • Second root letter (in the middle) has سُكُونٌ. • Second root letter is not weak, i.e., not و or ي.	

RESULT: In the plural, سُكُونٌ on the second root letter is replaced by فَتْحةٌ in the plural.

rings	حَلَقاتٌ	حَلْقةٌ		views	نَظَراتٌ	نَظْرةٌ

Remark: If there is a weak letter, the سُكُونٌ remains.

Pattern: فِعْلَةٌ or فُعْلَةٌ	II
• First letter has a كَسرةٌ or ضَمّةٌ. • Second root letter is not a weak letter.	

RESULT: You have three options.

1. You can put سُكُونٌ on the second letter;
2. You can put فَتْحةٌ on the second letter;
3. You use the first vowel, copy it and put it on the second letter.

meaning	option 3	option 2	option 1	singular
services	خِدِماتٌ	خَدَماتٌ	خِدْماتٌ	خِدْمَةٌ

rooms	حُجُراتٌ	حُجَراتٌ	حُجُراتٌ	حُجْرَةٌ

Eventually, it is a matter of taste. You can choose – but don't say what many people say: خَدَماتٌ! It is wrong.

Don't forget: a sound feminine plural (definite **and** indefinite) takes كَسْرةٌ in the accusative (مَنْصوبٌ) and never فَتْحةٌ.

I bought chicken.	إِشْتَرَيْتُ دَجاجاتٍ.
I want these cars.	أُريدُ هَذِهِ السَّيَّاراتِ.

119. *He jumped like a tiger. - How do you say that in Arabic?*

The most elegant way is to use a special type of مَصْدَرٌ.

If you want to describe how somebody did an action, e.g., *he jumped like a tiger*, you can use a special pattern in Arabic: the **noun of manner** (هَيْئةٌ;مَصْدَرُ هَيْئةٍ - إِسْمُ هَيْئةٍ) or (إِسْمُ نَوْع) means *form, shape*. Such nouns are rare. You can hardly find them in dictionaries.

They are difficult to translate because there is no English pendant. They can be rendered into English as *in the manner of* or in *the way of*. For ex.: *in the manner of walking* (مِشْيةٌ).

- If you want to produce such a noun, take the root and throw it into the pattern فِعْلةٌ.

- You can only form it from standard **triliteral verbs** (فِعْلٌ ثُلاثِيٌّ مُجَرَّدٌ) which means that their past tense form consists of only three letters. Therefore, this form is **only possible for I-verbs** (فَعَلَ).

- You need a إِضافَةٌ-construction to express the missing second part of *way of* ... Thus, you place the اِسْمُ هَيْئَةٍ as the first part of the إِضافَةٍ, the so-called مُضاف and add another noun.

- Since it serves as an object of the verb, it has to be in the accusative case (مَنْصُوبٌ).

He jumped like a tiger. Lit.: He jumped *the jump in the way* of the tiger.	قَفَزَ اللَّاعِبُ قَفْزَةَ النَّمِرِ.
I ate like someone who is hungry.	أَكَلْتُ إِكْلَةَ الْجائِعِ.
The mother looked at the child with a glance of love.	تَظَهَرَتِ الأُمُّ إِلَى طِفْلِها نِظْرَةَ الْحُبِّ.

Watch out: The اِسْمُ هَيْئَةٍ looks similar to the *noun of one act* or *instance* (اِسْمُ مَرَّةٍ.) Only the pronunciation is different! It is فِعْلةٌ ("fi3la") and not فَعْلةٌ ("fa3la") - *see #120.*

120. *To eat three times - How do you say that in Arabic?*

You use a special pattern of the noun.

Arabic knows a noun pattern to indicate the countable occurrences of an action. Let's check the following sentences:

قَفَزَ اللَّاعِبُ قَفْزًا.	1
قَفَزَ اللَّاعِبُ قَفْزَةً.	2

What is the difference? The first two words are the same and mean *the player jumped*. What about the last word, i.e., the object? First of all, both sentences are correct, but the meaning is different. In Arabic, there is a way to **emphasize...**

A. ...that a person has done an action in general.

You use the **standard مَصْدَر** and place it after the verb as the *absolute object* (مَفْعُولٌ مُطْلَقٌ); *see #122.* It emphasizes the core meaning of the action. You don't know how often the action was done.

The player jumped (vigorously).	قَفَزَ اللَّاعِبُ قَفْزًا.

B. ...that an action occurs only once (or a certain amount of times).

You use a **special type** of **مَصْدَر**, the *noun of one act* (اِسْمُ مَرَّةٍ). It denotes that the action was done only one time – however, by playing a number before it, you can denote the amount of times.

How do you build it? You use the pattern فَعْلةٌ → notice the فَتْحةٌ. It is the **مَصْدَر** plus ة. The plural is built by the usual patter for feminine nouns: ات. Since it serves as an object of the verb, it has to be in the accusative case (مَنْصُوبٌ). We can count the *noun of act* as a special case of the absolute, inner object (مَفْعُولٌ مُطْلَقٌ) → *see #122.*

The player jumped **once**.	قَفَزَ اللَّاعِبُ قَفْزَةً.
I ate in this restaurant **once**. (only/exactly one time)	أَكَلْتُ فِي هٰذا الْمَطْعَمِ أَكْلَةً.
I did eat in this restaurant. (unknown how often)	أَكَلْتُ فِي هٰذا الْمَطْعَمِ أَكْلًا.
I ate in this restaurant **three** times.	أَكَلْتُ فِي هٰذا الْمَطْعَمِ ثَلاثَ أَكَلاتٍ.

The player did jump.	قَفَزَ اللَّاعِبُ قَفْزًا.
The player jumped **once**.	قَفَزَ اللَّاعِبُ قَفْزَةً.
The player jumped **two times**. (dual!)	قَفَزَ اللَّاعِبُ قَفْزَتَيْنِ.
The player jumped **three times**.	قَفَزَ اللَّاعِبُ ثَلاثَ قَفَزاتٍ.

| The child smiled (one time only). | إِبْتَسَمَ الطِّفْلُ إِبْتِسامةً. |
| The child smiled (unknown how often). | إِبْتَسَمَ الطِّفْلُ إِبْتِسامًا. |

You have two options for the plural: قَفْزات or قَفَزات. The same is true for أَكَلات or أَكْلات. *See question #118.*

Remark: What happens if the standard مَصْدَر looks like the إِسْمُ الْمَرَّةِ؟ Let's see.

explanation	إِسْمُ مَرَّةٍ	verb
As the regular مَصْدَر of the verb is دَعْوةٌ, you need to add a **number** to make clear that you emphasize the amount of times.	دَعْوةٌ واحِدةٌ *one call*	*to call* (دَعا)
Same here: The standard مَصْدَر of the verb, رَحْمةٌ, looks like the إِسْمُ الْمَرَّةِ. You need additional information to indicate that you put the stress on the amount of times.	رَحْمةٌ واحِدةٌ *having compassion one time*	*to have mercy* (رَحِمَ)

121. What does لَسْتُ بِفاهِمٍ mean?

It conveys: I don't understand, really.

Not every preposition expresses a direction.

In Arabic, it is possible that a preposition amplifies a word and is therefore nothing but **additional** (حَرْفُ زائِدٌ or حَرْفُ زِيادةٍ). This often happens with بِ. Nevertheless, the grammatical impact is the same as if بِ worked as a classical preposition. In our example لَسْتُ بِفاهِم, the indefinite word فاهِم gets كَسرةٌ (nunation: "-*in*") as a noun after بِ takes the genitive (مَجْرُورٌ).

Regarding its function in the sentence, فاهِم is still placed in the location of the **predicate** (خَبَرُ لَيْسَ). A predicate of لَيْسَ gets the accusative case (مَنْصُوبٌ). Since the preposition drags the word visibly into the genitive case, we can only assign a place value (فِي مَحَلِّ نَصْبٍ) for the accusative case.

Let us see the difference:

Without the preposition (without emphasizing) the sentence means *I don't understand*.	لَسْتُ فاهِمًا. 1
فاهِمًا is the predicate of لَيْسَ; thus it is in the accusative (مَنْصُوبٌ).	

I don't understand, really.	لَسْتُ بِفاهِم. 2
Here, the preposition drags فاهِم into the genitive case (مَجْرُورٌ).	

122. What is an *absolute object* (مَفْعُولٌ مُطْلَقٌ)؟

It confirms or strengthens the action.

The infinitive noun in Arabic (مَصْدَرٌ) speaks of an action without any regard to the subject or the circumstances of time and mood under which it takes place.

This idea is very much found in the so-called *absolute* or *inner object* (مَفْعُولٌ مُطْلَقٌ).

The English term absolute or inner object is somewhat awkward. We should therefore turn to the term مُطْلَقٌ and see what it actually means. مُطْلَقٌ is the passive participle (اِسْمُ مَفْعُولٍ) of the IV-verb أَطْلَقَ which denotes *to undo; to set free.*

Thus, مُطْلَقٌ means *free; unrestricted (without exception), absolute (in any respect, under any circumstances); stark or perfect.* We can say that the term مَفْعُولٌ مُطْلَقٌ expresses an *unqualified thing done* – in the sense of not labeled as being one of the other objects. English does not have a stylistic device of this kind. To translate the meaning, we often need an adverb or a few auxiliary words.

So, what is the مَفْعُولٌ مُطْلَقٌ good for? With an *absolute object* you can **emphasize an action**. You need two steps:

1. Take the verb and build the مَصْدَر.

2. Add the مَصْدَر as the object of a sentence.

Finally, you have the verb and the corresponding infinitive in the same sentence. For English speakers, this sounds like a redundancy. In Arabic, however, it works perfectly well to emphasize the meaning this way, and it is used a lot. The مَفْعُولٌ مُطْلَقٌ occurs only in three forms:

translation	example	type of مَصْدَرٌ	
extraction	مُسْتَخْرَجًا	مَصْدَرٌ مِيمِيٌّ	1
thankfulness	شُكْرًا	مَصْدَرٌ أَصْلِيٌّ	2
shot, strike	ضَرْبَةً	اِسْمُ مَرَّةٍ	3

There are two ways to use the مَفْعُولٌ مُطْلَقٌ for **emphasis**:

1. For **confirmation** (تَأْكِيدٌ)

| I (definitely) hit Zayd. | ضَرَبْتُ زَيْدًا ضَرْبًا. |

2. For further **specification** (تَحْدِيدٌ)

| I hit Zayd hard / slightly. | ضَرَبْتُ زَيْدًا ضَرْبًا شَدِيدًا / خَفِيفًا. |

Watch out: In the place where you would expect an absolute object, you sometimes find phrases that represent it. You don't write the مَصْدَرٌ of the verb but choose something else.

The meaning is implicitly understood, and the idea to give emphasis remains. What could be a possible representative of the مَصْدَرٌ? We call them نَائِبٌ عَنِ الْمَفْعُولِ الْمُطْلَقِ. You have several options:

	original sentence	example of a substitute
1	فَرِحْتُ بِالنَّجاحِ فَرَحًا.	فَرِحْتُ بِالنَّجاحِ سُرُورًا.
	*I am **really** glad/delighted about the success.* A synonym (مُرادِفٌ) for *happiness* (سُرُورًا) is used instead of the original الْمَفْعُولُ الْمُطْلَقُ – which is فَرَحًا.	
2	تَكَلَّمَ الْخَطِيبُ تَكَلُّمًا حَسَنًا.	تَكَلَّمَ الْخَطِيبُ كَلامًا حَسَنًا.
	*The speaker talked **very well**.* Here, we use another form of the مَصْدَرٌ, the *noun of origin* (اسْمُ الْمَصْدَرِ), which is easier to pronounce – see *question #82*.	
3	رَجَعَ الْجَيْشُ رُجُوعَ الْقَهْقَرَى.	رَجَعَ الْجَيْشُ الْقَهْقَرَى.
	*The army moved **back**.* The word الْقَهْقَرَى already means *backward movement*, so the result is the same (نَوْعٌ مِن أَنْواعِهِ).	

4	وَثَبَ الْقِطُّ وُثُوبَ النَّمِرِ.	وَثَبَ الْقِطُّ وِثْبَةَ النَّمِرِ.

*The (male) cat jumped **like** a tiger.* We use the *noun of manner* (اِسْمُ الْهَيْئَة) instead of the basic مَصْدَر to describe how the cat jumped. Notice the difference between the *noun of one time* (اِسْمُ الْمَرَّة <- first vowel is "a": فَ) and the *noun of manner* (اِسْمُ الْهَيْئَة <- first vowel is "i": فِ).

5	فَهِمْتُ الدَّرْسَ فَهْمًا أَيَّ فَهم.	فَهِمْتُ الدَّرْسَ أَيَّ فَهْمٍ.

*I **totally** understood the lesson.* We use a إِضافةٌ with أَيّ.

6	فَهِمْتُ الدَّرْسَ الْفَهْمَ كُلَّهُ.	فَهِمْتُ الدَّرْسَ كُلَّ الْفَهْمِ.

*I **completely** understood the lesson.* We use a إِضافةٌ with كُلّ.

7	فَهِمْتُ الدَّرْسَ الْفَهْمَ بَعْضَهُ.	فَهِمْتُ الدَّرْسَ بَعْضَ الْفَهْمِ.

*I understood **some parts** of the lesson.* We use a إِضافةٌ with بَعْض.

8	فَهِمْتُ الدَّرْسَ فَهْمًا أَحْسَنَ الْفَهْمِ.	فَهِمْتُ الدَّرْسَ أَحْسَنَ الْفَهْمِ.

*I understood the lesson **as best as** I can.* We use a إِضافةٌ-construction with a noun of preference; comparative (اِسْمُ تَفْضِيل).

9	فَهِمْتُ الدَّرْسَ فَهْمًا جَيِّدًا.	فَهِمْتُ الدَّرْسَ جَيِّدًا.

*I understood the lesson **well**.* We use a word that was originally attached as an **adjective** (صِفةٌ) to the مَصْدَر.

10	قَفَزَ اللَّاعِبُ قَفَزَاتٍ ثَلَاثًا.	قَفَزَ اللَّاعِبُ ثَلَاثَ قَفَزَاتٍ.

*The player jumped **three times**.* We use a *noun of instance* (اِسْمُ مَرَّة) and a number (عَدَد) to focus on how often the action occurred.

11	سَقَيْتُ الظَّمآنَ سَقْيَ كُوبٍ.	سَقَيْتُ الظَّمآنَ كُوبًا.

*I gave the thirsty person **a cup**.* We use the plain noun denoting an instrument (آلة, وَسِيلة) that is meaning-wise related to the مَصدَرٌ and is able to replace it.

12	لَيْتَكَ تُعامِلُنِي مَعامَلَةً هذِهِ الْمُعامَلةِ.	لَيْتَكَ تُعامِلُنِي هذِهِ الْمُعامَلةَ.

*I wish you'd treat me **like** that.* We use a demonstrative (اِسْمُ إشارةٍ) instead of the original مَصْدَرٌ.

→ For an in-depth-analysis, see also *Arabic for Nerds 2, question #324.*

123. *Why not?* - How do you say that in Arabic?

You say: لِمَ لا؟

Let us start with a common mistake:

Strictly speaking, this wouldn't make sense unless the context is clear → which means that you dropped the verb as it is implicitly understood.	*Why not?*	لِماذا لا؟
Better style. لِمَ is the short version of لِما		لِمَ لا؟

As a rule, we could say that you only use لِماذا (= *for what*)

- if there is a **verb** in the sentence, similar to the interrogative particle ماذا (see *question #25*);
- if you need an **amplifier** for emphasis (ex. 4 below).

The word لِماذا is a compound (كَلِمَةٌ مُرَكَّبَةٌ) of:

demonstrative noun ذَا (this)		interrogative مَا (what)		preposition لِ (for); denotes cause
ذَا الْإِشَارِيَّة	+	مَا الْإِسْتِفْهَامِيَّة	+	لَامُ التَّعْلِيلِ

What's (why) the hurry?	لِمَ الْعَجَلَةُ؟	1
Why all this fear?	لِمَ كُلُّ هٰذا الْخَوْفِ؟	2
Why do you laugh? Note: We have a verb!	لِماذا تَضْحَكُ؟	3
Why (on earth)???	لِما ذَا؟؟؟	
Here we have actually a nominal sentence: *This* (ذا) *is what for* (لِما). The word مَا is the fronted predicate (خَبَرٌ مُقَدَّمٌ) and ذا is the subject (مُبْتَدَأٌ).		4

Note: For a grammatical analysis of sentences with ماذا, see *Arabic for Nerds 2*, question #161.

The interrogative *why not* can also be introduced by هَلَّا. It may denote *isn't...* or *doesn't...?* since it is built from the expression: هَلْ لا.

Why wasn't that possible?	هَلَّا كانَ هٰذا مُمْكِنًا؟
Wouldn't you like to sit down? With the second person, هَلَّا may express a polite request.	هَلَّا جَلَسْتَ؟

If the vowels aren't written, you need to watch out to correctly identify لم!

question		*Why does she answer?*	لِمَ تَسْتَجِيبُ؟	لم تستجيب

negation of past tense – verb in jussive (مَجْزُومٌ)	*She did not answer.*	لَمْ تَسْتَجِبْ.	لم تستجب

124. Why do you write دَعا (with ا) but مَشَى (with ى)?

It has to do with the root.

The I-verb مَشَى means *to walk* and I-verb دعا *to call*. The pronunciation of both last letters is the same: "*a*". How can you know the correct spelling of the last letter?

As always, you have to think about the root. For this, you have to build the **present tense** (الْمُضارِعُ):

translation	الْمُضارِعُ	ROOT	verb
to call, invite	يَدْعُو	د-ع-و	دَعا
to walk	يَمْشِي	م-ش-ي	مَشَى

The rule for this is simple:

- If you have و in the root – write ا at the end.
- If you have ي in the root – write ى.

125. *Barely, hardly* - How do you express that in Arabic?

Not by a single word. You need a work-around.

In many languages, it is often the simple words that give you a headache. In Arabic this is true for the words *barely* or *hardly*. There are many ways to express the idea that a statement is true to an insignificant degree.

1	Use قَلَّما **followed by** a verb (any tense).
The director hardly went to the office.	قَلَّما ذَهَبَ الْمُديرُ إِلَى الْمَكْتَبِ.

2	Use قَلَّما **plus** أَنْ **plus** verb in the subjunctive mood (مَنْصوبٌ).
I hardly study.	قَلَّما أَنْ أَدْرُسَ.

3	Use نادِرًا ما **plus** verb (any tense).
The director hardly (= rarely) went to the office.	نادِرًا ما ذَهَبَ الْمُديرُ إِلَى الْمَكْتَبِ.

4	Use نادِرًا ما **plus** أَنْ **plus** verb/subjunctive mood (مَنْصوبٌ).
I hardly (= rarely) study.	نادِرًا ما أَنْ أَدْرُسَ.
	= لا أَدْرُسُ إِلّا نادِرًا.

5	Use لَمْ **plus** يَكَدْ **plus** present tense verb (فِعْلٌ مُضارِعٌ).
You have to adjust the verb form (يَكَدْ) according to the person which talks. يَكَدْ is the 3rd person singular (*he*), jussive (مَجْزُومٌ), of the I-verb كادَ - يَكادُ. Alternatively, you could use the present tense or even the expression بِالكادِ	
I could hardly hear. (*See question #97*)	لَمْ أَكَدْ أَسْمَعُ.
I hardly know him.	لا أَكادُ أَعْرِفُهُ.

126. How many things can the letter ﻝ express?

Some say 10, some 12, some 31, some claim there are 40!

The letter ﻝ is probably the most powerful and sophisticated Arabic letter. It can denote many things: *to*; *because*; *I swear by*; *in view of*; *indeed*; *so that, that*; *then*; *with*, etc. During the Abbasid Caliphate (ﺍﻟْﺨِﻼﻓَﺔُ ﺍﻟْﻌَﺒَّﺎﺳِﻴَّﺔُ), which lasted from 750 (132 AH) to 1258 (656 AH), entire books were published about ﻻﻡ. Al-Zajjājī (ﺍﻟﺰَّﺟَّﺎﺟِﻲ), a Persian-born grammarian (892 - 952 CE), lists 31 types of the letter ﻻﻡ.

Around half of the applications of the letter ﻝ are very common. For example: The ﻝ is used as a **short form of** ﺇﻟَﻰ to show **directions**. It may express **possession**. ﻝ can also be used to express an aim: *in order to*:

I went to Egypt to study Arabic.	ﺫَﻫَﺒْﺖُ ﺇﻟَﻰ ﻣِﺼْﺮَ ﻟِﺪِﺭﺍﺳَﺔِ ﺍﻟﻠُّﻐﺔِ ﺍﻟْﻌَﺮَﺑِﻴّﺔِ.

It may be used to express **astonishment** (ﺗَﻌَﺠُّﺐٌ). In such application, ﻝ takes ﻓَﺘْﺤﺔٌ. This can happen in other situations too: If a (regular) ﻝ is followed by a pronoun, the ﻝ may also take ﻓَﺘْﺤﺔٌ, for example, *to/for him* (ﻟَﻪُ).

Let's take a look at a few concrete real-world examples. Note that in all the following examples, the letter ﻝ is not a classical preposition! It is used to emphasize (ﻻﻡُ ﺍﻟﺘَّﺄْﻛِﻴﺪ) a word. Such ﻝ is usually not translated, but you could render it as *indeed* if you want to display the emphasis explicitly.

The pollution is *(indeed)* harmful.	ﺇﻥَّ ﺍﻟﺘَّﻠَﻮُّﺙَ ﻟَﻤُﻀِﺮٌّ.
The solution of this problem is *(indeed)* very easy.	ﺇﻥَّ ﺣَﻞَّ ﻫٰﺬِﻩِ ﺍﻟْﻤُﺸْﻜِﻠﺔِ ﻟَﺴَﻬْﻞٌ ﺟِﺪًّﺍ.
You are *(indeed)* a clever student.	ﺇﻧَّﻚَ ﻟَﻄﺎﻟِﺐٌ ﺯَﻛِﻲٌّ.

- The ل has فَتْحة and is pronounced *"la"*. You have to be very careful when you hear a text or speech because you might confuse it with a negation! The negation, of course, is written with a long vowel: لا (*"lā"*).

- **Watch out:** The device ل <u>does not induce any case ending</u> in a word (اللَّامُ غَيْرُ الْعامِلةِ). A following noun (اِسْمٌ) is in the nominative case (مَرْفوعٌ).

- A hint: If you have to put case endings (إِعْرابٌ), read the sentence as if the letter ل was not there and vowel it.

It is essential to know the various jobs of the ل if you want to avoid bad translations. Let's take a look at what this fascinating letter is capable of! It's a playground for enthusiasts.

1	ل conveys a slight meaning of بَعْدَ (*after*). This ل takes كَسْرةٌ.

Fast when you see it (the new moon), and stop fasting when you see it (the new moon). (Hadith: Sahīh Muslim 1081)	صُومُوا لِرُؤْيَتِهِ، وَأَفْطِرُوا لِرُؤْيَتِهِ.

2	The ل to **strengthen** the meaning (تَقْوِية). Such ل is placed before the **object**. This ل takes كَسْرةٌ and the word after it gets the genitive case (مَجْرُورٌ). It is an **extra, additional preposition**.

Mastering your work is your duty.	إِتْقانُكَ لِلْعَمَلِ واجِبٌ عَلَيْكَ.
Of course I beat Zayd.	لِزَيْدٍ ضَرَبْتُ.

3	The device ل that induces the **jussive mood** (اللَّامُ الْجازِمةُ لِلْفِعْلِ الْمُضارِعِ). This ل is mostly used in the **imperative** (أَمْرٌ).

Such ل has كَسْرَةٌ and the verb which comes after it gets the jus-sive mood (مَجْزُومٌ). Grammarians call it *Lām of request* (لامُ الطَّلَبِ) or *Lām of the imperative* (لامُ الأَمْرِ).

Be a responsible man!	لِتَكُنْ مَسْؤُولًا!
Let us (two) be friends!	لِنَكُنْ صَدِيقَيْنِ!
Important: If the ل is used after فَ or وَ, the ل takes سُكُونٌ. You say: *"faltakun"*.	فَلْنَكُنْ صَدِيقَيْنِ!

4　The ل that induces the **subjunctive mood** (اللّامُ النَّاصِبَةُ لِلْفِعْلِ الْمُضارِعِ). This type is also called *Lām of denial* (لامُ الْجُحُودِ) or *Lām of negation* (لامُ النَّفْي). It is a *Lām* with *"i"* (كَسْرَةٌ): لِ.

Let us see how it works:

- Step 1 and 2: You have to use a negated form of كانَ at the beginning of the sentence.

- Step 3: Put ل after it.

- Step 4 and 5: The verb after ل has to be in the present tense (الْمُضارِعُ), subjunctive mood (مَنْصُوبٌ).

- All this together conveys the meaning of *something that is totally impossible*. It confirms the negative verb *to be*.

Here is the formula:

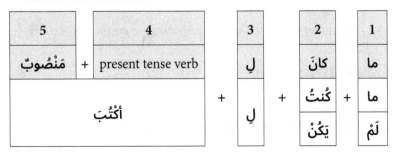

5		4	3	2	1
مَنْصُوبٌ	+	present tense verb	لِ	كانَ	ما
أَكْتُبَ			+ لِ	+ كُنتُ يَكُنْ	+ ما لَمْ

Some examples of the *Lām of denial* (لامُ الْجُحُودِ):

I was not a tyrant to people.	لَمْ أَكُنْ لِأَظْلِمَ النّاسَ
I didn't know that.	لَمْ أَكُنْ لِأَعْرَفَ ذلِكَ.
This student didn't neglect his studies.	ما كانَ هذا الطّالِبُ لِيُهْمِلَ دُرُوسَهُ.
I (indeed, truly) didn't neglect my studies. (pronunciation: *li'uhmila*)	ما كُنْتُ لِأُهْمِلَ دُرُوسِي.
Zayd was not late for the lecture.	لَمْ يَكُنْ زَيْدٌ لِيَتَأَخَّرَ عَنْ مَوْعِدِ بَدْءِ الْمُحاضَرَةِ.

...Allah will not forgive them, nor will He guide them on any path. *(Sura 4:137).*	...لَمْ يَكُنِ اللهُ لِيَغْفِرَ لَهُمْ وَلا لِيَهْدِيَهُمْ سَبِيلًا.

Note: Here we use the future tense for an appropriate translation as the meaning does not relate to something in the past.

5	The ل that **does not induce any case in any word**. In other words, a following word simply gets the case which it would also get without the preceding ل. Grammarians say that such type of ل has <u>no</u> ruling or governing power (لامُ غَيْرُ الْعامِلةِ).

There are some sub-species:

5.1	*Lām of introduction* (لامُ الْإِبْتِداءِ): the ل to emphasize a word.

Such ل can precede:

a) the subject (مُبْتَدَأٌ);

b) the words نِعْمَ or بِئْسَ - see *questions #155 and #183;*

c) the subject or predicate of إِنَّ;

d) the devices to denote the future tense: سَ or سَوْفَ;

Indeed, Karīm is present.	لَكَرِيمٌ حاضِرٌ. a)
Verily the best character is honesty.	لَنِعْمَ الْخُلُقُ الصِّدْقُ. b)
Indeed, the students are present.	إِنَّ الطُّلّابَ لَحاضِرُونَ. c)
Indeed, honesty is beneficial to the honest person.	إِنَّ الصِّدْقَ لَيَنْفَعُ صاحِبَهُ. c)
Indeed, success is found in hard work.	إِنَّ النَّجاحَ لَفِي الْعَمَلِ الْجادِّ. c)
Certainly the ceremony will be magnificent.	لَسَوْفَ يَكُونُ الْحَفْلُ جَمِيلا. d)
Indeed, in spring there is beauty.	إِنَّ فِي الرَّبِيعِ لَجَمالًا. c)

5.2	*Lām of the answer* (لامُ الْجَوابِ). Used to start the <u>main</u> (second) part of a conditional *if*-sentence or of an **oath**.

There are some sub-species as well:

5.2.1	The ـلَ which introduces the **main part of an oath** (لامُ الْقَسَمِ). This type of ل can also be placed after قَدْ plus verb in the past tense.

By God, Zayd is here!	وَاللهِ لَزَيْدٌ حاضِرٌ!
By God, I indeed/truly work hard!	وَاللهِ لَأَعْمَلَنَّ بِجِدٍّ!
By God, I will honor you!	وَاللهِ لَأُكْرِمَنَّكَ!

5.2.2	The ـَل which starts the **main (second) part** of an **if-sentence** (فِي جَوابِ لَوْ). Notice: The ل is not used if the second part of the conditional sentence is negated with ما or لَمْ.

If you had listened to the explanation, you would understand.	لَوْ أَنْصَتَّ لِلشَّرْحِ لَفَهِمْتَ.
If people cooperated, they wouldn't fail. → Since there is a negation, don't use ل!	لَوْ تَعاوَنَ النّاسُ ما أَخْفَقُوا.

5.2.3	This ل is used in the **second** part (فِي جَوابِ لَوْلا) of a sentence that starts with لَوْلا.
	You can only use ل if the answer (= second part) of the sentence consists of a verb in the past tense. **Watch out:** Don't use ل if the answer (part after لَوْلا) is negated by ما.

If it was not for schools, people would have been ignorant.	لَوْلا الْمَدارِسُ لَكانَ النّاسُ جُهَلاءَ.
If it was not for schools, no one would have learned. → Here, you don't use ل due to ما.	لَوْلا الْمَدارِسُ ما تَعَلَّمَ أَحَدٌ.
Hadn't it been you, I would have been lost.	لَوْلاكَ لَضَلَلْتُ.

6	In a complex sentence that combines an if-clause with an oath, you use the ل as a helping device – it introduces an oath.
	The ل intervenes in a conditional sentence (usually with إِنْ) and **paves the way** to another part of the sentence (لامٌ مُوَطِّئَةٌ): the part where the oath begins (جَوابُ الْقَسَمِ). By doing that the ل tells the reader or listener that the main part (جَوابٌ) after ل belongs to the oath.

| I swear if you come to visit us, we will be generous to you! | وَاللهِ لَئِنْ زُرْتَنا لَنُكْرِمَنَّكَ! |
| Allah! There is no god but Him! He will surely assemble you for [account on] the Day of Resurrection, about which there is no doubt. *(Sura 4:87)* | اللّهُ لَا إِلَهَ إِلَّا هُوَ لَيَجْمَعَنَّكُمْ إِلَى يَوْمِ الْقِيَامَةِ لَا رَيْبَ فِيهِ. |

In this verse, ل refers to the first part which includes an oath.

Remark: If you are not sure why we use the ending نّ in some sentences, have a look at *question #156.*

127. What is the difference between 3,000 and thousands?

The difference is the form of the plural you need.

The Arabic word for *thousand* (أَلْف) is of masculine gender (مُذَكَّر). There are two main plural forms: آلَاف and أُلُوف.

Does it matter what form we use? No!

a	For **small numbers** (three to ten thousands).	آلَاف
b	For **big (undefined) numbers**. It is actually the plural of the plural. أُلُوف can only be used if it is **indefinite** (no ال, not first part of إِضافة); it then donates *thousands.*	أُلُوف
c	Note: This is a rare plural form. It is only used and documented in the expression **3,000** (ثَلاثَة آلُفِ).	آلُف

Some examples (the numbers refer to the list above):

translation	example	type
for thousands of years	مُنْذُ آلَافِ السِّنِينَ	a
Since we have a إِضافةٌ-construction, آلاف is treated as definite (مَعْرِفَةٌ); so we cannot use option b).		
hundreds of thousands of...	مِئَاتُ الْآلافِ مِنْ....	a
The word آلاف is definite (مَعْرِفَةٌ); we can't use option b).		
Thousands and thousands (German: zigtausende).	آلَافٌ مُؤَلَّفَةٌ or أُلُوفٌ مُؤَلَّفَةٌ	a or b
Four thousand nine hundred and eighty-five (4985) girls	أَرْبَعَةُ آلَافٍ وَتِسْعُ مِئَةٍ وخَمْسٌ وَثَمانُونَ بِنْتًا	a

[Prophet], consider those people who abandoned their homeland in fear of death, even though there were thousands of them.... *(Sura 2:243)*	أَلَمْ تَرَ إِلَى الَّذِينَ خَرَجُوا مِن دِيَارِهِمْ وَهُمْ أُلُوفٌ حَذَرَ المَوْتِ...

Watch out: أَلْفٌ is masculine (مُذَكَّرٌ) which matters tremendously in numbers. So, don't mess up the gender-agreement!

4,000	أَرْبَعَةُ آلافٍ
400,000	أَرْبَعُمائَةِ أَلْفٍ

14,000	أَرْبَعَةَ عَشَرَ أَلْفًا

128. What is the plural of *month*? شُهُورٌ or أَشْهُرٌ؟

Both are correct forms - but are not always appropriate.

أَشْهُرٌ or شُهُورٌ are both **broken plural forms** (جَمْعُ التَّكْسِيرِ) of شَهْرٌ which means *month*.

The original meaning of شَهْرٌ is *the new moon, when it appears*. In Arabic, almost all words have more than one plural form, and so does شَهْرٌ. How can we know which form is appropriate? Well, it depends on the total number that the plural wants to express. In our example, on the number of months.

Few and many – the rules for choosing the correct plural:

1. The pattern فُعُولٌ is used for **big** (to infinite) **numbers** and called *major plural* (جَمْعُ كَثْرَةٍ). There are sixteen patterns of this kind. It is the default pattern.

2. The pattern أَفْعُلٌ is used for **small numbers** (3 to 10) and called *minor plural* (جَمْعُ قِلَّةٍ). Note أَفْعُلٌ is **not** a diptote (→ only أَفْعَلُ because it could be confused with a IV-verb). There are four patterns of this kind.

	1: plural; **big number**	2: plural; **small number**	singular
face	وُجُوهٌ	أَوْجُهٌ	وَجْهٌ
month	شُهُورٌ	أَشْهُرٌ	شَهْرٌ
line	سُطُورٌ	أَسْطُرٌ	سَطْرٌ
star	نُجُومٌ	أَنْجُمٌ	نَجْمٌ

Let's make it clearer:

several months	عِدَّةُ الشُّهُورِ	four months	أَرْبَعَةُ أَشْهُرٍ

Let's examine the most common patterns for the **minor plural** (جَمْعُ قِلَّةٍ), for things between 3 and 10 in number.

meaning	plural	singular pattern: فَعِيلٌ	**plural pattern**	1
loafs	أَرْغِفَةٌ	رَغِيفٌ	أَفْعِلَةٌ	

pillars	أَعْمِدَةٌ		عَمُودٌ	

meaning	plural	singular pattern: فَعْلٌ	plural pattern	2
months	أَشْهُرٌ	شَهْرٌ	أَفْعُلٌ	
souls	أَنْفُسٌ	نَفْسٌ		

The above words are masculine (مُذَكَّرٌ). It is important to note that the broken plural pattern أَفْعُلٌ is also used for feminine nouns (مُؤَنَّثٌ) consisting of <u>four letters</u> in total (رُبَاعِيٌّ - <u>not</u> 4 root letters). Such feminine nouns have a long vowel before the last letter:

meaning	plural	singular
tongue	أَلْسُنٌ	لِسَانٌ

meaning	plural	singular
arms	أَذْرُعٌ	ذِرَاعٌ

Remark: لِسَانٌ can be treated as masculine or feminine.

- If the meaning is *language*, it is mostly treated as masculine.
- If the meaning is *tongue*, it is mostly treated as feminine.

meaning	plural	singular pattern: فَعَلٌ	plural pattern	3
young men	فِتْيَةٌ	فَتًى	فِعْلَةٌ	

meaning	plural	singular patterns: فَعِلٌ • فُعْلٌ • فَعَلٌ فَعُولٌ • فَعِيلٌ	plural pattern	4
actions	أَعْمَالٌ	عَمَلٌ	أَفْعَالٌ	
vigilant people	أَيْقَاظٌ	يَقِظٌ		

enemies	أَعْداءٌ	عَدُوٌّ	
noble people	أَشْرافٌ	شَرِيفٌ	
sides	أَجْنابٌ	جُنْبٌ	

The word فتية – without vowels – can mean many things:

youthfulness	فَتِيَّةٌ
youthful (feminine, singular)	فَتِيَّةٌ
young men, juveniles; plural of فَتًى	فِتْيَةٌ

129. Which (Gregorian) year is 1435 Hijri?

It is the year 2014.

The term هِجْرةٌ (*hijrah*) denotes the migration of the Islamic prophet Muhammad and his followers from Mecca to Yathrib (later renamed by him to Medina) in 622 CE. It also marks the beginning of the Hijri calendar (التَّقْوِيمُ الْهِجْرِيُّ الْقَمَرِيُّ).

The Muslim calendar is a lunar calendar and doesn't follow the solar system like the Gregorian calendar. In Arabic, a Hijri year is marked by the letter هـ. It is written in this peculiar form, i.e., the form of the letter Hā᾽ when it starts a word (هـ) – and not the stand-alone form ه. Maybe so it is not confused with the number 5. The Gregorian (Christian) calendar is marked by the letter م which stands for مِيلادِيٌّ (A.D.).

Now let us return to our question: Which (Gregorian) year is 1435 Hijri? Let's do the math: One lunar year has about 354 days. 33 solar years correspond to 34 lunar years. The easiest way is to use a corrective factor (354 divided by 365) ≈ 0.97. From this, we can derive a formula:

1. If you want to convert a Hijri to a Gregorian date, you need to multiply the original Hijri year by 0.97 and add 622:

Year Gregorian ≈ Year Hijri × 0.97 + 622
You could also do the following: **G**= H-(H/33)+622

2. If you want to convert a Gregorian to a Hijri date, you have to subtract 622 from the year and multiply it by 1.03:

Year Hijri ≈ (Year Gregorian– 622) × 1.03
You could also do the following: **H**= G-622+(G-622)/32

In our example, the result is: 1435 x 0.97 + 622 = 2013.95. It is the year 2014.

130. ...has become unacceptable – How do you translate that?

You need to find a good way to express the prefix -un.

If you would like to express that *something has become unacceptable,* you should watch out. Why?

We will see.

Bad style!	أَصْبَحَ لَيْسَ مَقْبُولًا.
The verb أَصْبَحَ can't go along with the verb لَيْسَ directly as a predicate (خَبَرُ أَصْبَحَ) – this wouldn't make sense.	

Much better!	أَصْبَحَ غَيْرَ مَقْبُولٍ.

Here, the predicate (خَبَر) of أَصْبَحَ is a إِضافة-construction. The first part is the word غَيْر. Therefore, مَقْبُولٍ is in the genitive case.

Let's try to find a solution without أَصْبَحَ.

This is not acceptable (unacceptable).	لَمْ يَعُدْ مَقْبُولًا.
I could not stand it any longer.	لَمْ أَعُدْ أَسْتَطِيعُ صَبْرًا.

- These sentences may also express that something is not acceptable (anymore). In its original meaning, the I-verb عادَ / يَعُودُ (R2=و) denotes to *return* and is therefore usually connected with a **preposition**, e.g., إِلَى (*to return to*).

- However, if you don't use a preposition and add a **direct object** (مَفْعُولٌ بِهِ) instead, the verb will denote *to become xy again*. For example: *It became clean again* (عادَ نَقِيًّا).

- If عادَ (without a preposition) is **negated** and immediately followed by a **verb** in the **present tense** (الْمُضارِع), it will denote *to do something no more* or *no longer*. Note that you connect the second verb directly without أَنْ and conjugate it according to the subject indicated by عادَ.

131. Can the word ما unite with other words?

Yes, it can.

ما is a powerful device in Arabic. The meaning depends entirely on its function and position in the sentence (see #134).

In this *question*, we focus on ما as an interrogative noun (اِسْمُ
اِسْتِفْهامٍ). It is used to ask questions and means *what*.

Such type of ما can unite with other words – with the result
that the **Aleph vanishes**. Some of the resulting words are difficult to identify. As a general rule, ما does not form compounds with words ending in *"a"* (فَتْحةٌ) like بَعْدَ or قَبْلَ.

What happens grammatically when we combine ما with other
words? Then, ما is dragged into the genitive case (مَجْرُورٌ) due
to the preceding preposition.

Although we say interrogative *particle* in English, in Arabic
we deal with an interrogative *noun* (اِسْمُ اِسْتِفْهامٍ) as ما in this
application is a اِسْمٌ, and only a اِسْمٌ can get case endings.
However, you don't see all this because the expression has a
fixed, indeclinable shape.

Let's put, for example, عَمَّ under the microscope (إِعْرابٌ).

Preposition with a fixed shape; fixed on the سُكُونٌ. The ن will vanish during the merging process, however, we still say that in عَمَّ, there is the preposition عَنْ included having an inde- clinable, cemented shape on a deleted letter (حرفُ جَرٍّ مَبْنِيٌّ عَلَى السُّكُونِ عَلَى النُّونِ الْمَحْذُوفةِ).	عَنْ
Question word/interrogative noun. In its original form, the word has a fixed shape and سُكُونٌ on the letter Aleph. The ce- mented shape is the reason why we cannot put visible case markers. ما is a noun in Arabic, we have to assign a place value,. Since it follows a preposition, we say that it is placed in the location of a genitive case. Now comes the tricky part. The Aleph vanishes during the merging process. That's the reason why we say that ما is fixed (cemented) on سُكُونٌ on the deleted letter Aleph (اِسْمُ اِسْتِفْهامٍ مَبْنِيٌّ عَلَى السُّكُونِ عَلَى الْأَلِفِ الْمَحْذُوفةِ).	ما

Now we produce a few mergers.

meaning; question word	result	construction
about what?	عَمَّ or عَمَّا	عَنْ + ما
from what? of what?	مِمَّ or مِمَّا	مِنْ + ما
concerning what? what about?	عَلَامَ	عَلَى + ما
to what?	إِلَامَ	إِلَى + ما
concerning what? in what? why?	فِيمَ	فِي + ما
with what?	بِمَ	بِ + ما
why?	لِمَ	لِ + ما

Let's use some of these crafted question words in sentences.

What are you driving with?	بِمَ تُسافِرُ؟
And why not?	وَلِمَ (لِما) لا؟
How does it concern you?	فِيما يَتَعَلَّقُ بِكَ؟
What are you thinking about?	فِيمَ تُفَكِّرُ؟
He asked me about what had happened.	سَأَلَني عَمَّا حَصَلَ.
What does the river consist of?	مِمَّ يَتَكَوَّنُ النَّهْرُ؟

Watch out:

- فِيما = الَّذِي: Here, ما works as a <u>relative pronoun</u> (اِسْمٌ مَوْصُولٌ) and conveys *this* or *that; which*. In this application, you don't get rid of the Aleph!

- Furthermore, if the preposition consists of **three** or more **letters**, it does <u>not</u> merge with ما (i.e., when ما serves as a relative pronoun): عَلَى ما and إلَى ما.

Strive for what you desire!	إسْعَ إلَى ما تَبْتَغِي!
Note: We use the I-verb سَعَى in the imperative which explains why the last letter ى gets cut-off. The VIII-verb يَبْتَغِي - ابْتَغَى means *to desire; want* and is based on the root بَغَى/يَبْغِي (*to seek*).	
How does it concern you?	فِيما يَتَعَلَّقُ بِكَ؟

- From all this we can conclude that the expression فِيمَ is only used for questions.

132. Is there a difference whether you negate with ما or لَمْ؟

Yes, but it is subtle. Both convey almost the same meaning.

Let us start with ما which is one of the most versatile and powerful Arabic words. ما is suitable to work as a **negation particle** (حَرْفُ نَفْي). Hold on. We need to stop here for a second. In such application, ما is a particle and not a noun (إسْمٌ) as in the case of the ما which is used to ask questions (*what*).

There are a few special features here:

1. The negation device ما has to stand at the **beginning of a sentence**.

2. ما, if used to <u>negate the past tense</u>, **denies the entire matter** – it strengthens the meaning of the negation.

3. In the <u>present tense</u>, ما **denies** not only the action –but also its **possibility**.

4. Therefore, we may translate **ما** with *not at all*.

What about لَمْ? It is a negation particle (حَرْفُ نَفْي) that induces the <u>jussive</u> mood (مَجْزُومٌ) in a following verb.

- This device stands out because it **converts** the meaning of the present tense form **into** the **past tense** (يَقْلِبُ الْمُضارِعَ ماضِيًا).

- The negation particle لَمْ, which is used to negate the past tense, does **not express a complete denial**.

Some examples:

I did not hear a thing.	ما سَمِعْتُ شَيْئًا.
I didn't get (wasn't) thirsty at all.	ما عَطِشْتُ.
I wasn't thirsty.	لَمْ أَعْطَشْ.

Watch out: If you see **لا** before a verb in the **past tense**, it expresses a special meaning: usually a prayer or wish (قَسَمٌ)! Note that the past tense is used for wishes, curses and prayers irrespective of whether it is preceded by **لا** or not (see also *question #206*). For example:

May Allah spare you bad things!	لا أَراكَ اللّهُ مَكْرُوهًا!

133. Can you negate a nominal sentence with ما?

Yes, you can.

Normally, you negate a nominal sentence (جُمْلةٌ اِسْـمِيّةٌ) with the help of the defective verb لَيْسَ (*to to be*).

He is not a teacher.	هُوَ لَيْسَ مُدَرِّسًا.

It is possible to use ما as well even though you rarely encounter such constructions in Modern Standard Arabic.

There are two options: You treat ما with governmental power (a) or as a neutral negating device (b).

OPTION (a) ما can used in the way of لَيْسَ with severe grammatical impacts. Don't forget that لَيْسَ heavily interferes in a nominal sentence:

- The subject (مُبْتَدَأٌ), as usual, is nominative (مَرْفُوعٌ).
- The predicate (خَبَرٌ) in a sentence with لَيْسَ is in the **accusative** case (مَنْصُوبٌ).

If we treat ما like لَيْسَ, we get the above implications. This application of ما is called ما الْحِجازِيّةُ, named after the Hijaz region which Mecca falls within. It is only used in Classical Arabic and in the Qur'an.

The weather is not hot.	ما الجَوُّ حارًّا.
This is not a human being. (*Sura 12:31*). The sentence means *he cannot be mortal.*	ما هذا بَشَرًا.
In both examples, the predicate is in the accusative case (مَنْصُوبٌ).	

Watch out: You can only use ما as in option (a) if the subject <u>precedes</u> the predicate. You cannot use it if the word-order is reversed. → see *Arabic for Nerds 2, #142, #272.*

OPTION (b) ما does not induce any case endings and does not govern any word. Such ما is called ما التَّميميَّةُ, named after the Arabic tribe which applied it as such in their dialect.

He is not a teacher.	ما هُوَ مُدَرِّسٌ.
Karīm is not traveling.	ما كَريمٌ مُسافِرٌ.
Karīm doesn't understand.	ما كَريمٌ فاهِمٌ.
I have nothing. Note that عِنْدي is the fronted predicate!	ما عِنْدي شَيْءٌ = لَيْسَ عِنْدي شَيْءٌ = لا شَيْءَ عِنْدي.

In the above examples, we used the nominative case (مَرْفُوعٌ) for the predicate (خَبَرٌ).

Watch out: ما can be used with مِنْ to **strengthen** the meaning of the **negation**.

| Is there no alternative? | ما مِنْ بَديلٍ؟ |
| not a single person; nobody | ما مِنْ أَحَدٍ |

134. How many different jobs may ما have in Arabic?

More than ten.

ما is a genuine jack-of-all-trades. By throwing this tiny word into a sentence, you can dramatically change the meaning.

In my opinion, ما and لـ are the keys to a proper understanding of Arabic. Let's start with an appetizer:

| If it had been God's will, they would not | وَلَوْ شاءَ اللهُ ما أَشْرَكوا. |

have joined other gods with Him. (Sura 6:107)	

Without the conditional particle لَو, the **negation** device ما would have turned into a tool to form an (interpreted) **infinitive** (ما الْمَصْدَرِيّةُ). It would overthrow the entire meaning.

God willed their joining others with him.	شَاءَ اللّهُ مَا أَشْرَكُوا.

Let's look at the possibilities that ما offers us. Depending on the function, ما is sometimes treated as a noun (إِسْمٌ), sometimes as a particle (حَرْفٌ).

1	**Negation particle**	حَرْفٌ	ما النَّافِية

Normally ما is used to **negate a past tense verb** (الْماضِي). As shown in *question #133*, ما can also negate a nominal sentence (جُمْلةٌ إِسْمِيّةٌ). Furthermore, you could even negate the present tense (الْمُضارِعُ) with ما.

This is very rare. However, you may find it in the expression *still* (ما يَزالُ).

The students did not show up yesterday.	ما حَضَرَ الطُّلّابُ أَمْسِ.

2	**The question *what?*** (interrogative noun)	إِسْمٌ	ما الْإِسْتِفْهامِيّةُ

What is your name?	ما اسْمُكَ؟
What are you thinking about?	فِيمَ تُفَكِّرُ؟

3	**Relative pronoun** (def. conjunctive noun)	إِسْمٌ	ما الْمَوْصُولةُ

I found what I love.	وَجَدْتُ ما أُحِبُّ.
I do understand what you say.	إِنَّني أَفْهَمُ ما تَقُولُهُ.
Read what I wrote.	إِقْرَأْ ما كَتَبْتُهُ.

| 4 | Conditional noun | ما الشَّرْطِيّةُ | اِسْمٌ |

This ما induces the jussive mood (مَجْزُومٌ) in the entire conditional sentence (in the first and second part). → The verbs will get سُكُونٌ.

| What(ever) you sow, you will reap. | ما تَزْرَعْ تَحْصُدْ. |

| 5 | Used to strengthen the conditional meaning | ما لِتَأْكِيدِ مَعْنَى الشَّرْطِ | حَرْفٌ |

| If you had worked hard, you would have succeeded. (This is not a negation!) | إِذا ما عَمِلْتَ بِجِدٍّ نَجَحْتَ. |

| 6 | The ما that produces an (interpreted) infinitive. | ما الْمَصْدَرِيّةُ | حَرْفٌ |

Such ما is used like the particle أَنْ and has the same meaning and implications – see question #81. It introduces a clause equivalent to a حَرْفٌ مَصْدَرِيٌّ and oftentimes replaces an **adverb of time** (ظَرْفِيٌّ يَنُوبُ عَن ظَرْفِ الزَّمانِ الْمَحْذُوفِ الْمُضافِ إِلَى الْمَصْدَرِ الْمُؤَوَّلِ).

| The student came after the lesson had started. | حَضَرَ الطّالِبُ بَعْدَما بَدَأَ الدَّرْسُ. |
| I will fight as long as I live. | سَأُكافِحُ ما دُمْتُ حَيًّا. |

I will think of you as long as I live.	سَأَظَلُّ أَتَذَكَّرُكَ ما حَيِيتُ.

7	**The ما that denotes generality & vagueness** *some* (or *other*); *a certain*	ما الإِبْهامِيّة إِسْمٌ

In this application, **ما** has to be placed at the end of a sentence and must follow an indefinite noun. → **ما** functions as an **adjective** (صِفةٌ) describing the preceding word.

I came for a certain reason.	جِئْتُ لِأَمْرٍ ما.
The man who sat next to me in the plane was reading some book.	كانَ الرَّجُلُ الّذي جانِبِي في الطّائِرَةِ يَقْرَأُ كِتابًا ما.
There is certainly some mistake.	ثَمَّةَ بِالتَّأْكيدِ خَطَّأً ما.

Note: ثَمَّةَ (ثَمَّتَ) is a demonstrative (إِسْمَ إِشارَةٍ) and has the meaning of هُناكَ; it denotes *there is*. ثَمَّةَ does not change its shape and is negated with لَيْسَ ثَمَّةَ: *there isn't* (لَيْسَ ثَمَّةَ).

I lost something.	أَضَعْتُ شَيْئًا ما.
some day; sometime in the future	يَوْمًا ما
for some reason	لِسَبَبٍ ما

8	**The neutralizing (hindering) ما**	ما الْكافّةُ حَرْفٌ

Such **ما** neutralizes the governing power of a preceding word.

If you place **ما** after **إِنَّ**, the grammatical force of **إِنَّ** doesn't get through, so you won't have to think about special case endings. Such **ما** can neutralize the governing power of particles and verbs.

Indeed, the bird is free.	إنَّ الطَّائِرَ طَليقٌ.	1
	إنَّما الطَّائِرُ طَليقٌ.	2

In sentence 1, the particle إنَّ guards the word الطَّائِرَ ("subject" or اسْمُ إنَّ) in the accusative case (مَنْصُوبٌ). In sentence 2, ما is like a wall and neutralizes the power of إنَّ, so إنَّ can't get through with its grammatical force. However, both sentences mean the same!

The ما may also neutralize the demand of verbs for having a subject (الْكَافَّةُ عَنِ الْفاعِلِ). Such sentences have a sophisticated underbelly. We can say that the verb then cannot exercise its power to govern a word (= the subject) in the *nominative case*.

Examples of such verbs are *to be few* (قَلَّ), *to be often* (كَثُرَ), *to be extended* (طالَ), *to be extensive* (شَدَّ), etc.

sometimes, perhaps	رُبَّما	frequently; as long as	طالَما	seldom, rarely, hardly	قَلَّما

The lazy man rarely succeeds.	قَلَّما يَنْجَحُ الْكَسُولُ.
I have been looking for a suitable partner (wife) for a long time.	طالَما بَحَثْتُ عَنْ زَوْجَةٍ مُناسِبَةٍ.

If you place such ما after a preposition (حَرْفُ جَرٍّ) or an adverb of time or place (ظَرْفٌ), you neutralize their governing power; you neutralize the genitive case. This happens ins expressions such as *while* (بَيْنَما) or *as; just as* (كَما).

9	ما to denote **surprise** and **astonishment**	ما التَّعَجُّبِيّةُ اسْمٌ

What a nice spring!	ما أَجْمَلَ الرَّبِيعَ!

What fortunate I got here!	‫ما أَسْعَدَنِي بِوُجُودي هُنا!‬

We will examine this construction in *question #194*. See also *Arabic for Nerds 2*, questions #5, #294, #434.

135. Is there a word in Arabic which consists of only 1 letter?

Yes, وَ which means "and". But there are more exciting examples.

Arabic words consisting of only one letter are formed from verbs. They are rare and occur only in the **imperative** (أَمْرٌ). We need to look for verbs with **two weak root letters** (حَرْفُ عِلّةٍ). Only the strong consonant will survive our operation.

meaning	I-verb		imperative		meaning
to beware, preserve	‫وَقَى - يَقِي‬		‫قِ !‬	*qi!*	*Protect!*
to pay attention to	‫وَعَى - يَعِي‬	→	‫عِ !‬	*'i!*	*Pay attention!*
to live up a promise or agreement; to fulfill	‫وَفَى - يَفِي‬		‫فِ !‬	*fi!*	*Fulfill!*

It can be difficult to identify and understand such forms!

...protect us from the torment of the Fire! (*Sura 2:201*)	‫...قِنَا عَذَابَ النَّارِ!‬

Note the spelling! It is **impossible** to have a single stand-alone letter in Arabic. For example, the interrogative particle أَ is **always written together** with the word that follows it. Other examples are وَ • لِ • فَ • بِ. → Never use a space after them – you must connect them with the following word!

the book and the pen	not correct	الْكِتابُ وَ الْقَلَمُ
	correct – no space!	الْكِتابُ وَالْقَلَمُ
Is Zayd at home?	correct! (although it may be difficult to read)	أَفِي الْبَيْتِ زَيْدٌ؟
Didn't Zayd come?		أَلَمْ يَأْتِ زَيْدٌ؟

136. Because, since, as - How do you express that in Arabic?

There are several ways to express this idea.

As, because, and since are conjunctions and introduce subordinate clauses. They connect the result of something with its reason. An example: *I studied Arabic* (= **result**) *because I was in Egypt* (= **reason**). How would you express that in Arabic?

1	**Regular word order:** The *because*-part (= reason) appears later in the sentence.

because; since, as; in so far as	حَيْثُ أَنَّ	إِذْ أَنَّ	لِأَنَّ

He did not come (show up) **because** he was lazy.	لَمْ يَحْضُرْ حَيْثُ أَنَّهُ كانَ كَسُولًا.
I will go to Egypt **since** my heart tells me that I love you.	سَأَذْهَبُ إِلَى مِصْرَ إِذْ أَنَّ قَلْبِي يُحَدِّثُنِي أَنَّنِي أُحِبُّكِ.
He won't come tomorrow **because** he is ill.	لَنْ يَجِيءَ غَدًا لِأَنَّهُ مَرِيضٌ.

Spot the difference!

in order to	لِأَنْ	≠	لِأَنَّ	because

2	**Inverse word order:** The sentence starts with the *because*-part (i.e, the causative part).

as, since	بِما أَنَّ + فَ

Since I don't like the room I'll move (go) to another hotel.	بِما أَنَّ الغُرْفةَ لا تُناسِبُني فَسَأَذْهَبُ إِلَى فُنْدُقٍ آخَرَ.
Since the weather is nice, I will go to the garden.	بِما أَنَّ الْجَوَّ جَمِيلٌ فَسَأَذْهَبُ إِلَى الْحَدِيقَةِ.

137. *Because of...* How do you say that in Arabic?

It depends on the context.

Let's jump right in at the deep end and take a look at a common option: the word جَرّاءٌ which is a noun (اِسْمٌ) in Arabic.

because of; by what; as a result of	جَرّاءٌ ما + verb	1
because of what happened there	جَرّاءٌ ما لَحِقَ	
because of; due to	مِنْ جَرّاءِ + noun/pronoun	2

I did this for you.	قُمْتُ بِذَلِكَ مِنْ جَرّائِكَ.
	فَعَلْتُ ذَلِكَ مِنْ جَرّائِكَ.
→ The examples on the right mean the same as the above sentences!	بِسَبَبِكَ = وَمِنْ جَرّاكَ = مِنْ أَجْلِكَ

because of the money	مِنْ جَرَّاءِ الْمالِ
As a result, countless problems have occurred.	مِنْ جَرَّاءِ ذلكَ وَقَعَتْ مَشَاكِلُ لا حَصْرَ لَهَا.
A woman got into Hell-Fire because of a cat whom she had tied. (Hadith; Sahīh Muslim 2619)	دَخَلَتِ امْرَأَةٌ النَّارَ مِنْ جَرَّاءِ هِرَّةٍ لَهَا - أَوْ هِرٍّ - رَبَطَتْهَا.

There is an alternative spelling of جَرَّاءٌ without Hamza. The meaning is the same.

because of	مِن جَرَّى
because of you; on your account; for your sake	مِن جَرَّاكَ

Of course, it would be strange if Arabic did not offer other possibilities to express *because of.*

In the following expressions, you have to add a pronoun or noun as the second part of the إِضافة-construction. As always, watch out for the case endings!

because of this/as a result	لِذلِكَ + sentence	1
for the benefit of	عَلَى ذِمّةِ + noun	2
In view of; in regard to; seeing that; because of/for	نَظَرًا لِ + noun	3
for the sake of	مِنْ أَجْلِ or لِأَجْلِ + noun/pronoun	4
because of	بِسَبَبِ + noun	5

Since you have helped him in the past...	نَظَرًا لِمُساعَدَتِكَ لَهُ فِي الْماضِي...	3

The meeting was canceled because of the weather.	أُلْغِيَ الاجْتِماعُ بِسَبَبِ الْجَوِّ.	5

Remark: In Egyptian Arabic, you can use the very flexible words عَلَشان or عَشان. They both denote **(a)** *for the sake of;* **(b)** *because of;* **(c)** *in order to;* **(d)** *because.*

What for? Why?	'ashaan eeh?	عشان ايه؟	a
This room is for travelers.	el-'ooda di 'ashaan el-musafreen.	الأوضة دي عشان المسافرين.	a
for that reason	'ashaan kedda	عشان كده	b
A palm tree needs time in order to grow.	en-nakhla betaakhud wa't 'ashaan tikbar.	النخلة بيتاخد وقت عشان تكبر.	c
I came to Egypt because of the weather.	geet masr 'ashaan el-gaww.	جيت مصر عشان الجوّ.	d

138. What do أَخْرَجَ، عَلَّمَ and ناقَشَ have in common?

The pronunciation of the first letter in the present tense.

To get to the bottom of this, let's check the three verbs.

meaning	present tense	past tense	stem
to discuss	يُناقِشُ	ناقَشَ	III
to oust, to extract	يُخْرِجُ	أَخْرَجَ	IV
to teach	يُعَلِّمُ	عَلَّمَ	II

All three verbs consist of four letters (__not__ root letters). Grammarians call them *triliteral augmented verbs* (فِعْلٌ مَزِيدٌ ثُلاثِيٌّ). They have one thing in common: the **pronunciation**.

In the present tense (الْمُضارِعُ), the **first vowel** is ضَمّةٌ ("*u*") and not فَتْحةٌ ("*a*") as in all other verb patterns: **I** and **V to X**.

comparison: verb pattern I		meaning		مُضارِعٌ	وَزْنٌ	stem
he leaves	يَخْرُجُ	he extracts	yukhriju	يُخْرِجُ	أَفْعَلَ	IV
he paints	يَنْقُشُ	he discusses	yunāqishu	يُناقِشُ	فاعَلَ	III
he learns	يَعْلَمُ	he teaches	yu'allimu	يُعَلِّمُ	فَعَّلَ	II

Therefore, we can say that when you see a verb consisting of four letters, you can be sure that the first vowel is "*u*".

139. Does a weak letter cause trouble in the مَصْدَر-form?

Of course it does.

If you spot و or ي in the root, roll up your sleeves! There will be work to be done.

- Sometimes the weak letter (حَرْفُ عِلّةٍ) just disappears.
- Sometimes the letter transforms into another letter.

	problem	meaning	مَصْدَرٌ	verb	stem
1	و at the beginning	*stopping*	إيقافٌ	أَوْقَفَ	IV
2	I in the middle	*desire; will*	إرادةٌ	أَرادَ	IV

3	ء at the beginning plus ى at the end	damage; injury	إيذاءٌ	آذَى	IV
4	و in the middle and ى at the end	takeover; seizure	اِسْتيلاءٌ	اِسْتَوْلَى	X
5	و in the root; instead of تَفْعيلٌ, you use تَفْعِلة	education; pedagogy	تَرْبِيةٌ	رَبَّى	II

The following rules summarize how to build a مَصْدَر if there are troublemakers involved:

1. و becomes ي

2. ‏ا (Aleph) in the middle stays, but you have to add ة

3. آ (Aleph madda) turns into ي

4. ى at the end becomes ء

5. Exception: ى at the end of a II-verb becomes ية

140. What does the تّ do in اِتِّصالٌ (connection)?

It is the result of an assimilation.

اِتِّصالٌ denotes *connection; communication; relation* and is the مَصْدَر of the VIII-verb اِتَّصَلَ - يَتَّصِلُ (R1=و). How can we explain the doubled تّ? Where does the extra ت come from?

If و is the first letter of a root, و will transform into ت with a شَدّةٌ in the VIII-stem اِفْتَعَلَ. Some examples:

meaning	مَصْدَر	present t.	past t.	root
to form a union	اِتِّحادٌ	يَتَّحِدُ	اِتَّحَدَ	و-ح-د

to agree on (عَلَى)	إِتِّفاقٌ	يَتَّفِقُ	إِتَّفَقَ	و-ف-ق
to get in touch with	إِتِّصالٌ	يَتَّصِلُ	إِتَّصَلَ	و-ص-ل

141. Why does سَماءٌ take nunation ("un") but زَرْقاءُ doesn't?

Because زَرْقاءُ is a so-called diptote (مَمْنُوعٌ مِن الصَّرْفِ).

سَماءٌ means *sky;* زَرْقاءُ means *blue* (feminine form). We see that both words end with اء. So why do we have to use different case markers when we put nunation (تَنْوِينٌ)? Let's use both words in one phrase.

In a blue sky	فِي سَماءٍ زَرْقاءَ

We see that سَماءٍ gets nunation (تَنْوِينٌ) but زَرقاءَ not. Why is that? We need to examine the root.

explanation	root	
ء is part of the root; ء is just a transformed و.	س - م - و	سَماءٌ
The ء is **extra** (زِيادَةٌ) and **not part of the root.** This is the reason why it does not take nunation (تَنْوِينٌ). The extra هَمْزَةٌ is part of a pattern which counts as a diptote (مَمْنُوعٌ مِن الصَّرْفِ).	ز - ر - ق	زَرْقاءُ

142. مَساءً or مَساءًا - Which spelling is correct?

It is مَساءً and means: in the evening.

Our question is about the correct spelling of the ending: Should you place an Aleph at the end? First of all, we need to write the nunation (تَنْوِينٌ) above the هَمْزةٌ, this is for sure.

Let's check similar examples to understand the problem:

Aleph?	meaning; explanation		root	word
yes	The Hamza is part of the root. If the word functions as a direct object, it will get the accusative case (مَنْصُوبٌ). It will be written like this: جُزْءًا *I want a piece.* (أُرِيدُ جُزْءًا)	*a piece; portion*	ء-ز-ج	جُزْءًا

| **no** | The ء belongs to the root. | *in winter* | ش-ت-و | شِتاءً |
| | It was originally و that became ء. | *in the evening* | م-س-و | مَساءً |

The rules are quite simple:

1. If there is an <u>Aleph</u> before هَمْزةٌ, you <u>don't write</u> an Aleph after هَمْزةٌ if the word is in the accusative case (مَنْصُوبٌ).

2. If there is **no** <u>Aleph</u> before هَمْزةٌ, you have to put an Aleph after it. Why? Because the هَمْزةٌ belongs to the root!

143. عَظِيمٌ and رَحِيمٌ - Same pattern, same form?

No, they are of different kind although they share a pattern.

Although both words visually follow the same pattern, they have different DNA.

- In English, both words would be **adjectives**. رَجِيمٌ means *merciful*; عَظِيمٌ means *great*.

- In Arabic, it is actually the same. Both words usually work as adjectives or attributes (نَعْتٌ or صِفةٌ). However, unlike English which knows the word type adjective, we can only say for the Arabic words that they are adjectives according to their **function** in the sentence. Regarding the word type, they are nouns (اِسْمٌ).

So far, so good. Let's see why رَجِيمٌ and عَظِيمٌ have a different morphological personality and character. For our analysis, we first try to build an **active participle** (اِسْمُ فاعِلٍ) of the root:

1. The root ر-ح-م means *to have mercy; to have compassion*. An active participle, literally meaning *somebody who has compassion*, makes sense.

2. The root ع-ظ-م means *to become grandiose*. An active participle **wouldn't** make sense.

Now, let's see where رَجِيمٌ and عَظِيمٌ would fit.

الصِّفةُ الْمُشَبَّهةِ	صِيغةُ الْمُبالَغةِ	اِسْمُ الْفاعِلِ	root
---	رَجِيمٌ	راجِم	ر-ح-م
عَظِيمٌ	---	---	ع-ظ-م

What should we make out of that?

- The صِيغةُ الْمُبالَغةِ describes that an action is done extensively or often. It indicates exaggeration or superlativeness. We could say that it is a relative of the *active participle* - see *question #86*.

Let's move on to the الصِّفَةُ الْمُشَبَّهةِ.

- An *active participle* (إِسْمُ فاعِلٍ) always points to the oc-currence/happening (الْحُدُوثُ) of an action.

- On the contrary, a صِفَةٌ مُشَبَّهةٌ (*quasi participle; similar quality*) is describing a <u>quality</u> (state, action) as natural and <u>permanent</u>! It indicates a meaning of **firmness** and **constancy**.

- *Similar quality* here means that they indicate a quality similar to the active participle. The long version of the term is *adjectives which are made like the participles* (صِفةٌ مُشَبَّهةٌ بِاسْم الْفاعِلِ وَالْمَفْعُولِ).

- Since there are roots which can't form an active participle (إِسْمُ الْفاعِلِ) but only a صِفَةٌ مُشَبَّهةٌ, we could say that a صِفَةٌ مُشَبَّهةٌ is a substitute for the non-existing active par-ticiple. Therefore, we could call them *pseudo participles* or *quasi-participles*.

- Regarding the morphology (صَرْفٌ), the صِفَةٌ مُشَبَّهةٌ be-longs to the *derived nouns* (إِسْمٌ مُشْتَقٌّ).

- The صِفَةٌ مُشَبَّهةٌ can only be built from triliteral, intran-sitive verbs (فِعْلٌ ثُلاثِيٌّ لازِمٌ). An intransitive verb cannot carry a direct object.

There is **one important rule** you should know about:

- You <u>cannot</u> build the <u>active participle</u> (إِسْمُ فاعِلٍ) of a I-verb if it has the vowel *"u"* (ضَمّةٌ) on the <u>second</u> root let-ter in the past tense. Such verbs don't form an active par-ticiple (إِسْمُ فاعِلٍ). This gap is filled by the صِفَةٌ مُشَبَّهةٌ.

  Notice: This rule also applies for some verbs which have the vowel *"i"* (كَسْرةٌ) under the second root letter.

Some examples:

	صِفةٌ مُشَبَّهةٌ	اِسْمُ الْفاعِلِ	past tense verb		root
many	كَثِيرٌ	---	to be much	كَثُرَ	ك-ث-ر
big	كَبِيرٌ	---	to be big	كَبُرَ	ك-ب-ر
small	صَغِيرٌ	---	to be small	صَغُرَ	ص-غ-ر
generous	كَرِيمٌ	---	to be generous	كَرُمَ	ك-ر-م
brave	شُجاعٌ	---	to be courageous	شَجُعَ	ش-ج-ع

How do we know which pattern we should use? We need to check the **vowel of the second root letter** – if it is "*u*" or "*i*". A few comments in advance:

- Some forms are diptotes (مَمْنُوعٌ مِن الصَّرْفِ) and don't take nunation (تَنْوِينٌ) - they are marked in black.
- If I don't mention the feminine form, you simply add ة.

A	Verbs with "*i*" (كَسْرةٌ) under the second root letter (فَعِلَ).

	صِفةٌ مُشَبَّهةٌ	past tense verb		pattern	
happy	فَرِحٌ	to be glad	فَرِحَ	فَعِلٌ	1
lame	أَعْرَجُ - عَرْجاءُ	to be lame	عَرِجَ	أَفْعَلُ - فَعْلاءُ	2
green	أَخْضَرُ - خَضْراءُ	to be green	خَضِرَ		
thirsty	عَطْشانُ - عَطْشَى	to be thirsty	عَطِشَ	فَعْلانُ - فَعْلَى	3

B	Verbs with "*u*" (ضَمّةٌ) on the second root letter (فَعُلَ).

	صِفةٌ مُشَبَّهةٌ	past tense verb		pattern	
noble	شَرِيفٌ	to be noble	شَرُفَ	فَعِيلٌ	1
clean	نَظِيفٌ	to be clean	نَظُفَ		
difficult	صَعْبٌ	to be hard	صَعُبَ	فَعْلٌ	2
easy	سَهْلٌ	to be easy	سَهُلَ		
brave	شُجاعٌ	to be brave	شَجُعَ	فُعالٌ	3
coward(ly)	جَبانٌ	to be a coward	جَبُنَ	فَعالٌ	4
brave	بَطَلٌ	to be brave	بَطُلَ	فَعَلٌ	5
beautiful	حَسَنٌ	to be fine	حَسُنَ		
hard; solid	صُلْبٌ	to be firm	صَلُبَ	فُعْلٌ	6
sweet	حُلْوٌ	to be sweet	حَلُوَ		

144. Is there a mistake? - رَأَيْتُ السَّيّارَةَ الْجَمِيلَ لَوْنُها...

No, there isn't!

If you thought that الْجَمِيلُ should be written with ة, you might have misunderstood the meaning of the sentence.

I saw the car **whose color is beautiful**.	رَأَيْتُ السَّيّارَةَ الْجَمِيلَ لَوْنُها.

I saw the car with the **beautiful color**.	
The sentence does not mean: I saw the **beautiful car**.	

That's confusing because the adjective – often an active participle – structurally qualifies the preceding noun but logically qualifies a following noun!

The second part of the sentence is a so-called *causative description* or *semantically linked adjective* (نَعْتٌ سَبَبِيٌّ), referring to the pronoun which always links the second noun to the first. I prefer the term *connected description*.

		second part		head	
ها		لَوْنُ	الْجَمِيلَ	السَّيَّارَةَ	رَأَيْتُ
binder or connector (سَبَبٌ) which links the second part to the first word. It is a referring pronoun.	This is the word to which the adjective relates in meaning.		*the connected* (مُسَبَّبٌ)	The main word which we want to describe.	
	Both together function as an adjective (صِفَةٌ) for *car*. Grammarians call it a qualificative clause.			direct object (مَفْعُولٌ بِهِ)	verb + subject

In such constructions, the **adjective** is also called the *connected* (مُسَبَّبٌ) and belongs to the **following** noun. To make the construction work, we need a **binder** or **connector** (سَبَبٌ) which is usually a **referring pronoun**. The adjective plus the word after it both together form an adjective/attribute for the word earlier in the sentence. Let's do the إِعْرابٌ:

Adjective/attribute for *car*; it follows *car* regarding the case (نَعْتٌ لِسَيّارة تابِعٌ لَها فِي النَّصْبِ).	الْجَمِيلَ

Subject (فاعِلٌ) of the quasi participle (صِفةٌ مُشَبَّهةٌ)! Such forms have similar powers like a verb which explains why we have a "verbal" subject here. Since it is the subject, it gets the nominative case (مَرْفُوعٌ). First part of the إضافةٌ.	لَوْنُ
Second part of the إضافةٌ; virtually in the genitive case.	ها

This construction is really confusing, which is why we should look at it calmly.

نَعْتٌ حَقِيقِيٌّ	the successful student	الطَّالِبُ النَّاجِحُ
نَعْتٌ سَبَبِيٌّ	the student whose sister is successful	الطَّالِبُ النَّاجِحَةُ أُخْتُهُ

What are the different parts of the نَعْتٌ سَبَبِيٌّ?

نَعْتٌ مُؤَنَّثٌ	Although it is a نَعْتٌ, it doesn't describe the word before but after it! The word *sister* (أُخْت) is the logical target of the adjective because it is not the (male) *student*, who is successful.	النَّاجِحَةُ
فاعِلٌ	subject; the thing which is described (مَنْعُوتٌ).	أُخْتُهُ

Don't get confused! The above sentence does not start with a verb. Therefore, the main, primary sentence is a nominal sentence (جُمْلةٌ اِسْمِيّةٌ). The word الطَّالِبُ is the subject (مُبْتَدَأٌ) as the مُبْتَدَأٌ has to be placed at the beginning of a sentence.

Now, what about أُخْتُهُ? Why do we say that it is the الْفاعِلُ? Well, grammarians regard it as the الْفاعِلُ. That might sound strange. But it is a tricky construction (two sentences combined). The word النَّاجِحَةُ is an active participle (اِسْم فاعِلٍ) which does the job of a verb here (تَعْمَلُ عَمَلَ فِعْلِها).

Still difficult? Let's rewrite the sentence and use a relative clause (اِسْمُ إِشارةٍ).	الطَّالِبُ الَّذِي نَجَحَتْ أُخْتُهُ.

Let's stop for a moment and repeat the main points:

- In Arabic, the "adjective" must follow the noun. In this construction it is the opposite. The adjective (الْمُسَبَّبُ) belongs to the <u>following</u> noun. So the adjective isn't for the person/thing which we primarily want to describe – but for someone/something that is related to it.

- The noun after the adjective needs a *connector; binder*, also called *semantic link* (السَّبَبُ). This is almost always a referring pronoun to mark the relation with the word earlier in the sentence.

- The two together (*the connected* and *the word after the adjective*) form the description (نَعْتٌ) for the preceding noun (مَنْعُوتٌ), with which the adjective agrees in case only by attraction.

In practice, you need to check 5 steps:

1. The نَعْتٌ سَبَبِيٌّ is <u>always</u> **singular**.

2. It is placed **before** the word to which it logically (and in meaning) refers.

3. It agrees with this <u>preceding</u> noun in **determination** (definite/indefinite) and **case** (إِعْرابٌ).

4. It agrees with the <u>following</u> noun in **gender** (masculine/feminine). Furthermore, it is the regent (عامِلٌ) of the following noun which means that the adjective works like a verb. So, the following noun is always the **subject** (فاعِلٌ) of the adjective (which does the job of a verb) – and has to be in the **nominative case** (مَرْفُوعٌ).

5. The noun after the adjective needs a suitable **pronoun** which refers to the head (main word) in the sentence!

A few example sentences will help to better understand and practice the construction.

The man whose brother is honorable came.	جاءَ الرَّجُلُ الْفاضِلُ أَخُوهُ.
The man whose two brothers are honorable came.	جاءَ الرَّجُلُ الْفاضِلُ أَخَواهُ.
Two men whose two brothers are honorable came.	جاءَ رَجُلانِ فاضِلٌ أَخَواهُما.
The two men whose sisters are honorable came.	جاءَ الرَّجُلانِ الْفاضِلَةُ أَخَواتُهُما.
Ladies whose sisters are honorable came.	جاءَتْ سَيِّداتٌ فاضِلَةٌ أَخَواتُهُنَّ.

Now that we have analyzed the complicated construction, we can compare it to a normal adjective.

1	I passed by a handsome man.	مَرَرْتُ بِرَجُلٍ حَسَنٍ.
	Standard adjective (نَعْتٌ حَقِيقِيٌّ). حَسَنٍ agrees in gender, number, case, and determination (definiteness) with its **head** (رَجُلٍ).	

2	I passed by a man with a beautiful mother (lit.: I passed by a man beautiful his mother.)	مَرَرْتُ بِرَجُلٍ حَسَنةٍ أُمُّهُ.
	The adjective حَسَنةٍ agrees only in **case** (مَجْرُورٌ) and **determination** (indefinite) with its <u>grammatical</u> **head** (رَجُلٍ). However, it agrees in **gender** (feminine) with its <u>logical</u> **head** (أُمُّهُ).	

Here, the adjective (نَعْت) has a dual function:

- <u>Syntactically</u> (regarding the grammatical arrangement), it is an attribute of *man* (رَجُل).
- <u>Semantically</u> (logically; in meaning), it is a predicate of *mother* (أُمّ).
- The <u>connection</u> (سَبَبٌ) is expressed by a referring pronoun: هُ

Some more examples.

The students with the following names succeeded. Or: The students whose names follow (are listed below) succeeded.	الطُّلّابُ الْآتِيةُ أَسْماؤُهُمْ نَجَحُوا.

الْآتِيةُ is the نَعْتٌ and has verbal power. The word أَسْماؤُ is the subject (فاعِلٌ) and therefore in the nominative case (مَرْفُوعٌ).

If you are not sure about the meaning, rewrite the sentence and use a relative clause:	الطُّلّابُ الَّذِينَ أَتَتْ أَسْماؤُهُمْ نَجَحُوا.

This is a man whose mother is standing.	هٰذا رَجُلٌ قائِمَةٌ أُمُّهُ.

The word قائِمَةٌ is the نَعْتٌ; the word أُمّ is the subject (فاعِلٌ).

To sum it up:

- The نَعْتٌ حَقِيقِيٌّ comes <u>after the noun</u> which it describes. It follows the noun in gender (m./f.), case, determination (definite, indefinite) and number (singular/dual/plural).
- The نَعْتٌ سَبَبِيٌّ comes <u>before the word</u> which it describes. It is always singular!

→ For a detailed analysis, see *Arabic for Nerds 2, #172 and #175.*

145. What is the إِسْمُ الْفَاعِلِ of أَتَى (*to come*)?

It is آتٍ.

The I-verb يَأْتِي - أَتَى is tricky because of two things:

1. The **first** root letter (R1) which is هَمْزةٌ.

2. The **last** root letter (R3) which is ي.

So you don't have to be a clairvoyant to realize that we are dealing with a very special verb here. For the construction of the active participle (*coming*), we use the pattern فاعِلٌ.

1. Let us first deal with the هَمْزةٌ. The rule is: ء + ا equals آ

2. Now, let's turn to ى. The rules for weak letters apply. If the active participle is **indefinite**, we drop ى and add nunation (تَنْوِينٌ) under the second root letter – the result is آتٍ. If the active participle is **definite**, ى will turn into ي.

Finally, we get:

definite	الآتِي	*the coming*

indefinite (*ātin*)	آتٍ	*coming*

146. أَفْعَلُ - This is the comparative pattern, isn't it?

Yes and no.

The pattern أَفْعَلُ is highly versatile in Arabic and occurs in verbs and nouns. We now focus only on two patterns, used in two very common derived nouns (مُشْتَقّاتٌ):

1. The *measure of preference* (إِسْمُ التَّفْضِيلِ): comparative or superlative.

2. The *pseudo participle* (صِفةٌ مُشَبَّهةٌ): the adjective that resembles an active participle. It denotes a firm and durable
state or condition and usually indicates color, deficiency,
or ornament. See *question #143*.

Now, why does all this matter?

1. They both share the same pattern for the masculine form.
Note that أَفْعَلُ is a diptote (مَمْنُوعٌ مِن الصَّرْفِ) and does
not take nunation (تَنْوِينٌ).

2. The <u>feminine</u> form, however, is different.

Let us check both patterns in depths.

meaning	feminine pattern	feminine form	إِسْمُ التَّفْضِيلِ
bigger/biggest	فُعْلَى	كُبْرَى	أَكْبَرُ
smaller/smallest		صُغْرَى	أَصْغَرُ

meaning	feminine pattern	feminine form	الصِّفةُ الْمُشَبَّهةُ
shining	فَعْلاءُ	زَهْراءُ	أَزْهَرُ
red	Used for colors and handicaps; it	حَمْراءُ	أَحْمَرُ
blind	is also a diptote.	عَمْياءُ	أَعْمَى

147. What does the word دُنْيا mean?

دُنْيا *is translated as "world" – but that's not the literal meaning.*

دُنْيا is generally used with the definite article: الدُّنْيا. The plural of دُنْيا is دُنًى or دُنْيَياتٌ.

Students learn this word relatively quickly at the beginning. Most textbooks only mention that it means *world; earth*. If we want to translate it, that usually fits – most of the time. However, as soon as we examine the root, we will notice that it means something completely different.

Let us check the root: د-ن-و. The I-verb دَنا - يَدْنو denotes *to be close*.

If we look at the DNA of دُنْيا, we identify the pattern فُعْلَى. This is the feminine form of the pattern أَفْعَلُ which is a noun of preference (اِسْمُ تَفْضِيلٍ), the comparative or superlative (elative) form. The pattern فُعْلَى is tricky: if the last root letter is و, it gets converted into ي; and the ى becomes l.

meaning	comparative; feminine form	comparative; masculine form	root
closer; closest	دُنْيا	أَدْنَى	د-ن-و
higher; highest	عُلْيا	أَعْلَى	ع-ل-ى
further; furthest	قُصْوَى	أَقْصَى	ق-ص-و

Notice the feminine form in the last example! It's an exception that became the norm. According to the rule it should be قُصْيا.

The literal meaning of الدُّنْيا is *the lowest; the closest; the nearest* – but definitely not: *the world*. So, how on earth do we translate it as *world*?

In ancient times, people used the term الْحَياةُ الدُّنْيا (*the closest, nearest life*) to describe the present life (الْحَياةُ الْحاضِرَةُ). Eventually, الْحَياةُ was deleted and all that remained was الدُّنْيا.

The expression الدُّنْيا is already found in the Qur'an.

| ...there is a reward in this **present world** for those who do good, but their home in the Hereafter is far better:... (Sura 16:30) | ... لِلَّذِينَ أَحْسَنُوا فِي هَذِهِ الدُّنْيَا حَسَنَةٌ وَلَدَارُ الْآخِرَةِ خَيْرٌ... |

- The same can be said about *afterlife/hereafter*. The expression الْحَيَاةُ الْأُخْرَى denotes *the other life* (which we don't know). Eventually, الْحَيَاةُ was dropped and we got الْأُخْرَى. Another expression for *afterlife* is الْآخِرَة.

- The most famous mosque in Jerusalem, which is also one of the most important in Islam, is called *al-Aqsa-Mosque*. It is called الْأَقْصَى as in ancient times it was the mosque that was the most remote from Mecca (الْمَسْجِدُ الْأَقْصَى). The word الْأَقْصَى literally means *the farthest*.

| I said, "O Allah's Messenger! Which mosque was built first?" He replied, "Al-Masjid-u-l-Haram." I asked, "Which (was built) next?" He replied, "Al-Masjidu-l-Aqsa." (Hadith Sahīh al-Bukhārī 3425) | قُلْتُ: يَا رَسُولَ اللَّهِ أَيُّ مَسْجِدٍ وُضِعَ أَوَّلُ؟ قَالَ: الْمَسْجِدُ الْحَرَامُ. قُلْتُ: ثُمَّ أَيُّ؟ قَالَ: ثُمَّ الْمَسْجِدُ الْأَقْصَى. |

148. How do you mark the مَجْرُورٌ - case in the word الدُّنْيَا؟

Just do nothing.

The Aleph at the end of الدُّنْيَا (*the world* or *the nearest/closest*) doesn't change in any case. It always remains an Aleph.

الدُّنْيَا is a *noun with shortened ending* (إِسْمٌ مَقْصُورٌ), *see question #13*. These are special nouns that like to cause trouble – but not when it comes to case endings.

As a noun, it may get any of the three cases: the nominative (مَرْفُوعٌ), genitive (مَجْرُورٌ), or accusative (مَنْصُوبٌ) case. However, you can't see that optically. Case markers are always hidden. We can only use **virtual, presumptive markers** (مُقَدَّرَة). When you see such a word, keep these two things in mind:

1. The case marker it is not pronounced.

2. The word looks the same in any case.

An example.

king of the world	مَلِكُ الدُّنْيَا

الدُّنْيَا is the second part of a إِضافةٌ and has to be in the genitive case. However, we can't visibly mark it as such and can only apply virtual markers in the sense of a place value (فِي مَحَلِّ رجَرٍّ).

149. Why is عُلْيَا written with an Aleph but كُبْرَى not?

This is related to the last root letter, which has a different nature.

عُلْيَا means *higher* and كُبْرَى *larger/greater*. Both words are a *noun of preference* (اِسْمُ تَفْضِيلٍ), to be precise, a comparative/superlative in the **feminine** form (مُؤَنَّثٌ). The pattern is فُعْلَى. The masculine form would follow the pattern أَفْعَلُ.

But that's not the end of the common ground. They are also both *nouns with shortened endings* (اِسْمٌ مَقْصُورٌ). The last letter is pronounced as a long *ā*-vowel (see #13). Nevertheless, the **spelling** is different.

It has to do with the last <u>root</u> letter.

إِسْمُ التَّفْضِيلِ (f.)	root	explanation
دُنْيا	د-ن-و	The last root letter is **weak.** → You have to write an Aleph at the end. Why do we write ي before Aleph? This is related to the phonetic nature of the pattern فُعْلَى! The final root letter و is converted into ي because if you simply apply the pattern without conversion, we would get the hard to pronounce دُنْوَى. Thus, we opt for دُنْيا.
كُبْرَى	ك-ب-ر	The last root letter is ر (**not** weak). → You have to write ى, pronounced as long *ā*.

150. How do you express *still* in Arabic?

Unfortunately, there is no simple word for still.

The English adverb *still* is a very flexible word that can express many ideas. In this *question*, we will analyze how to express that something is **continuing to happen** now.

In Arabic, this cannot be achieved by a simple word. You can express this idea of *still* by a **negated verb**, which is the most common, elegant, and convenient solution. But which verbs are suitable for this job? Answer: *Sisters of* كانَ (كانَ وَأَخَواتُها). They follow the rules of كانَ. A quick reminder:

كانَ الْجَوُّ جَمِيلًا.	The weather was nice.
Weather is the "subject" (إِسْمُ كانَ); it is nominative (مَرْفُوعٌ). *Nice* is the predicate (خَبَرُ كانَ) and takes the accusative case (مَنْصُوبٌ).	

The striking thing about the verbs which we are going to examine is the **tense.** You can use them in the present or past
tense – the **meaning in Arabic is the same.**

Still, there are a few subtleties to consider here:

- The <u>present</u> tense (الْمُضارِعُ) is negated with لا.

- If you want to express the <u>future</u>, you negate the present
  tense with لَنْ and use the subjunctive mood (مَنْصُوبٌ) of
  the verb. → You use the vowel "*a*" (فَتْحةٌ) on the final letter.

- The <u>past</u> tense (الْماضِي) is negated with لَمْ or ما. After ما,
  you simply use a verb in the past tense. After لَمْ, you need
  the jussive mood (مَجْزُومٌ) which means that you use the
  present tense and put سُكُونْ on the final letter.

Notice that you can place a verb (فِعْلٌ) or a noun (اِسْمٌ) directly after the following expressions:

still; yet	ما زالَ • لا يَزالُ
If you don't negate the I-verb زالَ - يَزالُ (R2=و), it means *to come to an end; to vanish; to abandon.*	

He is still sick.	ما زالَ مَريضًا.
She is still sitting.	لا تَزالُ جالِسةً.
He still needs it.	لا يَزالُ فِي حاجةٍ إِلَيْهِ.
Zayd is still a student.	ما زالَ زَيْدٌ طالِبًا.
He's still as crazy as ever!	ما زالَ مَجْنُونًا كَما كانَ!
He was still in Damascus.	كانَ لا يَزالُ (باقِيًا) فِي دَمَشْقَ.
Do you want anything else?	أَما زِلْتَ تُرِيدُ شَيْئًا؟

not stop doing; keep doing	ما اِنْفَكَّ • لَمْ يَنْفَكَّ • لا يَنْفَكُّ

It is a VII-verb following the pattern اِنْفَعَلَ (يَنْفَعِلُ). If it is not negated, it denotes *to be separated; be disconnected; be undone*. The I-verb فَكَّ - يَفُكُّ denotes *to separate; disconnect; to take apart*.

The man is still writing.	ما اِنْفَكَّ الرَّجُلُ كاتِبًا.

not to cease to be	ما فَتِئَ • لَمْ يَفْتَأْ • لا يَفْتَأُ

Without negation, the I-verb فَتِئَ - يَفْتَأُ (R3=ء) means *to desist, to refrain*, or *to stop*.

He is still doing...	ما فَتِئَ يَفْعَلُ...
He is still thinking about her.	ما فَتِئَ يَذْكُرُها.
He always will be.	لَنْ يَفْتَأَ.
Khalid is always trying to travel.	مَا فَتِئَ خالِدٌ يُحَاوِلُ السَّفَرَ.
He is still a prisoner.	لَمْ يَفْتَأْ أَسِيرًا.

to continue to be	ما بَرِحَ • لَم يَبْرَحْ • لا يَبْرَحُ

Not negated, the I-verb بَرِحَ - يَبْرَحُ means *to leave; to depart*.

He is still rich.	ما بَرِحَ غَنِيًّا.
They are still in Egypt.	ما بَرِحُوا في مِصْرَ.
He is still speaking.	ما بَرِحَ يَقُولُ.

151. How do you say *yet* and *not yet* in Arabic?

This is more sophisticated in Arabic than in English.

Even in English, the expressions *yet* and *not yet* are tricky. We use *yet* usually in **questions** and **negatives** when we talk about things which are expected but which have not happened. *Yes* is related to *still* – yet, there is a difference: If you use *still* in a negated sentence, you suggest that the situation should have changed, but it has not. For example:

- *I haven't finished **yet**.* → yet is put **after** the main **verb.**

- *I **still** haven't finished.* Meaning: I've been working on it for quite some time and should have finished it by now. → still is placed **after** the **subject.**

Let's see how these little related words work in Arabic. We will check *still; yet; not yet; not any more.*

1	*yet (still); in spite of it*	مَعَ أَنَّ • مَعَ ذلِكَ

He is still your brother!	مَعَ ذلِكَ كُلُّهُ فَهُوَ أَخُوكَ!
She forbade it, but he did it anyway.	فَعَلَ ذلِكَ مَعَ أَنَّها قَدْ مَنَعَتْهُ مِنْهُ.

2	*not yet*	حَتَّى الآنَ

He has not written yet.	لَمْ يَكْتُبْ حَتَّى الآنَ.

3.1	*not yet; not any more*	negated verb plus بَعْدُ

- In this function, بَعْدُ has a special shape (مَبْنِيٌّ عَلَى الضَّمِّ).
  How come? You have to write بَعْدُ with final "u" if it is cut
  off from a إضافةٌ, i.e., if no other word follows it. There's
  a clever idea behind it. Although the second part of the
  إضافةٌ is missing, the meaning is still understood; we can
  say that it is cut off from the إضافةٌ by pronunciation, but
  not by meaning. Where should بَعْدُ be put? In verbal sentences it sounds most natural to put it at the end of a sentence (and not between the verb and the direct object).

- **Watch out:** It is possible to use بَعْدُ without a negation
  which often changes the meaning to *still*.

- **Notice the difference:** بَعْدَ with "a" (فَتْحةٌ) means *after*
  and serves as the **first** part of a إضافةٌ. *See #221.* بَعْدُ with
  "u" (ضَمّةٌ) is not followed by a word and may even be
  preceded by a preposition. Since the shape of بَعْدُ is cemented, the preposition does not influence بَعْدُ visually.

not yet	لَيْسَ بَعْدُ
He has not written the letter yet.	لَمْ يَكْتُبْ بَعْدُ الْجَوابَ.
	ما كَتَبَ الْجَوابَ بَعْدُ.

Notice: It is usually better to put بَعْدُ at the end of the sentence. But
to place it immediately after the verb would also be correct.

He had not written the letter yet.	لَمْ يَكُنْ قَدْ كَتَبَ بَعْدُ الْجَوابَ.
	ما كانَ قَدْ كَتَبَ بَعْدُ الْجَوابَ.
He won't have written the letter yet.	كانَ لَنْ يَكْتُبَ بَعْدُ الْجَوابَ.
	كانَ سَوْفَ لا يَكْتُبُ بَعْدُ الْجَوابَ.
Nobody else came then (after).	لَمْ يَأْتِ أَحَدٌ بَعْدُ.

| She doesn't write anymore. | هِيَ لا تَكْتُبُ بَعْدُ. |

Watch out: A negation particle may change the meaning.

not yet; not longer; not any more	لَيْسَ بَعْدُ
She is still young. (She is only a small girl.) Notice that we don't use the negation.	هِيَ بَعْدُ صَغِيرَةٌ.
He is yet to come.	سَيَأْتِي بَعْدُ.
He has not come yet.	لَمْ يَأْتِ بَعْدُ.

| 3.2 | *never* | مِنْ قَبْلُ |

| I have never seen her. | لَمْ أَرَاها مِنْ قَبْلُ |
| | لَمْ أَرَاها قَطُّ. |

| 4 | *not yet* | particle لَمَّا plus verb in the jussive mood (مَجْزُومٌ) |

Here, لَمَّا is a particle of negation which induces the jussive mood in a following verb (حَرْفُ نَفْيٍ وَجَزْمٍ لِلْمُضارِعِ). Watch out: It is possible to **delete** the verb → and the meaning is still understood.

He has not written the letter yet.	لَمَّا يَكْتُبْ الْجَوابَ.
The train hasn't arrived yet.	لَمَّا يَأْتِ الْقِطارُ.
I came close to the city yet. Notice: We have deleted the verb here!	قارَبْتُ الْمَدِينةَ وَلَمَّا.

I came close to the city (but) haven't arrived yet.	قَارَبْتُ الْمَدِينَةَ وَلَمَّا أَصِلْ إِلَيْهَا.

5	*not any more*	negation (مَا - لَمْ - لَا) plus عَادَ / يَعُودُ plus verb in the present tense.

The director did not go to the office any more.	لَمْ يَعُدْ الْمُدِيرُ يَذْهَبُ إِلَى الْمَكْتَبِ.
	مَا عَادَ الْمُدِيرُ يَذْهَبُ إِلَى الْمَكْتَبِ.
The director doesn't go to the office any more.	لَا يَعُودُ الْمُدِيرُ يَذْهَبُ إِلَى الْمَكْتَبِ.

The director did not go to the office any more.	لَمْ يَعُدْ الْمُدِيرُ يَذْهَبُ إِلَى الْمَكْتَبِ.
	مَا عَادَ الْمُدِيرُ يَذْهَبُ إِلَى الْمَكْتَبِ.
The director doesn't go to the office any more.	لَا يَعُودُ الْمُدِيرُ يَذْهَبُ إِلَى الْمَكْتَبِ.

152. Does the Egyptian word لِسَّه mean *still* or *yet*?

It can mean both depending on the situation.

When I started learning Egyptian Arabic, there was one word which really gave me a headache: *lissa* (لِسَّه), sometimes also written لِسَّى or لِسّة. Let's see why.

- *Lissa means **not yet** in negated sentence. This is also true when *lissa* is used as a stand-alone expression.

- In non-negated sentences (affirmative), *lissa* usually denotes **still** or **just**.

1 *Just* versus *not yet.*

This can be quite confusing for beginners.

| 1.1 | *Lissa* in the meaning of *just* or *only recently.* |

lissa is frequently used in combination with an **active partici-ple** (اِسْمُ فاعِلٍ) to denote a past tense meaning (in the sense of *just*): اِسْمُ فاعِلٍ plus لِسَّه.

I have just arrived.	لِسَّه واصِل.
They just came.	لِسَّه جايِّين.
He was standing next to me just a second ago.	ده لِسَّه واقِف جَنْبِي مِن ثانْية.

| 1.2 | The meaning of *not yet.* |

Note: If you want to express *not yet*, you should use the **past tense** (الْماضِي) combined with a negation (ما+ش).

I haven't arrived yet.	ما وَصَلْتش لِسَّه.
They haven't come yet.	لِسَّه ماجُوش.
It is not yet a month since he has left.	سافِر لِسَّه مافِيش شَهْر.

2 The meaning of *still.*

| 2.1 | There is **no verb** (action) involved. |

How do we use *lissa* if there is no action (= no verb) men-tioned in the sentence, but an **adjective** or **adverb of time**?

It is still early.	لِسَّه بَدْرِي.
There is still time.	لِسَّه فيه وَقْت.
There is still one week (to go);	لِسَّه أُسْبُوع.
He's still young.	هُوَّ لِسَّه صُغَيَّر.
It's still to soon for...	لِسَّه بَدْرِي عَلَى...
She is still young.	هِيَ لِسَّه صُغَيَّرة.
Still three dollars (to go; owing).	لِسَّه ثلاثة دولار.

| 2.2 | There is a **verb** involved. |

Which **verb** form and tense do you use if you want to express
still? You use the **present tense** (فِعْلٌ مُضارِعٌ+ب) if the action
happens right now or the future if the action is yet to happen.
You should not use the active participle (اِسْمُ فاعِلٍ) because
this would express *just* – see number 1.

I am still eating.	لِسَّه بآكُل.
I am still studying at the center.	لِسَّه بادْرِس في الْمَرْكَز.
I've still to deliver the menu (food).	لِسَّه حاوَدِّي الْوَجْبة.
I've still to read the magazine.	لِسَّه هأقْرَأ الْمَجَلّة.

| 3 | *Just* in the meaning of *just **now**; only recently.* |

lissa is often used with the Egyptian Arabic expression for
now, i.e., *dilwa'ti* (دِلْوَقْتِي).

They just now left.	لِسَّه طِلْعوا دِلْوَقْتِي.
She was standing next to me just a sec-ond ago.	دي لِسَّه كانِت واقِفة جنبي من ثانية.
The lady who had just come from the doctor...	السِتّ اللّي كانِت لِسَّه جايّة مِن عَنْد الدُّكْتُور...

4   *Lissa* as a stand-alone word

| 4.1 | *Lissa* conveys the meaning of: *Have... yet?* |

Oftentimes, *lissa* is used in **yes-or-no-questions**.

| Question: Have you written it? | كِتِبْتُه وَلا لِسَّه؟ |
| Answer: Not yet. | لِسَّه. |

Haven't you gone yet?	إنتَ لِسَّه مارُحْتِش؟
Has he come yet or not?	جاء ولّا لِسَّه؟
Have you seen the student? - Not yet.	شُفْت الطَّالِب؟ - لِسَّه.

| 4.2 | *Lissa* is directly connected to a sentence. |

| She put up with a lot, and there's more to come. | إسْتَحْمِلِتْ كْتِير، وَلِسَّه. |

153. مَتْحَفٌ or مُتْحَفٌ - **What is the Arabic word for *museum*?**

In Standard Arabic, it is مُتْحَفٌ *("mut-haf").*

Many native Arabic speakers call a *museum* مَتْحَفٌ, pronounced with the vowel *"a"* (فَتْحةٌ) on the first letter. Although there is only a tiny difference, it is strictly speaking wrong although the *Academy of the Arabic Language* in Cairo has approved it in the meantime.

Let's analyze it. مُتْحَفٌ is based on the Arabic root ت-ح-ف which denotes *to present; to show*. However, this root is only used as a IV-verb following the pattern أَفْعَلَ.

If we want to build the *noun of place* (إِسْمُ مَكانٍ) of this action (= the place where something is being displayed), we need to be careful.

meaning	إِسْمُ الْمَكانِ	verb	pattern
museum	مُتْحَفٌ	to present أَتْحَفَ	أَفْعَلَ

The word is pronounced with *"u"* (ضَمّةٌ) at the beginning. So why to people say مَتْحَف then?

مَتْحَفٌ would be the إِسْمُ الْمَكانِ of a I-verb (ثُلاثِيٌّ مُجَرَّدٌ). But this stem is not used. The I-verb تَحَفَ doesn't exist.

From this we can distill an important rule:

- To build the إِسْمُ الْمَكانِ of the stems II to X, you use the **same pattern** as for the **passive participle** (إِسْمُ مَفْعُولٍ).

Let's take the word مُنْبَعَثٌ. Depending on the context, it can mean *source* (إِسْمُ الْمَكانِ) or *sent* (إِسْمُ الْمَفْعُولِ). Some other examples:

stem	verb	meaning	إِسْمُ الْمَكانِ	meaning
II	صَلَّى	to pray	مُصَلَّى	place of prayer
IV	أَتْحَفَ	to present	مُتْحَفٌ	museum
VII	إِنْبَعَثَ	to originate	مُنْبَعَثٌ	place of origin
VIII	إِجْتَمَعَ	to gather together	مُجْتَمَعٌ	gathering place
X	إِسْتَشْفَى	to seek a cure	مُسْتَشْفَى	hospital

154. مُبْتَدَأٌ - Why do we use this grammar term for subject?

It is the key figure in a sentence. The term describes what a subject, in fact, is: that with which a beginning is made (الْمُبْتَدَأُ بِهِ).

In grammar, we call the subject of a nominal sentence (جُمْلةٌ اِسْمِيّةٌ) the مُبْتَدَأٌ. But have you ever thought about what مُبْتَدَأٌ actually means?

The root of مُبْتَدَأٌ is ب-د-ء. Let's try to form the VIII-verb by using the pattern اِفْتَعَلَ. Now, we get the verb يَبْتَدِئُ - اِبْتَدَأَ which denotes *to begin; to start; to bring out something*. Now we are ready to determine the nature of مُبْتَدَأٌ.

We have two options:

1. The *passive participle* (اِسْمُ الْمَفْعُولِ) of the verb اِبْتَدَأَ → the meaning would be *begun*.

2. The *noun of place* (اِسْمُ الْمَكانِ) → then it would mean: *the place where it* (the sentence) *begins*.

How can this be? Well, the إِسْمُ الْمَكانِ and إِسْمُ الْمَفْعُولِ of a VIII-verb share the same pattern (see *question #172*).

From all this we can deduce the following: If we use the term *subject of a nominal sentence*, we basically mean the first word. **What are the main features of the مُبْتَدَأ in Arabic?**

- A verb and a prepositional/adverbial phrase (شِبْهُ الْجُمْلةِ) <u>cannot</u> work as the مُبْتَدَأ.

- If a nominal sentence starts with a preposition or an adverb, then it is the **predicate** – more precisely, the *fronted predicate* (خَبَرٌ مُقَدَّمٌ). You reverse the word-order if you want to emphasize a certain part of the sentence.

Since we have just mentioned the predicate (خَبَرٌ) of a nominal sentence, we should take the opportunity to quickly look at its features. It may consist of:

- a single noun;

- a verbal or nominal sentence;

- a prepositional or adverbial phrase (شِبْهُ الْجُمْلةِ);

Now that we have broken down the nominal sentence into its component parts, it is still advisable to look at how it differs from a verbal sentence.

1	ذَهَبَ مُحَمَّدٌ إِلَى الْمَدِينةِ.	verbal sentence (جُمْلةٌ فِعْلِيّةٌ)
2	مُحَمَّدٌ ذَهَبَ إِلَى الْمَدِينةِ.	nominal sentence (جُمْلةٌ إِسْمِيّةٌ)

Both sentences more or less mean the same: *Muhammad went to the city*. However, if we look at them from a grammatical perspective, there is a big difference. Let's see why.

- In the <u>first sentence</u>, مُحَمَّدٌ is the subject of a **verbal** sentence (فَاعِلٌ). If we only used the first word of this sentence, it would be enough to form a meaningful sentence, even without *Muhammad*. Simply put, the expression ذَهَبَ is already a complete sentence: *he went*. There is a hidden, implied pronoun in ذَهَبَ which stands for *he*. This hidden pronoun is the subject (فَاعِلٌ) of the verb.

- In the <u>second sentence</u>, مُحَمَّدٌ is the subject of a **nominal** sentence (مُبْتَدَأ). If we only used the first word (Muhammad), it wouldn't be enough to form a sentence.

The subject of a nominal sentence needs a **predicate**. The predicate completes the meaning.

Now, what is the function of the verb in a nominal sentence? It is the predicate! We will have a full sentence serving as the predicate: *Muhammad, he went to the city.*

	element 2		**element 1**
First sentence:	ذَهَبَ إِلَى الْمَدِينةِ.		مُحَمَّدٌ
Element 1 plus 2: *Muhammad went to the city.*	The predicate (خَبَرٌ) is a full verbal sentence!	+	subject (مُبْتَدَأ)
Second sentence: Only element 2: *He went to the city.*	If we dropped the word *Muhammad*, we would still have a full sentence.		

Note: If you want to know how nominal and verbal sentences differ in meaning, see *Arabic for Nerds 2, question #208ff.*

155. Can you use the letter ل to emphasize a word in Arabic?

Yes, you can.

In Arabic, *emphasis* (تَأْكِيدٌ or تَوْكِيدٌ) is a huge playground for language lovers.

You can use additional words, change the word-order – or use the letter *Lām* (ل). We limit ourselves here to looking at how we can use ل as an amplifier. Note that if we use ل to convey emphasis, it has the vowel "*a*" on top (لَ).

1	The *Lām of introduction*	لامُ الْإِبْتِداءِ

إِبْتِداءٌ means *beginning*. This type of ل is <u>never</u> combined with a **verb**! Notice that it does not influence any word regarding cases.

Such ل is placed...

   a) before the <u>subject</u> of a nominal sentence (مُبْتَدَأٌ) or

   b) before the <u>fronted predicate</u> (خَبَرٌ مُقَدَّمٌ);

You are (truly, indeed) a faithful friend.	لَأَنْتَ صَدِيقٌ وَفِيٌّ.	a)
(Indeed,) Zayd is courageous.	لَزَيْدٌ شُجاعٌ.	
You are great. (Indeed great you are.)	لَعَظِيمٌ أَنْتَ.	b)

2	*What a wonderful... What a bad...!*	نِعْمَ • بِئْسَ

Both expressions can be used with ل in order to boost the emphasis. See *question #183* for more details.

The best thing a person can do is to seek knowledge.	لَنِعْمَ ما يَفْعَلُهُ الْإِنْسانُ طَلَبُ الْعِلْمِ.

| The worst character is lying. | لَبِئْسَ خُلُقًا الْكَذِبُ. |

| 3 | ل plus **far future** with سَوْفَ | لَسَوْفَ |

| I will (definitely) attend the party. | لَسَوْفَ أَحْضُرُ الْحَفْلَ. |

| 4 | The *Lām of the answer* (حَرْفُ جَوابٍ). This type of ل is used in the 2nd part of an **if-clause** with لَوْ or لَوْلا. | لامُ الْواقِعِ |

If he studied, he would succeed.	لَوْ دَرَسَ لَنَجَحَ.
If it weren't for the doctor, the situation of the patient would become bad.	لَوْلا الطَّبِيبُ لَساءَتْ حالةَ الْمَرِيضِ.
Were it not for you, I would have been lost.	لَوْلاكَ لَضَلَلْتُ.

| 5 | ل before the **predicate** of إنَّ | خَبَرُ إنَّ |

| Zayd is indeed generous. | إنَّ زَيْدًا لَكَرِيمٌ. |
| The satisfaction of people is difficult indeed. | إنَّ رِضا النّاسِ لَصَعْبٌ. |

| 6 | ل before the **delayed "subject"** of إنَّ (اِسْمُ إنَّ). We call this type of *Lām* also the slipping or wandering *Lām* (لامٌ مُزَحْلَقة). For an in-depth analysis, *see Arabic for Nerds 2, question #260.* | |

| There is (indeed) benefit in traveling. | إنَّ فِي السَّفَرِ لَمَنافِعَ. |
| Indeed, in history there are many | إنَّ فِي التّارِيخِ لَعِبَرًا. |

lessons.	

7	ل before قَدْ →to express *already* or the past perfect

Zayd is already gone.	لَقَدْ ذَهَبَ زَيْدٌ.

→ For other ways to convey emphasis, see *questions #155, 157, 159.*

156. Can you use an extra ن to give emphasis?

Yes, you can.

Nūn (ن), when added to a conjugated verb, has enough power to function as an amplifier and convey emphasis. We call it *a Nūn of confirmation* (نُونُ التَّوْكِيدِ) *or energetic Nun*. The idea of adding a *Nūn* to the verb is to show the speaker's determination to carry out the action without hesitation. Note that the *Nūn of confirmation* may be left untranslated.

Such ن can appear in a "light" or "strong" version. It is used with the **present tense** (الْمُضارِعُ) and the **imperative** (الْأَمْرُ) – but you <u>can't</u> use it with a past tense verb (الْماضِي). Let's see how it works – an instruction manual:

1. Delete the ضَمّة on the verb (marker of the indicative mood) or delete the final ن if the verb form belongs to the so-called *five verbs* (أَفْعالٌ خَمْسةٌ) → see question #83.

2. Put the vowel "a" (فَتْحةٌ) on the last letter. We cement the construction with this vowel (مَبْنِيٌّ عَلَى الْفَتْحِ).

3. Finally, add ـَنَّ for the heavy *Nūn* or ـَنْ for the light *Nūn*.

   Note: For the imperative, you do exactly the same.

| A | The *light Nūn of confirmation* is formed by adding **نْ** with **سُكُونٌ** to the verb. | نُونٌ خَفِيفَةٌ |

| Obey your parents! Note: This is the imperative of the IV-verb يُطِيعُ - أَطاعَ (R2=و). | أَطِعَنْ والِدَّيْكَ! |
| Will you go certainly? | هَلْ تَذْهَبَنْ؟ |

| B | The *strong* or *heavy Nūn of confirmation* is more common and its confirmation is bolder. | نُونٌ ثَقِيلَةٌ |

| Do you (certainly) help your friend? | هَلْ تُساعِدَنَّ زَمِيلَكَ؟ |

Let's now turn to the *heavy Nūn* and see it in action.

| 1. | **نَّ** - used to express a **demand** or **inquiry** | مُضارِعٌ جائِزٌ |

| 1.1 | Used with the imperative | أَمْرٌ |

| In this application, you have to use the *Lām of request* (لامُ الطَّلَبِ), which is **لِ**, before the imperative. See *question #126*. |

| Beware of overeating! | لِتَحْذَرَنَّ الإِفْراطِ فِي الطَّعامِ! |
| Oh our people, be cautious! | يا قَوْمَنا إحْذَرَنَّ! |

| 1.2 | Used to express warnings or prohibitions | نَهْيٌ |

| Don't think that success in life is easy! | لاَ تَحْسَبَنَّ النَّجاحَ فِي الْحَياةِ سَهْلًا! |

1.3	Used with questions to express a request	إِسْتِفْهامٌ

Could you help your colleague?	هَلْ تُساعِدَنَّ زَمِيلَكَ؟

1.4	Used to give advice/offer	عَرْضٌ

Shouldn't you certainly help your colleague!	أَلا تُساعِدَنَّ زَمِيلَكَ!

1.5	Used to goad somebody	تَحْضِيضٌ

Would you stop lying!	هَلَّا تَتْرُكَنَّ الْكَذِبَ!

1.6	Used to express a wish, hope, or desire	تَمَنٍّ

I wish that you would do good deeds!	لَيْتَكَ تَعْمَلَنَّ طَيِّبًا!

2	After the **negation** with لا. → To put stress on the thing you won't do or won't accept.

I like honesty and I (certainly) won't tolerate lying.	أُحِبُّ الصِّدْقَ وَلا أَرْضَيَنَّ الْكَذِبَ.

3	After إِمّا in a conditional sentence (شَرْطِيَّةٌ)

Notice the سُكُون in the second part of the sentence as the verb has to be مَجْزُومٌ.

| If you really work hard you will certainly succeed in your life. | إِمَّا تَعْمَلَنَّ بِجِدٍّ تَنْجَحْ فِي حَيَاتِكَ. |

| 4 | After an **oath** if there is a conditional meaning involved. You need to use a combination of ل and ن in the so-called *answer* (جَوابُ الْقَسَم). |

The verb gives the details why you swear and what you prom-ise (جَوابُ قَسَم).

It is not negated and although the verb is in the present tense, it has a future meaning. Notice: After an oath you need the particle ل – see *question #205*.

I swear, I will definitely work hard!	وَاللهِ لَأَعْمَلَنَّ بِجِدٍّ!
I swear, I write a letter now!	وَاللهِ لَأَكْتُبُ رِسالَةَ الآنَ!
If there is no conditional meaning involved, you usually don't use the ن of confirmation.	

→ For an in-depth analysis of the *Nūn of confirmation*, see *Arabic for Nerds 2, question #94*.

157. What are the particles of attention?

Tools used to call someone's attention like "hey!"

Particles of attention (حَرْفُ تَنْبِيهٍ) are devices which help to clarify the matter for the listener. The word تَنْبِيهٌ means *notification; warning*. These little words are often a bit confusing that they tend to get mixed up. Let's take a closer look.

أَلَا

أَلَا literally means *is it not*. It is an **intensifying interjection** which introduces sentences. It is often found in the Qur'an.

It may be translated as *nay; verily; truly; indeed; oh yes*.

It works mainly as a *particle of inauguration* (حَرْفُ إِسْتِفْتاح). The word إِسْتِفْتاح means *beginning, opening*. However, it can also occur as a *particle of premonition* (= a strong feeling that something is about to happen, often something unpleasant).

Nay, it is with knowledge that nations advance.	أَلَا بِالْعِلْمِ تَتَقَدَّمُ الْأُمَمُ.
Unquestionably, it is Allah who is the Forgiving, the Merciful. *(Sura 42:5)*	أَلَا إِنَّ اللهَ هُوَ الْغَفُورُ الرَّحِيمُ.
O guilty one, won't you amend yourself?	أَلَا أَيُّهَا الْمُذْنِبُ كَفِّرْ عَنْكَ؟

أَما

Same meaning as أَلَا (i.e., *isn't it*) – but watch out! أَما is usually combined with an **oath** (قَسَمٌ).

Furthermore, أَما can be placed at the beginning since it is a *particle of inauguration* (حَرْفُ إِسْتِفْتاحٍ).

I swear he is truly honest!	أَما وَاللهِ إِنَّهُ لَصادِقٌ!
By God, who made you cry and made you laugh!	أَما وَاللهِ الَّذِي أَبْكَى وَأَضْحَكَ!

ها

ها basically just expresses *look here, oh!*

It an emphatic meaning and is used to express attention. It may be connected with other words, especially with pronouns and demonstratives (*this, that*).

Here I am.	هاأَنَذا حاضِرٌ.
Here	هاهُنا
and so forth (and so on)	وَهَكَذا
Hey you there!	ها أَنْتَ ذا!!
Hey you (fem.) there!	ها أَنْتِ ذي!
Here, take it! There you are! There you have!	هاكَ / هاكُم (.pl)

158. Can you use بِ and مِنْ to emphasize?

Yes, this is possible.

The prepositions بِ and مِنْ can be used to give emphasis.

In this type of application, they do not exercise their original job which is to direct or give direction. Instead, they are **extra, additional particles** (حَرْفٌ زائِدٌ). Nevertheless, they do keep their governing power which means that the word which comes after بِ or مِنْ has to be in the genitive case (مَجْرُورٌ).

The letter بِ

Traveling is not difficult at all.	لَيْسَ السَّفَرُ بِصَعْبٍ.
Knowledge is sufficient to advance.	كَفَى بِالْعِلْمِ وَسِيلةً لِلتَّقَدُّمِ.
Allah is the best protector!	كَفَى بِاللهِ وَكِيلًا!
Note: The I-verb كَفَى - يَكْفِي (R3=ي) basically means *to be enough.* However, it can also denote *to protect; to spare.* It is used <u>without</u> a	

preposition. The preposition بـ here is only there to give emphasis.

The preposition مِنْ

You have to place a singular noun (اِسْمٌ نَكِرةٌ) after it. Unlike a real preposition (حَرْفُ الْجَرِّ), the extra preposition مِنْ doesn't change the meaning dramatically. As a حَرْفٌ زائِدٌ it is just there for emphasis!

| Nobody came to me. | ما جاءَنِي مِنْ أَحَدٍ. |

→ See also *Arabic for Nerds 2, question #178.*

159. What does a (separate) personal pronoun express?

It can express emphasis and may help to identify the predicate.

You can easily emphasize a noun (اِسْمٌ) by adding the corresponding, independent personal pronoun.

This form is called *pronoun of separation* (ضَمِيرُ فَصْلٍ) because it separates the subject (مُبْتَدَأٌ) from the predicate (خَبَرٌ) and provides some space in-between. Why can that be useful?

Usually, the predicate in a nominal sentence is <u>indefinite</u>. However, if both the subject and the predicate are <u>definite</u>, it may be difficult to grasp the correct meaning of the sentence.

For example, you may mistake the predicate for an adjective (صِفةٌ) since an adjective, among other things, has to agree in *determination* (i.e., the definite article) with the word to which it refers. Thus, a pronoun helps us to distinguish the predicate and clarify the subject. Some examples.

It is **Khalid** who sits there.	خالِدٌ هُوَ الْجالِسُ هُناكَ.
The **engineers** were the ones responsible for the success of the project.	كانَ الْمُهَنْدِسُونَ هُم الْمَسْؤُولينَ عَنْ نَجاحِ الْمَشْروعِ.
I have done my duty.	قُمْتُ أَنا بِالْواجِبِ.
He wrote the lesson himself.	كَتَبَ هُوَ الدَّرْسَ.
Zayd, **he** is the generous.	زَيْدٌ هُوَ الْكَريمُ.
The mothers, **they** are the most virtuous.	الْأُمَّهاتُ هُنَّ الْفاضِلاتُ.

There are also other applications.

In sentences with إنَّ (*verily, indeed*), the *pronoun of separation* (ضَميرُ فَصْلٍ) appears as well. It is actually the same situation as above. Before إنَّ entered the sentence, we had a standard nominal sentence (جُمْلَةٌ اسْمِيَّةٌ) with subject (مُبْتَدَأٌ) and predicate (خَبَرٌ). If both are **definite** (مَعْرِفَةٌ), the sentence may be difficult to understand. The *pronoun of separation* helps to identify both parts clearly. Once the particle إنَّ enters the sentence, the subject is called اسْمُ إنَّ and the predicate خَبَرُ إنَّ.

Indeed, the boy (he) is diligent.	إنَّ الْوَلَدَ هُوَ الْمُجْتَهِدُ.
Let's delete إنَّ and we get: الْوَلَدُ الْمُجْتَهِدُ	
This is a nominal sentence with both subject and predicate having the definite article. Therefore, we should use a personal pronoun.	

Watch out: We also use a *pronoun of separation* if the predicate is **close to a definite noun**. This happens when a *noun of preference* (اسْمُ تَفْضيلٍ) is involved.

| Nobody (he) is more knowledgeable than your brother. | لَيْسَ أَحَدٌ هُوَ أَعْلَمَ مِنْ أَخِيكَ. |

Usually, such a pronoun does not have a job in the sentence. It is merely there for **separation**. We say that it has no place in the analysis (لا مَحَلَّ لَهُ مِن الإِعْرابِ). In other words, it cannot function as the subject, predicate, object, etc.

However, there is one tricky situation when we have to treat it differently and assign a grammatical function (which means we need to think about a *virtual* case ending since it has a fixed, cemented shape): a nominal sentence (جُمْلةٌ اِسْمِيّةٌ) in which the **second noun** is connected to the **first noun** by the *pronoun of separation*. The personal pronoun then functions as the subject (مُبْتَدَأٌ) of the second nominal sentence.

Sounds complicated? Here is an example:

| The student was (he is/himself) Zayd. | كانَ الطّالِبُ هُوَ زَيْدٌ. |

- Let's first check the sub-sentence. The pronoun هُوَ is the subject (مُبْتَدَأٌ) and زَيْدٌ is its predicate (خَبَرٌ).
- What about the main, primary sentence? The word الطّالِبُ is the "subject" of كانَ (اِسْمُ كانَ) and the **entire sentence** هُوَ زَيْدٌ is the predicate of كانَ (خَبَرُ كانَ).

160. Can you use a negation to emphasize in Arabic?

Yes. A very proven option for that is the absolute negation.

If you want to add weight to your statement, there are plenty of options to choose from in Arabic. A simple and elegant solution is the *generic, absolute negation* (لا النّافِيَةُ لِلْجِنْسِ) which literally translates as *there is **no**...*

If you use this type of negation, the "subject" (اِسْمُ لا) will take the accusative case (مَنْصُوبٌ). Although the "subject" has to be indefinite (نَكِرَةٌ - no definite article!), it does not take nunation (تَنْوِينٌ). It only gets one فَتْحَةٌ: "*a*". → See *quest. #248.*

Such constructions are usually followed by a prepositional or adverbial phrase. However, the preposition (فِي or مِنْ) therein is often dropped. For example, you see that in the expression *it is unavoidable* (لَا بُدَّ مِنْ أَنَّ); lit: *no avoiding [exists].* Furthermore, people tend to use the conjunction وَ instead resulting in لَا بُدَّ وَأَنَّ.

doubtless; not doubt that...	لا رَيْبَ فِي...
There is no doubt about it.	لا رَيْبَ فِيهِ.
She will come, no doubt about it.	سَتَحْضُرُ وَلا رَيْبَ.

doubtless; without doubt	لا شَكَّ أَنَّ...
You know him, without doubt.	تَعْرِفُهُ وَلا شَكَّ.

Note: Such expressions are often introduced with the conjunction وَ and are placed at the end of the sentence.

There is absolutely no doubt that many of you did not go.	لا شَكَّ أَبَدًا أَنَّ الْكَثِيرَ مِنْكُمْ لَمْ يَذْهَبْ.

You have certainly crossed the line.	لا بُدَّ وَأَنَّكَ تَجاوَزْتَ الْخَطَّ.
I must know it.	لا بُدَّ أَنْ أَعْرِفَهُ.

Notice: In the last example, we he expression is followed by a verb and not a noun; thus, we used أَنْ plus verb instead of أَنَّ plus noun.

| indisputably | لا جِدالَ أَنَّ... |
| unquestionable | لا مِراءَ أَنَّ... |

161. When do you use a pronoun in a relative clause?

When you would decline the relative pronoun in English.

In German, you have to decline relative pronouns according to their position in a sentence (*welch - welcher - welche – welches*). Even in English, this sometimes happens! For example, you use *who* if it relates back to the subject and *whom* if it is linked to the object.

In Arabic, you **almost never** decline relative pronouns (اِسْمُ مَوْصُولٍ). Let's take, for example, الَّذِي (*which, that*). It stays the same in all cases, no matter if it denotes *which, who,* or *whom.* There is only one exception: the dual! see *#113.*

So, what happens in Arabic? Depending on the case, we may need a **connector**, a *referential pronoun* (ضَمِيرٌ عائِدٌ) which relates back to the main word. Let's look at both cases:

Without a referring, referential pronoun: the nominative case (مَرْفُوعٌ)	
the lazy man	الرَّجُلُ الْكَسُولُ
= the man who is lazy	= الرَّجُلُ الَّذِي هُوَ كَسُولٌ
Here, the relative pronoun would be in the <u>nominative case</u> in English. The information in the relative clause takes the same case as the subject. Since we do not have any other person or object involved, there is **no need for a connector/link.**	

The man who came...	...الرَّجُلُ الَّذِي جاءَ

You wouldn't decline the relative pronoun in English. Imagine the sentence without a relative pronoun: الرَّجُلُ جاءَ. (*The man came.*) This would make sense → you don't need a referential pronoun.

With a referring, referential pronoun: the genitive (مَجْرُورٌ) or accusative case (مَنْصُوبٌ)	
The man whom I knew.... (attached to a verb)	...الرَّجُلُ الَّذِي عَرَفْتُهُ
Have you found the keys that you lost? (attached to a verb)	هَلْ وَجَدْتَ الْمَفاتِيحَ الَّتِي فَقَدْتَها؟
This is the pen which you asked for. (attached to a preposition)	هٰذا هُوَ الْقَلَمُ الَّذِي سَأَلْتَ عَنْهُ.
This is the professor whose book I read. (attached to a noun)	هٰذا هُوَ الْأُسْتاذُ الَّذِي قَرَأْتُ كِتابَهُ.

In the above table, try to imagine the sentences without the relative pronoun – they wouldn't make sense. In English, the relative pronoun **would be declined** (*whom*), which is true for German as well (*Der Mann, den...*).

We can work out a rule from the Arabic examples. When the main word (*antecedent*) is <u>not</u> the <u>subject</u> of the verb in the <u>clause</u>, then you need a **link (returning pronoun)**.

Let's illustrate this with the last sentence:

هٰذا هُوَ الْأُسْتاذُ الَّذِي قَرَأْتُ كِتابَهُ

The subject of the verb in the clause is "*I*" and not *this* or *the professor*. Since we talk about the book of the professor, we need an object pronoun that refers to the professor. The object pronoun agrees with the main word (*professor*).

Excursus I: The nature of the relative pronoun/noun الَّذِي.

In Arabic, الَّذِي is considered a **definite** (مَعْرِفةٌ) and **indeclinable** (مَبْنِيٌّ) noun. We cannot put case endings and can only assign a place value. We say that it is فِي مَحَلِّ رَفْعٍ (*in the position of a nominative*), نَصْبٍ (*accusative*) or جَرٍّ (*genitive*).

Lit.: *He came, he who...*	...جَاءَ الَّذِي

الَّذِي is the **subject** (فَاعِلٌ) of the verbal sentence! It gets the nominative case (مَرْفُوعٌ). However, since it has a fixed shape, we can only **assign a place value** – that of a nominative (فِي مَحَلِّ رَفْعٍ).

Wait a second! Why do we say that the relative "pronoun" can be charged with a grammatical function in the sentence? This is because of its origin and character. Contrary to English, the relative noun in Arabic has a **demonstrative nature**. It is a compound of لَ plus ذِي which got enhanced by the definite article (الـ) resulting in الَّذِي. Let's see what this means.

I hit the man who came.	ضَرَبْتُ الرَّجُلَ الَّذِي جَاءَ.

If we apply the core nature of الَّذِي, the meaning of the sentence is as follows: *I hit the man, **this one (t)here**, he came.* (German: Ich schlug den Mann, **den da**, er kam.)

Excursus II: What kind of stuff can be used in a relative clause (صِلةُ الْمَوْصُولِ)? You have four options.

The man who lives there.	الرَّجُلُ الَّذِي يَسْكُنُ هُناكَ.	verbal sentence (جُمْلةٌ فِعْلِيّةٌ)	1
He came, he who was	حَضَرَ الَّذِي كانَ غائِبًا.		

absent.			

Those who are my friends attended.	حَضَرَ الَّذِينَ هُمْ أَصْدِقَائِي.	nominal sentence (جُمْلَةٌ إِسْمِيّةٌ)	2

Notice: When the relative clause is a nominal sentence, the subject (مُبْتَدَأٌ) serves as the *referential pronoun*! In the example: هُمْ.

	أُنْظُرْ إِلَى اللَّوْحَةِ الَّتِي أَمَامَكَ.	adverbial phrase (ظَرْفٌ)	3

Look at the panel that is in front of you.

	قُطِفَتْ الْأَزْهَارُ الَّتِي فِي الحَدِيقَةِ.	prepositional p.. (جَارٌّ وَمَجْرُورٌ)	4

The flowers which were in the garden, were picked up.

In 3 and 4, we assume that there is a virtual, estimated verb or active participle to which the adverbial or prepositional phrase relates (for example, كائِنٌ or اِسْتَمَرَّ). or a deeper discussion about that (التَّعَلُّقُ), see *Arabic for Nerds 2, question #140.*

Watch out: It is impossible to have only a single word after الَّذِي. If you have such a situation, just insert a personal pronoun, and the sentence works.

162. الَّذِي and مَنْ - When do you use which word for *who*?

It depends on whether you talk about a specific person or not.

First of all, both words express the meaning of a **relative pronoun** (اِسْمُ مَوْصُولٍ): *this; that; the one; which; whom; who.*

to refer to a **specific person**	الَّذِي	1

to express a **general statement**	مَنْ	2

I like the professor who cares about his students.	أُحِبُّ الأُسْتاذَ الَّذِي يَهْتَمُّ بِطُلّابِهِ.	1
I like (one) who cares about students.	أُحِبُّ مَنْ يَهْتَمُّ بِطُلّابٍ.	2

This is similar to ما which is used for general statements too.

I like the (two) dresses that my (two) friends have bought.	أُحِبُّ الفُسْتانَيْنِ اللَّتَيْنِ اِشْتَرَتْهُما صَدِيقَتَي.	1
I like what I bought.	أُحِبُّ ما اِشْتَرَيْتُهُ.	2
Watch out: Why did we use ه and not ها in the second sentence? In <u>general statements</u>, normally the <u>masculine pronoun</u> is used!		

163. *Exactly twenty or more than twenty. How do you know?*

If there's مِنْ involved, you know that the number is a bit vague.

In Arabic, there is a nice way to express whether you are talking about an exact number of people/things or just an approximate number.

Look at these two examples:

I met (*exactly*) twenty students.	قابَلْتُ عِشْرِينَ طالِبًا.	1
I met (*about/more than*) twenty students.	قابَلْتُ عِشْرِينَ مِن الطُّلّابِ.	2

In short, if you use the construction مِنْ plus the **plural form** of a noun, you indicate that you are not talking about an exact number. But watch out: This nuance is often not translated. You would just say: *I met twenty students.*

164. If a verb is transitive, what does that mean?

A transitive verb is a verb that can take a direct object.

Let's take a quick look at how a **transitive** verb (فِعْلٌ مُتَعَدٍّ) works in English.

He	sends	her	a letter.
subject	(**transitive**) verb	**indirect** object	**direct** object

An **intransitive** verb (فِعْلٌ لازِمٌ) doesn't have a direct object.

We	walked	for hours.
subject	(**intransitive**) verb	adverb

Now we switch to the Arabic world.

The player ran. (There is no object.)	جَرَى اللّاعِبُ.	intransitive
The child sat down.	جَلَسَ الْوَلَدُ.	

It is impossible to use a direct object with *to sit*. The action can only be done by the doer – but the doer can't do it to a thing or an object.

The child broke the cup.	كَسَرَ الطِّفْلُ الْكُوبَ.	transitive

The verb needs an object (*cup*); otherwise the sentence would not work. The object is the answer to the question: ***what?***

Note: In Arabic, there are **verbs** which can have **two** or even **three objects**. If a verb can carry only one object, we call it مُتَعدٍّ إلَى مَفْعُولٍ واحِدٍ. If a verb can carry two objects, we say مُتَعَدٍّ إلَى مَفْعُولَيْنِ. See *question #109* for more details.

165. What is the root of the word تَارِيخٌ (*history*)?

The root is ء-ر-خ.

It is worth putting this root on the operating table.

- The corresponding **verb** for *history* is أَرَّخَ - يُؤَرِّخُ which is a II-verb following the paradigm فَعَّلَ.
- The active participle (اِسْمُ الْفَاعِلِ) of the II-verb, the person *who writes down the history*, is the مُؤَرِّخٌ.
- The مَصْدَرٌ of II-verbs is formed using the pattern تَفْعِيلٌ. Thus, the مَصْدَرٌ of أَرَّخَ is تَأْرِيخٌ – notice the هَمْزةٌ on top of the Aleph.
- The word تَأْرِيخٌ describes the **process** of *writing down history* or *dates*.
- The **result** of تَأْرِيخٌ is تاريخٌ = *history*. The plural is تَوارِيخُ (diptote!). Notice that the هَمْزةٌ is gone!

In a nutshell:

➤ تاريخٌ is a noun (اِسْمٌ) denoting the **result**. This idea is often found in the اِسْمُ الْمَصْدَرِ.

➤ تَأْرِيخٌ, the مَصْدَرٌ of the II-verb, denotes the **process** of reaching the goal (هَدَفٌ) of the action.

Remark: ء-ر-خ is probably not an Arabic root. It is already found in Accadian, Aramaic, and Hebrew. The Hebrew word יָרֵחַ (yareah) means *moon* and יֶרַח means *month* from which the idea of a *calendar* and *date* might be derived. However, some scholars stated that it is a pure Arabic root or that تَأْرِيخ was formed by transposition from تَأْخِيرٌ (*delay*).

166. How do you convert transitive into intransitive verbs?

You play with the stems: you add or delete letters.

Every verb has a subject, but not every verb has an object. A verb which is capable of carrying an object is a so-called transitive verb (فِعْلٌ مُتَعَدٍّ).

A verb which **can't** carry an object and thus only has a subject is called *intransitive* verb (فِعْلٌ لَازِمٌ). A single letter, which we add or delete, can **convert a transitive verb into an intransitive verb** or vice versa.

Let's see how it works and start with the conversion operation transitive → **intransitive.**

	translation	**transitive**		translation	**intransitive**
1	The policeman threw the thief out of the house.	أَخْرَجَ الشُّرْطِيُّ اللِّصَّ مِن البَيْتِ.	→	The thief got out of the house.	خَرَجَ اللِّصُّ مِن البَيْتِ.

2	فاعَلَ		→	فَعَلَ	
Muhammad sat with the guest.	جالَسَ مُحَمَّدٌ الضَّيْفَ.			The guest sat.	جَلَسَ الضَّيْفُ.

3	إسْتَفْعَلَ		→	فَعِلَ	
The company brought tourists to Egypt.	إسْتَقْدَمَتِ الشَّرِكَةُ السُّيّاحَ إلَى مِصْرَ.			The tourists came to Egypt.	قَدِمَ السُّيّاحُ إلَى مِصْرَ.

4	فَعَّلَ		→	فَعُلَ	
The student improved his handwriting.	حَسَّنَ الطّالِبُ خَطَّهُ.			The handwriting of the student is nice.	حَسُنَ خَطُّ الطّالِبِ.

What about the other direction? Let's see some options for this type of operation, the conversion intransitive → **transitive.**

	translation	**intransitive**		translation	<u>**transitive**</u>
1		إنْفَعَلَ, تَفَعَّلَ	→		فَعَلَ
	The cup got broken.	إنْكَسَرَ الْكُوبُ.		The child broke the cup.	كَسَرَ الطِّفْلُ الْكُوبَ.

2		إفْتَعَلَ	→		فَعَلَ
	The cup is filled with water.	إمْتَلَأَ الْكُوبُ بِالْماءِ.		The child filled the cup with water.	مَلَأَ الطِّفْلُ الْكُوبَ بِالْماءِ.

167. What is so special about *a kilogram of sugar* in Arabic?

In Arabic, it is the grammar.

When you say *I buy a kilo, a liter,* or *a hectare,* it is a vague information because you don't say what kind of good you are buying. The sentence becomes clearer as soon as you add a *specification* (تَمْيِيزٌ). It answers the question *what?* (مَاذَا؟)

However, there are several grammar issues we have to solve. Let us first check the grammar terms.

I have one pound (a *ratl* ~ half a kilo) of honey.	عِنْدِي رَطْلٌ عَسَلًا.
He gives me a liter (of) milk.	يُعْطِينِي لِتْرًا لَبَنًا.

رَطْلٌ in example 1 is the *subject* (مُبْتَدَأٌ); in example 2, لِتْرًا is the *direct object* (مَفْعُولٌ بِهِ). We also call them the *distinguished (specified):* الْمُمَيَّزُ.	*liter* *ratl*	لِتْرًا رَطْلٌ
This is the *specification* or *distinctive* (التَّمْيِيزُ). It clears the ambiguity of *liter* and *ratl* (one pound).	*milk* *honey*	لَبَنًا عَسَلًا

Rule: The standard *specification* (تَمْيِيزٌ) has to be a **singular** (مُفْرَدٌ) word in the **accusative** case (مَنْصُوبٌ).

But that's not all. If you want to express *one pound (of) oil,* you have **four different options** which all express the same. However, the case markers may be different!

You add the word *oil* directly as a تَمْيِيزٌ	عِنْدِي رَطْلٌ زَيْتًا.	1
Oil has to be in the accusative case (مَنْصُوبٌ) because it is a classical, standard **specification** (تَمْيِيزٌ).	

You use a **إِضافةٌ**-construction	عِنْدِي رَطْلُ زَيْتٍ.	2
Oil is the second part of the **إِضافةٌ** and has to be **مَجْرُورٌ**.		

You use a construction with **مِن**	عِنْدِي رَطْلٌ مِن زَيْتٍ.	3
Oil follows a preposition and therefore has to be **مَجْرُورٌ**.		

You use an apposition (**بَدَلٌ**)	عِنْدِي رَطْلٌ زَيْتٌ.	4
Oil stands in apposition to one pound (*ratl*). It therefore takes the same case → here it is the nominative case (**مَرْفُوعٌ**) since the word **رَطْلٌ** is the subject (**مُبْتَدَأٌ**) of the nominal sentence.		

The specification doesn't have to be a classical unit like *kg*, *liter*, etc. It can also be an abstract entity (no measurement).

I bought (a bouquet) of flowers.	اِشْتَرَيْتُ باقةً زَهْرًا.
I bought a bag (sack) of tea.	اِشْتَرَيْتُ كِيسًّا شايًّا.

كَمْ (*how much, how many*) is also followed by a *specification*. Furthermore, almost all numbers in Arabic follow the logic of the specification. Some use a **إِضافةٌ**-construction (option 2), other numbers carry the *distinctive* as a **تَمْيِيزٌ** (option 1) which is the reason for the accusative case (**مَنْصُوبٌ**). The numbers marked in gray use a **specification** (**تَمْيِيزٌ**).

	distinctive	translation	example
3-10	plural in the genitive (**جَمْعٌ مَجْرُورٌ**) (**إِضافةٌ**-construction)	*In the room are 7 students.*	فِي الْغُرْفةِ سَبْعةُ طُلّابٍ.
11 - 99	singular in the accu-	*In the room*	فِي الْغُرْفةِ أَحَدَ عَشَرَ

20, 30, 40, ...	sative (مُفْرَدٌ مَنْصُوبٌ) specification (تَمْيِيزٌ)	are 11 students.	طالِبًا.
		There are 20 men in the house.	فِي الدَّارِ عِشْرُونَ رَجُلًا.
100	singular in the genitive (مُفْرَدٌ مَجْرُورٌ) (إِضافَةٌ construction)	The faculty has 100 professors.	فِي الْكُلِّيَّةِ مِئَةُ أُسْتاذٍ.
1000		The faculty has 4000 students.	فِي الْكُلِّيَّةِ أَرْبَعةُ آلافِ طالِبٍ.
how many	singular in the accusative (مُفْرَدٌ مَنْصُوبٌ) specification (تَمْيِيزٌ)	How many books do you have?	كَمْ كِتابًا عِنْدَكَ؟

There are two <u>exceptions</u>: the **numbers 1** and **2**. They use a different idea – the adjective.

In the office, there is one (male) employee and two (female) employees.	فِي الْمَكْتَبِ مُوَظَّفٌ واحِدٌ، وَمُوَظَّفَتانِ اِثْنَتانِ.
The number comes **after** the noun! It is an **adjective** (صِفةٌ) and needs agreement. It corresponds in number, case, gender, and determination (definite, indefinite) with the preceding noun.	

Remark: Also a **comparison** may be a specification (تَمْيِيزٌ).

Cairo is more crowded than Alexandria.	الْقاهِرةُ أَكْثَرُ اِزْدِحامًا مِن الإِسْكَنْدَرِيِّة.
اِزْدِحامًا is a **specification** (تَمْيِيزٌ). It tells the reader or listener what you are talking about; the sentence wouldn't make sense without it.	

168. اِمْتَلَأَتْ الْبُحَيْرَةُ سَمَكًا. - **How do you translate that?**

The lake is full of fish.

The underlying construction of اِمْتَلَأَتْ الْبُحَيْرَةُ سَمَكًا is pretty sophisticated. In fact, we deal with a sentence that has changed its word order.

In Arabic grammar, such constructions are called *distinctive/specification of the sentence* (تَمْيِيزُ الْجُمْلةِ) or *distinctive/ specification of the relation* (تَمْيِيزُ النِّسْبةِ).

Let's break the sentence apart. If we dropped the last word سَمَكًا, the sentence would still work.

The lake was filled.	اِمْتَلَأَتْ الْبُحَيْرَةُ.

That would be a general saying as you have removed the additional information, the specification (التَّمْيِيزُ), which made it specific. We only know that the lake is filled now, but filled with what? Water, garbage, or fish? That's the reason why we need the additional information, to tell the reader what the lake was filled with. Another example:

يَخْتَلِفُ النَّاسُ ثَقافةً. - *People differ culture-wise.*

The culture of people differs.	تَخْتَلِفُ ثَقافةُ النَّاسِ.	1

This was the original sentence. We used a إضافة-construction.

People differ culture-wise.	يَخْتَلِفُ النَّاسُ ثَقافةً.	2

This is how we can rewrite the first sentence – without changing the meaning. Notice three things:

1. The different form of the verb. Now, we use the masculine form; above, we used the feminine form = تَخْتَلِفُ.

> 2. *Culture* gets the accusative case (مَنْصُوبٌ) because it is a تَمْيِيزٌ.
>
> 3. The subject in both sentences is different. In example 1, it is ثَقافةٌ; in example 2, it is النَّاسُ.

What we have seen can be applied to different parts of a sentence as well. In the following examples, the original sentence and the sentence with the specification (تَمْيِيزٌ) mean the same.

what has changed	with **specification** (تَمْيِيزٌ)	original sentence
subject	اِشْتَعَلَتِ النَّارُ فِي الْبَيْتِ.	اِشْتَعَلَ الْبَيْتُ نارًا.
	The house caught fire.	
object	نَظَّمَ الْقائِدُ الْجُنُودَ صُفُوفًا.	نَظَّمَ الْقائِدُ صُفُوفَ الْجُنُودِ.
	The leader organized the soldiers to stand in a line.	
	Notice: You have to change the order of the إضافةٌ and delete the definite article.	
comparative, superlative	هذا الطَّالِبُ أَشَدُّ ذَكاءً.	---
	This student is the most intelligent.	

169. What is the passive participle (إِسْمُ الْمَفْعُولِ) of دَعا?

It is مَدْعُوٌّ.

The I-verb دَعا - يَدْعُو means *to call, to invite*.

The passive participle (اِسْمُ مَفْعُولٍ) of the verb is مَدْعُوٌّ which means *called*. How did we end up with such a weird form?

To build the passive participle of a I-verb, we use the pattern مَفْعُولٌ. Some examples:

meaning	اِسْمُ مَفْعُولٍ	I-verb
to understand - *understood*	مَفْهُومٌ	فَهِمَ - يَفْهَمُ
to read - *was read*	مَقْرُوءٌ	قَرَأَ - يَقْرَأُ
to break - *broken*	مَكْسُورٌ	كَسَرَ - يَكْسِرُ

Remember that the glottal stop – the Hamza (هَمْزَةٌ) – is **not** a weak letter! The verb قَرَأَ (*to read*) follows the standard rules, except that you need to be careful how to spell the هَمْزَةٌ correctly → مَقْرُوءٌ.

Now, what happens if we have a root that contains و or ي, i.e., a **weak letter** (حَرْفُ عِلّةٍ)? It gets tricky.

- Verbs with a weak letter in the **middle** (مُعْتَلُّ الْوَسَطِ) are called *hollow* (فِعْلٌ أَجْوَفُ). For example: قالَ.

- Verbs with a weak letter **at the end** (مُعْتَلُّ الآخِرِ) are called *defective* (فِعْلٌ ناقِصٌ - مُعْتَلٌّ). See *question #98*.

Some examples.

meaning	اِسْمُ مَفْعُولٍ	verb	root
to call - *invited* or *called*	مَدْعُوٌّ	دَعا - يَدْعُو	د-ع-و
to say - *said*	مَقُولٌ	قالَ - يَقُولُ	ق-و-ل
to sell - *sold*	مَبِيعٌ	باعَ - يَبِيعُ	ب-ي-ع

meaning	اِسْمُ مَفْعُولٍ	verb	root
to forget - *forgotten*	مَنْسِيٌّ	نَسِيَ - يَنْسَى	ن-س-ي
to throw - *thrown*	مَرمِيٌّ	رَمَى - يَرْمِي	ر-م-ي

But how do know the correct (middle or last) letter of the passive participle? → You should have a look at the present tense form (الْمُضارِعُ) which shows you how the weak letter changes.

> **Rule:** If the present tense verb ends in و or ى, the passive participle will have شَدّةٌ on the last letter.

What about the other verb stems II to X? The passive participle of such verbs is an easy task.

- You just have to add an initial مُ to the **past** tense verb.
- If it starts with ا, then you additionally have to delete ا.

Watch out: The active participle (اِسْمُ فاعِلٍ) looks optically the same if the vowels are not written. In fact, the only difference is just **one** vowel. For ex., the VIII-verb *to respect* (اِحْتَرَمَ):

passive participle (اِسْمُ الْمَفْعُولِ)	*respected*	مُحْتَرَمٌ	1
	The vowel on the second root letter is فَتْحةٌ.		
active participle (اِسْمُ الْفاعِلِ)	*one who respects*	مُحْتَرِمٌ	2
	The vowel of the second root letter is كَسْرةٌ.		

How does the plural of the passive participle مَدْعُوٌّ look like? You add the usual suffix وُنَ. Hence, you have to write two و!

the invited students	الطُّلّابُ الْمَدْعُوُّونَ

170. How do you build the *noun of place* (اِسْمُ مَكانٍ)?

You use the pattern مَفْعَلٌ *or* مَفْعِلٌ.

In Arabic, it is easy to craft a word for the place where the action happens. It is called *noun of place* (اِسْمُ مَكانٍ) and belongs to the derived nouns of the root (اِسْمٌ مُشْتَقٌّ).

For a **I-verb** (ثُلاثِيٌّ) there are two patterns:

A. The pattern مَفْعَلٌ

It is used in two situations:

1. if the verb has a **weak** letter <u>at the end</u> (defective ending);
2. if the second root letter takes the vowel "*a*" (فَتْحَةٌ) or the vowel "*u*" (ضَمّةٌ) in the **present tense**.

translation	اِسْمُ مَكانٍ	translation	verb		
principle; basis	مَبْدَأٌ	to begin	*a*	يَبْدَأُ	بَدَأَ
playground	مَلْعَبٌ	to play	*a*	يَلْعَبُ	لَعِبَ
amusement center	مَلْهَى	to be amused	*u*	يَلْهُو	لَهَا

However, some roots do not use this pattern. There's hardly any logic behind. It is just based on how people use them.

translation	اِسْمُ مَكانٍ	translation	verb		
school	مَدْرَسةٌ	to learn	*u*	يَدْرُسُ	دَرَسَ
farm	مَزْرَعةٌ	to plant	*a*	يَزْرَعُ	زَرَعَ
place of sunset*	مَغْرِب	to depart	*u*	يَغْرُبُ	غَرَبَ

mosque*	مَسْجِدٌ	to bow down	u	يَسْجُدُ	سَجَدَ
graveyard	مَقْبَرَةٌ	to bury	u	يَقْبُرُ	قَبَرَ

* Notice: According to the rules it should be مَسْجَدٌ and مَغْرَبٌ.

B. The pattern مَفْعِلٌ

It is used either...

1. if the verb has a <u>weak letter</u> at the **beginning**;

2. if the second root letter takes the vowel *"i"* (كَسرةٌ) in the **present tense**.

translation	إِسْمُ مَكانٍ	translation	verb	
position, station	مَوْقِفٌ	to stop	يَقِفُ	وَقَفَ
appointment	مَوْعِدٌ	to promise	يَعِدُ	وَعَدَ
birthplace	مَوْلِدٌ	to give birth to	يَلِدُ	وَلَدَ
native country	مَوْطِنٌ	to settle down	*"i"* يَطِنُ	وَطَنَ
runway	مَهْبِطٌ	to descend	يَهْبِطُ	هَبَطَ
place of retreat	مَرْجِعٌ	to return	يَرْجِعُ	رَجَعَ
residence	مَنْزِلٌ	to stay	يَنْزِلُ	نَزَلَ

There are well-known exceptions:

airport*	مَطارٌ	to fly	يَطِيرُ	طارَ

* Notice: According to the rules it should be مَطِيرٌ

→ If you want to know how to build the اِسْمُ مَكانٍ for other verb forms (II to X), have a look at *question #172*.

171. Does مَوْلِدٌ mean *birthday* or *birthplace*?

It can mean both.

Depending on the context, the pattern used for the اِسْمُ مَكانٍ functions as the *noun of time* (اِسْمُ زَمانٍ). This may happen because in certain verbs, they share the same pattern.

The *noun of time* indicates the time (moment) when the action happens. Sometimes it is hard to tell the two apart. Moreover, they may denote approximately the same idea.

An example:

اِسْمُ زَمانٍ	My <u>birthday</u> is in October.	مَوْلِدِي فِي شَهْرِ أَكْتُوبِر.
اِسْمُ مَكانٍ	My <u>birthplace</u> is in London.	مَوْلِدِي فِي مَدِينَةِ لَنْدُن.

172. What do verbs of stem II to X have in common?

In each stem, four types of derived nouns look the same: noun of place, noun of time, passive participle, and مَصْدَرٌ مِيمِيٌّ.

Augmented in Arabic means that you add extra letters to the root. One result of this is the different verb stems. Augmented verbs (فِعْلٌ مَزِيدٌ) have one big advantage.

They are easier to handle than plain I-verbs. There are only few patterns and almost no exceptions. But when something is very simple, it usually also means that this comes at the expense of accuracy.

Let us examine the VIII-verb يَلْتَقِي - إِلْتَقَى بِ which means *to meet (someone); to encounter*. It uses the past tense pattern إِفْتَعَلَ. We formed it by adding the letters ا and ت to the basic I-verb لَقِيَ - يَلْقَى (R3=ي) expressing *to find, to meet*. What happens if we want to derive nouns from a VIII-verb? For example, we want to build the passive participle, the noun of place or time? Answer: We will end up with the same word.

This does not only happen to VIII-verbs – but to all augmented verbs (stem II to X). In other words, some of the derived nouns (إِسْمٌ مُشْتَقٌّ) use exactly the same pattern!

1	إِسْمُ مَكانٍ	The center is the meeting point of the students.	المَرْكَزُ مُلْتَقَى الطُّلّابِ.
2	إِسْمُ زَمانٍ	The students meet at nine o'clock.	السّاعةُ التّاسِعة مُلْتَقَى الطُّلّابِ.
3	إِسْمُ مَفْعُولٍ	The students have met.	الطُّلّابُ مُلْتَقَى بِهِمْ.
4	مَصْدَرٌ مِيمِيٌّ	The meeting of the students was nice.	كانَ مُلْتَقَى الطُّلّابِ جَمِيلا.
		The original مَصْدَرٌ (مَصْدَرٌ أَصْلِيٌّ) is إِلْتِقاءٌ.	

Let's summarize the most important points:

- The إِسْمُ مَفْعُولٍ and إِسْمُ مَكانٍ and إِسْمُ زَمانٍ as well as the share the same pattern. This is true for all stems except for the most basic, bare I-verb.

- Only a I-verb has special patterns for the إِسْمُ زَمانٍ and إِسْمُ مَكانٍ. They are مَفْعَلٌ and مَفْعِلٌ.

Let's get right into it and look at a few examples.

pas. p. (اِسْمُ مَفْعُولٍ)	pattern	passive	meaning	verb	
decided	مُقَرَّرٌ	مُفَعَّلٌ	قُرِّرَ	to decide	قَرَّرَ	II
controlled	مُراعًى	مُفاعَلٌ	رُوعِيَ	to control	راعَى	III
closed	مُغْلَقٌ	مُفْعَلٌ	أُغْلِقَ	to close	أَغْلَقَ	IV
instructed	مُتَعَلَّمٌ	مُتَفَعَّلٌ	تُعُلِّمَ	to study	تَعَلَّمَ	V
prevented	مُتَدارَكٌ	مُتَفاعَلٌ	تُدورِكَ	to prevent	تَدارَكَ	VI
depressed	مُنْحَدَرٌ	مُنْفَعَلٌ	---	to descend	إِنْحَدَرَ	VII
concise	مُخْتَصَرٌ	مُفْتَعَلٌ	أُخْتُصِرَ	to shorten	إِخْتَصَرَ	VIII
The passive participle is not used with IX-verbs. However, the active participle (اِسْمُ فاعِلٍ) of this stem is often mistaken as the passive participle. It follows the pattern مُفْعَلٌّ. For example, the active participle of to be black (إِسْوَدَّ) is مُسْوَدٌّ.					IX
extracted	مُسْتَخْرَجٌ	مُسْتَفْعَلٌ	أُسْتُخْرِجَ	to extract	إِسْتَخْرَجَ	X

173. What is the root of مُسْتَشْفًى (hospital)?

It is ش - ف - ي.

مُسْتَشْفًى (plural: مَشافٍ or مُسْتَشْفَياتٌ) means *hospital*.

It is the *noun of place* (اِسْمُ مَكانٍ) of the X-verb *to seek a cure* (يَسْتَشْفِي - إِسْتَشْفَى) and uses the pattern مُسْتَفْعَلٌ. It literally denotes *the place to seek cure*.

In order to identify the root, you need to remove the extra letters م-س-ت until you are left with فْعَلٌ. In our example, the last part is crucial: فًى. If you see such an ending, you can be sure that it is a *noun with a shortened ending* (إسْمُ الْمَقْصُور) with the characteristic permanent Aleph (أَلِفٌ لازِمةٌ); *see #13.*

Such Aleph is never followed by Hamza (هَمْزةٌ) and cannot be extended.

The *noun of place* (إسْمُ مَكانٍ) and the *passive participle* (إسْم مَفْعُولٍ) of a X-verb share the same pattern! *See question #172.*

translation	إسْمُ مَكانٍ
meeting place	مُلْتَقًى
hospital	مُسْتَشْفًى
society	مُجْتَمَعٌ

translation	X-verb
to meet	إلْتَقَى
to seek a cure	إسْتَشْفَى
to meet	إجْتَمَعَ

174. Is مُسْتَشْفًى (hospital) masculine or feminine?

It is masculine (مُذَكَّرٌ).

Wait a second! Isn't it true that a final ى indicates a feminine word? Yes, this is true. But there are exceptions.

Rule: Most *nouns of place* (إسْمُ مَكانٍ) are **masculine!**

Now, what happens if we add an adjective? What about the agreement? The adjective has to take the masculine form!

a nightclub	مَلْهًى لَيْلِيٌّ (not لَيْلِيّةٌ)
a big hospital	مُسْتَشْفًى كَبِيرٌ
university hospital	مُسْتَشْفًى جامِعِيٌّ

private hospital	مُسْتَشْفًى خاصٌّ

175. How do you build words for tools (إِسْمُ آلَةٍ)?

There are many patterns.

Arabic has a remarkable feature. Using the root, you can easily compile nouns for **tools** and **instruments** with which the action (of the verb) is being done; for example, scissors, spoon, or car.

We call such words *noun of instrument* (إِسْمُ آلَةٍ); the word آلَةٌ means *instrument* or *machine*. The noun of instrument belongs to the derived nouns (إِسْمٌ مُشْتَقٌّ). There are several patterns to build a إِسْمُ آلَةٍ.

pattern: مِفْعَلٌ

instrument	plural	إِسْمُ آلَةٍ		I-verb
microscope	مَجَاهِرُ	مِجْهَرٌ	to be brought to light	جَهَرَ - يَجْهَرُ
scissors	مَقَاصُّ or مِقَصَّاتٌ	مِقَصٌّ	to cut	قَصَّ - يَقُصُّ

pattern: مِفْعَلةٌ

instrument	plural	إِسْمُ آلَةٍ		I-verb
sweeper	مَكَانِسُ	مِكْنَسةٌ	to sweep	كَنَسَ - يَكْنِسُ
spoon	مَلَاعِقُ	مِلْعَقةٌ	to lick	لَعِقَ - يَلْعَقُ

pattern: مِفْعالٌ

instrument	plural	اِسْمُ آلِةٍ		I-verb
key	مَفاتِيح	مِفْتاحٌ	to open	فَتَحَ - يَفْتَحُ
weight scales	مَوازِين	مِيزانٌ	to weigh	وَزَنَ - يَزِنُ

pattern: فَعّالةٌ

instrument	plural	اِسْمُ آلِةٍ		I-verb
eyeglasses	نَظّاراتٌ	نَظّارةٌ	to see	نَظَرَ - يَنْظُرُ
car; vehicle	سَيّاراتٌ	سَيّارةٌ	to ride	سارَ - يَسِيرُ

Sometimes we use the active participle to name the tool.

active participle (اِسْمُ فاعِلٍ)

meaning	plural	اِسْمُ آلِةٍ		verb	
air plane	طائِراتٌ	طائِرةٌ	to fly	طارَ - يَطِيرُ	I
air conditioner	مُكَيِّفاتٌ	مُكَيِّفةٌ	to adjust	كَيَّفَ - يُكَيِّفُ	II

Watch out: Not all words for tools and instruments are derived from roots. They are **inert, static nouns** (اِسْمٌ جامِدٌ).

Not related to roots – inert, static noun (اِسْمٌ جامِدٌ)

plural	instrument	
أَقْلامٌ	قَلَمٌ	pen

plural	instrument	
أَسْيافٌ or سُيوفٌ	سَيْفٌ	sword

plural	instrument	
سَكاكِينُ	سِكِّينٌ	knife

plural	instrument	
رِماحٌ or أَرْماحٌ	رُمْحٌ	spear

176. مِئْذَنةٌ or مَأْذَنةٌ - What is the word for *minaret*?

Both are used – however, there is a difference in meaning.

If we take a closer look at both words, we notice that the first vowel is different. Today, most people use مَأْذَنةٌ with the vowel "*a*" (فَتْحةٌ) on the first letter.

In the early times of Islam, however, the spelling and pronunciation of *minaret* was مِئْذَنةٌ – with the vowel "*i*" (كَسْرةٌ). *Lane's Lexicon* even calls مَأْذَنةٌ a *vulgar word*. Let's examine both possibilities. The root is ء-ذ-ن which denotes *to hear*.

- The II-verb أَذَّنَ - يُؤَذِّنُ means *to call to prayer*.
- The IV-verb آذَنَ - يُؤاذِنُ: *to make public; to announce.*

So, why do مِئْذَنة and مَأْذَنة have different prefixes? First of all, both are derived nouns (إِسْمٌ مُشْتَقٌّ).

1. مِئْذَنةٌ is a *noun of instrument* (إِسْمُ آلةٍ). → مِئْذَنة is an **instrument** to do the call to prayer.
2. مَأْذَنة is a *noun of place* (إِسْمُ مَكانٍ). It is the **place** where the call to prayer happens.

If we take that seriously, it could probably mean that the مِئْذَنةٌ was originally a structure small enough justifiably to be called an instrument.

Remark: In the film *The Message* (1976), which was approved by several Islamic scholars, the first muezzin, Bilāl, went up to the roof to make the very first call to prayer in Islam. The earliest mosques most probably lacked minarets.

According to Islamic tradition, Bilāl and his early successors gave the call to prayer from a high or public place such as the doorway or roof of a mosque, an elevated structure or the city wall, but never from a tall tower. The idea of a minaret first arose under the Umayyad Caliphate (الْخِلافَةُ الأُمَوِيَّةُ) in Syria where Muslims came in contact with church towers. They converted the churches into mosques and adapted the towers.

177. How do you say *write!* in Arabic?

You use the imperative (اُكْتُبْ) - but there are other options too.

In spoken language, you will only use the imperative (أَمْرٌ). In very sophisticated Arabic, however, you may encounter a different construction: *Be a responsible man!* (لِتَكُنْ مَسْؤُولًا!).

The following two examples basically both express *write!* Notice that the verbs – in both constructions – end with سُكُونٌ as we need the jussive mood (مَجْزُومٌ).

construction and remarks			prefix
This is the standard imperative.	'uktub	اُكْتُبْ!	---
We use the *Lām of the imperative* (لامُ أَمْرٍ). This type of لِ takes the vowel "*i*" (كَسرةٌ). We use the conjugated present tense verb in the jussive mood (مَجْزُومٌ) - note the تَ.	litaktub	لِتَكْتُبْ!	لِ

The *Lām of the imperative* can also be used with فَ or وَ. Since the لِ is in between, لْ has no vowel! This is necessary because otherwise it would be difficult to combine و with لْ. Try to pronounce both letters very quickly – eventually, you will end up producing *"wal"* and *"fal"*.

falyastajībū	Let them comply, **and** let them be-	فَلْ...	فَلْيَسْتَجِيبُوا
walyu'minū	lieve! Note: We mark the jussive mood by dropping the final ن.	وَلْ...	وَلْيُؤْمِنُوا!

178. ذٰلِكُم الْكِتابُ مُفِيدٌ يا أَصْدِقائِي - Is there a mistake?

No, there isn't. But let us check why.

The sentence means: *That book is useful, my friends!* The first expression ذٰلِكُم looks strange. Since the meaning is *that book,* why is it not just ذٰلِكَ الْكِتابُ؟

For English speakers, it is not logical that the *demonstrative* (اِسْمُ إشارةٍ) **agrees** in **gender** and **number** (singular/plural) with the person that gets called – in our example: *my friends!* In Arabic, however, this happens if the *Kāf of allocution* (كافُ الْخِطابِ) is involved. Such ك is attached to demonstratives producing the expression *that*.

Hey Karīm, that notebook is useful!	ذٰلِكَ الدَّفْتَرُ مُفِيدٌ يا كَرِيمُ!
Hey my (two) friends, that notebook is useful!	ذٰلِكُما الدَّفْتَرُ مُفِيدٌ يا صَدِيقَيَّ!
Hey my friends, that notebook is useful!	ذٰلِكُم الدَّفْتَرُ مُفِيدٌ يا أَصْدِقائِي!

Hey (my)ladies, that notebook is useful!	ذٰلِكُنَّ الدَّفْتَرُ مُفِيدٌ يا سَيِّداتِي!

Rarely, you find such ك also in special expressions.

tell me	أَرَأَيْتَكَ		slowly!	رُوَيْدَكَ

→ See also *Arabic for Nerds 2, question #95.*

179. What does إِمَّا mean?

The word إِمَّا *could be translated as: either.... (or).*

The English word *either* is used when you refer to a choice between two possibilities. In Arabic, we use إِمَّا which is a particle (حَرْفٌ). Having this nature, it implies that it can't get case endings and can't take one of the usual grammar functions (لا مَحَلَّ لَها مِن الْإِعْرابِ); furthermore, إِمَّا always stays the same.

If there is doubt (شَكٌّ) - particle of **separation**	حَرْفُ تَفْصِيلٍ
This man is either stupid or insane.	هٰذا الرَّجُلُ إِمَّا أَحْمَقُ وَإِمَّا مَجنُونٌ.
Either Samīr or Zayd will pay me a visit.	يَنْزُورُنِي إِمَّا زَيْدٌ وَإِمَّا سَمِيرٌ.

Letting choose – particle of **selection**	حَرْفُ تَخْيِيرٍ
You have to meet either the director or the secretary.	يَجِبُ عَلَيْكَ أَنْ تُقابِلَ إِمَّا الْمُدِيرَ وَإِمَّا السِّكْرِتِيرَ.

| You have to choose, either diligence or laziness! | اِخْتَرْ إِمَّا الْجِدَّ وَإِمَّا الْكَسَلَ! |

What you should keep in mind:

- You have to put إِمَّا <u>twice</u> → and in the second part, you have to connect it with وَ.

- إِمَّا <u>does not influence</u> other words; it does not govern any word and therefore, it does not induce cases.

180. What type of word is لَيْسَ (*not to be*)?

It is a defective verb (فِعْلُ مَاضٍ نَاقِصٌ) which means that it does not form all tenses and moods.

The verb لَيْسَ literally denotes *not to be; not to exist*. In fact, the existence itself is absolutely denied. لَيْسَ is used to negate a nominal sentence (جُمْلَةٌ اِسْمِيّةٌ), which is a sentence that does not include a verb. It changes the meaning from affirmative to negative (مِن الْإِثْباتِ إِلَى النَّفْيِ). We can say that لَيْسَ **excludes the predicate from the subject.**

لَيْسَ is a remarkable device. The verb **only** exists in the **past tense** (الْماضِي). It **cannot** form the **imperative** (الْأَمْرُ) and cannot be used in the present tense (الْمُضارِعُ).

- In Arabic, verbs like لَيْسَ which are only used in the past tense are called *inert, aplastic verbs* (فِعْلٌ جامِدٌ). Another example is the verb عَسَى which means *to wish*.

- The reason for this name (*inertia*) is the similarity to particles (حَرْفٌ) which do not change their forms. For example, the particles of negation: لَمْ, لَنْ

- All other verbs are called *variable verbs* (فِعْلٌ مُتَصَرِّفٌ).

Watch out! لَيْسَ is a *sister of* كانَ. This implies that the...

- **"subject"** (اِسْمُ لَيْسَ) is in the **nominative** case (مَرْفُوعٌ);
- **predicate** (خَبَرُ لَيْسَ) is in the **accusative** case (مَنْصُوبٌ).

The idea of being and not being entails that we translate the idea and not the literal meaning.

> Although لَيْسَ is only used in the past tense,
> it conveys the **meaning of the present tense!**

Only in very few situations, when the context is clear, you could translate لَيْسَ with a past tense meaning. Since لَيْسَ is a verb, you don't need to add a personal pronoun (هُوَ, أَنا, ...) as it is already included in the verb. We call that an implied, hidden pronoun (ضَمِيرٌ مُسْتَتِرٌ). There are various ways to negate a nominal sentence.

Let's see an example: *She is not generous.*

كَرِيمَةً is in the accusative case (مَنْصُوبٌ) because it is the predicate of لَيْسَ, similar to the خَبَرُ كانَ.	لَيْسَتْ كَرِيمَةً 1

We use an extra بـ to emphasize the negation. This can be combined with the definite article.	لَيْسَتْ بِكَرِيمَةٍ 2

Also here, كَرِيمَة is the predicate (خَبَرُ لَيْسَ). However, the additional, extra preposition for emphasis drags the word visually into the genitive case (مَجْرُورٌ). This is the reason for "-in" (two كَسْرة). For a deep analysis, see *Arabic for Nerds 2, question #128.*

Here, we use a construction with غَيْرُ instead of	هِيَ غَيْرُ كَرِيمَةٍ 3

لَيْسَ. This is a إِضافَةٌ-construction. Thus, كَرِيمَةٍ takes the genitive case.	

Similar to بـ, also the preposition مِنْ can be used to accentuate the negation:

No one knows everything.	لَيْسَ مِنْ إِنْسانٍ يَعْرِفُ كُلَّ شَيْءٍ.

181. لَيْسَ لَدَيْهِ سَيَّارَةٌ. - Is there a mistake?

No, there isn't. The sentence means: He doesn't have a car.

If you translate لَيْسَ لَدَيْهِ سَيَّارَةٌ into English, you'll probably choose *he* as the subject and *car* as the predicate. But that's not that obvious in Arabic because the construction is quite tricky.

The verb لَيْسَ has to agree with the subject (إِسْمُ لَيْسَ). You can easily identify the subject in a sentence with لَيْسَ by the marker for the nominative case (مَرْفُوع) because the predicate has to be in the accusative case (مَنْصُوبٌ). Therefore, in the Arabic sentence, the subject is *car*!

The director is **not in the** office.	لَيْسَ الْمُدِيرُ فِي الْمَكْتَبِ.	subject of لَيْسَ 1
He is **not the director** in the office.	لَيْسَ الْمُدِيرَ فِي الْمَكْتَبِ.	predicate of لَيْسَ 2
The subject is the hidden pronoun *he* (هُوَ) found in لَيْسَ.		

There are a few other peculiarities in our example: *Car* (سَيَّارَةٌ) is **feminine** in Arabic and لَيْسَ has the third person singular

masculine form. Is this a mistake? **No!** The feminine subject *car* is separated from the other parts of the sentence.

That is why لَيْسَ can have the masculine form. This is pretty common in Arabic.

The predicate (خَبَرُ لَيْسَ) in our example is لَدَيْهِ, which is an adverbial phrase (ظَرْفُ مَكَانٍ). In sentences of this construction, the predicate of لَيْسَ is often mistaken as the subject, especially in sentences that express possession which is due to the **inverted word-order.** Let us remember what inverted word order means.

He has a book. (Lit.: At/with him is a book.)	عِنْدَهُ كِتابٌ.

This adverbial phrase (ظَرْفُ مَكَانٍ) is the fronted predicate (خَبَرٌ مُقَدَّمٌ). The predicate appears at the first position where you would expect the subject = inverted word order. عِنْدَهُ is the predicate of the sentence and should be in the accusative (مَنْصُوبٌ) – but you don't see that because you cannot put case markers on عِنْدَهُ. We can only assign virtual case markers, i.e., the place value of an accusative case. Note: Some say that it is not entirely correct to say that the adverbial phrase (ظَرْفُ مَكَانٍ) is the predicate, which is true, but it doesn't really matter in the practical world. If you are interested in this discussion, see *Arabic for Nerds 2, #220.*	عِنْدَهُ
Subject (مُبْتَدَأٌ) of the nominal sentence (جُمْلَةٌ اِسْمِيَّةٌ).	كِتابٌ

He does not have a book. (Lit: At him a book does not exist.)	لَيْسَ عِنْدَهُ كِتابٌ.

Which part is actually negated? The subject or the predicate? We say that لَيْسَ **excludes the <u>predicate</u> from the subject.**

Let's play with this sentence.

wrong	If you rearrange the sentence in such way, it looks wrong – and it is wrong!	لَيْسَ سَيَّارَةٌ لَدَيْهِ.
correct	This is a correct sentence because the "subject" is **not** <u>separated</u> from لَيْسَ.	لَيْسَتْ سَيَّارَةٌ لَدَيْهِ.
correct	This looks correct and most scholars say that it is indeed – although the verb doesn't agree with the "subject"!	لَيْسَ لَدَيْهِ سَيَّارَةٌ.
	This needs some explanation. There is another part of the sentence (لَدَيْهِ) between the اِسْمُ لَيْسَ ("subject") and the verb لَيْسَ, which is the reason why this is approved.	

Remark: If you use لَيْسَ similar to a particle (→ you don't conjugate it), it often **negates single elements** of the sentence:

It was not I who killed him.	لَيْسَ أَنَا قَتَلْتُهُ

182. لَسْتُ أَدْرِي - Is there a mistake?

No, there isn't.

The expression لَسْتُ أَدْرِي means *I don't know*.

Usually, we use the verb لَيْسَ only to negate a nominal sentence (جُمْلَةٌ اِسْمِيّةٌ).

Here we have a verb after لَيْسَ. It is the I-verb يَدْرِي - دَرَى (R3=ي) which means *to know; to be aware.*

The negation with لَيْسَ conveys a very strong idea of non-existence and is mainly used in literature. You may negate any verbal sentence with لَيْسَ. Such constructions are rare and mostly used with the first person singular: *I.* When you negate a verb with لَيْسَ, you change the DNA of the sentence. Suddenly, the verbal sentence works as the predicate (خَبَر) of لَيْسَ.

Don't forget: Although لَيْسَ is a past tense verb, you **negate the present tense**.

| We do not come to you. | لَسْنا نَصِلُ إِلَيْكَ. |
| I don't remember. | لَسْتُ أَذْكُرُ. |

183. Can you praise or condemn something with one word?

Yes, you can. You use نِعْمَ for the good and بِئْسَ for the bad.

نِعْمَ and بِئْسَ are two extraordinary **verbs** which convey an emphatic meaning. Both are used in a special sentence construction called *praise* and *criticism* (أُسْلُوبُ الْمَدْحِ وَالذَّمِّ).

| what a good / superb / perfect / wonderful / truly excellent ... | نِعْمَ |
| what bad / miserable ... | بِئْسَ |

We don't deal with ordinary verbs here. Both are *inert, static verbs* (فِعْلٌ جامِدٌ) similar to لَيْسَ. Such verbs do not form all tenses. نِعْمَ and بِئْسَ are only used in the past tense (الْماضِي). They cannot be conjugated in the present tense (الْمُضارِعُ), they also cannot be used in the imperative (الأَمْرُ).

- Moreover, these two verbs never change their form. They have a fixed, **cemented shape**.
- The word after نِعْمَ or بِئْسَ (the word being qualified) must be a **definite noun** in the **nominative** case (مَرْفُوعٌ).
- The feminine forms نِعْمَتْ / بِئْسَتْ are rarely used.

It's probably best to see them both in action.

What an excellent man Karīm is! → ل at the beginning is used to intensify the meaning!	لَنِعْمَ الرَّجُلُ كَرِيمٌ!
He is a wonderful friend indeed. → The particle إِنَّ is used for emphasis.	إِنَّهُ نِعْمَ الْخَلِيلُ.
What bad men you both are!	لَبِئْسَ الرَّجُلانِ أَنْتُما!

نِعْمَ and بِئْسَ can also be used with a relative pronoun (اِسْمٌ مَوْصُولٌ), i.e., with ما or مَن. Merged with the particle ما, the meaning is slightly different and often translated as *indeed*.

Indeed, bad things you did! (German: *Gar Schlechtes hast du getan!*)	بِئْسَما صَنَعْتَ!

There are other Arabic words which follow the same rules, meaning: they are unchangeable, connected to a noun in the nominative case, and used emphatically!

what/how a great..., monumental...	جَلَّ	عَزَّ
	شَدَّ	هَدَّ
what a big...		كَبُرَ
what a bad..., wicked...		ساءَ

what a nice..., beautiful...	حَسُنَ - حُسْنَ - حَسْنَ
what a great..., powerful...	عَظُمَ - عُظْمَ - عَظْمَ
how lovely..., what lovely...	حَبَّ + ذا
how terrible, bad...	لا حَبَّ + ذا

Some examples.

How lovely you are!	حَبَّذا أَنْتَ!
How dear/strong you loved her!	لَشَدَّ ما أَحْبَبْتَها!
What big/bad word comes out of your mouth!	كَبُرَتْ كَلِمةً تَخْرُجُ مِن أَفْواهِكُمْ.

In the last example, we used the feminine form. But this is optional! You can also use just كَبُرَ. Watch out: The word فَمٌ is tricky!. If you want to say *your mouth* (singular), you say فِيكَ or فَمِكَ (if مَجْرُورٌ).

| What an annoying hypocrisy! | لا حَبَّذا النَّفاقُ! |

A few remarks about حَبَّ:

- The verb حَبَّ is used as a static verb (فِعْلٌ جامِدٌ) and is merged with a demonstrative pronoun (اِسْمُ إشارةٍ).
- The demonstrative pronoun ذا is the subject (فاعِلٌ) and thus should get the nominative case. Since it has a fixed shape, we can only use a virtual case marker and assign the place value of a nominative case (فِي مَحَلِّ رَفْعٍ).
- If you want to express criticism, use the negation: لا حَبَّذا

Note: For an analysis of such sentences, see *Arabic for Nerds 2, #446*.

184. When does a verb need the مَنْصُوبٌ-mood?

This mood indicates that an action is intended or expected.

Certain devices induce the *subjunctive* mood (مَنْصُوبٌ) in Arabic verbs. In grammar, مَنْصُوبٌ means basically *with open ending*. *Open* here means that the last vowel is "*a*" (فَتْحةٌ).

What does such a vowel at the end of a verb tell us? There are several possibilities. The verb may relate to a state or act that you want to do; that you won't do; that you would like to have; that you could do.

Therefore, the subjunctive mood cannot be used on its own. **It is connected to a possibility, to a wish or a duty** (which usually stands at the beginning of the sentence). Certain words and particles ignite this mood in the verb.

that; in order to	Device to mold an interpreted infinitive (أَنْ المَصْدَرِيّةُ). See *question #81*.	أَنْ	1

not to; don't	لا is a *particle of interdiction* (حَرْفُ نَهْي). Used to request leaving a matter, to refuse it, to forbid it.	أَنْ لا = أَلّا	2

I wrote to him not to slow down = that he should not slow down.	كَتَبْتُ إِلَيْهِ أَلّا تُبْطِئَ.

in order to; so that; so	Lām of causality and *justification* (لَامُ تَعْلِيلٍ). لِ can also be used to mold an interpreted infinitive (مَصْدَرٌ مُؤَوَّلٌ).	لِ	3

We assume that the particle أَنْ is implicitly there. Thus, in fact, we have لِأَنْ, but usually, you only write لِ. However, if you want to negate the verb, you need to write أَنْ. The result is: لِئَلّا.

Be audacious in order to reach glory!	غَامِرْ لِتَبْلُغَ الْمَجْدَ!
Study so that you don't fail!	اُدْرُسْ لِئَلَّا تَرْسُبَ!
He said: "So that there would not be any hardship on his Ummah." (Hadith; Sunan al-Nasāʾī 609).	قَالَ لِئَلَّا يَكُونَ عَلَى أُمَّتِهِ حَرَجٌ.

(emphasis) *Lām of denial* (لامُ الْجُحُودِ). It occurs after the negated form of *to be* (كَانَ) in order to confirm the negation.	لِ	4

I was not a tyrant to people.	لَمْ أَكُنْ لِأَظْلِمَ النّاسَ.

so that	*Fāʾ of occasion* or *causality* (فاءٌ سَبَبِيَّةٌ). Used if a preceding word indicates a wish, command, question or prohibition – usually expressed by an imperative.	فَ	5

Be generous, so that you will prevail.	جُودُوا فَتَسُودُوا.
Stand up, then I will stand up!	قُمْ فَأَقُومَ!

in order to; so that	*Kāf of causality* and *justification* (كافُ تَعْلِيلِ). It can be used instead of أَنْ to build an interpreted infinitive (مَصْدَرٌ مُؤَوَّلٌ).	كَيْ لِكَيْ	6

Be active, so that you can succeed!	إِعْمَلْ كَيْ تَنْجَحَ!

in order not to	This works similar to أَلَّا – see number 2.	كَيْ لا = كَيْلا لِكَيْ لا = لِكَيْلا	7

until; so that; in order to	حَتَّى can convey many meanings take on several jobs in a sentence.	حَتَّى	8

Here, we only look at two functions:

a) حَتَّى as a *particle of causality* (حَرْفُ تَعْلِيلٍ). It is a synonym of the *Lām of causality* and *justification* (لامُ تَعْلِيلٍ). We have to use the subjunctive mood because we assume that the particle أَنْ is implicitly involved and virtually understood.

b) حَتَّى as a *particle of finality* (حَرْفُ غايةٍ). It is used to indicate an intention or the result plus its consequences.

Be active, so that you can succeed !	إِعْمَلْ كَيْ تَنْجَحَ!	a)

I ate the fish in order to leave only its head. (See *Arabic for Nerds 2*, #189)	أَكَلْتُ السَّمَكَةَ حَتَّى رَأْسِها.	b)

Cases matter! The genitive case (مَجْرُورٌ) in رَأْسِها expresses that the *head* is **not** eaten because it is a particle of finality! If رَأْسَها was in the accusative case (مَنْصُوبٌ), then حَتَّى would work as a conjunction (حَرْفُ الْعَطْفِ) expressing: *I ate all the fish, even its head*. Then, the head would be eaten as well!

will not	Particle to deny or negate the occurrence of the verb in the future (حَرْفُ مَعْنًى مَبْنِيٌّ يَنْفِي وُقُوعَهُ فِي الْمُستقْبَلِ).	لَنْ	9

I will not help the corrupt people.	لَنْ أَكُونَ مُناصِرًّ لِلْفاسِدِينَ.	

in that case;	Particle (حَرْفٌ) with a fixed shape (مَبْنِيٌّ).	إِذَنْ	10

| therefore; so; then | It is placed at the start of an answer clause (صَدْرُ الْجَوابِ). Note: The verb after إِذَنْ in the subjunctive mood expresses the <u>future</u>! | |

| In that case you will succeed. | إِذَنْ تَنْجَحَ. |
| In that case I will leave after your visit. | إِذَنْ أَذْهَبَ بَعْدَ زِيارَتِكَ. |

What about the usual killjoys و or ي؟

If the **last root** letter is weak (حَرْفُ عِلّةٍ) and you need the subjunctive (مَنْصُوبٌ), you need to check the vowels.

What matters is the **vowel** of the **second root-letter** in the **present tense**!

	example		What is the مَنْصُوبٌ-ending?	last letter	verb	
he won't be pleased	لَنْ يَرْضَى		hidden "a"	ى	يَرْضَى	1
he won't complain	لَنْ يَشْكُوَ		فَتْحَةٌ on top of و	و	يَشْكُو	2
he won't throw	لَنْ يَرْمِيَ		فَتْحَةٌ on top of ي	ي	يَرْمِي	3

185. *Nice flowers.* Should you say زَهْرٌ جَمِيلٌ or زَهْرٌ جَمِيلَةٌ؟

You should say زَهْرٌ جَمِيلٌ.

زَهْرٌ is the *collective plural* (اِسْمُ جِنْسٍ جَمْعِيٌّ) for *flowers*. It indicates the meaning of the plural as well as its genus.

In biology, genus describes a group of animals or plants that share some characteristics in a larger biological group.

Usually, you start from the singular to build a plural. Here, we do the opposite! You basically **convert a plural into a singular** if you want to express one unit. This is achieved by adding ة or building a Nisba adjective (يَاءُ النِّسْبَةِ). The singular form of زَهْرٌ is زَهْرَةٌ which means *a flower* or *blossom*.

عَرَبِيٌّ	an Arab		عَرَبٌ	Arabs
عَسْكَرِيٌّ	a soldier		عَسْكَرٌ	army (camp)
تُفَّاحَةٌ	an apple	◀	تُفَّاحٌ	apples
زَهْرَةٌ	a flower		زَهْرٌ	flowers
دَمْعَةٌ	a tear		دَمْعٌ	tears
حَدِيدَةٌ	a piece of iron		حَدِيدٌ	iron

We can thus say that we do not form the regular plural of the singular unit. Otherwise, we would get plural nouns like زَهْرَاتٌ or تُفَّاحَاتٌ. Since we do not have real plural forms, we call words like زَهْرٌ *quasi-plurals* (شِبْهُ الْجَمْعِ).

Collective nouns don't describe a specific group, but species. For example: شَجَرٌ (*trees*); عِلْمُ الشَّجَرِ (*dendrology; science of trees*); لَحْمُ الْبَقَرِ (*beef; meat*). Collective nouns, in comparison to English, tend to have a distinction between being collective and being countable, often related to elements in nature.

This explains why we have different plural forms in Arabic. The difference between شَجَرٌ and أَشْجَارٌ is like the difference between *Gebirge* (species) and *Berge* in German. Both mean *mountains*. Regarding *Gebirge*, you are thinking of the mountains as **one entity**; regarding *Berge*, you are thinking of them as **individual entities**.

There is a remarkable thing about collective nouns – **the gender**:

> Generic collectives (collective plurals) are **masculine** (مُذَكَّر).

Since adjectives need to agree with the word they describe, collective plurals go along with a **masculine** singular adjective. That is striking because in Arabic, we normally use the feminine form of the adjective when they relate to a plural.

tall trees	شَجَرٌ طَوِيلٌ

This is only true for the pseudo-plural. There is another plural of زَهْرةٌ which is: أَزْهارٌ. It is used to describe a small amount of flowers, like a bouquet or a bunch of. In this situation, the adjective follows the regular rules of plurals. So, we need the feminine form: أَزْهارٌ جَميلةٌ (*beautiful flowers*).

But there is one exception: Only **collective names** of **tribes** and **people** are treated as feminine!

يَهُودِيٌّ	a Jew	◄	يَهُودٌ	Jews
هِنْدِيٌّ	an Indian		هِنْدٌ	Indians
قُرَيْشِيٌّ	a Qurayshite		قُرَيْشٌ	Quraysh

Watch out: Some collective plurals do not form a singular unit. For example, طَيْرٌ means *bird* <u>or</u> *birds*! The collective plural is understood to be the individual noun as well. If you want to express flocks of birds, you may use the plural form طُيُورٌ.

186. How do you say *not at all* in Arabic?

You have several options.

In English, you use *not at all* if you want to emphasize the fact that you have not done anything or that you have never done a certain thing. In Arabic, you could use the following expressions to convey this idea:

with negation: *not at all; never; by no means.* Since it is used as an adverb of time, the noun غَيْرَ has the vowel "*a*" (فَتْحَةٌ).	غَيْرَ مَرَّةٍ لا...بِالْمَرَّةِ	1
never; not at any point; in any respect; by no means	مُطْلَقًا لا...عَلَى الإِطلاقِ	2
never; not at all (with the future tense only! See *Arabic for Nerds 2*, question #350).	أَبَدًا	3
not at all; in the first place	أَصْلًا	4
totally not; not at all	بِأَكْمَلِها	5
not at all (acknowledging thanks)	عَفْوًا ! = العَفْوَ!	6
absolutely not, definitely not. It comes from the root ب-ت-ت which means *to complete.*	بَتَّةَ or الْبَتَّةَ	7

Let's look at how these expressions behave in sentences.

I've seen him more than once.	رَأَيْتُهُ غَيْرَ مَرَّةٍ.	1
I haven't seen him at all.	لا رَأَيْتُهُ غَيْرَ مَرَّةٍ.	
It will not be accepted at all.	لَنْ يُقبَلَ مُطْلَقًا.	2
not a thing	لا شَيْءَ مُطْلَقًا	

I won't scream at all!	لَنْ أَصْرُخَ أَبَدًا!	3
There were no people there at all.	لَمْ يَكُنْ هُناكَ ناسّ أَصْلًا.	4
She won't be in Cairo at all.	لَنْ تَكُونَ فِي الْقاهِرة بِأَكْمَلِها.	5
A: Thank you very much! B: You are welcome/Not at all.	شُكْرًا جَزِيلًا! الْعَفْوُ = لا شُكْرَ عَلَى واجِبٍ!	6
A: Are you ill? B: Not at all!	أَأَنْتَ مَرِيضٌ؟ لا لَسْتُ مَرِيضًا أَلْبَتَّةَ.	7

187. *The girl is bigger than... - Why is that tricky in Arabic?*

You need to decide whether you should use أَكْبَرُ or كُبْرَى.

For the translation of this sentence, you need to form a **comparative**. In linguistics, a comparative is the form of an adjective that expresses a difference in amount, number, degree, or quality.

An adjective (in English) can exist in three forms: positive, comparative, and superlative.

You will encounter several grammar terms:

positive	comparative	superlative	elative
big	*bigger*	*biggest*	*very big; especially big*

For example:

This boy is bigger than his brothers.	هذا الْوَلَدُ أَكْبَرُ مِن إِخْوَتِهِ.

	term	explanation
الْوَلَدُ	الْمُفَضَّلُ	*The preferred.* The thing which has more of it. It is placed <u>before</u> the comparative.
أَكْبَرُ	اِسْمُ تَفْضِيلٍ	*Noun of preference* (اِسْمُ تَفْضِيلٍ); a derived noun (اِسْمٌ مُشْتَقٌّ). It uses the pattern أَفْعَلُ. In its pure form, it is an **elative**. By using certain constructions, you can give it the meaning of a **comparative** or **superlative**.
إِخْوَتِه	الْمُفَضَّلُ عَلَيْهِ	*The thing which is inferior.* Placed <u>after</u> مِنْ of the comparative. Note that there is no الْمُفَضَّلُ عَلَيْهِ in the superlative.

For example, the comparative of *big* (كَبِيرٌ) is *bigger* (أَكْبَرُ). This is the **masculine** (مُذَكَّرٌ) form. However, in the sentence *The girl is bigger than...* we talk about a girl. So, does that mean that we have to use the feminine form of *bigger*, which would be كُبْرَى? Well, we will see.

We have many options to translate our example into Arabic. Let's go through them. Pay attention to the vowels at the end!

1	Comparative meaning: *bigger than*	أَنْ يَكُونَ مُجَرَّدًا مِن أل وَالإِضافة

It is always أَكْبَرُ مِن. You always use the **masculine** form! There are some important things you should know:

- Don't use the definite article. It is only أَكْبَرُ and not الْأَكْبَرُ.
- This isn't an إِضافةٌ-construction. Note the preposition مِن after أَكْبَرُ.

<table>
<tr><th>English translation</th><th colspan="3">example</th></tr>
<tr><td>This boy is bigger than his brothers.</td><td>إِخْوَتِهِ.</td><td rowspan="6">أَكْبَرُ مِن</td><td>هٰذا الْوَلَدُ</td></tr>
<tr><td>This girl is bigger than her sisters.</td><td>أَخَواتِها.</td><td>هٰذِهِ الْبِنْتُ</td></tr>
<tr><td>These two boys are bigger than their brothers.</td><td>إِخْوَتِهِما.</td><td>هٰذانِ الْوَلَدانِ</td></tr>
<tr><td>These two girls are bigger than their sisters.</td><td>أَخَواتِهِما.</td><td>هاتانِ الْبِنْتانِ</td></tr>
<tr><td>These boys are bigger than their brothers.</td><td>إِخْوَتِهِمْ.</td><td>هٰؤلاء الْأَوْلادُ</td></tr>
<tr><td>These girls are bigger than their sisters.</td><td>أَخَواتِهِنَّ.</td><td>هٰؤلاء الْبَناتُ</td></tr>
</table>

Notice that أَكْبَرُ مِن stays the same in every sentence! In the comparative, we don't use the feminine form nor dual/plural, and there is no agreement!

- It **always** has the same form: **masculine** and **singular**.
- أَكْبَرُ doesn't take nunation (تَنْوِينٌ) because this pattern (morpheme) is a diptote (مَمنُوعٌ مَن الصَّرْفِ).

Therefore, the answer to our question is: ...الْبِنْتُ أَكْبَرُ مِن

2	Superlative meaning: ***the biggest***	أَنْ يَكُونَ مَعْرِفًا بِأَل

- أَكْبَرُ changes its gender and number. It needs the **definite article**.
- The *preferred thing* (الْمُفَضَّلُ) also gets the **definite article**.
- We need to apply the rules of <u>adjectives</u> (صِفةٌ).

English translation	إِسْمُ التَّفْضِيلِ	الْمُفَضَّلُ		
This is the biggest boy.	الْأَكْبَرُ.	الْوَلَدُ	هوَ	هٰذا
This is the biggest girl.	الْكُبْرَى.	الْبِنْتُ	هِيَ	هٰذِهِ
These two are the biggest (two) boys.	الْأَكْبَرانِ.	الْوَلَدانِ	هُما	هٰذانِ
These two are the biggest (two) girls.	الْكُبْرَيانِ.	الْبِنْتانِ	هُما	هاتانِ
These boys are the biggest.	الْأَكْبَرُونَ or الْأَكْبَرُ.	الْأَوْلادُ	هُمْ	هٰؤُلاء
These girls are the biggest.	الْكُبْرَياتُ or الْكُبَرُ.	الْبَناتُ	هُنَّ	هٰؤُلاءِ

Some remarks:

- For the correct agreement, the إِسْمُ التَّفْضِيلِ has to follow the الْمُفَضَّلُ.

- If you have a feminine dual, you have to write ي and not ت because there is ى at the end of the feminine form! For example, الْكُبْرَيانِ.

- When the إِسْمُ التَّفْضِيلِ is the object of a sentence, then it has to be in the accusative case (مَنْصُوبٌ)! For example:

I saw the two big (biggest) girls.	شاهَدْتُ الْبِنْتَينِ الْكُبْرَيَيْنِ.

3	Superlative meaning: *the biggest*	أَنْ يَكُونَ مُضافًا إِلَى نَكِرَةٍ

- We only use أَكْبَرُ.

- The إِسْمُ التَّفْضِيلِ is <u>always</u> **masculine** and **singular**.

- We use a إِضافةٌ-construction.
- The *preferred thing* (الْمُفَضَّلُ) is **indefinite** and serves as the second part of the إِضافةٌ → it is in the genitive case.
- This type conveys the **strongest** superlative meaning!

English translation	الْمُفَضَّلُ	اِسْمُ التَّفْضيلِ		
This is the biggest boy.	وَلَدٍ.		هُوَ	هذا
This is the biggest girl.	بِنْتٍ.		هِيَ	هٰذِهِ
These two are the biggest boys.	وَلَدَيْنِ.	أَكْبَرُ	هُما	هذانِ
These two are the biggest girls.	بِنْتَيْنِ.		هُما	هاتانِ
These are the biggest boys.	أَوْلادٍ.		هُمَ	هؤُلاءِ
These are the biggest girls.	بَناتٍ.		هُنَّ	هؤُلاءِ

4	Superlative meaning: *the biggest*	أَنْ يَكُونَ مُضافًا إِلَى مَعْرِفَةٍ

1. You have the choice: You can use أَكْبَرُ or the appropriate form that corresponds in gender and number with the *preferred thing* (الْمُفَضَّلُ).
2. The الْمُفَضَّلُ has the **definite** article.
3. The comparative (اِسْمُ التَّفْضيلِ) is indefinite (نَكِرَةٌ).

English translation	الْمُفَضَّلُ	اِسْمُ التَّفْضيلِ		
This is the biggest boy.	الأَوْلادِ	أَكْبَرُ	هوَ	هذا
This is the biggest girl.	الْبَناتِ	أَكْبَرُ - كُبْرَى	هِيَ	هذه

These two are the biggest boys.	الأَوْلادِ	أَكْبَرُ - أَكْبَرا	هُما	هذانِ
These two are the biggest girls.	الْبَناتِ	أَكْبَرُ - أَكْبَريا	هُما	هاتانِ
These are the biggest boys.	الأَوْلادِ	أَكْبَرُ - أَكْبَروا	هُمْ	هؤُلاء
These are the biggest girls.	الْبَناتِ	أَكْبَرُ - كُبْرَياتُ	هُنَّ	هؤُلاء

Now, does it matter which construction you use? No, it doesn't. Most sentences are translated in the same way. But there are finesses and nuances.

In this constructions, we can't tell how many children we compare. It may be only two.	هذا هُوَ أَكْبَرُ الأَوْلادِ.
The superlative here has an **absolute sense**: the biggest **(known)** child.	هذا هُوَ أَكْبَرُ وَلَدٍ.

the highest of the mountains	أَعْلَى الْجِبالِ
the highest (known) mountain	أَعْلَى جَبَلٍ

188. What is the stem of the verb *to be reassured* (إِطْمَأَنَّ)?

It is a IV-verb – with four root letters!

The root of يَطْمَئِنُّ - اطْمَأَنَّ contains **four** letters: ط-م-ء-ن. The basic I-verb of this root with four letters is يُطَمْئِنُ - طَمْأَنَ which means *to pacify, to reassure*.

Which pattern should we use for a IV-verb with 4 root letters? ➔ It is اِفْعَلَلَّ.

You put a connecting هَمْزَة at the beginning and double the last radical (فِعْلٌ مَزِيدٌ رُباعِيٌّ). The conjugation of a IV-verb of four root letters is similar to the conjugation of a IX-verb based on three root letters. For example, the IX-verb *to turn red; to blush* (اِحْمَرَّ).

- Many IV-verbs (four root letters) express a **reflexive** or **superlative meaning**. Reflexive verbs indicate that the person who does the action is also the person who is affected by it. What is meant by superlative? Two examples:

The hair trembled. This means that the hair rose up and stood upright because of fear, weather, or any other reason.	اِقْشَعَرَّ الشَّعرُ.
The night was dark. Here, the verb tells you that darkness grew up and blackened.	اِكْفَهَرَّ اللَّيْلُ.

- Many of these verbs don't form the passive voice. Thus, also the passive participle (اِسْمُ مَفْعُولٍ) is rarely used. Theoretically, you would use the pattern مُفْعَلَلٌّ. In our example, we would get مُطْمَأَنٌّ.

Let's check the **derived nouns** of اِطْمَأَنَّ:

meaning	pattern	type	word
he was reassured	اِفْعَلَلَّ	الْماضِي	اِطْمَأَنَّ
he is reassured	يَفْعَلِلُّ	الْمُضارِعُ	يَطْمَئِنُّ
tranquility; serenity	اِفْعِلّالٌ	الْمَصْدَرُ	اِطْمِئْنانٌ
be reassured!	masculine	الْأَمْرُ (imperative)	اِطْمَأْنِنْ
	feminine		اِطْمَئِنِّي
	plural		اِطْمَئِنُّوا

مُطْمَئِنٌّ	اِسْمُ الْفَاعِلِ	مُفْعَلِلٌّ	calm

189. How do you say *more crowded* in Arabic?

Not by a single word. You can't express "more crowded" by building the comparative of "crowded" – it is simply impossible.

So how can we solve the problem? Adjectives in Arabic are not a certain type of word like the English word *beautiful*. In Arabic, we use nouns that can qualify to work as adjectives. These nouns are derived from the root (اِسْمٌ مُشْتَقٌّ) and have different shapes, patterns, and grammatical origins.

There are seven conditions that need to be fulfilled if we want to build the *noun of preference* (اِسْمُ تَفْضِيلٍ).

1	Our source must be the most basic form of the verb: **stem I** of a **triliteral** root.	فِعْلٌ ثُلاثِيٌّ
2	The word of which we want to build the comparative **isn't a quasi participle** (an active participle-like adjective). In other words, it is not an adjective that indicates firmness. → It should not be derived from a static verb which describe a state rather than an action.	أَلّا تَكُونَ صِفَةً مُشَبَّهَةً
3	Our starting point is the **active voice** – not the passive.	أَنْ يَكُونَ الْفِعْلُ مَبْنِيًّا لِلمَعْلُومِ
4	The verb is **not negated** (i.e., affirmative).	أَنْ يَكُونَ الْفِعْلُ مُثْبَتًا, لَيْسَ مَنْفِيًّا
5	The verb is **not defective** and has a **subject**.	أَنْ يَكُونَ الْفِعْلُ تامًّا, لَهُ فاعِلٌ

6	The verb can be **conjugated in all tenses and moods**.	أَنْ يَكُونَ الفِعْلُ مُتَصَرِّفًا
7	A **comparison** is **meaningful** and does make sense.	أَنْ يَكُونَ الْفِعْلُ قابِلًا لِلتَفاوُتِ

This all sounds quite theoretical. It becomes practical as soon as one of the above conditions is violated. You run into this situation when you need to translate expressions like *more respected; more crowded; more intense red; feeling more not like going to*. We will now go through each of the seven conditions and see what happens when the condition is violated.

CONDITION 1: It is not a I-verb, so its pattern has more than three letters.	possible

We can fix this by a construction called أُسلُوبُ التَّفْضِيلِ. Let us take the VIII-verb اِزْدَحَمَ - يَزْدَحِمُ (R1=ز) which means *to be crowded*. Now, we want to say the following: *Cairo is more crowded than Beirut*. How do you translate that into Arabic? Here is a step by step guide:

▷ **1. Build the مَصْدَرٌ**. The root of اِزْدَحَمَ is زَحَمَ. Note that the letter د is not part of the root. Since we have a VIII-verb of the pattern اِفْتَعَلَ, it should actually be ت, but it was replaced by a د to make the pronunciation easier. The مَصْدَرٌ is اِزْدِحامٌ.

▷ **2. Choose an auxiliary word (اِسْمُ تَفْضِيلٍ)**. Usually you use one of the following words (مُساعِدٌ) for the construction.

more; bigger	أَكْثَرُ		more; more intense	أَشَدُّ		less	أَقَلُّ

> **3. Combine both words.** We use a trick here. We do not use a إضافةٌ-construction. We use a **specification** (تَمْييزٌ) which is the reason for the accusative case (مَنْصوبٌ); see *question #167* and *Arabic for Nerds 2, question #381*.

Cairo is more crowded than Beirut.	الْقاهِرةُ أَكْثَرُ ازْدِحامًا مِن بَيْروتَ.

CONDITION 2: The comparative of an active participle-like adjective (الصِّفةُ الْمُشَبَّهةُ).	possible

These two patterns form pseudo participles (صِفةٌ مُشَبَّهةٌ):

masculine	أَفْعَلُ		feminine	فَعْلاءُ

In the pattern فَعْلاءُ, notice the فَتْحةٌ above the first letter! If it was ضَمّةٌ, it would be a regular comparative form and not a صِفةٌ مُشَبَّهةٌ! For example, the feminine form of *bigger*: كُبْرَى.

Some examples of a صِفةٌ مُشَبَّهةٌ:

meaning	feminine form	masculine form	root/verb
red	حَمْراءُ	أَحْمَرُ	حَمِرَ
blind	عَمْياءُ	أَعْمَى	عَمِىَ

A صِفةٌ مُشَبَّهةٌ cannot form a comparative in Arabic! If we insist on expressing the idea, we need a helping construction. Here is a step by step guide:

> **1. Build the مَصْدَرٌ**. Let us take a look at these examples:

meaning	مَصْدَرٌ	pattern	root
redness; red color	حُمْرةٌ	فُعْلةٌ	ح-م-ر

blueness; blue color	زُرْقَةٌ		ز-ر-ق

Watch out – there are two famous exceptions:

meaning	مَصْدَرٌ	root
whiteness; white color	بَياضٌ	ب-ي-ض
blackness; black color	سَوادٌ	س-و-د

➤ 2. Choose an auxiliary word (إِسْمُ تَفْضِيلٍ).

more; bigger	أَكْثَرُ		more; more intense	أَشَدُّ		less	أَقَلُّ

This is the result – also here, we use a **specification** (تَمْيِيزٌ).

The flower has more red-ness than the other flower.	الْوَرْدَةُ أَشَدُّ حُمْرَةً مِن الْوَرْدَةِ الأُخْرى.

CONDITION 3: The comparative of a passive voice.	possible

In Arabic, you can't build a comparative form by using the passive voice itself. For example: *more respected*. Before we dig into this matter, let us quickly check what we are talking about. The passive voice of a I-verb is built by the pattern فُعِلَ for the past tense and يُفْعَلُ for the present tense.

active voice (مَعْلُومٌ) of the verb *to listen*	يَسْمَعُ	سَمِعَ
passive voice (مَجْهُولٌ) of the verb *to listen*	يُسْمَعُ	سُمِعَ

Let's check now the VIII-verb *to respect* (اِحْتَرَمَ).

passive, present tense		past tense		pattern	root
he is respected	يُحْتَرَمُ	he respected	اِحْتَرَمَ	اِفْتَعَلَ	حَرِمَ

If we want to express *more crowded*, we need another solution and can apply a new trick. Here is a step by step guide.

▷ 1. Build an interpreted infinitive (مَصْدَرٌ مُؤَوَّلٌ) → see question #81. This is easy.

interpreted infinitive (مَصْدَرٌ مُؤَوَّلٌ)	original infinitive (مَصْدَرٌ أَصْلِيٌّ)
أَنْ يُحْتَرَمَ	اِحْتِرامٌ

▷ 2. Choose an auxiliary word (اِسْمُ تَفْضِيلٍ).

The following words mean basically the same, you can choose any of them. Don't forget that all of them are diptotes and don't take nunation (مَمْنُوعٌ مِن الصَّرْفِ).

meaning	اِسْمُ تَفْضِيلٍ	root
worthier; more deserving	أَحَقُّ	حَقَّ
more appropriate, suitable, deserving	أَوْلَى	وَلَى
worthier; more suitable	أَجْدَرُ	جَدَرَ

▷ 3. Combine both. Here is the result:

The father is more respected.	الأَبُّ أَحَقُّ أَنْ يُحْتَرَمَ.

| CONDITION 4: The verb is negated. | possible |

Let's see how we can fix a sentence if we have **لا يَعْرِفُ**. We will follow and apply the same procedure as shown in CONDITION 3. The only thing we must not forget is the negation!

➤ 1. Build an interpreted infinitive (مَصْدَرٌ مُؤَوَّلٌ).

This is tricky since we have a negation (see *question #208*).

| أَلّا يَعْرِفَ | = | يَعْرِفُ | + | لا | + | أَنْ |

Notice that أَنْ plus لا becomes أَلّا

➤ 2. Choose an auxiliary word (اِسْمُ تَفْضِيلٍ).

As explained above, the following words mean basically the same, you can choose any of them: أَحَقُّ • أَوْلَى • أَجْدَرُ

➤ 3. Combine both. Here is the result:

| It is better for humans not to lie. | الإنْسانُ أَجْدَرُ أَلّا يَعْرِفَ الْكِذْبَ. |
| My colleague deserves not to go. | زَمِيلي أَحَقُّ أَلّا يَذْهَبَ. |

| CONDITION 5: We have a verb that does not have a subject/doer of the action (فاعِلٌ). Furthermore, it is *defective*. | impossible |

There are verbs in Arabic which are not satisfied with only a subject. Unless you add a **predicate**, they would not provide a meaningful sentence. That is the reason why such verbs are called *deficient* (فِعْلٌ ناقِصٌ) opposite to *complete* verbs (فِعْلٌ

تامٌّ). A deficient verb does not give you information by itself. A well-known example is the verb *to be* (كانَ).

The weather was nice.	كانَ الْجَوُّ جَمِيلًا.

As for كانَ, there is no way to express a comparison. Sounds logical, because what should be the comparative of *to be*?

CONDITION 6: The verb can't be conjugated in all tenses and moods.	**impossible**

There are verbs in Arabic which can't be conjugated in all tenses and moods (فِعْلٌ ناقِصُ التَّصْرِيفِ). For example, لَيْسَ which is used to negate nominal sentences (جُمْلةٌ اِسْمِيّةٌ) is only known in the past tense (الْماضِي). It cannot form the present tense (الْمُضارِعُ), nor the imperative (الْأَمْرُ).

Such verbs are also called inert, static verbs (فِعْلٌ جامِدٌ). They do not accept changes in their forms which also makes them close to particles (حَرْفٌ). Regarding لَيْسَ, there is no way to express a comparison. Therefore, we absolutely need a complete/full verb (فِعْلٌ مُتَصَرِّفٌ).

CONDITION 7: You can't make a real comparison.	**possible**

If someone is dead, he is dead. You can't be *more dead*. But what if it is meant in the sense of time? For example: *he has died before...* A similar example of another idea: *he has been sitting on the chair longer than...* That makes sense.

We could form the comparative of such words if we have the idea of time in mind (the amount of time; length). Let us use the I-verb يَجْلِسُ - جَلَسَ which means *to sit*.

> **1. Build the original infinitive (مَصْدَرٌ أَصْلِيٌّ).**

This is easy: جُلُوسٌ.

> **2. Choose an auxiliary word (إِسْمُ تَفْضِيلٍ).**

Here we need words connected to time.

meaning	إِسْمُ تَفْضِيلٍ	root
previous; former; earlier	أَسْبَقُ	سَبَقَ

> **3. Combine both.** We use a **specification (تَمْيِيزٌ).**

Here is the result:

Meaning: The child sat down before the teacher.	الطِّفْلُ أَسْبَقُ جُلُوسًا مِن الْمُدَرِّسِ.
Meaning: 'Abd al-Naser died earlier than al-Sadāt.	عَبْدُ النَّاصِرِ أَسْبَقُ مَوْتًا مِن السَّداتِ.

190. Why shouldn't you say *I bought the Qur'an* in Arabic?

Since we assume that you want to buy a physical book, the word
الْقُرْآنُ *doesn't really fit.*

The root of الْقُرْآنُ is ق-ر-ء. Many dictionaries say that it is the infinitive noun (مَصْدَرٌ) of the verb *to read* (قَرَأَ / يَقْرَأُ). Hence, قُرْآن denotes the action of *to read* or *to recite*.

The origin of the word is not entirely clear. Mainly Western scholars say that the word is borrowed from Aramaic. Others say that the word الْقُرْآنُ uses the pattern فُعْلانٌ. This pattern is used for the مَصْدَرٌ of a triliteral verb, but it is not the standard pattern, it is **common usage** (وَزْنٌ سَماعِيٌّ). Other examples of this pattern are *thankfulness* (شُكْرانٌ) or *pardon* (غُفْرانٌ).

According to *Lane's Lexicon*, some scholars had suggested that الْقُرآن was originally the *noun of origin* (اِسْمُ الْمَصْدَرِ) of the expression: قَرَأْتُ الشَّيْءَ which means *I **collected** together the thing* or of قَرَأْتُ الْكِتابَ which means *I read (or recited) the book or scripture*. It was later conventionally applied *to signify the Book of God that was revealed to Muhammad.*

Precisely speaking, قُرآن describes all the words that are in the book. So it doesn't make sense to use this term if you want to say that you want a physical copy of the book.

Instead, it is better to use the expression الْمُصْحَفُ الشَّرِيفُ to denote *(a physical copy of) the Holy Qur'an.*

مُصْحَفٌ (plural: مَصاحِفُ) means *volume* or *binder*. It is the passive participle of the IV-verb أَصْحَفَ denoting *collected in it; put in it* (=أُصْحِفَ). A word related to this root is صَحِيفةٌ (plural: صُحُفٌ or صَحائِفُ) which means *newspaper*. Now, let's try to translate the sentence: *I bought the Qur'an (= a copy).*

understandable (poor style)	I bought the Qur'an.	إِشْتَرَيْتُ الْقُرآنَ.
better style		إِشْتَرَيْتُ الْمُصْحَفَ الشَّرِيفَ

191. Why is the verb *to wish* (عَسَى) of special kind?

It is immune to morphological changes.

The original meaning of عَسَى is *to be possible; it could be*. It belongs to a special group of verbs. They are called *inert, static verbs* (فِعْلٌ جامِدٌ) because they lack the flexibility to form tenses and moods.

عَسَى is only used in the past tense (الْماضِي). Present tense, future tense, the imperative simply don't exist. Furthermore, عَسَى is only used in the third person singular (masculine)! So, basically, it is never conjugated and always remains عَسَى.

The verb is usually followed by أَنْ plus verb in the subjunctive mood (مَنْصُوبٌ). It can be followed by the subject of a sentence which then has to be in the accusative case (مَنْصُوبٌ) because عَسَى follows the same rules as كادَ (see *questions #97* and *#98*). Remember that the predicate of كادَ has to be in the nominative case (مَرْفُوعٌ).

The verb عَسَى can get a personal pronoun suffix which makes the expression personal: *perhaps you; perhaps we, ...*

It could be; it was possible; wishfully; maybe. عَسَى expresses a wish or rhetorical question.	
What should I do?	ماذا عَسَى أَنْ أَفْعَلَ؟
What could he say?	ماذا عَساهُ يَقُولَ؟
The weather should be nice.	عَسَى الْجَوُّ يَكونَ جَميلًا.
Perhaps you are lazy?	عَساكَ كَسُولٌ؟
Perhaps I... (ن is needed to connect ي)	عَساني...
Maybe Allah (مَنْصُوبٌ!) will...	عَسَى اللهَ أَنْ...

For a deep analysis of عَسَى, see *Arabic for Nerds 2, #241 and #242*.

192. How do you say *dark/deep red*?

You use a construction which is pretty similar to English.

دَاكِن (plural: دَوَاكِنُ) means *dark* or *blackish* and is what we need for our translation. It is the active participle (إِسْمُ فَاعِلٍ) of the I-verb دَكِنَ - يَدْكَنُ which means *to darken*.

Since دَاكِن functions as an adjective (صِفَةٌ), you have to place it **after** the color. Hence, a possible translation of *dark red* is أَحْمَرُ دَاكِنٌ. Some examples – notice the gender of داكِن!

	dark skin	بَشرةٌ داكِنةٌ		dark green	أَخْضَرُ داكِنٌ
f.			m.		
	dark eyes	عُيونٌ داكِنةٌ		dark eyes	شَعْرٌ داكِنٌ

However, we can also use a different construction. Like any other صِفَةٌ, the word دَاكِن can be used in a *figurative (impure) possessive construction* (إِضافةٌ غَيْرُ مَحْضةٍ) which entails that the صِفَةٌ precedes the noun. Let's see the difference:

Zayd's book (the book of Zayd)	كِتابُ زَيْدٍ

This is a **pure possessive construction** (إِضافةٌ حَقيقيّةٌ). Why? Because it would be impossible to use a different case marker in the second part (*Zayd*)! It has to be the genitive case (مَجْرُورٌ).

In a pure إِضافةٌ-construction, you find its core, original idea: *determination* (تَعْرِيفٌ) and *specification* (تَخْصِيصٌ).

the thief of the house	سارِقُ الْمَنْزِلِ

This is an **impure إِضافةٌ**-construction (إِضافةٌ غَيْرُ حَقيقيّةٍ). How can we tell? The first part of the إِضافةٌ is an active participle (إِسْمُ فاعِلٍ). It has verbal power and could theoretically take a direct object (مَفْعُولٌ بِه). An active participle includes a hidden pronoun (in the nominative case). This hidden pronoun brings a separation between the first and second part of the إِضافةٌ. Any type of **separation** weakens the bond and link between the two words.

Theoretically, we could interpret the sentence differently. When we use the hidden pronoun *he*, we could transform the phrase into a meaningful sentence. We just need to use the verbal power of the active participle (it can work as a regent for the direct object). Thus, we use the accusative case (مَنْصُوبٌ) in the second word. What would be the result? هُوَ سارِقٌ الْمَنْزِلَ - *He steals the house.*

Let's return to our task: *dark/deep red.*

The active participle (اِسْمُ فاعِلٍ), the passive participle (اِسْمُ مَفْعُولٍ) as well as the quasi-participle (صِفَةٌ مُشَبَّهَةٌ) may be put as the first part of a إِضافةٌ. The very same words could also work as adjectives (with the effect that they switch places).

An adjective has to agree with the word which it wants to describe. When the modified noun is definite, the adjective has to be definite as well. This reveals our dilemma! We cannot have two visibly definite nouns in a إِضافةٌ. We can solve that by a figurative إِضافةٌ.

dark green	دَاكِنُ الْخُضْرةِ	*dark red*	دَاكِنُ الْحُمْرةِ
dark blue	دَاكِنُ الزُّرقةِ	*pitch black*	دَاكِنُ السَّوادِ

Look again closely at the words we used for the colors. The second part of the إِضافةٌ must be the **infinitive** noun (مَصْدَرٌ; *redness, blueness*) and not the **adjective** (صِفةٌ; *red, blue*).

dark black	دَاكِنُ السُّوداءِ	
dark red, deeply red	داكِنُ الأَحْمَرِ	**incorrect**

Remark: What we showed here has nothing to do with the **inverted word-order** when the predicate (خَبَرٌ) precedes the subject (مُبْتَدَأٌ) in a nominal sentence. For example:

Smoking is forbidden.	مَمْنُوعٌ التَّدْخِينُ.

Fronted predicate (خَبَرٌ مُقَدَّمٌ); it gets the nominative case (مَرْفُوعٌ بِالضَّمّةِ): "un".	مَمْنُوعٌ
Delayed subject (مُبْتَدَأٌ مُؤَخَّرٌ); it also gets the nominative case (مَرْفُوعٌ بِالضَّمّةِ).	التَّدْخِينُ

193. بَيْتًا or بَيْتاً - Where do you add the two lines at the end?

*The very correct view is that you should put it **before** the Aleph.*

The two lines plus the Aleph are used to mark nouns (اِسْم) with certain characteristics: **indefinite nouns** (اِسْمٌ نَكِرَةٌ) that need the **accusative** case (مَنْصُوبٌ). The marker symbolizes *nunation* (تَنْوِينٌ). In practice, two spellings are common: on top of the Aleph (بَيْتاً) and before the Aleph (بَيْتًا). Which one is correct? Well, it's a debate.

Especially Egyptian linguists argue that the تَنْوِينٌ should be written on the letter <u>before the Aleph</u>. They justify it with the fact that the Aleph is a silent letter (حَرْفٌ سَاكِنٌ) and can't take any vowel. It always carries سُكُونٌ and looks like اْ.

If we explicitly wrote out the ن of nunation, we would get بَيْتَنْ. It looks reasonable now that the vowel "*a*" of the nunation "*an*" should be put on the last letter of the word (in our ex., the ت). The same is true for the other two cases. You can find an extensive analysis in *Arabic for Nerds 2*, question #59.

Some people break this rule on purpose in one concrete situation: If a word ends in ل and Aleph is added, the result is لا. In this situation, some people write the تَنْوِينٌ on top of the Aleph resulting in لاً and not on the letter before the Aleph (لًا).

Let's check two examples: كَسُولٌ (lazy), رَسُولٌ (prophet).

alternative spelling	correct
رَسُولاً	رَسُولًا
كَسُولاً	كَسُولًا

What happens if a word ends in ى pronounced as Aleph? Let's see and check the Arabic word for *meaning*.

incorrect	مَعْنىً
correct	مَعْنًى

A few subtleties: There are **four situations** when you don't add an Aleph after the last letter in the مَنْصُوبٌ-case. Then, the تَنْوِينٌ will be put on the last letter – except when the last letter is already a long Aleph like in example 2 below:

	last letter:	
water (ماءٌ), *finishing* (إنْتِهاءً)	isolated Hamza (هَمْزَةٌ)	1
stick (عَصًا), *Mustafa* (مُصْطَفَى)	shortened Aleph (أَلِفٌ مَقْصُورةٌ)	2
library (مَكْتَبةً)	feminine ending ة (تاءُ تَأْنِيثٍ)	3
refuge (مَلْجَأً)	Hamza written as أ	4

194. When would you use the word أَجْمَلَ in Arabic?

If you want to express astonishment or admiration.

If we just look at the word أَجْمَلُ, it can be a *noun of preference* (اِسْمُ تَفْضِيلٍ) expressing a comparative: *more beautiful.*

But there is another possibility. أَجْمَلَ can also express **astonishment, admiration,** or **surprise** (أُسْلُوبُ التَّعَجُّبِ). This, however, changes the character of the word dramatically: أَجْمَلَ is then not treated as a noun (اِسْمٌ), because a noun of this pattern would express the *comparative* – instead, it is regarded as a <u>verb</u> (فِعْلُ التَّعَجُّبِ). To be precise, أَجْمَلَ is an *inert, static verb* (فِعْلٌ جامِدٌ), it has a cemented shape and is always in the singular. Let's see two examples to illustrate this rather confusing information:

What a beautiful view of the sea!	ما أَجْمَلَ مَنْظَرَ الْبَحْرِ!
How beautiful is the rose!	ما أَجْمَلَ الْوَرْدَةَ!

Like أَجْمَلَ, also other I-verbs are capable to be used in this fashion and pattern:

كَبُرَ	كَثُرَ	صَدَقَ	عَظُمَ	عَذُبَ	جَمُلَ
to be big	*to be many*	*to be sincere*	*to be great*	*to be sweet*	*to be beautiful*

There are two Arabic patterns which convey such a meaning. A hint: You use the same source and method (and apply the same conditions) which you would opt for to form a *noun of preference* (اِسْمُ تَفْضِيلٍ); see #189. So, let's see how it works.

You use the particle **ما plus** the pattern for astonishment (فِعْلٌ ماضٍ عَلَى وَزْنِ أَفْعَلَ) and add a direct object in the **accusative case** (اِسْمٌ مَنْصُوبٌ).	ما + أَفْعَلَ	1

What a beautiful sky!	!مَا أَجْمَلَ السَّماءَ

Subject (مُبْتَدَأٌ) of the nominal sentence (جُمْلَةٌ اِسْمِيّةٌ). Since we cannot mark this word with visible case markers, we can only apply a place value (اِسْمٌ نَكِرَةٌ فِي مَحَلِّ رَفْعٍ). Note: مَا here has the implicit meaning of *something great*.	مَا
The **predicate** (خَبَرٌ). This is an inert, static past tense verb; the (verbal) subject (فاعِلٌ) is a hidden/implied pronoun.	أَجْمَلَ
Direct object (مَفْعُولٌ بِهِ) of the verb. Therefore, it takes the accusative case (مَنْصُوبٌ).	السَّماءَ

Use the other pattern of astonishment (فِعْلٌ ماضٍ عَلَى وَزْنِ أَفْعِـلْ) plus the extra **preposition** بِ. Then you may add the subject (فاعِلٌ) and a specification in the accusative case (تَمْييزٌ مَنْصُوبٌ).	أَفْعِلْ + ب	2

What a beautiful sky!	!أَجْمِلْ بِالسَّماءِ
What a noble woman is she!	!أَكْرِمْ بِها فَتاةً
	!أَكْرِمْ بِها مِن فَتاةٍ =

Inert, static past tense verb in the imperative (فِعْلُ أَمْرٍ جامِدٌ).	أَكْرِمْ
Redundant/extra preposition (حَرْفُ جَرٍّ زائِدٌ).	بِ
This is the **subject** (فاعِلٌ)! The preceding preposition forces the genitive case (مَجْرُورٌ) which you cannot see because the pronoun suffix has an indeclinable, fixed shape. From a grammatical perspective, ها is located in the position of a nominative case (فِي مَحَلِّ رَفْعٍ).	ها

This is a **specification** (تَمْيِيزٌ) which is the reason why it takes the accusative case (مَنْصُوبٌ).	فَتاةً

→ See *Arabic for Nerds 2, question #382*, for a detailed analysis.

What about the other verb stems II to X? What happens, if we have a negation or the passive voice? The good news is that the أُسْلُوبُ التَّعَجُّبِ is still possible, albeit a more complicated. We can fix these constructions with the help of some tricks which work similar to the *comparative* (see *question #189*).

Expressing astonishment if there is *to be* (كَانَ) involved.	1
The rain was heavy.	كَانَ الْمَطَرُ شَدِيدًا.

What a heavy rain!	ما أَصْعَبَ كَوْنَ الْمَطَرِ شَدِيدًا !
Construction: auxiliary word + مَصْدَرٌ.	

What a heavy rain!	ما أَصْعَبَ أَنْ يَكُونَ الْمَطَرُ شَدِيدًا !
Construction: instead of the regular مَصْدَرٌ, you use an interpreted infinitive (مَصْدَرٌ مُؤَوَّلٌ) molded by أَنْ.	

Expressing admiration using verbs other than stem I (الْفِعْلُ غَيْرُ ثُلاثِيٍّ).	2
The professor made an effort. (VIII-verb اِجْتَهَدَ - يَجْتَهِدُ)	اِجْتَهَدَ الْأُسْتاذُ.

What an effort of the professor!	ما أَحْسَنَ اِجْتِهادَ الْأُسْتاذِ!
Construction: auxiliary word + مَصْدَرٌ.	

What an effort of the professor!	ما أَحْسَنَ أَنْ يَجْتَهِدَ الأُسْتاذُ!
Instead of the مَصْدَرٌ, use an interpreted infinitive (مَصْدَرٌ مُؤَوَّلٌ).	

195. الْمَدِينةُ قَرطاجُ or مَدِينةُ قَرطاجَ - What is correct?

Both are correct.

At first glance, they almost look the same. If you look closer, you'll see that in one example we use the article, and the vowels are different. This is because we are dealing with completely different constructions. Let us analyze the differences:

Carthage is an **apposition** (بَدَلٌ) and must get the same case as *city*: the **nominative** case (مَرْفُوعٌ). It literally means: *The city, Carthage, ...*	الْمَدِينةُ قَرطاجُ
Carthage is the **second part** of a إضافةٌ and thus needs the **genitive** case (مَجْرُورٌ). Watch out! Foreign city names are diptotes (مَمْنُوعٌ مِن الصَّرْفِ) which is the reason for the vowel "*a*". It literally means: *The city of Carthage...*	مَدِينةُ قَرطاجَ

196. Why do we read numbers from left to right in Arabic?

Actually, you could also read them from right to left.

Arabic is written from right to left. Strangely, numbers are usually written (and spoken) from left to right. There is no clear rationale for this. Some say that this is linked to Modern

Arabic which is influenced by the West. But that doesn't really explain it. Ibn 'Abbās (ابْن عَبَّاس), the cousin of the Islamic prophet Muhammad and one of the early scholars of the Qur'an, is said to have already used the numbers in the direction from left to right! It is a matter of taste as both reading directions are regarded as correct. For example, the year 1997.

| 7+90+ 900+1000 | فِي عامِ سَبْعةٍ وَتِسْعِينَ وَتِسْعِ مِئةٍ وَأَلْفِ |
| 1000+900+7+90 | فِي عامِ أَلْفِ وَتِسْعِ مِئةٍ وَسَبْعةٍ وَتِسْعِينَ |

Note that the word *hundred* in Arabic is written as a compound and with a long Aleph before the Hamza: تِسْعِمائةٍ.

If you want to know if the reading direction affects the grammar, see *Arabic for Nerds 2*, #194.

197. Why are there "an"-endings in أَهْلًا وَسَهْلًا؟

Because we assume that there is an underlying, virtual verb.

In Arabic, several words are often used with the ending *"an"* – with nunation (تَنْوِينٌ) in the accusative case (مَنْصُوبٌ).

These words were originally part of a sentence, but the verbs responsible for the case endings were deleted. The only thing that remains is a مَصْدَرٌ in the مَنْصُوبٌ-case.

In most situations, the words in the accusative case served as an **absolute** or **inner object** (مَفْعُولٌ مُطْلَقٌ) which is regularly used to confirm or emphasize the verb or show its nature – see *#122*. This is true for words such as شُكْرًا (*thanks*). Sometimes, it may also be a **direct object** (مَفْعُولٌ بِه) of a deleted verb as in the word أَهْلًا (*welcome*).

Many of such words have become independent expressions.

	original sentence	expression (عِبَارَةٌ)
أَهْلًا وَسَهْلًا	*welcome!*	صَادَفْتَ أَهْلًا لاَ غُرَبَاءَ وَوَطِئْتَ سَهْلًا لاَ وَعْرًا.
	Literal meaning: You have found (met with) kinsfolk, not strangers, and set foot on a place that is even and not rugged. (May you arrive as part of the family, and tread an easy path as you enter.)	
شُكْرًا	*thanks!*	أَشْكُرُكَ شُكْرًا.
	I really want to thank you.	
أَيْضًا	*as well*	آضَ or يَئِيضُ إِلَى شَيْءٍ أَيْضًا.
	He returned to the thing, i.e., to the doing of the thing; he did the thing again.	

Some words, especially adjectives (صِفَةٌ), may lose their case ending because they are not a مَصْدَرٌ and do not function as a مَفْعُولٌ مُطْلَقٌ. Since you pause after the only existing word, put سُكُونٌ at the end.

wonderful!	عَظِيمْ!
Quasi participle (صِفَةٌ مُشَبَّهَةٌ) of the I-verb عَظُمَ - يَعْظُمُ.	

congratulations!	مَبْرُوكْ!
lit.: *blessed; passive participle* (اِسْمُ مَفْعُولٍ) of I-verb بَرَكَ.	

198. النَّوْمَ, النَّوْمَ! - Why do these words get فَتْحَةٌ؟

Because they convey a warning.

Arabic offers a unique construction if you want to warn or instigate someone.

It is called أُسْلُوبُ التَّحْذِيرِ وَالْإِغْراءِ (lit.: *warning and instigation*). When a student almost falls asleep, the teacher can warn the person by saying النَّوْمَ, النَّوْمُ! which means *beware of sleep*!

The tricky thing about this construction is the case ending. We need the **accusative** case (مَنْصُوبٌ). Some examples:

Fire!	النَّارَ!
Fire and drowning!	النَّارَ وَالْفَرَقَ!

You can enhance the construction by adding the receiver of the warning.

All three sentences mean the same: *(you) beware of fire!*	إِيَّاكَ النَّارَ!	1
	إِيَّاكَ وَالنَّارَ!	2
	إِيَّاكَ مِن النَّارِ!	3
• The pronoun إِيَّاكَ is the accusative (مَنْصُوبٌ) of *you*. • If the fire is confirmed, repeat the vocative: إِيَّاكَ إِيَّاكَ النَّارَ !		

See also *Arabic for Nerds 2, question #421ff* if you want to understand why we use the accusative case.

199. How do you express *although; despite* in Arabic?

Not so easy. It depends on where you want to place them.

We need to build a so-called *concessive clause*.

This subordinate clause refers to a situation that contrasts with the one described in the main clause.

subordinate clause; final clause	main clause
Although he was tired,	*he couldn't sleep.*

In Arabic, such sentences are often difficult to grasp because you don't use simple words like in English.

1	Words that may stand at the **start** of the **main** <u>or</u> **subordinate** clause. They always go along with a <u>nominal sentence</u> (جُمْلةٌ اسْمِيّةٌ) which means that you can never have a verb after them.

although; even though	رَغْمَ أَنَّ	عَلَى الرَّغْمِ مِنْ أَنَّ	بِالرَّغْمِ مِنْ أَنَّ

Note: The expressions بِالرَّغْمِ مِنْ أَنَّ with ب is widespread, but it is not found in the classical works of Arabic. You cannot find بِالرَّغْمِ but only عَلَى الرَّغْمِ. Why? Probably because the preposition عَلَى simply fits better as it denotes **compulsion** (الإِجْبارُ). The ب, on the other hand, conveys accompanying (الْمُصاحَبةُ).

although; whereas; nevertheless; however	مَعَ أَنَّ	بَيْدَ أَنَّ	غَيْرَ أَنَّ

He showed up **although** he was lazy.	حَضَرَ مَعَ أَنَّهُ كانَ كَسُولًا.
Although he was sick, he decided to attend the lecture.	عَلَى الرَّغْمِ مِنْ أَنَّهُ كانَ مَرِيضًا فَقَدْ قَرَّرَ أَنْ يَحْضُرَ الْمُحاضَرَةَ.
He has a lot of money, **however,** he is stingy.	هُوَ كَثِيرُ الْمالِ بَيْدَ أَنَّهُ بَخِيلٌ.
I left the house **although** the weather was cold (despite the cold weather).	خَرَجْتُ مِنَ الْبَيْتِ عَلَى الرَّغْمِ مِنْ أَنَّ الطَّقْسَ كانَ بارِدًا.

2 | The expression إِلّا أَنَّ is put at the **start** of the **main clause**. It is common to use it with expressions containing رَغْم (see above).

| yet; however; but; nevertheless | إِلّا أَنَّ |

Although the hotel was nice, it **nevertheless** had no toilet.	مَعَ أَنَّ الْفُنْدُقَ كانَ جَمِيلًا إِلّا أَنَّهُ يَخْلُو مِنْ دَوْرَةِ مِياهٍ.
Although this company is famous, **yet** its output has become little and weak.	مَعَ أَنَّ هَذِهِ الشَّرِكَةَ مَشْهُورَةٌ إِلّا أَنَّ إِنْتاجَها صارَ قَلِيلًا وَضَعِيفًا.
Even though the test was difficult, **yet** I answered all the questions.	عَلَى الرَّغْمِ أَنَّ الْإِمْتِحانَ كانَ صَعْبًا إِلّا أَنَّنِي أَجَبْتُ عَلَى كُلِّ الْأَسْئِلَةِ.

3 | Devices that are placed **in-between** a sentence or at the beginning of the **subordinate** clause. See also *question #265*.

| even if; though | وَإِنْ |
| even if (Note: Although you use a past tense verb, it conveys the meaning of the present tense.) | وَلَوْ |

| Call me, <u>even if</u> you are on the train! | كَلِّمْنِي بِالْمَحْمُولِ وَلَوْ كُنْتَ فِي الْقِطارِ! |
| You will visit Cairo again <u>even if</u> you have visited Cairo before. | أَنْتَ - وَإِنْ زُرْتَ الْقاهِرَةَ مِنْ قَبْلُ - سَوْفَ تَزُورُها مَرَّةً أُخْرَى. |

200. بَعَدَ ما or بَعَدَما (with space) - How do you spell *after*...?

It depends on whether you want to use ما as a relative pronoun (which, that) or if ما should produce an interpreted infinitive.

Both applications of ما are often misunderstood. Let's do it the other way around and start the analysis with the result. The following two rules almost always work:

- You **leave space** before ما when it is used as a **relative pronoun** (ما الْمَوْصُولةُ). A good indicator for this type of ما is when the verb after ما has a pronoun suffix.

- You **connect** ما with the preceding word (without space) if ما works as a device to produce an expression that can be interpreted as a مَصْدَرٌ (ما الْمَصْدَرِيّة).

The whole issue has been subject of a long debate. Take, for example, the following sentence:

1	أُحِبُّ ما كَتَبْتَ.

Theoretically, ما could be **both**: a relative pronoun or a device for an interpreted infinitive.

But what about the meaning?

type of ما	How could we rewrite the sentence?
ما الْمَصْدَرِيّة	أُحِبُّ كِتابَتَكَ.
Meaning: *I like the way you write* (طَرِيقَتُكَ في الْكِتابَةِ).	
ما الْمَوْصُولةُ	أُحِبُّ الَّذي كَتَبْتَ.
Meaning: *I like what is written on the paper* (الْمَكْتُوبُ في الْوَرَقِ).	

In the following sentence, however, ما can **only** be a **relative pronoun**.

2	أُحِبُّ ما كَتَبْتَهُ.

Why can ما here only have on function?

We have a *binder, connector*: the *returning or referential pronoun* (ضَمِيرُ الْعائِدِ). The ه is referring to the word ما. That fact, that the referrer may be omitted sometimes, doesn't make it easier for us. All that matters if other words come into play like عِنْدَ before ما.

ما الْمَصْدَرِيّة	I stop talking when I want.	أَتَوَقَّفُ فِي الْحَدِيثِ عِنْدَما أَرْغَبُ.	correct
Meaning: *at/when my wish is to stop* (عِنْدَ رَغْبَتِي التَّوَقُّفَ).			

ما الْمَوْصُولة	I stop talking (at the position that) when I want.	أَتَوَقَّفُ فِي الْحَدِيثِ عِنْدَما أَرْغَبُهُ.	**incorrect** You need space.
Notice the pronoun! This hints that ما is a relative pronoun. The ه here is a returning, referential **pronoun**. The meaning is عِنْدَ الَّذِي أَرْغَبُهُ. It denotes *when my wish is to stop* (عِنْدَ رَغْبَتِي التَّوَقُّفَ).			

ما الْمَوْصُولة	I stop talking (at the position that) when I want.	أَتَوَقَّفُ فِي الْحَدِيثِ عِنْدَ ما أَرْغَبُهُ.	correct
Remark: We would also use a space if the pronominal suffix, the ه in our example, would be concealed/hidden which occasionally happens in such sentences with ما in Classical Arabic. The ه here is the **direct object** (مَفْعُولٌ بِهِ) of the verb أَرْغَبُ.			

Now we use *after* (بَعْد) and analyze the difference.

ما الْمَصْدَرِيَّةُ	I came after we had finished.	جِئْتُ بَعَدَما إنْتَهَيْنا.	correct
ما الْمَوْصُولةُ		جِئْتُ بَعَدَ ما إنْتَهَيْنا.	incorrect

ما الْمَوْصُولةُ	I came after what happened.	جِئْتُ بَعَدَ ما حَدَثَ.	correct
ما الْمَصْدَرِيَّةُ		جِئْتُ بَعَدَما حَدَثَ.	incorrect

If ما is preceded by a preposition, mistakes are likely to happen. Only if the preposition before ما is very short (1 or 2 letters), you write them together – otherwise, you should leave a space in-between.

	صحِّحْ فيما يَلِي!	understandable
Correct what follows!	صحِّحْ فِي ما يَلِي!	better (الصَّوابُ)
	The meaning of ما here is: صحِّحْ فِي الَّذِي يَلِي	

Excursus: How do you build and use adverbs of time?

Adverbs have many meanings and functions. They are especially important for indicating the time, manner, place, degree, and frequency of something. Adverbs work very differently in Arabic. What is the most important step to a correct identification? → You have to identify the appropriate **location** in a sentence where an adverb of time, place, or manner fits.

Once you find the spot, you have a choice of different types of words and forms appropriate for that location. You may use *particles* (حَرْفٌ), *indeclinable nouns* (إسْمٌ مَبْنِيٌّ) but also *absolute objects* (مَفْعُولٌ مُطْلَقٌ) or *specifications* (تَمْيِيزٌ). Let's see some expressions that function as *adverbs of time*. Note that in the following expressions, ما is either a particle to produce an **infinitive** (ما الْمَصْدَرِيّةُ) or a **relative pronoun** (ما الْمَوْصُولةُ).

I Constructions in which ما is a **relative pronoun** (ما الْمَوْصُولةُ).	

1	*after; later; in the future*	فِيما بَعْدُ

فِيما denotes *while, as* (and may be followed by a nominal or verbal sentence). The ما here is a **relative pronoun** (ما الْمَوْصُولةُ). The expression together literally denotes *in what is after* (فِي الّذِي بَعْدَهُ).

Why do we write فِيما together? This is optional. Only if the word before ما has more than 3 letters, you have to write them together.

He came **later**.	جاءَ فِيما بَعْدُ.
She remembered the word **later**.	تَذَكَّرَت الْكَلِمةَ فِيما بَعْدُ.

2	*before; earlier; in the past*	فِيما مَضَى

The Prophet said: "Amongst the people **preceding you** there used to be *Muhaddithun* (i.e. persons who can guess things that come true later on, as if those persons have been inspired by a divine power), and if there are any such persons amongst my followers, it is Umar bin al-Khattāb. (*Sahīh al-Bukhārī 3469*)	قَالَ: انّهُ قَدْ كَانَ فِيمَا مَضَى قَبْلَكُمْ مِنَ الأُمَم مُحَدَّثُونَ، وَإِنّهُ إِنْ كَانَ فِي أُمّتِي هَذِهِ مِنْهُمْ، فَإِنّهُ عُمَرُ بْنُ الْخَطّابِ.

3	*as much as; to the same extent as*	بِقَدْرِ ما

You are as free as I am.	أَنْتَ حُرٌّ بِقَدْرِ ما أَنا حُرٌّ.

4	as soon as; the moment when	أَوَّلَ ما

As soon as the negotiations started...	...أَوَّلَ ما بَدَأَت الْمُحادَثاتُ

II Constructions in which ما forms an **interpreted infinitive** (ما الْمَصْدَرِيّةُ) that has the same meaning as the مَصْدَر itself.

5	after...	past tense verb + ما + بَعْدَ/قَبْلَ
	before...	بَعْدَ/قَبْلَ + أَنْ + present tense subjunctive / مَنْصُوبٌ

Both of the above constructions produce an **interpreted infinitive** (مَصْدَرٌ مُؤَوَّلٌ). This explains why we need ما or أَنْ because after بَعْدَ only a noun can follow.

The interpreted infinitive, as an entity, can replace the مَصْدَر and means exactly the same.

After he had left...	بَعْدَما إنْصَرَفَ = بَعْدَ إنْصِرافِهِ

Caution, risk of confusion! بعْدُ with "*u*" means *yet* or *later*.

He is yet to come. (Or: He will come later.) *See # 151.*	سَيَأْتِي بَعْدُ.

6	*when; whenever; as soon as*	past or present tense + عِنْدَما

عِنْدَما is used to indicate the time in which the action expressed in the main clause takes place (فِي الْوَقْتِ الَّذِي). It may precede or follow the main clause. Note that the عِنْدَما was not used in the prime of Classical Arabic!

When he came...	...عِنْدَما جاءَ
When he goes...	...عِنْدَما يَذْهَبُ
Whenever he began to walk...	...عِنْدَما يَبْدَأُ الْمَشْيَ

| 7 | *until; while; as long as* | رَيْثَما or رَيْثَ أَنْ |

| Sit down while I am out – until I am back. | إِجْلِسْ رَيْثَما أَعُودُ. |

| 8 | *often; frequently* | طالَما + past tense verb |
| | *Lit.: as long as. Related to I-verb* طالَ - يَطُولُ (R2=و); *to be long.* |

| that occurred often | طالَما حَدَثَ ذَلِكَ |

Watch out: Some people use طالَما as a synonym of ما دامَ:

| As long as you fear, Allah will be with you. | طالَما تَتَّقِي اللّهَ فَسَيَكُونَ مَعَكَ. | incorrect |
| | ما دُمْتَ تَتَّقِي اللّهَ فَسَيَكُونَ مَعَكَ. | correct |

Strictly speaking, this doesn't make sense. Why is that? The **verb** طالَ denotes that its subject (فاعِلٌ) is present during the entire period of the action.

If we say, for example, طالَما سِرْنا مَعًا (*as long as we walked together*), the meaning would be that the duration of the act of walking (=subject) was long. The interpretation of the sentence would be: طالَ سَيْرُنا مَعًا because the ما in this expression produces an interpreted infinitive! However, the actual subject نا (we) is suddenly the second part of the إِضافةٌ and the main subject is *walking*.

The expression ما دامَ, on the other hand, needs a subject and a predicate – because it is a sister of كانَ. An example:

As long as the truth is among the people, ignorance won't spread.	ما دامَ الْحَقُّ بَيْنَ النّاسِ فَلَنْ يَنْتَشِرَ الْجَهْلَ.

الْحَقُّ is the "subject"; بَيْنَ النّاسِ. is the predicate. The answer or result is فَلَنْ يَنْتَشِرَ الْجَهْلَ which is what we want to express.

Remark: Some scholars say that ما in type II is a **hindering (neutralizing) particle (حَرْف كافّ)**. See *Arabic for Nerds 2, #296*.

III   A special type: the ما which produces an **adverbial interpreted infinitive (ما الْمَصْدَرِيّة الزَّمانِيّةُ).**

9	*every time when; whenever*	كُلَّما

- Although we use past tense verbs, they usually express a **present tense** or even conditional **meaning.**

- The ما is special (ما الْمَصْدَرِيّةُ الزَّمانِيّةُ). This particle produces a *circumstantial, adverbial infinitive* (حَرْفٌ مَصْدَرِيٌّ ظَرْفِيٌّ). In such constructions, a lot happens invisibly: the ما replaces the *adverb of time* (ظَرْفُ الزَّمانِ) which was deleted and had been holding the place of the first part of the إِضافةٌ. Therefore, if we look at its position, it gets the place value of an adverb in the accusative case (فِي مَحَلِّ نَصْبِ). We can picture ما as conveying a notion of time which expresses **simultaneousness.**

Whenever he studies, he is happy.	كُلَّما دَرَسَ فَرِحَ.

Whenever they are given sustenance from the fruits of these Gardens, they will say, "We have been given this before" (Sura 2:25)	كُلَّما رُزِقُوا مِنْهَا مِن ثَمَرَةٍ رِّزْقًا قَالُوا هُذَا الَّذِي رُزِقْنَا مِن قَبْلُ

IV Expressions with ما that include special verbs such as *to be many* (كَثُرَ), *to be few* (قَلَّ), *to be often* (شَدَّ), etc.

- The ما here is a *hindering, neutralizing device* (ما الْكَافَّة). It neutralizes the verb's action and – regarding verbs like *to be many* (كَثُرَ), *to be few* (قَلَّ), *to be often* (شَدَّ), – its necessity to have a subject (ما الْكَافَّة عَن الْفَاعِلِ). This is possible in certain verbs and means that they verbs do not request a subject (an agent; the doer of the action) anymore.

- If we add a **verb** in the past tense, it denotes a conditional or future meaning.

The lazy man can scarcely succeed.	قَلَّما يَنْجَحُ الْكَسُولُ.

10	*maybe; possibly; perhaps; sometimes*	رُبَّما

Perhaps Zayd is in the house.	رُبَّما زَيْدٌ فِي الْبَيْتِ.
Maybe I would leave Egypt; perhaps I shall leave Egypt.	رُبَّما غادَرْتُ مِصْرَ.

رُبَّما may be introduced by the emphatic particle لَ. Note that رُبَّما is a tricky expression – for an analysis, see *Arabic for Nerds 2, qu. #137*.

Perhaps he has escaped.	لَرُبَّما نَجا.

201. How do you say *so that* in Arabic?

There are many options.

Sentences starting with *so that...* are subordinate clauses and give a cause or result. In Arabic, there are many possibilities to express this idea. We'll examine three common constructions.

so that; to the point where; in such a manner that	بِحَيْثُ	1

After بِحَيْثُ, you usually have a verbal sentence (جُمْلة فِعْلِيّة) in the present or past tense. Sometimes, it can be followed by أَنَّ and a جُمْلةٌ اِسْمِيّةٌ.

You have a lot of money, **so (that)** you can travel to Germany.	لَدَيْكَ مالٌ كَثِيرٌ بِحَيْثُ تَسْتَطِيعُ أَنْ تُسافِرَ إِلَى أَلْمانِيا.
I am ill, so I cannot study.	أَنا مَرِيضةٌ بِحَيْثُ لا أَسْتَطِيعُ الدِّراسةُ.

فَ can also denote *so that* and expresses a wish, command, or question. What's important: The verb needs the **subjunctive** mood (مَنْصُوبٌ)!	فَ	2

He hoped/wished to see me so that we could discuss the topic.	تَمَنَّى لَوْ رَآني فَنُناقِشَ الْمَوْضُوعَ.

حَتَّى is usually translated as *until*. Nevertheless, it can also express *so that*. If the **situation** or event you describe is still **ongoing**, you must use the present tense, **subjunctive** mood (مَنْصُوبٌ) because there is a virtual, estimated أَنْ which is understood, but not visible. If the **action** is already **over**, you should use the **past tense** after حَتَّى.	حَتَّى	3

Do good, so that you (can) enter the Garden.	إعْمَلْ الْخَيْرَ حَتَّى تَدْخُلَ الْجَنَّةَ.
I saved the files on the computer so it wouldn't be lost.	حَفِظْتُ الْمِلَفَّاتَ في الْحاسُوبِ حَتَّى لا تَضيعَ.

202. How do you recognize a reported (indirect) speech?

After قالَ, you will have the particle إنَّ.

In Arabic, there is little difference between direct and indirect/reported speech (كَلامٌ مَنْقُولٌ, غَيْرُ مُباشِرٍ). You don't have to worry about different tenses or word order or expressions you have to change (unlike English where *yesterday* becomes *the day before)*. In German, the reported speech is easily recognized as you have to use the *Konjunktiv I*.

And in Arabic?

1	**Direct speech**	
	He said: "I wrote you a letter."	قالَ: "(إنَّني) كَتَبْتُ لَكَ رِسالةً."

2	**Reported speech**	
	He said that he had written me a letter. (Both mean the same.)	قالَ إنَّهُ كَتَبَ لِي رِسالةً.
		قالَ بِأَنَّهُ كَتَبَ لِي رِسالةً.

A hint: If you want to make clear that a sentence is a reported speech you could use بِأَنَّ = *that*. Notice the vowel *"a"* (فَتْحةٌ) in بِأَنَّ. Since there is the preposition بِ involved, you don't have to use إنَّ with *"i"* (كَسْرةٌ) – for more information about إنَّ, *see question #231*.

203. How do you build reported questions?

This is more difficult than the reported speech.

The issue is mainly about the expression *whether/if* for which we have to find a solution. We also have to consider whether we need to adjust the tenses. Let's try to translate the following rather simple sentence: *He asked me whether/if...*

whether / if...	إنْ + كانَ ...		1
	إذا + كانَ (ما) ...		2
→ If you have a verb with a preposition, e.g., سَأَلَ عَنْ (to ask about).	عَمّا إذا	ما إذا + عَنْ	3
	فِيما إذا	ما إذا + فِي	

Now let us check the tenses.

direct question			reported question
present tense	الْمُضارِعُ	▷	الْماضِي or كانَ + الْمُضارِعُ
past tense	الْماضِي		كانَ + قَدْ + الْماضِي
future tense	الْمُسْتَقْبَلُ		كانَ + الْمُسْتقْبَلُ
nominal sentence	جُمْلَةٌ اِسْمِيّةٌ		كانَ + خَبَرٌ

Some examples.

direct question	reported question
لا أَعْرِفُ: "هَلْ ذَهَبَ أَمْ لا؟"	لا أَعْرِفُ ما إذا (=إنْ) كانَ قَدْ ذَهَبَ أَمْ لا.
I don't know: "Did he go or	I don't know whether he had

سَأَلْتُهُ: "هَلْ تُحِبُّ الْقَهْوَةَ أَمْ الشَّايَ؟"	سَأَلْتُهُ إِنْ (= عَمَّا إذا) كَانَ يُحِبُّ الْقَهْوَةَ أَمْ الشَّايَ.
I asked him: "Do you like coffee or tea?"	I asked him whether he liked coffee or tea.

204. لَبَّيْكَ (*at your service*) - What form is that?

It is pretty sophisticated which has to do with the dual.

Muslims use لَبَّيْكَ many times. It means *Praise Allah!* Or *Allah be praised!* The most famous example is لَبَّيْكَ اللَّهُمَّ لَبَّيْكَ which is said during the Islamic pilgrimage before the pilgrims enter Mecca. It means *Here I am! At your service!*

The expression is tricky and worth drilling down into it.

1. What is the root? It is ل-ب-ي. It is only used in the II-verb لَبَّى - يُلَبِّي (*to follow, to accept a call or an invitation*).

2. We need a مَصْدَر. The مَصْدَر-pattern for a II-verb (فَعَّلَ) with a final weak letter would produce تَلْبِيَةٌ. This noun, however, is not used in the expression لَبَّيْكَ. Instead, we use لَبٌّ which is the *noun of origin* (اِسْمُ الْمَصْدَرِ). Unlike the regular مَصْدَر, the اِسْمُ الْمَصْدَرِ does not refer to the ongoing action but to the result of the action. (*See #82 and Arabic for Nerds 2, #110*).

3. We need the dual. لَبٌّ is changed into the dual form for the sake of corroboration (emphasis) meaning *answer after answer, saying after saying* (إِلبَابًا بَعْدَ إِلبَابٍ, وإجابةً بَعْدَ إجابةٍ). In We get لَبَّانِ in in the nominative (مَرْفُوعٌ) and for the genitive case (مَجْرُورٌ) and accusative case (مَنْصُوبٌ), we get لَبَّيْنِ.

4. We need the مَنْصُوبٌ case: لَبَّيْنِ. This expression in the accusative case (see below) is used as an exclamation of admiration, as an expression of admiration (أُسْلُوبُ التَّعَجُّبِ).

5. Add the personal pronoun. Since we want to add the personal pronoun *you* (→ *you* refers to Allah) to لَبَّيْنِ, we need to think a for a moment. لَبَّيْنِ is used as an absolute, inner object (مَفْعُولٌ مُطْلَقٌ) which will serve as the first part of a إضافةٌ. Remember, if we add a pronoun to the first part of a إضافةٌ and this first part is a dual, the ن of the dual is dropped.

6. Result: Finally, we get لَبَّيْكَ.

There is a bunch of expressions that are similarly constructed using an **absolute object** (مَفْعُولٌ مُطْلَقٌ); sometimes in the dual form, e.g., (سَعْدَيْكَ).

meaning	original meaning	expression
Praise God!	أُسَبِّحُ اللهَ تَسْبِيحًا.	سُبْحانَ اللهِ!
God forbid! God save (protect) me (us) from that!	أَعُوذُ بِاللهِ مَعاذًا.	مَعاذَ اللهِ!
Here I am! At your service!	أُلَبِّيكَ تَلْبِيةً بَعْدَ تَلْبِيةٍ أَيْ أُلَبِّيكَ كَثِيرًا.	لَبَّيْكَ!
And all good is in your hands. (here, we use the dual!)	أَسْعَدْتُكَ إِسْعادًا بَعْدَ إِسْعادٍ.	سَعْدَيْكَ!

Other expressions which use an **exclamation of admiration** or surprise (أُسْلُوبُ التَّعَجُّبِ). You often see the expression يا لَهُ من which you translate as an exclamation: *"what a ...!"*

Meaning: *how capable, how excellent he is!* Lit.: *His achievement is due to God.*	لِلّٰهِ دَرُّهُ !

What a hero!	يا لَهُ مِنْ بَطَلٍ!
What a lovely apartment!	يا لَها مِن شَقّةٍ جَميلةٍ!

Excursus: Why do Muslims use اللَّهُمَّ ("*allahumma*") for God? اللَّهُمَّ occurs already in the Qur'an five times. The origin of the expression is not entirely clear. Some ideas:

- Muslim scholars say that it just means يا اللّٰه (O God!). The م, they say, was added to compensate the omission/suppression of the vocative particle يا.

- Others say it is a short form of يا اللّٰهُ أُمَّنا بِخَيْرٍ which means *O God! Bring us good!* Or: *O God! Instruct us in righteousness!*

- There is even another idea: Bible scholars suggested that it comes from Biblical Hebrew because a word for *God* is אֱלֹהִים which is pronounced *ĕlohīm*. However, Muslim scholars claim that God's name in Hebrew is the plural form of God which would contradict the idea of *one God*. אֱלֹהִים is, in fact, the plural of אֱלוֹהַּ or אֱלָהַּ (*Eloah*).

  Jewish scholars hold that אֱלֹהִים is singular (it does govern a singular verb or adjective) when referring to the Hebrew God, but grammatically in the plural (taking a plural verb or adjective) when used to denote pagan divinities. The Hebrew plural can be explained by a *plural of respect* (*pluralis excellentiae*). And what do secular scholars say? They attribute the plural אֱלֹהִים to a polytheistic origin of the Israelite religion.

205. Why do you have to be careful when you say وَاللّٰهِ?

At least because the grammar is tricky.

In Arabic, the word قَسَم means *oath*. The principle meaning of the root is *to share, to part*; but also *to destine*. From this root, the IV-verb يُقْسِمُ - أَقْسَمَ بِ عَلَى expresses *to swear*. The preposition بِ here means *by*.

The most famous oath is وَاللهِ which literally means *by God!* It is usually translated (according to the meaning) as *I swear*.

Now comes the exciting part. Do you know why the Arabic word for God gets the genitive case (مَجْرُورٌ)? Interestingly, the device و stands for the meaning of a verb: أَقْسَمَ بِ. This suppressed and unpronounced verb is the reason for the case → after بِ we need the genitive! This type of وَ is called وَاوُ الْقَسَمِ.

Hence, in Arabic, the person or thing you swear by (الْاِسْمُ الْمُقْسَمُ بِهِ) has to take the genitive case.

There are three helping devices which are used to introduce an oath (أَدَواتُ الْقَسَمِ):

- وَ: The most common particle; never use it with a verb. So never say: أُقْسِمُ وَاللهِ

- بِ: The only particle that may be used with the core verb itself: *I swear by* (أُقْسِمُ بِ)

- تَ: exclusively used with *God* (اللهُ or رَبّ).

By the sky with its towering constellations (Sura 85:1)	وَالسَّمَاءِ ذَاتِ الْبُرُوجِ

What does this mean for us in terms of grammar?

1. If the sentence after the oath is a <u>nominal sentence</u> (جُمْلَةٌ اسْمِيَّةٌ), you'll have to use either إِنَّ or إِنَّ combined with لِ.

I swear that (certainly) life is a struggle!	وَاللهِ إِنَّ الْحَيَاةَ كِفَاحٌ!
I swear that (certainly) life is a struggle! In this sentence we use لِ. The meaning is the same.	وَاللهِ إِنَّ الْحَيَاةَ لِكِفَاحٌ!

2. If the sentence after the oath is a <u>verbal sentence</u> (جُمْلَةٌ فِعْلِيَّةٌ) in the <u>past tense</u>, you'll have to use قَدْ or لَقَدْ.

| By Allah, I have obeyed your command! | تَاللَّهِ لَقَدْ أَطَعْتُ أَمْرَكَ! |
| By Allah, I obeyed your command! | تَاللَّهِ قَدْ أَطَعْتُ أَمْرَكَ! |

3. If the sentence after the oath is a <u>verbal sentence</u> (جُمْلَةٌ فِعْلِيَّةٌ) in the <u>present tense</u>, you'll have to add the letter لَ after the oath and use the letter ن for emphasis (the so-called نُونُ التَّوْكِيدِ; see *question #156*). In short: you put فَتْحَةٌ at the end of a verb and add نّ.

| I swear, I will certainly do it! | وَاللَّهِ لَأَفْعَلَنَّ! |

4. If the sentence after the oath is <u>negated</u>, there is no need to add any kind of emphasis (تَأْكِيدٌ).

| By God, there is no success with laziness! | وَاللَّهِ لا نَجَاحَ مَعَ الْكَسَلِ! |
| After the oath there is a negated nominal sentence (جُمْلَةٌ إِسْمِيَّةٌ). | |

| By God, I do not agree! | وَاللَّهِ لَمْ أُوَافِقْ! |
| After the oath there is a negated verbal sentence (جُمْلَةٌ فِعْلِيَّةٌ). | |

206. If we curse in the name of God, why do we use the past?

Because we want to express a wish.

Kind of weird: When we curse in the name of God, we use a past tense verb to express the present or future tense. The same applies to wishes that refer to God. Some examples:

God kill them!	قَتَلَهُمُ اللّٰهُ!
God assist you!	نَصَرَكَ اللّٰهُ!
May God protect you from diseases!	حَماكَ اللّٰهُ مِن الأَمْراضِ!

| May God not make you prosper! | لا أَصْلَحَكَ اللّٰهُ! |

If you want to negate a verb (and want to express a curse or wish), you use لا plus past tense (الْماضِي). This is a rare exception! Normally, you only negate the present tense (الْمُضارِعُ) with لا.

207. Can you use مَنْ to start a conditional sentence?

Yes, you can.

In literature and formal Arabic, you can choose from a variety of words to start a conditional sentence (*if; when*).

Even مَنْ, which generally denotes *who*, can be used to introduce an (indefinite) conditional sentence. مَنْ then conveys the meaning of *whoever; whatever; wherever; however.* مَنْ is used for general assumptions. For example: *Whatever you do, you will be my friend.*

When you use مَنْ, you must pay attention to the correct mood of the verbs. → We need the jussive mood (مَجْزُومٌ).

| Whoever strives, succeeds in life. | مَنْ يَجْتَهِدْ يَنْجَحْ فِي حَياتِهِ. |

The verb يَنْجَحْ ends in سُكُونٌ which is the standard way of marking the jussive mood (مَجْزُومٌ) in regular verbs.

| Whoever visits Egypt meets a friend. | مَنْ يَزُرْ مِصْرَ يَلْقَ صَدِيقًا. |

The verb يَزُورُ becomes يَزُرْ in the jussive mood (مَجْزُومٌ); in verbs with a weak letter in the middle (second root letter), you delete the weak letter to mark the jussive. Thus, we got rid of **و**.

يَلْقَ, on the other hand, ends with *"a"* (فَتْحَةٌ). The present tense (indicative mood) of this I-verb is يَلْقَى. We got rid of the last letter because it is weak (حَرْفُ عِلَّةٍ). The vowel on top of the second (and now last letter) is فَتْحَةٌ and works as a compensation for the deletion.

This is true for verbs which have **و** or **ي** as the final root letter and follow the past tense pattern فَعِلَ like *to meet* (لَقِيَ). The same would happen to the I-verbs *to remain* (يَبْقَى - بَقِيَ), *to be pleased* (يَرْضَى - رَضِيَ), *to forget* (يَنْسَى - نَسِيَ) in the jussive mood (مَجْزُومٌ).

208. What is the difference between أَلَّا and إِلَّا?

إِلَّا means *"except"*. أَلَّا expresses *"not to"*.

These two words almost look the same. The only difference is the Hamza (هَمْزَةٌ).

It is written either on top (أَلَّا) or at the bottom (إِلَّا). The position is decisive.

- إِلَّا is a *particle of exception* (حَرْفُ اسْتِثْنَاءٍ). It means *except* (see *question #215*).

- أَلَّا is a combination of two words (تَكُونُ مُرَكَّبَةً مِنْ أَنَّ النَّاصِبَةِ لِلْمُضَارِعِ وَلاَ النَّافِيَةِ) and means *not to*.

أَلَّا has فَتْحَةٌ on هَمْزَةٌ. It expresses the meaning of *that not*; *unless*; *if not* and is the result of the following construction:

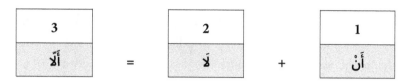

3		2		1
أَلَّا	=	لا	+	أَنْ

The verb after أَلَّا must get the subjunctive mood (مَنْصُوبٌ) due to the particle أَنْ. Here are some examples:

...that you don't travel...	أَلَّا تُسافِرَ = أَنْ لا تُسافِرَ
that you don't (didn't) do it...	أَلَّا تَفْعَلَهُ...
I think that he didn't drink.	أَظُنُّ أَلَّا يَشْرَبَ.
I want you not to pull back.	أُرِيدُ أَلَّا تَتَراجَعَ.

Let us look at a sentence in which you find both words:

He decided not to take anything with him except the book.	قَرَّرَ أَلَّا يَأْخُذَ مَعَهُ إِلَّا الْكِتابَ.

After أَنْ the verb is in the subjunctive (مَنْصُوبٌ); so the verb has to take فَتْحَةٌ at the end (يَأْخُذَ).	أَنْ + لا = أَلَّا

In the above example, why has الْكِتابَ a فَتْحَةٌ? Here, إِلَّا means *except*. The construction is called أُسْلُوبُ الْقَصْرِ and follows certain rules. If you don't know them, have a look at #217.	إِلَّا

A hint: If you have to add the correct case endings, just delete the negation in your mind – and you'll get: يَأْخُذُ الْكِتابَ. The word الْكِتاب is the direct object (مَفْعُولٌ بِهِ) and has to be in the accusative case (مَنْصُوبٌ).

Watch out: إِلَّا may express a <u>conditional meaning</u>. How come? إِلَّا then is, in fact, a compound of the *conditional* إِنَّ (إِنَّ) and the *negation device* لا (لا النَّافِيَةُ).

If you don't study, you will fail.	إِلَّا تَدْرُسْ تَرْسُب.
Even if you do not help the Prophet, God helped him. *(Sura 9:40)*	إِلَّا تَنْصُرُوهُ فَقَدْ نَصَرَهُ اللّٰهُ.

209. What is the function of a بَدَلٌ (apposition)?

An apposition refers to a person or thing which is already mentioned in a sentence.

In Arabic, an apposition is called بَدَلٌ which means *substitute*. An apposition takes the same case as the word it is accompanying.

Karīm, the driver, was in the house.	كانَ كَرِيمٌ السَّائِقُ فِي الْبَيْتِ.
→ This is the origin of the above sentence!	كانَ كَرِيمٌ, كانَ السَّائِقُ, فِي الْبَيْتِ.

We need to introduce two grammar terms:

- The first part (*Karīm*) is called مُبْدَلٌ مِنْهُ (*substituted for*).
- The second part (*the driver*) is the بَدَلٌ (*apposition*).

What about the **position** of the بَدَلٌ in a sentence? There are several options:

1. The بَدَلٌ follows the subject of a sentence.

This student came.	جاءَ هذا الطَّالِبُ.

This is the subject of the sentence.	فاعِلٌ / مُبْدَلٌ مِنْهُ	هذا

The student <u>is not</u> the subject of the sentence. It is an apposition.	بَدَلٌ	الطَّالِبُ

2. The بَدَلٌ follows the object of a sentence.

I met this student.	قابَلْتُ هذا الطَّالِبَ.

Direct object of the sentence. The word هذا never changes its shape.	مَفْعُولٌ بِهِ مُبْدَلٌ مِنْهُ	هذا
The student is <u>not</u> the object of the sentence! It is an apposition and needs agreement. Therefore, you have to use the accusative case (مَنْصُوبٌ) as well.	بَدَلٌ	الطَّالِبُ

Now a tricky example.

The بَدَلٌ has an attributive meaning. See also *Arabic for Nerds 2, question #185.*

The doctor treated the leg of the patient. (Lit. meaning: The doctor treated the patient, his leg.)	عالَجَ الطَّبِيبُ الْمَرِيضَ رِجْلَهُ.

Direct object (مَفْعُولٌ بِهِ)	الْمَرِيضَ
Apposition (بَدَلُ الْبَعْضِ مِن الْكُلِّ). This type of apposition needs a **connector** (رابِطٌ) which is usually a possessive pronoun. Such pronoun may be shown or is implicitly understood (unwritten).	رِجْلَهُ
This pronoun always ends in ضَمَّةٌ because its shape is cemented, fixed, indeclinable (مَبْنِيٌّ). Grammatically speaking, the pronoun is the second part of a إِضافةٌ-construction (مُضافٌ إِلَيْهِ).	ه

210. What is the root of the verb *to examine; to study* (اِطَّلَعَ)؟

The root is ط-ل-ع.

The VIII-verb اِطَّلَعَ - يَطَّلِعُ (R1=ط) means *to examine; to study; to check*. It follows the pattern اِفْتَعَلَ.

For that reason, watch out! According to the verb pattern, the verb should be اِطْتَلَعَ. Since this would be difficult to pronounce, ت and ط merge to double ط – written as ط.

- The مَصْدَر is اِطِّلَاع and means *inspection; examination*.
- The IV-verb أَطْلَعَ - يُطْلِعُ (*to inform; to tell*) almost looks the same. So, what's the difference? The IV-verb doesn't have شَدَّة and it starts with *Hamza of rupture* (هَمْزَة قَطْعِ), the ء in form of أ which you have to pronounce.

211. How do you use وَ, فَ, and ثُمَّ؟

They describe a sequence and do not influence case endings.

All three particles are found between two words which have the same case. وَ, فَ and ثُمَّ are so-called conjunctions, "couplers" (حَرْفُ عَطْفِ).

Practically, this means that two words mirror many grammatical properties. They need to agree. That's for the grammar part. Let's focus on the meaning. All three words are used to describe a chronological sequence.

- وَ means *and*;
- فَ could be translated as *and*; *and so*; *then*. It implies a closer relationship, some development, or a logical order between the words or sentences.

- ثُمَّ could be translated as *then; after that; thereupon*. It shows that one event is over, and that a new thing starts.

Ahmed **and** Khalid came. We don't know who came first or if they came at the same time. The chronological sequence doesn't matter.	جاءَ أَحْمَدُ وَخالِدٌ.	1
Ahmad came, **and right after him** (immediately after) Khalid.	جاءَ أَحْمَدُ فَخالِدٌ.	2
Ahmad came, and **thereupon** Khalid.	جاءَ أَحْمَدُ ثُمَّ خالِدٌ.	3

Note that words consisting of only one letter are combined with the subsequent word. Thus, you have to attach وَ and فَ to the word which comes after them.

212. What does the verb عاد mean?

It depends on what you add.

The I-verb عادَ - يَعُودُ (R2=و) is a sly verb. It can denote many things and go along with many constructions. For example, you add verbs without أَنْ directly, which looks a bit unusual. Let's see the most common constructions.

No longer to be; to become. → present or past tense meaning	عادَ (only in the **past tense**) is **negated** and you have **two nouns**. → Then, we treat عادَ as a *sister of* كانَ. The subject (اِسْمُ عادَ) takes the **nominative case** (مَرْفُوعٌ) and the **predicate** (خَبَرُ عادَ) gets the **accusative** case (مَنْصُوبٌ).	1

I am no longer a child.	أَنا لَمْ أَعُدْ صَغِيرًا.
She never became angry with him.	لَمْ تَعُدْ مَرَّةً واحِدَةً غاضِبَةً مِنْهُ.
He was no longer interested in the matter. Literally, it means: The case did no longer arouse his interest.	لَمْ يَعُدْ الْأَمْرُ يُثيرُ اِهْتِمامَهُ.

| 2 | *to return* (= the core meaning) | عَادَ or يَعُودُ (present or past tense) used with إِلَى. → Then, there is no other verb involved. عَادَ is thus treated as a full, **complete verb** (فِعْلٌ تامٌّ). |

| The student returned to Egypt. | عَادَ الطَّالِبُ إِلَى مِصْرَ. |

| 3 | *no longer to be* | عَادَ (only past tense) is **negated.** → لَمْ يَعُدْ plus verb in the present tense, **indicative.** You don't use أَنْ! |

I no longer remember....	لَمْ أَعُدْ أَذْكُرُ...
I no longer think...	لَمْ أَعُدْ أُفَكِّرُ...
He didn't (or doesn't) feel anymore.	لَمْ يَعُدْ يَشْعُرُ.
He no longer walked.	ما عادَ يَذْهَبُ.

| 4 | *to do again; to repeat* | عَادَ (only past tense) is **not** negated: → عَادَ plus verb in the present tense, **indicative.** You don't use أَنْ! |

| He hit me again. | عَادَ فَضَرَبَنِي. |

He walked again.	عادَ يَذْهَبُ.

to do again	عادَ or يَعُودُ (present or past tense), **not** negated, plus فَ. → You add a verb in the present tense, indicative mood (الْمُضارِعُ الْمَرْفُوعُ) or past tense (الْماضِي).	5

He kissed her again.	عادَ فَقَبَّلَها.
I convinced myself again.	عُدْتُ فَأَقْنَعْتُ نَفْسِي.
I forget again.	أَعُودُ فَأَنْسَى.

213. Do إذا and إذًا and إذَنْ and إذْ mean the same?

No way! Only in rare situations, they may denote the same idea.

Three Arabic words almost look the same but mean very different things.

Let's see the main points.

1	when, if; as suddenly	إذا

- إذا is normally introducing a conditional sentence. The verbal sentence after it is usually in the past tense – but it has the meaning of the present tense or even future tense!

- إذا can only be used if the situation in the conditional sentence can theoretically be achieved (if it is possible or if it has happened).

- This is different to إِنْ because إِنَّ may be used to introduce a <u>possible or impossible</u> condition – see below.
- إذا ما is only used to emphasize a sentence (تَأْكِيدٌ).

If you work hard, you will be successful in your life. (This leaves open if you are successful or not; you could be both.)	إِنْ تَجْتَهِدْ فِي عَمَلِكَ تَنْجَحْ فِي حَيَاتِكَ.
When the sun rises (and the sun does rise every day without an exception), people will go to their work.	إذا طَلَعَتِ الشَّمْسُ ذَهَبَ النَّاسُ إِلَى عَمَلِهِمْ.
When/if angels come, devils will go. Note: This is an Arabic proverb which means that good and bad do not meet.	إذا حَضَرَتِ الْمَلائِكَةُ، ذَهَبَتِ الشَّيَاطِينُ.

2	since; as, because; at that time, when	إِذْ

- It may explain or **indicate the reason** for the preceding event ("*as*", "*since*" → causal). Note that such إِذْ may be followed by a verb or noun.
- إِذْ may be used to express that two actions happen at the **same time** ("*when*" → temporal); see *Arabic for Nerds 2, question #342*. Normally, a verbal sentence in the past tense will follow after إِذْ, very rarely you see a nominal sentence. It has usually the meaning of عِنْدَ ما.

She cried because she was sick.	بَكَيَتْ إِذْ كانَتْ مَرِيضَةً.
Do they hear you when you call?	هَلْ يَسْمَعُونَكُمْ إِذْ تَدْعُونَ؟
I was late. I made a mistake since I didn't use the train.	وَصَلْتُ مُتَأَخِّرًا. أَخْطَأْتُ إِذْ لَمْ أُسافِرْ بِالْقِطارِ.

| 3 | therefore; so; then | إِذًا |

It denotes a **response**. So, it is not surprising that إِذًا is often used in dialogues in response to what was said before. Most grammarians say that it does not change any case or mood and thus has **no governing power**.

| A: We will meet at the center. | سَنَلْتَقِي فِي الْمَرْكَزِ. |
| B: Let's have a coffee together then. | إِذًا نَشْرَبُ قَهْوَةً مَعًا. |

| So, what's the problem? | إِذًا مَا الْمُشْكِلَةُ؟ |

| 4 | in that case; if the case be so; well then | إِذَنْ |

It occurs at the start of the main clause, (صَدْرُ الْجَوابِ).

It is followed by a verb which has to be in the **subjunctive mood** (مَنْصُوبٌ). The verb expresses the **future**! Thus, we call this device حَرْفُ جَوابٍ وَجَزَاءٍ وَنَصْبٍ وَاسْتِقْبَالٍ.

In that case you will succeed.	إِذَنْ تَنْجَحَ.
In that case I will leave after your visit.	إِذَنْ أَذْهَبَ بَعْدَ زِيارَتِكَ.
Note the subjunctive mood – the vowel "*a*"!	

214. Can إِذَا and إِذْ express something unexpected?

Yes, they can.

إِذَا and إِذْ may have a **special job** in a sentence:

- Both can be a *particle of surprise* (حَرْفُ مُفاجَأَةٍ). They then express that something is unexpected or surprising: *behold! see! wow! suddenly! and all of a sudden there was...*

- إذا (إذا الْفُجائِيَّةُ) is more common. You have to use a **nominal sentence** (جُمْلةٌ اسْمِيّةٌ) after it. Furthermore, إذا is usually preceded by فَ; but you can also use وَ.

- إذْ, when used to express *when suddenly*, is used after *while* (بَيْنَما). See *Arabic for Nerds 2*, question #349.

I entered the room and (surprisingly) all the students were absent.	دَخَلْتُ الْحُجْرةَ فَإذا جَمِيعُ الطُّلّابِ غائِبُونَ.
I opened my bag, and (strangely/surprisingly) it was empty.	فَتَحْتُ حَقِيبَتِي فَإذا هِيَ خالِيَةٌ.
While I was studying, suddenly my friend came.	بَيْنَما أَنا أَدْرُس إذْ دَخَلَ صَدِيقِي.
While we were sitting, suddenly, a man came up to us.	بَيْنَما نَحْنُ جُلُوس إذْ طَلَعَ عَلَيْنَا رَجُلٌ.
I went out, and all of a sudden, Zayd was at the door.	خَرَجْتُ فَإذًا زَيْدٌ بِالْبابِ.

215. How many words may be used to express *except*?

Around ten.

Arabic knows many words and expressions to denote *except*. They all belong to a special construction called أُسْلُوبُ الإِسْتِثْناءِ. The word اسْتِثْناءٌ means *exclusion, exception*.

All the following words and expressions mean basically the same: *except; but; excluding; save*:

إلّا • غَيْر • سِوَى • عَدَا • ما عَدَا • خَلا • ما خَلا • حاشا

Note: The expression ما حاشا doesn't exist. حاشا literally means *far be it*. خَلا means *outside of*. عَدَا means *save*. All three may be treated as inert, static past tense verbs or prepositions.

We need two grammar terms for our analysis:

- The **excluded thing** is called الْمُسْتَثْنَى. It occurs <u>after</u> the particle of exception (e.g., إلّا). The grammarians regard the الْمُسْتَثْنَى as a **variety of the direct object** (مَفْعُولٌ بِهِ). Therefore, it takes the accusative case (مَنْصُوبٌ). For more details, see *Arabic for Nerds 2, #401.*

- The **all-included thing** (the majority from which the exception is taken) is called الْمُسْتَثْنَى مِنْهُ. It is placed <u>before</u> the particle denoting *except*.

1. The construction with إلّا *(except).* It is a particle of exception (حَرْفُ اسْتِثْناءٍ).

There are three ways to encounter and use this device.

1	All students came except one.	جاءَ الطُّلّابُ إلّا طالِبًا.

الطُّلّابُ is the الْمُسْتَثْنَى مِنْهُ. The word طالِبًا is the الْمُسْتَثْنَى. It has to be in the accusative case (مَنْصُوبٌ) because we assume that طالِبًا is the direct object (مَفْعُولٌ بِهِ) of a suppressed, underlying verb. The hidden/virtual, implicitly understood verb may express: **I exclude** *students.*

| 2 | Only one student came. | ما جاءَ الطُّلّابُ إلّا طالِبًا. |
| | | ما جاءَ الطُّلّابُ إلّا طالِبٌ. |

Both are correct. You can choose between the nominative case (مَرْفُوعٌ) or the accusative case (مَنْصُوبٌ).

- The word طالِبًا in the accusative case (مَنْصُوبٌ) is the **excluded** (الْمُسْتَثْنَى).

- In the second sentence, we use the nominative (مَرْفُوعٌ). Thus, the grammatical function is different! طالِبٌ is an **apposition** (بَدَلٌ) and thus has to copy the grammatical features of the word to which it refers (i.e., the الْمُسْتَثْنَى مِنْهُ). In our example, it mirrors the features of الطُّلّابُ.

3	Only one student is here.	ما جاءَ إلّا طالِبٌ.

This form is called أُسْلُوبُ الْقَصْرِ and describes **exclusivity** (see *question #217*). The word طالِبٌ is the subject (فاعِلٌ).

Good to know: Delete the negation in your mind if you want to find the correct cases. Once you have only جاءَ الطُّلّابُ, putting case endings is suddenly quite simple.

The following sentence is quite tricky.

There is only one student in the room.	لَيْسَ فِي الْغُرْفةِ إلّا طالِبٌ.
لَيْسَ, a verb, usually stands in the singular form at the beginning!   • فِي الْغُرْفةِ is the predicate (خَبَرُ لَيْسَ);   • طالِبٌ is the "subject" (إسْمُ لَيْسَ);

Watch out: If the subject is inherent in the verb, e.g., *they*, the situation is totally different: لَيْسُوا فِي الْبَيْتِ – *They are not at home.*)

2. The construction <u>with</u> ما

In such application, ما is not a negation particle, but a device to form an infinitive noun (مَصْدَر). The resulting expression has the power of a verb which explains why we can have a direct object, guarded in the accusative case.

All students came except one.	جاءَ الطُّلّابُ ما عَدَا طالِبًا.
	جاءَ الطُّلّابُ ما خَلا طالِبًا.

- In both examples, the word for *except* is expressed by an interpreted **infinitive** (ما الْمَصْدَرِيّةُ) which expresses the same meaning as the basic مَصْدَرٌ. It has verbal power.

- Expressions like ما عَدَا can guard a direct object (مَفْعُولٌ بِهِ) which is the reason for the accusative case (مَنْصُوبٌ).

- The entire expression ما عَدَا طالِبًا is located in the position of a *circumstantial description; status* (حال)

→ For a deep analysis, see *Arabic for Nerds 2, question #408.*

3. The construction <u>without</u> ما

How could you interpret these special devices (خَلا, عَدَا, etc.) then? You have two options:

Option I: Verbs like عَدَا are treated as inert, static past tense verbs which can have a direct object. This explains why we use the accusative case (مَنْصُوبٌ) for the *excluded* (= the object).

1	All students came except one.	جاءَ الطُّلّابُ عَدَا طالِبًا.
	Same meaning as above with ما. The word طالِبًا is a regular object (مَفْعُول بِه) of the verb عَدَا.	

Option II: We treat them as prepositions → we need the genitive case (مَجْرُورٌ) for the *excluded*.

2	All students came except one.	جاءَ الطُّلّابُ خَلا طالِبٍ.
		جاءَ الطُّلّابُ حاشا طالِبٍ.
	Here, we treat خَلا and حاشا as prepositions (حَرْفُ جَرٍّ). Thus, the word after it has to be in the genitive case (مَجْرُورٌ).	

4. The construction using غَيْر • سِوَى

Both غَيْر and سِوَى are **nouns** (إِسْمُ إِسْتِثْناءٍ). The word غَيْر means *other*. سِوَى expresses *other than*. Both nouns are considered to be *indefinite* – see *#216*.

You have **five** (!) **options**:

Option I: Use an <u>indefinite</u> noun before غَيْر.

The most elegant way of treating غَيْر is to treat it as an **adjective** (صِفةٌ) for an **indefinite** (نَكِرةٌ) noun. But there's an issue: غَيْر cannot stand alone and thus needs to be the first part of a إِضافةٌ. As soon as we add the second part, the entire expression will become definite (مَعْرِفةٌ). Looks like a mismatch (indefinite noun ↔ definite adjective), but it isn't! In Arabic, both غَيْر and سِوَى are always treated as indefinite nouns.

A man came to me other than you.	جاءَني رَجُلٌ غَيْرُكَ.
Theoretically, the expression غَيْرُكَ is **definite** due to the pronoun suffix كَ. The expression غَيْرُكَ is an adjective for the **indefinite** word *a man*. Wait, but how can it be an adjective for an indefinite word when the expression itself is definite? Good question.	

The grammarians say that the pronoun كَ which is attached to غَيْر does not strip the word غَيْر from its indefiniteness. That is also the reason why it takes the nominative (مَرْفُوعٌ) – the case of the word to which it refers since adjectives need agreement (الْمُطابَقةُ).

Option II: Use a <u>definite</u> noun before غَيْر.

We treat غَيْر itself as *the excluded* (الْمُسْتَثْنَى) with the effect that we have to mark it with the accusative (مَنْصُوبٌ). So we actually treat غَيْر like a word that is placed after إِلّا! Why? We assume that إِلّا was originally involved and placed before غَيْر. The word غَيْر serves as the first part of a إِضافةٌ-construction and drags a following word into the genitive case (مَجْرُورٌ).

All students came except one.	جاءَ الطُّلّابُ غَيْرَ طالِبٍ. جاءَ الطُّلّابُ سِوَى طالِبٍ.
The word طالِب is the second part of a إِضافة-construction, so it has to be in the genitive case (مَجْرُورٌ). Since the sentence is **not** *negated*, the word غَيْرَ has to be in the accusative case.	

Option III: Use a negated sentence before غَيْر.

Only one student came. (The students didn't come, except for Zayd.)	ما جاءَ الطُّلّابُ غَيْرَ طالِبٍ. ما جاءَ الطُّلّابُ غَيْرُ طالِبٍ.

You have a choice: You can either write غَيْرَ or غَيْرُ. Both are correct. After a negated sentence (جُمْلَةٌ مَنْفِيَّةٌ), you have two possibilities. You can either treat غَيْر as *the excluded* (مَنْصُوبٌ عَلَى الْإِسْتِثْناءِ) → the <u>accusative</u> case. Or you say that it stands in *apposition* (بَدَلٌ) to the preceding word → in our example, the nominative case (in apposition to *students*).

Option IV: Use a negated sentence before غَيْر, but leave out the الْمُسْتَثْنَى مِنْهُ. → Only *the excluded* is mentioned.

Only one student came.	ما جاءَ غَيْرُ طالِبٍ. ما جاءَ سِوَى طالِبٍ.

This type of construction is called أُسْلُوبُ الْقَصْرِ. The word طالِب is the second part of a إِضافةٌ-construction; hence, it has to be in the genitive case (مَجْرُورٌ). We mark the word غَيْر according to its function in the sentence. In our examples, it is the **subject** (فاعِلٌ) since the الْمُسْتَثْنَى مِنْهُ is not mentioned. It has to take ضَمّةٌ.

Also here, just delete the negation in your mind if you have to add the case markers – the result will be correct! Note: In the sentence with سِوَى, the case marker is hidden/presumptive (مُقَدَّرة).

Option V: It is cut off from the إِضافةٌ – which can only happen if لَيْسَ is involved.

I have one penny, nothing more.	قبضتُ دِرْهَمًا لَيْسَ غَيْرُ.
This is the meaning →	لَيْسَ غَيْرُها مَقْبُوضًا

We deleted the second part of the إِضافةٌ as well as the predicate of لَيْسَ (marked in gray above). In this situation, we fix the word غَيْرُ on the vowel "*u*" (مَبْنِيٌّ عَلَى الضَّمِّ). This happens also with words like قَبْلُ in the expression مِنْ قَبْلُ - see #221.

Now, which **job** may غَيْر have in a sentence? It depends on the position in the sentence.

Someone else visited me.	زارَنِي غَيْرُكَ.
Subject (فاعِلٌ) of the verb → nominative case.	

I asked someone else.	سَأَلْتُ غَيْرَكَ.
Direct object (مَفْعُولٌ بِهِ) → accusative case.	

I looked at someone else (other than you).	نَظَرْتُ إِلَى غَيْرِكَ.
After a preposition, in the genitive case (مَجْرُورٌ بِحَرْفِ جَرٍّ).	

I didn't look at the students, except for Zayd.	ما نَظَرْتُ إِلَى الطُّلّابِ غَيْرَ زَيْدٍ.
	ما نَظَرْتُ إِلَى الطُّلّابِ غَيْرِ زَيْدٍ.
Negated sentence (جُمْلَةٌ مَنْفِيَّةٌ); so we have a choice. The accusative case or the case of the preceding word (apposition) – see option III.	

Buy another book than this!	إِشْتَرِ كِتابًا غَيْرَ هٰذا!
Adjective (نَعْتٌ) → it mirrors the case; accusative here (like كِتابًا).	

The students succeeded, except for Zayd.	نَجَحَ الطُّلّابُ غَيْرَ زَيْدٍ.
The excluded (مَنْصُوبٌ عَلَى الْإِسْتِثْناءِ), thus in the accusative case.	

Zayd traveled unsatisfactorily.	سافَرَ زَيْدٌ غَيْرَ راضٍ.
Circumstantial description; status (حالٌ) → accusative case.	

216. Is the word بَعْضٌ (*some*) definite or indefinite?

That's disputed – and an almost philosophical question.

بَعْضٌ means *some* and is a remarkable word. Some say that it denotes the greater part of a portion (e.g., eight of ten). In the world of Arabic, it is noun that *is impregnated with incertitude, obscurity* (مُتَوَغِّلٌ فِي الإِبْهامِ). Some other nouns share this characteristic too: *one* (أَحَدٌ), *like* (مِثْلٌ), *similar to* (شِبْهٌ), *except/other than* (غَيْر and سِوَى).

There has been a century-long debate revolving around بَعْضٌ: Would you say that بَعْضٌ can receive the definite article ال or not? It is not trivial. One more thing: What we say here about بَعْض is basically also true for كُلّ.

In the Qur'an, you don't find بَعْض with ال. Perfect, so we can stop the analysis – the Qur'an is always right. Furthermore, also in Classical Arabic poetry, you can't find الْبَعْض.

On the other hand, languages are not in a frozen state. Especially nowadays you often see الْبَعْضُ and الْكُلُّ. In early times, people seem to have used الْبَعْضُ and الْكُلُّ since they are both recorded in books of the first grammarians. So is الْبَعْض incorrect? Most importantly, given this is true, why should الْبَعْض be wrong?

Let's look at what the grammarians can agree on.

- The conservative view is that you can't prefix ال to بَعْض and كُلّ. They are **determinate without it** (مَعْرِفةٌ بِغَيْرِ ال).
- The moderate view, accepted by the majority, states that both words (كُلّ and بَعْض) are **definite**, but that the Arabs **don't use it with the definite article.**

- From a logical point of view, بَعْض in the meaning of *some* **cannot get the definite article** الـ because such a device would cancel the inherently indefinite meaning.

- بَعْض and كُلّ are **understood as prefixed**. They are originally only used as prefixed nouns and as such **determinate** either literally or virtually, which means that they **do not admit another cause of being determinate**. So, what would happen, if the second part of the إِضافةٌ gets الـ?

This would mean that also بَعْض becomes definite, because the second part of the إِضافةٌ decides whether the entire expression is definite or indefinite. Since we said that بَعْض does not accept being "determined" by others, we have to distinguish between reality and appearance. Although the إِضافةٌ appears definite, the entire construction will be treated as being indefinite. For ex.: *some/one of their books* (بَعْضُ كُتُبِهِم) – indefinite! This becomes relevant as soon as we deal with adjectives.

So why do people use الـ before بَعْضٌ?

- Some argue that the article is meant to be a **substitute** for the noun to which بَعْض should be prefixed – so to say, to compensate that the second part of the إِضافةٌ is missing.

- Others suggested that you can use الـ with بَعْض because it is equivalent to جُزْءٌ which receives the article الـ.

Now let's look at how we can understand such constructions grammatically.

one of them	Although the pronoun suffix would make the whole إِضافةٌ definite, we treat the en-	أَحَدُهُم
a youth like me	tire expression as **indefinite**. This has	فَتَّى مِثْلِي

men other than you	huge implications. For example, in the last two examples, we use a إضافة-construction (which looks **definite** on paper) as an adjective for an **indefinite** word!	رِجالٌ غَيْرُكُمْ

...except some who got to the Prophet.	...إِلّا بَعْضَهُمْ لَحِقُوا بِالنَّبِيِّ.

The construction with بَعْضَهُمْ would suggest that you need to introduce the relative clause with the word الَّذي, but that didn't happen. بَعْضَهُمْ is a إضافة-construction, which is automatically turned **definite** by the pronoun suffix. However, in Arabic, the expression بَعْضُهُمْ is treated as **indefinite**! See also *question #87*.

Some of us watched the others (We watched each other.)	راقَبَ بَعْضُنا بَعْضًا.	1
بَعْضُنا is the subject (فاعِلٌ); بَعْضًا is the direct object (مَفْعُولٌ بِه).		

We raised some of them above the others.	رَفَعْنا بَعْضَهُمْ فَوْقَ بَعْضٍ.	2
بَعْضٍ is part of an adverbial phrase (second part of the إضافةٌ).		

...the people could hardly recognize one another. *(Sahīh Muslim 614)*	...النّاسُ لاَ تَكادُ يَعْرِفُ بَعْضُهُمْ بَعْضًا.	3
بَعْضُهُمْ is the subject (فاعِلٌ); بَعْضًا is is the direct object (مَفْعُولٌ بِه). The entire sentence after النّاسُ is the predicate (خَبَرٌ).		

Watch out! If you want to express *give me some*, you could say أَعْطِني بَعْضًا مِنْهُ ← with the preposition مِنْ.

If you want to express that a person should read *something*, you should avoid a literal translation. Instead, use the absolute object (مَفْعُولٌ مُطْلَقٌ) because in a إِضافةٌ-construction بَعْض prefers to go along with an object derived from verb.

bad style	Read something!	إِقْرَأْ بَعْضَ الشَّيْءِ!
better!		إِقْرَأْ بَعْضَ الْقِراءَةِ!

Good to know:

- بَعْض, especially in Classical Arabic, may express **one of**.
- *Some* is not always expressed in Arabic. For ex.: *I bring you some water* → أُحْضِرُ لَكَ ماءً ← Here, don't use بَعْض!
- If you see in English *some of*, don't use the preposition مِنْ as its meaning (*of*) is included in the إِضافةٌ anyway.

correct	some of the students	بَعْضُ الطُّلابِ
bad style		بَعْضٌ مِنْ الطُّلابِ

217. How do you express exclusiveness in Arabic?

There are many options.

If you want to emphasize a fact or person, you can use the words *except* or *only* in English. In Arabic, there are plenty of ways to express this idea (أُسْلُوبُ الْقَصْرِ).

1	Negation plus exception	النَّفْيُ والْإِسْتِثْناءُ
	Only the serious workers are successful.	لا يَنْجَحُ إِلّا الْعامِلُونَ بِجِدٍّ.
	Note: To put case endings, imagine the sentence without لا and إِلّا.	

إِنَّما	2	Use a combination of إِنَّ + ما

After **إِنَّما**, you can use a nominal (**جُمْلَةٌ اِسْمِيّةٌ**) or verbal sentence (**جُمْلَةٌ فِعْلِيّةٌ**). The **ما** included in **إِنَّما** is a *neutralizing particle* (**ما الْكافّةُ**)! Such **ما** is like an absorbing wall through which the grammatical force of **إِنَّ** doesn't penetrate. In other words, you don't have to think about special case endings.

Success is for serious workers only.	إِنَّما النَّجاحُ لِلْعامِلِينَ بِجِدٍّ or إِنَّما يَنْجَحُ الْعامِلُونَ بِجِدٍّ.

بَلْ	لٰكِنْ	3	*but ; rather ; on the contrary*

The particle **بَلْ** corrects a statement and confirms and verifies what follows (**حَرْفُ إِضْرابٍ**). If you see **بَلْ** in a sentence, you know at least that the information after **بَلْ** is more important or correct than the statement earlier.

You have to use a **single word** after **بَلْ** and not a sentence. Only if you do so, you can treat **بَلْ** as a **conjunction**/"coupler" (**حَرْفُ عَطْفٍ**) with the effect that both words which directly surround **بَلْ** take the **same case**.

If we want to **overturn** the information that is given before **بَلْ**, we need to start with a **negation**. Then, **بَلْ** is a *particle of correction* (**حَرْفُ اِسْتِدْراكٍ**), an *adversative particle*, which corrects the previous statement.

Note that what we said so far about **بَلْ** is also true for **لٰكِنْ**.

Khalid wasn't present but absent.	ما كانَ خالِدٌ حاضِرًا بَلْ غائِبًا.
Fairouz is not a writer, she is a singer.	ما فَيْرُوزُ كاتِبةٌ لٰكِنْ مُغَنِّيةٌ.
	ما فَيْرُوزُ كاتِبةٌ بَلْ مُغَنِّيةٌ.

There is a tricky situation. If you use لَيْسَ (or ما in the sense of لَيْسَ) in a sentence with بَلْ, you have to apply the **nominative case (مَرْفُوعٌ)** after بَلْ and not the accusative case which we would expect for the predicate of لَيْسَ.

| Zayd is not standing, but (he is) sitting. | مَا زَيْدٌ قَائِمًا بَلْ قَاعِدٌ. |
| Zayd is not standing; no, is not sitting. (This is not what you want to express!) | مَا زَيْدٌ قَائِمًا بَلْ قَاعِدًا. |

Some grammarians even say that you can only use بَلْ after a negation. If you encounter بَلْ in an affirmative (not negated) sentence, you should be careful. If you **don't have a negation** before or if you use an **imperative**, then بَلْ may...

a) ...indicate that the earlier information was incorrect or not important. The information after بَلْ is the <u>correction</u>.

b) ...indicate the <u>opposite</u> of what was previously stated in the sentence.

→ The command or instruction relates only to **what follows بَلْ**!

Drink water, rather, milk! (Drink water; no, milk!)	إِشْرَبْ مَاءً، بَلْ حَلِيبًا!	a
Zayd came; no, Khalid.	جَاءَ زَيْدٌ، بَلْ خَالِدٌ.	
We don't visit the enemy, but the friend.	لَا نَزُورُ الْعَدُوَّ، بَلْ الصَّدِيقَ.	b

| 5 | Emphasis by word-order | التَّقْدِيمُ وَالتَّأْخِيرُ |

I address my words to you.	إِلَيْكَ أُوَجِّهُ كَلَامِي or أُوَجِّهُ كَلَامِي إِلَيْكَ.

Watch out for the correct cases and use of grammar!

The friendship with an idiot is a burden.	صَداقَةُ الْأَحْمَقِ تَعَبٌ.

Only a burden is the friendship with an idiot.	لَيْسَتْ صَداقَةُ الْأَحْمَقِ إِلّا تَعَبًا.

You have to negate the noun with لَيْسَ The predicate (خَبَرُ لَيْسَ) has to be in the accusative case (مَنْصُوبٌ).

I am a **student** (feminine).	أَنا طالِبَةٌ.
I am (only) a **student**.	لَسْتُ إِلّا طالِبَةً.
(It is that; because; only) I am a **student**.	إِنَّما أَنا طالِبَةٌ.
I am **student**, not a teacher.	أَنا طالِبَةٌ لا مُدَرِّسَةٌ.

218. How do you express *I can* in Arabic?

You have many verbs to choose from.

In colloquial Arabic, you will hear مُمْكِن a lot. In Standard Arabic you often use verbs. Which one you choose, however, depends on what you actually want to express with *can*.

I. *Can* in the meaning of *to master*

to master, to do well (a skill)	أَحْسَنَ / يُحْسِنُ	IV-

to master (a language)	أَجَادَ / يُجِيدُ	verb
to bring to perfection; to be proficient	أَتْقَنَ / يُتْقِنُ	

He speaks Arabic very well.	يُجِيدُ الْعَرَبِيَّةَ.
	يُتْقِنُ الْعَرَبِيَّةَ.

II. *Can* in the meaning of *to be able to*

ط-و-ع	X-verb إِسْتَطاعَ / يَسْتَطِيعُ	+	أَنْ + verb subjunctive
			مَصْدَرٌ

Alternatively, you could also use the following construction.

مَصْدَرٌ of X-verb	بِاسْتِطاعَةِ	+	person	+	a	أَنْ + verb subjunctive
					b	noun in the nominative (= what the person can do)
					c	فِي plus noun

He can travel.	يَسْتَطِيعُ السَّفَرَ.
	يَسْتَطِيعُ أَنْ يُسافِرَ.

lit. *to know* (used for things that you need to learn in order to exercise them).	عَرَفَ - يَعْرِفُ	ع-ر-ف

He can swim.	يَعْرِفُ الْعَوْمَ.

| with my capacity, possibility | بِمَقْدُورِي أَنْ | |
| to be able to (often associated with physical capability) | قَدَرَ - يَقْدُرُ أَنْ or عَلَى | ق-د-ر |

| He can walk. | يَقْدُرُ عَلَى الْمَشْيِ. |
| | يَقْدُرُ أَنْ يَمْشِي. |

| to enable someone to do something (IV-verb!) | أَمْكَنَ - يُمْكِنُ أَنْ or مِنْ | |
| it is possible that... | مِن الْمُمْكِنِ أَنْ | م-ك-ن |

Can I go with you? (Is it possible for me that...)	هَلْ يُمْكِنُنِي أَنْ أَذْهَبَ مَعَكَ؟
he can do...	يُمْكِنُهُ أَنْ
it is possible that; it may be that...	يُمْكِنُ أَنْ
as much as possible	...أَكْثَرَ مَا يُمْكِنُ

III. If you want to express: *not to be able; to be incapable*

| to be unable to do | عَجَزَ - يَعْجَزُ عَنْ | ع-ج-ز |

| He couldn't do it. | عَجَزَ عَنْ فِعْلِ الْأَمْرِ |
| | عَجَزَ أَنْ يَفْعَلَ الْأَمْرَ. |

IV. *Can* in the meaning of *not to be possible*

negated: not to be possible for someone	وَسِعَ - يَسَعُ	و-س-ع

I couldn't stop her.	ما وَسِعَني مَنْعُها.
She defended him as good as possible.	دافَعَتْ عَنْهُ ما وَسِعَها الدِّفاعُ (ما سَمَحَ الْجَهْدُ)
I cannot say.	لا يَسَعُني أَنْ أَقولَ.
I can't do that.	ما أَسَعُ ذلِكَ.

V. *Can* in the meaning of *to be allowed to*

to allow; to permit	سَمَحَ - يَسْمَحُ لِ + بْ + أَنْ	س-م-ح

Can (may) I enter? (Do you allow me to enter?)	هَلْ تَسْمَحُ لي بِأَنْ أَدْخُلَ؟ or يُسْمَحُ لَكَ بِأَنْ تَدْخُلَ.
Smoking is permitted.	التَّدْخِينُ مَسْموحٌ.

219. Does a simple sentence also mean simple grammar?

Most of the time, unfortunately, no.

Sometimes a tiny, single word can change the grammar and the meaning of an Arabic sentence dramatically. This happens oftentimes when you emphasize words.

Let us look at three examples.

1	*The student is in the house.*		الطَّالِبُ فِي الْبَيْتِ.
	The second part of the sentence is a prepositional phrase (شِبْهُ جُمْلَةٍ). It is located in the position of a nominative case (مَرْفُوعٌ) – but you cannot see that. ➤ We can only assign a place value (فِي مَحَلِّ رَفْعٍ).	subject (مُبْتَدَأٌ)	الطَّالِبُ
		predicate (خَبَرٌ)	فِي الْبَيْتِ

For a discussion whether the prepositional phrase can be called the predicate or not, see *Arabic for Nerds 2, question #219.*

2	*Indeed, safety lies in slowness.*		إِنَّ السَّلَامَةَ فِي التَّأَنِّي.
	The "subject" (اِسْمُ إِنَّ) is in the accusative case (مَنْصُوبٌ). The predicate is in the nominative case (مَرْفُوعٌ).	اِسْمُ إِنَّ	السَّلَامَةَ
		خَبَرُ إِنَّ	فِي التَّأَنِّي

3	*Indeed, safety lies in slowness.*		إِنَّما السَّلَامَةُ فِي التَّأَنِّي.
	We use a neutralizer (ما الْكَافَّة) with the effect that إِنَّ can't use its grammatical force. Thus, we have a standard nominal sentence after the particle of emphasis (إِنَّما).	مُبْتَدَأٌ مَرْفُوعٌ	السَّلَامَةُ
		خَبَرٌ مَرْفُوعٌ	فِي التَّأَنِّي

220. What are the so-called five nouns in Arabic?

Father, brother, mother-in-law, owner of, mouth

Clearly, these words are not really related by meaning. It has to be something completely different that connects them.

They are called *the five nouns* (الْأَسْماءُ الْخَمْسة) because they are five in number. Some say there are six of them.

These nouns are special because they change their form dramatically when they are connected with a pronoun or when they are part of a إِضافة. It all depends on the case they need!

Let's take a closer look at these words in all cases.

meaning	مَنْصُوبٌ	مَجْرُورٌ	مَرْفُوعٌ	word	
his father	أَباهُ	أَبِيهِ	أَبُوهُ	أَبٌّ	1
his brother	أَخاهُ	أَخِيهِ	أَخُوهُ	أَخٌّ	2
his mother in law	حَماهُ	حَمِيهِ	حَمُوهُ	حَمٌّ	3
owner of; with	ذا	ذِي	ذُو	ذُو	4
his mouth	فاهُ	فِيهِ	فُوهُ	فُو (فَمٌّ)	5

221. What is the correct spelling of *before?* قَبْلُ or قَبْلَ؟

Both are correct – but you have to know in which situation.

Let's start with the solution, which is easy to remember:

> *Before* (قَبْلَ) and *after* (بَعْدَ) end in *"a"* (فَتْحةٌ).
> Only when preceded by مِنْ they get *"u"* (ضَمّةٌ).

Arabic is quite sophisticated. The ضَمّةٌ replaces a **deleted phrase** which is still understood: ...مِنْ قَبْلِ ذٰلِكَ الْوَقْتِ.

That's why you write one ضَمّةٌ on the last letter of بَعْدُ or قَبْلُ when it is preceded by مِنْ. Let us look at some examples.

previously; before	مِنْ قَبْلُ
I have not visited Luxor before (this day).	لَمْ أَزُرْ الْأُقْصُرَ قَبْلَ الْيَوْمِ.
I have not visited Luxor before.	لَمْ أَزُرْ الْأُقْصُرَ مِنْ قَبْلُ.

Let's focus on the difference:

before; previously. It doesn't require further specification. قَبْلُ gets a fixed ضَمّةٌ-ending since we don't have a إِضافةٌ.	مِنْ قَبْلُ

before xyz	قَبْلَ + إِضافةٌ
before the lesson	قَبْلَ الدَّرسِ

After مِنْ, the word قَبْلِ takes كَسْرةٌ since it is placed after a preposition.	مِنْ قَبْلِ + إِضافةٌ
before that	مِنْ قَبْلِ ذٰلِكَ

222. How do you express *never* in Arabic?

It depends on whether you talk about the past or future.

In Arabic, there is no universal word for *never*. Many people think that أَبَدًا would do the job, but in fact, it is often misused. أَبَدًا only works when the time frame fits to it.

(1) **negation** of the <u>past</u> tense + (2) قَطُّ	*never*
قَطُّ is an *adverb of time* which always looks like that; it has a cemented shape (ظَرْفُ زَمانٍ مَبْنيٌّ عَلَى الضَّمِّ). You negate the past	

tense with لَمْ plus verb in the **jussive** mood (مَجْزُومٌ).	
The director has never gone to the office. (Note: You'd need a helping vowel in يَذْهَبْ).	لَمْ يَذْهَبِ الْمُديرُ قَطُّ إِلَى الْمَكْتَبِ.
I've never done that (before).	لَمْ أَفْعَلْ هذا قَطُّ

(1) **negation** of the **future** + (2) أَبَدًا	*never*
أَبَدًا (lit.: *eternally*) is an *adverb of time* which can get case endings and is always declined! (ظَرْفُ زَمانٍ مُعْرَبٌ).	
➤ You negate the future with لَنْ plus a verb in the **subjunctive** mood (مَنْصُوبٌ).	

I will never study.	لَنْ أَدْرُسَ أَبَدًا.
He will never do that.	لَنْ يَفْعَلَ ذلك أَبَدًا.

(1) **negation** of the **present** tense + (2) مُطْلَقًا	*never*
The word مُطْلَقٌ means *free; absolute; unlimited*. It is the passive participle (إِسْمُ الْمَفْعُولِ) of the IV-verb أَطْلَقَ - يُطْلِقُ. The same word is used in the grammar term absolute object (مَفْعُولٌ مُطْلَقٌ).	

I never study. (lit.: I absolutely don't study.)	لا أَدْرُسُ مُطْلَقًا.
In such constructions, مُطْلَقًا serves as a substitute of the absolute object (نائِبُ الْمَفْعُولِ الْمُطْلَقِ).	

For a deep analysis, see *Arabic for Nerds 2*, question #350.

223. كانَ and إِنَّ are somehow the opposite, aren't they?

Yes, they are – regarding case endings.

If you see the verb كانَ (*to be*) or the particle إِنَّ (*indeed; that*) in a sentence, you have to be very careful.

The standard rules for case endings are overthrown. Both كانَ and إِنَّ have "sisters", i.e., other words that share the same grammar rules.

Let us analyze both groups since they are crucial for understanding Arabic grammar.

All sisters of كانَ are **verbs** (فِعْلٌ).	كانَ وَأَخَواتُها
All sisters of إِنَّ are **particles** (حَرْفٌ).	إِنَّ وَأَخَواتُها

كانَ	إِنَّ
Past tense of the verb *to be*.	To emphasize a **nominal sentence** (جُمْلةٌ إِسْمِيّةٌ)
كانَ • أَصْبَحَ • أَضْحَى • أَمْسَى • ظَلَّ • باتَ *to be or to become* صارَ to describe a transformation لَيْسَ for negation ما دامَ for proof of duration ما إنْفَكَّ • ما فَتِئَ • ما زالَ • ما بَرِحَ to express continuation; *still, as long as* (all have a present tense meaning)	إِنَّ • أَنَّ • كَأَنَّ • لِكِنَّ • لَيْتَ (if only) • لَعَلَّ (perhaps) The "sisters" are conjunctions, most of them express doubt or objection. Since these particles emphasize a nominal sentence, the word after إِنَّ has to be a noun or a pronoun (ها, ه, ...) which turns it, in fact, into a nominal sentence.
subject: nominative (مَرْفُوعٌ)	**subject**: accusative (مَنْصُوبٌ)

| predicate: accusative (مَنْصُوبٌ) | predicate: nominative (مَرْفُوعٌ) |

An example:

أَصْبَحَ الرَّجُلُ مُدِيرًا.	كَأَنَّ الْحَيَاةَ حُلْمٌ.
The man became director.	It seems that life is a dream.

224. What is the plural of the word *year* (سَنةٌ)?

There are two correct plural forms: سَنَواتٌ *and* سِنُونَ.

سَنةٌ is a feminine word (مُؤَنَّثٌ). So it is not surprise that one plural form is سَنَواتٌ. Nevertheless, you can also form a **sound masculine plural** (جَمْعُ الْمُذَكَّرِ السَّالِمُ).How come?

type	explanation, remarks	plural
A	regular feminine plural	سَنَواتٌ
B	sound masculine plural pattern for the nominative case (مَرْفُوع)	سِنُونَ
	sound masculine plural pattern for the genitive case (مَجْرُورٌ) and the accusative case (مَنْصُوبٌ)	سِنِينَ

Form B is a sound masculine plural (جَمْعُ الْمُذَكَّرِ السَّالِمُ). Therefore, you have to apply the standard rules of sound masculine plurals, i.e., you have to omit the ن if the word serves as the first part of a إضافة.

Such examples are rare, but you shouldn't be surprised if you see a sound masculine plural although the singular form wouldn't necessarily suggest that. If you want to know why we are allowed to do that, see *Arabic for Nerds 2, question #100.*

225. What does the word أُولُو mean?

أُولُو *is the plural of the demonstrative* ذُو *which basically means: master of; in possession of.*

أُولُو is a very strange plural form. Such atypical patterns are rare, but occur in common words. For example, the Arabic word for *son:* اِبْنٌ.

sons of Israel	بَنُو إِسْرائِيلَ
Send with us the Children of Israel. *(Sura 26:17)*	أَنْ أَرْسِلْ مَعَنَا بَنِي إِسْرائِيلَ.
→ In both examples, the ن was dropped due to the إِضافةٌ.	

We should put the words اِبْنٌ and ذُو on the operating table.

- A: broken plural (جَمْعُ التَّكْسِيرِ)
- B: sound masculine plural pattern (جَمْعُ الْمُذَكَّرِ السَّالِمُ)

	meaning; explanation	plural	type	
	Meaning: *sons.* This is the broken plural.	أَبْناءٌ	A	
	sound masculine plural, nominative (مَرْفُوعٌ)	بَنُونَ	B	اِبْنٌ
	sound masculine plural, مَجْرُورٌ and مَنْصُوبٌ	بَنِينَ	B	
	Type B is more common in religious texts.			بَنُو إِسْرائِيلَ

Note that the ن disappears in إِضافةٌ-constructions because it is a sound masculine plural!		

owner; people. أُولُو is the masculine plural of ذُو for the nominative case (مَرْفُوعٌ) You can't use it alone; it must be placed as the first part of a إِضافةٌ which is why there's no ن as it drops.	أُولُو	B	ذُو
sound masculine plural, مَجْرُورٌ and مَنْصُوبٌ	أُولِي	B	
Meaning: *men of understanding.* Note: لُبٌّ (plural: أَلْبابٌ) *means reason; mind* but also *core, heart; essence.*		أُولُو الْأَلْبابِ	

وَلَكُمْ فِي الْقِصاصِ حَياةٌ يا أُولِي الْأَلْبابِ لَعَلَّكُمْ تَتَّقُونَ.
Fair retribution saves life for you, people of understanding, so that you may guard yourselves against what is wrong. When death approaches one of you who leaves wealth *(Sura 2:179)*

Watch out: The word ذُو is sometimes mistaken with the demonstrative اذ and mistranslated as *that.*

226. What is correct? - قَضَيْتُ أَوْقاتًا or قَضَيْتُ أَوْقاتٍ

Correct is قَضَيْتُ أَوْقاتًا. *The sentence means: I spent time.*

Don't let the last part fool you. It is true that sound feminine plurals (جَمْعُ الْمُؤَنَّثِ السّالِمُ) never receive the case ending "*-an*" (اتً) in the accusative case (مَنْصُوبٌ); see #34. For example:

I saw (female) teachers.	رَأَيْتُ مُعَلِّماتٍ.

In قَضَيْتُ أُوقاتًا, *time* is the direct object (مَفْعُولٌ بِهِ). At first glance, you spot the feminine ات-ending in أُوقاتٌ. But this is not correct. أُوقاتٌ is not a feminine plural! The ت is part of the root! Therefore, it has to be قَضَيْتُ أُوقاتًا.

meaning	broken plural	noun	root
time; period	أَوْقاتٌ	وَقْتٌ	و-ق-ت
I had a great time.	قَضَيْتُ أَوْقاتًا سَعِيدةً.		
sound; voice	أَصْواتٌ	صَوْتٌ	ص-و-ت
I heard sounds.	سَمِعْتُ أَصْواتًا.		

227. What is the Arabic active participle of *to point out* (دَلَّ)?

It is دَالٌّ *and means: indicating; pointing; showing.*

Arabic verbs with two root letters having one doubled can be nasty. The active participle (اِسْمُ فاعِلٍ) of such roots is often misread because the typical vowel "*i*" (كَسْرةٌ) is missing.

	مَصْدَرٌ	passive p. اِسْمُ الْمَفْعُول	active p. اِسْمُ الْفاعِلِ	present الْمُضارِعُ	past ten. الْماضِي	root
to show; point out	دَلالةٌ	مَدْلُولٌ	دَالٌّ	يَدُلُّ	دَلَّ عَلَى	د-ل-ل
to split; to divide	شَقٌّ / مَشَقّةٌ	مَشْقُوقٌ	شاقٌّ	يَشُقُّ	شَقَّ	ش-ق-ق

→ The only thing you should keep in mind is that the **doubled root letter is not written twice.** Instead, it gets شَدّةٌ.

228. How do you express *on the same day* in Arabic?

You use a word expressing time and add إذْ *resulting in* يَوْمَئِذٍ.

There are many ways to express that something happened on the same day, in the same year, etc. We will focus here on a **universal formula** that works smoothly. Our main ingredient is إذْ, a word denoting past time: *at the time of; then.*

We need to take three steps to produce such expressions.

Step 1	Take a word indicating time (or place), e.g., *hour.*	ساعةٌ

Step 2	Place the vowel "*a*" (فَتْحةٌ) at the end of the word because it will be used as an adverb (ظَرْفٌ). This word will later merge with another which explains why we convert ة into ت. The word ساعَتَ is the first part of a إضافةٌ.	ساعَتَ

Watch out: This is **not the marker** of the accusative case! Although the result is often simplistically presented as "accusative", it is the result of a complex operation which happened in the background. First, we fixed (cemented) the word on the vowel "*a*". (مَبْنِيٌّ عَلَى الْفَتْحِ). By this operation, however, the word became **indeclinable** → we can't put visible case endings! We can only say that the word is placed in the **position of an accusative case** (فِي مَحَلِّ نَصْبٍ).

Step 3	Add إذْ as the second part of the إضافةٌ. Thus, it has to take the genitive case, so we get ئِذٍ. The expression means *at the same time; in this/that hour.*	ساعَتَئِذٍ

If you want to know why إذْ in this situation is capable of taking case endings, see *Arabic for Nerds 2*, question #343.

Let's see some examples:

They all express more or less the same: *then* or *at that time*.	وَقْتَئِذٍ	عِنْدَئِذٍ	آنَئِذٍ
	ساعَتَئِذٍ	حِينَئِذٍ	فِي ذَاكَ الْوَقْتِ

You can use إِذْ with other words as well, e.g., *day* or *year*.

at the same moment/second	لَحْظَتَئِذٍ
on the same day	يَوْمَئِذٍ
in the same year	سَنَتَئِذٍ

229. What is the difference between إِنَّ and أَنَّ?

The spelling of the Hamza (هَمْزة). But there is more, of course.

You may have noticed that after *to say* (قالَ - يَقُولُ), the particle إِنَّ is used and not أَنَّ. Why is that?

We should begin our investigation by taking a closer look at DNA إِنَّ and أَنَّ.

إِنَّ is a particle with **properties that resemble a verbal nature**. (حَرْفٌ مُشَبَّهٌ بِالْفِعْلِ). What does that mean? Well, it expresses the meaning of a verb: *I confirm* (= أُؤَكِّدُ). Hence, the grammarians say that إِنَّ and its *sisters* resemble verbs which is also one explanation for the accusative case (مَنْصُوبٌ) which can be interpreted as the object of a virtual, estimated verb.

أَنَّ is a sister of إِنَّ. Together with the noun after it, أَنَّ produces an expression which can be interpreted as an infinitive in Arabic (تُؤَوَّلُ مَعَ ما بَعْدَها بِمَصْدَرٍ).

Both particles intervene in nominal sentences (جُمْلة اِسْمِيّةٌ) and give it a special nature. Both need **two ingredients**:

- a "subject" (إِسْمُ إِنَّ or إِسْمُ أَنَّ) which takes the **accusative** case (مَنْصُوبٌ);

- a predicate (خَبَرُ إِنَّ or خَبَرُ أَنَّ) which has to be in the **nominative** case (مَرْفُوعٌ).

We are now doing an analysis and will develop three rules.

RULE 1:
أَنَّ ('anna) can never occur at the beginning of a sentence.

إِنَّ ('inna), on the other hand, can only be used in the following situations:

- To **start a full, nominal sentence** (جُمْلةٌ اِسْمِيّةٌ). إِنَّ then functions as an emphatic particle (*indeed, truly, verily*).

- **After** verbs that don't necessarily take an object (*to say*).

- In the **reported speech** when you use *to say* (قَالَ); sometimes also with the verb عَلِمَ (*to get to know*).

RULE 2:
إِنَّ ('inna) can never be used before a verb.

Which, conversely, means: إِنَّ is never followed by a verb.

That's why you often see a dummy pronoun after إِنَّ, grammatically speaking, a *pronoun of the matter* (ضَمِيرُ شَأْنٍ) in form of a pronoun suffix; for example, ه which results in إِنَّه.

Instead of starting the sentence directly with a noun (إِسْمٌ), the verb is placed after إِنَّه, and everything is fine. But you should check something else then: case endings! With a dummy pronoun, the sentence suddenly follows the regular rules of a verbal sentence (جُمْلةٌ فِعْلِيةٌ). Therefore, you don't need to think about weird case endings.

Let us look at an example. Both sentences mean the same: *He said that the teacher came.*

→ Here we use a dummy pronoun.	**قالَ إنَّهُ جاءَ المُدَرِّسُ.**
Teacher (المُدَرِّسُ) takes a ضَمّة as it is the subject (فاعِلٌ) of the verb جاءَ (!) and thus must get the **nominative** case (مَرْفُوعٌ). The entire sentence after إنَّهُ is located in the spot of the predicate of إنَّ (خَبَرُ إنَّ). And what about the إسْمُ إنَّ؟ → It is the dummy pronoun.	
→ The regular construction (**without** a dummy).	**قالَ إنَّ المُدَرِّسَ جاءَ.**
المُدَرِّسَ is the "subject", the so called noun of إنَّ (إسْمُ إنَّ); it takes the vowel "*a*" (فَتْحة) because it is in the **accusative** case (مَنْصُوبٌ).	

We should dig deeper into the sentence structure.

I said that the lesson is easy.	**قُلْتُ إنَّ الدَّرْسَ سَهْلٌ.**
There has to be a full (nominal) sentence after إنَّ. This is rooted in the nature of the verb *to say* because *to say* doesn't need an object!	

We are ready now for another rule.

RULE 3:
قالَ is **always followed by a sentence** or clause – and <u>never</u> by a single word.

If you have إنَّ, a مَصْدَرٌ alone would not be enough. What about أنَّ (with فَتْحةٌ on ن)? That's a whole new story! Try to imagine the following examples with a مَصْدَرٌ instead of أنَّ plus verb. Notice also the case endings.

I am pleased that you arrived.	**أسْعَدَني أنَّكَ وَصَلْتَ. =** **أسْعَدَني وُصُولُكَ.**

| I mentioned to Karīm that you arrived. | ذَكَرْتُ لِكَرِيمٍ أَنَّكَ وَصَلْتَ. = ذَكَرْتُ لِكَرِيمٍ وُصُولَكَ. |
| I was happy that you arrived. (or: with the fact that you arrived.) | فَرِحْتُ بِأَنَّكَ وَصَلْتَ. = فَرِحْتُ بِوُصُولِكَ. |

Now everything becomes clearer. The expression أَنَّكَ وَصَلْتَ (*that you arrived*) could be replaced by وُصُولُكَ (*your arriving/your arrival*) which is the مَصْدَر. The meaning is the same. In English, we occasionally leave the word *that* out.

إِنَّ, however, **cannot be paraphrased** like that! The sentence قَالَ إِنَّكَ وَصَلْتَ (*He said: truly, indeed, you arrived.*) cannot be replaced by قَالَ وُصُولَكَ (*He said: your arriving/arrival*) because the latter doesn't make sense.

Now we get the answer to where the subtle but important difference between the two lies: إِنَّكَ وَصَلْتَ has the status of a full clause and not that of a مَصْدَر (infinitive)!

A couple of subtleties:

➤ You have to use إِنَّ after قَالَ if you **trust** the information which comes after it.

➤ If you **doubt** it, you can use a construction with ب and أَنَّ to indicate that it may not be the absolute truth. Notice: This construction is also used for the reported speech! (see #202). Let us check an example (taken from a Syrian textbook):

| Some scientists say that the universe is expanding. | يَقُولُ بَعْضُ الْعُلَمَاءِ بِأَنَّ الْكَوْنَ يَتَمَدَّدُ. |

➤ أَنَّ can start a sentence. But it is another type of أَنَّ!

| The child moaned. | أَنَّ الطّفْلُ. |
| The child moans. | يَئِنُّ الطّفْلُ. |

Don't let that fool you. We said that أَنَّ can't be placed at the beginning! This is correct. In both examples, أَنَّ is not a particle (حَرْفٌ) – it is a I-verb (فِعْلٌ) and means *to groan; moan*.

| past tense (الْماضِي) | أَنَّ | | present tense (الْمُضارِعُ) | يَئِنُّ |

➤ Sometimes, you find the letter لـ after a sentence with إِنَّ.

| It is you whom I know. | إِنّي بِكَ لَعارِفٌ. |

إِنَّ here is combined with the first person أَنا expressed by the pronoun suffix ي. The information after it (i.e., the predicate) is introduced by لـ, which is **not** a negation nor a preposition. It is a *wandering* or *slipping Lām* (اللّامُ الْمُزَحْلَقةُ). Inserting such لـ happens often ins such constructions.

The لـ was initially put before the "subject"/noun of إِنَّ (اِسْمُ إِنَّ), but since Arabic does not like to have two devices of emphasis next to each other targeting the same word, it slipped towards the end and is now placed before the predicate. **Watch out:** This type of لـ does not have any influence on cases!

For specialists: When you use the I-verb عَلِمَ in the meaning of *to hear about; to be told; to get to know*, you can choose between إِنَّ or أَنَّ. See also *Arabic for Nerds 2*, question #306.

| Both sentences mean the same: *I was told/got to know that the lesson is easy.* | عَلِمْتُ أَنَّ الدّرْسَ سَهْلٌ. |
| | عَلِمْتُ إِنَّ الدّرْسَ سَهْلٌ. |

Note: For an analysis of إِنَّ and أَنَّ, see *Arabic for Nerds 2, q. #253 to #267.*

230. What kind of word do you put after the particle أَنَّ?

*Certainly **not** a verb (فِعْلٌ).*

After the particle أَنَّ, you usually find a pronoun suffix or a مَصْدَر. If you have an English sentence in mind that starts with *I think that..*, oftentimes you should not translate it bit by bit. You may need some tuning. Let's see why.

I think that it isn't clear if...	أَظُنُّ أَنَّ لَيْسَ مِن الْواضِح إذا... 1
There is a mistake! After أَنَّ you can **never** put a verb – and لَيْسَ is a verb! In this sentence, the إسْمُ أَنَّ would be missing!	

The solution: You can fix the sentence with a pronoun serving as the إسْمُ أَنَّ.	أَظُنُّ أَنَّهُ لَيْسَ مِن الْواضِح إذا... 2
The word after أَنَّ is not a verb anymore! It is a pronoun that converts the sentence into a nominal sentence (جُمْلَةٌ اِسْمِيّةٌ). Notice the pronunciation: 'annahu.	

231. When do you have to use the particle إِنَّ?

There are at least nine important situations.

إِنَّ is translated as *verily; indeed; certainly; that* – or is even left untranslated.

It all depends on the context.

1	At the beginning of a nominal sentence (جُمْلَةٌ اِسْمِيّةٌ)
Certainly (indeed), work is important for people.	إِنَّ الْعَمَلَ ضَرُورِيٌّ لِلإِنْسانِ.

| 2 | After a quotation |

| My professor said: "Indeed, the prices in this shop are high." | قَالَ أُسْتَاذِي:"إِنَّ الأَسْعَارَ فِي هٰذا الْمَحَلَّ مُرْتَفِعَةٌ." |

Good to know: almost always use إِنَّ after قَالَ - يَقُولُ (و=R2)!

| I say firmly that... | أَقُولُ جَازِمًا إِنَّ... |
| I say for sure that... | أَقُولُ عَنْ يَقِينٍ إِنَّ... |

| 3 | After أَلَا, a so-called *intensifying interjection* or *particle of inauguration* (حَرْفُ اسْتِفْتَاح). The expression أَلَا can be rendered as *oh yes, indeed, truly, verily*. It literally means: *is it not*. |

Oh yes, everything is ephemeral (lasting for a short time; not permanent)!	أَلَا إِنَّ كُلَّ شَيْءٍ زَائِلٌ!
By all means they are themselves the conquerors!	أَلَا إِنَّهُمْ هُمْ الظَّافِرُونَ!
Unquestionably, [for] the allies of Allah there will be no fear concerning them, nor will they grieve. *(Sura 10:62)*	أَلَا إِنَّ أَوْلِيَاءَ اللّٰهِ لَا خَوْفٌ عَلَيْهِمْ وَلَا هُمْ يَحْزَنُونَ.

| 4 | After the word كَلَّا which denotes *not at all; on the contrary; by no means! Certainly not! Never! No!* |

| On the contrary! Health is more important than money! | كَلَّا إِنَّ الصِّحَّةَ أَهَمُّ مِنَ الْمَالِ! |
| No! He has been stubbornly hostile to Our revelation. *(Sura 74:16)* | كَلَّا إِنَّهُ كَانَ لِآيَاتِنَا عَنِيدًا. |

5	After the particle إِذْ. In such constructions, إِذْ usually means *in view of the fact that; since; as*

Don't associate with him because he is not trustworthy.	لا تُعاشِرْهُ إِذْ إِنَّهُ غَيْرُ أَمِينٍ.

6	After حَيْثُ and حَتَّى • حَيْثُ usually means *where* (not used in questions!) and is used as an adverb of place (ظَرْف مَكان). With إِنَّ, it may denote *since, as, due to the fact that; in that…* • حَتَّى in such constructions denotes *so that; in such a way*.

I sat since the colleagues were sitting.	جَلَسْتُ حَيْثُ إِنَّ الزُّمَلاءَ جالِسُونَ.
Fire, since (as, because) it is hot, heats water.	النَّارُ مِنْ حَيْثُ إِنَّها حارَّةٌ تُسَخِّنُ الماءَ.
Zayd became ill in such a way that they have no hope for him.	مَرِضَ زَيْدٌ حَتَّى إِنَّهُمْ لا يَرْجُونَهُ.

7	To start a sentence used as a *circumstantial description* (حال)

I said goodbye to my colleague while he was leaving.	وَدَّعْتُ زَمِيلِي وَإِنَّهُ مُنْصَرِفٌ.

8	At the beginning of a relative clause (جُمْلَةُ الصِّلةِ)

I met those who master five languages.	قابَلْتُ مَنْ إِنَّهُمْ يُجِيدُونَ خَمْسَ لُغاتٍ.

| 9 | To start the sentence after an oath (جَوابُ الْقَسَمِ) |

| I swear that the temperature has reached fifty below zero. | وَاللهِ إِنَّ دَرَجَةَ الْحَرارةِ وَصَلَتْ إِلَى خَمْسِينَ تَحْتَ الصِّفرِ. |

232. Can you use قالَ (to say) together with أَنَّ?

Yes, you can – but you have to place أَنَّ later in the sentence.

The indirect (reported) speech after قالَ is introduced by إِنَّ. But what happens if you have more information? For example: *It is said that... and that...* Can you use إِنَّ a second time?

In grammatical terms, if you have two noun clauses in an indirect speech with قالَ, there is a good way to deal with it:

- The **first part** is introduced with إِنَّ and
- the **second part** with أَنَّ.

Let us look at an example:

| It is said **that** they are still alive and **that** they need water. | يُقالُ إِنَّهُمْ ما زالُوا أَحْياءً، وَأَنَّهُمْ يَحْتاجُونَ إِلَى مِياهٍ. |
| We have two occurrences of *that*. Notice the spelling! The first *that* is إِنَّهُمْ (*’inna*) and the second *that* is أَنَّهُمْ (*’anna*). |

233. When does a noun (إِسْمٌ) in Arabic need the nominative case (مَرْفُوعٌ)?

There are six situations.

Subject of a nominal sentence (جُمْلة اِسْمِيّةٌ). The word مُبْتَدَأ literally denotes *where it begins*. It is usually the **first word** of a sentence.	مُبْتَدَأ	1
Predicate of a nominal sentence (جُمْلة اِسْمِيّةٌ). It completes the meaning of the مُبْتَدَأ. Without the خَبَر, a nominal sentence wouldn't make sense.	خَبَرٌ	2
"Subject" (usually the first noun) in sentences with كان. All its *sisters* work similar: *verbs of approximation* (فِعْلٌ مُقارَبةٍ), *verbs of hope* (فِعْلُ رَجاءٍ), and *verbs of beginning* (فِعْلُ شُرُوعٍ). See #101, #102, #103.	إِسْمُ كانَ and its sis- ters	3
Predicate of a sentence starting with إِنَّ. Its *sisters* work likewise: أَنَّ • كَأَنَّ • لٰكِنَّ • لَعَلَّ • لَيْتَ , the absolute, generic negation (لا النّافِية لِلْجِنْسِ). For ex.: *There is no lasting pleasure* (لا سُرُورَ دائِمٌ).	خَبَرُ إِنَّ and its sisters	4
Subject of a verbal sentence	فاعِلٌ	5
Subject of a verbal sentence in the passive voice	نائِبُ فاعِلٍ	6

234. What is the difference between تَمَّ الْقَتْلُ and قُتِلَ؟

The meaning is the same: was killed. But there is a finesse.

Both constructions express the passive voice.

- قُتِلَ is the regular passive voice of the I-verb قَتَلَ - يَقْتُلُ (*to kill*). Therefore, it is translated as: *was killed*.

- تَمَّ الْقَتْلُ expresses roughly the same. We use the construction تَمَّ plus مَصْدَرٌ. The I-verb تَمَّ - يَتِمُّ means *to be* or *become complete/finished*. Therefore, تَمَّ الْقَتْلُ literally means *the killing was completed*.

Is there also a difference in meaning? We will see.

| The man was killed. | قُتِلَ الرَّجُلُ. | 1 |

We use the verb *to kill* in the passive voice. We don't know who the killer was. *Man* is now the **subject** of the passive voice (نائِبُ فاعِلٍ) and used to be the direct object (مَفْعُولٌ بِهِ).

| The man was killed. | تَمَّ قَتْلُ الرَّجُلِ. | 2 |

The meaning of example 2 is slightly different. It's more in the direction of: *the killing was completed*. تَمَّ is an intransitive verb; it cannot carry a direct object.

If you use this sentence without further information, it will express that there was an *order/assignment that has been fully completed*. It conveys the meaning of: *Okay, I did it; it is done.*

Killing (قَتْلُ) is an infinitive noun (مَصْدَرٌ) and functions as the regular **subject** (فاعِلٌ) of the verbal sentence (جُمْلَةٌ فِعْلِيّةٌ) – and not, like in the previous sentence, as the نائِبُ فاعِلٍ.

Note that the مَصْدَرٌ after تَمَّ must be **definite** (مَعْرِفةٌ): by the article الـ, by being the first part of a إِضافةٌ-construction (our example), or by a pronoun suffix.

Two more examples to illustrate this:

| The lesson was completed. | تَمَّ الدَّرْسُ. |

If you use this sentence *without* further information, it will mean: *I have finished the lesson; I did it.* (Rather than just: *The lesson is over*).

The work will be finished.	سَيَتِمُّ الْعَمَلُ.

In this sentence, we express a *future* action by conjugating the verb تَمَّ. Note: الْعَمَلُ here is the subject of the sentence (فَاعِلٌ).

235. What may the word أَيّ express?

Various things. For example: which, each, what a...!, or: that is.

أَيّ is one of those flexible words that can express a wide variety of things. A careless translation can quickly end in disaster. There are different ways of using أَيّ • أَيّةٌ (feminine form) – and each way may change the meaning of the sentence.

Usually, أَيّ serves as the first part of a إِضافةٌ-construction and drags the word which follows into the genitive (مَجْرُورٌ). أَيّ may take any of the three case endings according to its position in the sentence. Let us examine how you can use أَيّ:

A	Meaning: *which?*	الْإِسْتِفْهامُ

Which book is this?	أَيُّ كِتابٍ هذا؟	1

أَيّ is the **predicate** (خَبَرٌ) of a nominal sentence (جُمْلةٌ اِسْمِيّةٌ) and thus takes the **nominative** case (مَرْفُوعٌ); هذا is the subject (مُبْتَدَأٌ).

Which book did you read?	أَيَّ كِتابٍ قَرَأْتَ؟	2

أَيّ is the **direct object** (مَفْعُولٌ بِهِ) in the **accusative** case (مَنْصُوبٌ).

which is unexpected as it starts the sentence → inverted word-order! أيّ can also function as other types of objects. For example:

- أيّ is placed as a **circumstantial qualifier** (حالٌ): *I passed by Zayd, what a well-mannered man!* = مَرَرْتُ بِزَيْدٍ أيَّ مُهَذَّبٍ
- أيّ is placed as an **absolute object** (مَفْعُولٌ مُطْلَقٌ). It usually expresses the exclamatory meaning of *"what a..!"*. For example: *She was very happy with this book.* = سُرَّتْ بِهذا الْكِتابِ أيَّ سُرُورٍ

Which book did you read? (same meaning as 2)	أيُّ كِتابٍ قَرَأْتَهُ؟ 3

What is the difference to example 2? أيُّ in example 3 is the **subject** (مُبْتَدَأ) of a nominal sentence (جُمْلَةٌ اسْمِيّةٌ) and takes the nominative case (مَرْفُوعٌ). This is why you have to refer to the word *book* again with the help of a referential, returning pronoun: هـ.

Rule: If you use a **transitive** verb (a verb that can carry an object), you have to attach a pronoun. If you have an **intransitive** verb, you don't need a pronoun.

Which student came?	أيُّ تِلْمِيذٍ حَضَرَ؟ 4

أيُّ is the **subject** (مُبْتَدَأ) of the nominal sentence (جُمْلَةٌ اسْمِيّةٌ). *To come* is an intransitive verb → You don't need a pronoun suffix!

Which nationality?	مِنْ أيِّ جِنْسِيةٍ؟ 5

أيِّ is placed after a preposition; we need the genitive case (مَجْرُورٌ).

Which (female) student?	أيَّةُ طالِبةٍ؟ 6

We use the feminine form أيَّةُ because طالِبةٍ is feminine. Nevertheless, you may also encounter the masculine form in such constructions despite that the word after أيّ is feminine.

B	Meaning: anyhow; anyone; anyway

It may rain; but anyhow, I shall go out.	قَدْ تُمْطِرُ وَلكِنِّي سَأَخْرُجُ عَلَى أَيّةِ حالٍ.
I did not hear anything of...	لَمْ أَسْمَعْ أَيَّ شَيْءٍ مَنْ...
I like anything you like.	أَيُّ شَيْءٍ تُحِبُّهُ فَأَنا أُحِبُّهُ.

We have two sentences which are combined. Watch out: The verb تُحِبُّ in the last example does not take the jussive mood (مَجْزُومٌ) because this is not a conditional sentence (see type C).

C	Conditional meaning	اِسْمُ شَرْطٍ

| A (each/every) student who works hard will succeed. | أَيُّ طالِبٍ يَجْتَهِدْ يَنْجَحْ. |

Both verbs are in the jussive mood (مَجْزُومٌ) since the sentence has a conditional meaning!

| Whomever you honor shall praise you. | أَيًّا تُكرِمْ يَحْمَدْكَ. |

If you skip the second part of the إِضافةٌ-construction after أيّ, you have to put nunation (تَنْوِينٌ) as a **compensation**. In the accusative case (مَنْصُوبٌ), we get أَيًّا (with "an"). Notice: Both verbs are in the jussive mood (مَجْزُومٌ).

D	Meaning of a relative pronoun: which, that. See Arabic for Nerds 2, question #120.	اِسْمٌ مَوْصُولٌ

| I like the one who carries out his work. | يُعْجِبُنِي أَيُّ أَدَّى عَمَلَهُ. |

| → For a better understanding, we could rewrite the sentence like this. | أَيْ يُعجِبُني مَنْ أَدَّى عَمَلَهُ. |

| E | **Adjective** describing an <u>indefinite</u> noun (نَعْتٌ بَعْدَ نَكِرَةٍ) | نَعْتٌ |

| Zayd is a man, what a man! | زَيْدٌ رَجُلٌ أَيُّ رَجُلٍ. |
| It is of greatest importance (lit.: it is of importance, and of what importance!) | إِنَّ لَهُ شَأْنًا أَيَّ شَأْنٍ. |

Watch out: أَيْ without شَدّةٌ denotes *that is (to say); namely.*

| أَيْ is used to explain a preceding word or information. It can be translated as *this means; that is to say; namely.* It is also used to address somebody (حَرْفُ نِداءٍ). | أَيْ = يَعْني |

| You are accusing me of a crime, **namely**, that I am a thief. | تَتَّهِمُني بِالجُرْمِ، أَيْ أنا مُجْرِمٌ. |

| O Lord! (Note: It is read with inclination of voice.) | أَيْ رَبِّ! |

236. How do you express *when I was eleven...* in Arabic?

There are several possibilities.

We will now have a look at a more complicated solution.

| When I was eleven... | كُنْتُ فِي الْحادِيةَ عَشْرَةَ مِنْ عُمْري... |

1. Is الْحادِيةَ **in the accusative case** (مَنْصُوبٌ)? No, it is not!

الْحادِيَةَ is located in the position of a genitive case (مَجْرُورٌ) since it is placed after a preposition. What you see is not the case marker of the accusative case (مَنْصُوبٌ)!

All numbers between 11 and 19 (cardinal and ordinal) end in "*a*" (فَتْحةٌ) whatever the case may be. They have a cemented shape which is fixed and thus indeclinable (مَبْنِيٌّ).

2. Why do you use the feminine form of the numbers? Originally, the sentence included the word سَنة (*year*) after the preposition فِي. Even it is not written, the numbers are still declined according to the feminine word سَنَةٌ.

When I was twelve...	كُنْتُ فِي الثّانِيةَ عَشْرَةَ مِنْ عُمْرِي...
I am 22 (variation one).	عُمْرِي اثْنانِ وَعِشْرُونَ عامًا.
I am 22 (variation two).	أَنا فِي الثّانِيةِ وَالْعِشْرِينَ مِنْ عُمْرِي.

Watch out: In the last sentence, the number after فِي gets كَسْرةٌ ("I"). It is in the genitive case (مَجْرُورٌ) and follows the standard rules (unlike numbers between 11 and 19 – see first example!)

237. What is a causal object (مَفْعُولٌ لِأَجْلِهِ)?

It gives the purpose of an action and the reason why it is done.

The مَفْعُولٌ لِأَجْلِهِ or مَفْعُولٌ لَهُ explains the reason why the act has been done. As a causal object, it clarifies the reason for the occurrence of an action which originates from the doer (subject).

It normally includes the idea of *because of* or *out of.*

In order to identify it, you ask: **Why did the subject/agent do it?** Or: **What for** *(reason)*? Let's take a look at its properties:

- The **مَفْعُولٌ لِأَجْلِهِ** is a dependent element – an object – and thus receives the accusative case (مَنْصُوبٌ).

- It is **not derived from the main verb** in the sentence, but from a verb related to feelings and emotions.

- It must be **indefinite** (نَكِرَةٌ); otherwise, you need to paraphrase it and use a different construction with لِ, the so-called *Lām of causality* and *justification* (لامُ تَعْلِيلٍ).

- It has to be **one word only**: a مَصْدَرٌ alone; otherwise, you also need to use لِ. It is usually related to emotions, feelings, etc. to express the purpose of the action.

- However, there is an exception: the **مَفْعُولٌ لِأَجْلِهِ** is not always just a single word alone; it can also be an adverbial phrase (شِبْهُ جُمْلةٍ).

- What is the difference to the *circumstantial description* or *status* (حالٌ)? If you want to identify a حالٌ, you ask: *how?*

causal object (مَفْعُولٌ لِأَجْلِهِ)	

| I went to Egypt **to study Arabic**. (Question: **Why** did I go to Egypt?) | جِئْتُ إِلَى مِصْرَ رَغْبَةً في تَعَلُّمِ العَرَبِيَّةِ. |
| The word رَغْبَةً describes the cause, the reason why I went to Egypt. | رَغْبَةً في = السَّبَب |

He cried of fear. (Question: **Why** did he cry?)	بَكَى خَوْفًا.
I am not saying it **to be nice**.	لا أَقُولُهُ مُجامَلةً.
→ Both خَوْفًا and مُجامَلةً are transporting feelings and emotions. They are prime examples of purposive, causal objects.	

In the following examples, we are **not able** to use a causative object (مَفْعُولٌ لِأَجْلِهِ). Let's see why.

I came for water. (Question: **Why** did I come?)	جِئْتُ لِلْماءِ.
ماءٌ is **not a** مَصْدَرٌ! Therefore, we use لِ.	

I came to you for my benefit/interest (to take advantage). (Question: **Why** did I come?)	جِئْتُكَ لِلْإِسْتِفادَةِ.
الْإِسْتِفادَةُ (*profit, gain*) is **definite** (مَعْرِفةٌ)! Therefore, we need to insert the preposition لِ.	

I went to school for learning. (Question: **Why** did I go to school?)	قَصَدْتُ الْمَدْرَسةَ لِلدَّرْسِ.
دَرْسٌ is not connected to emotions, feelings, or affectivity; therefore, we use لِ.	

circumstantial description (حالٌ)

He came laughing.	جاءَ ضاحِكًا.
Question: **How** did he come? It describes the **subject** while it was doing the action. It does **not** explain **why** he came because he certainly did not come to laugh but was already laughing.	

238. How do you express: *at the beginning of the century?*

You could almost use a direct translation – but there's one issue.

We should first look at what ingredients we need.

In Arabic, we will need the **plural form** of the word that **determines** the time. Let's have a look.

At the beginning of the 20th century	الْقَرْنِ الْعِشْرِينَ	أَوَائِلِ	
In the middle of the month	الشَّهْرِ	أَواسِطِ	خِلال or فِي
At the end of the year	السَّنةِ	أَواخِرِ	

at the very outset; at the beginning of; in the early stages of	فِي أَوَائِلِ
at the beginning of the fifties	فِي أَوَائِلِ الْخَمْسِينَاتِ
since its beginnings; from the very beginning	مِن أَوَائِلِهِ

The word after خِلال (*during; through*) or فِي has to be in the genitive case (مَجْرُورٌ). In our examples, they are broken plurals (جَمْعُ تَكْسِيرٍ) and diptotes (مَمْنُوعٌ مِن الصَّرفِ). Since they are treated as definite (first part of a إِضافةٌ), they take the regular ending, i.e., a كَسْرةٌ.

Watch out: Don't mix خِلال with the expression مِنْ خِلالِ which means *across; on the basis of; by means of.*

239. What is special about diptotes (مَمْنُوعٌ مِن الصَّرفِ)؟

They do not take nunation (تَنْوِينٌ).

Diptote is a strange word that most people see for the first time when they learn Arabic. It usually denotes a noun with only two cases. The term is derived from Greek: δі- (dí-;

"two") plus πτῶσις (ptôsis; "case"). A *triptote* (having three cases) describes a standard Arabic noun (→ fully inflected).

The Arabic term is easier to grasp and targets a deeper level, مَمْنُوعٌ مِن الصَّرْفِ, which means *prohibited from variation/declension*. الصَّرْف is used for the area of morphology, a science which studies the forms of a word and its transformation.

In Arabic, indefinite words get **nunation** (تَنْوِينٌ). The term *Tanwīn* (تَنْوِينٌ) is the مَصْدَر of the II-verb نَوَّنَ - يُنَوِّنُ (R2=و) which denotes *adding nunation to a noun*. At the very beginning of Arabic, تَنْوِينٌ indicated the nasalization of the final vowel of the word, especially in the case ending of the noun. Precisely speaking, the main function of nunation is to mark the absence of the definite article الـ.

What we are going to analyze now is only relevant for **indefinite** (نَكِرةٌ) **nouns**, e.g., *friends* (أَصْدِقاءُ) or *desert* (صَحْراءُ). Words definite by الـ or by serving as the first part of a إِضافةٌ follow the standard rules. That's not our topic here.

> **RULE:** If a noun is a *diptote*, you **don't write nunation.**

Practically speaking, you don't write nor pronounce the endings "*-un*", "*-in*" or "*-an*". Instead, you use just a simple vowel without the n-sound.

Several types of nouns are مَمْنُوعٌ مِن الصَّرْفِ. We will check them now in detail.

I. proper names (عَلَمّ)

- All names of men and women are diptotes.

- All names of cities are **feminine** and are also diptotes.

Feminine proper nouns (عَلَمٌ مُؤَنَّثٌ)		A
Zaynab (زَيْنَبُ), Suʿād (سُعادُ), Damascus (دِمَشْقُ)	They look masculine – but have a feminine meaning.	1
Osama (أُسامةُ), Hamza (حَمْزةُ)	They look feminine – but have a masculine meaning.	2
Mecca (مَكَّةُ), Fatima (فاطِمةُ), Khadīja (خَدِيجةُ)	They look feminine – and have a feminine gender.	3
Sun (شَمْسُ), Egypt (مِصْرُ), India (هِنْدُ)	They consist of three letters; the second letter has سُكُونٌ.	4
→ You can choose if you want to add تَنْوِينٌ or not: مِصْرٌ or مِصْرُ; هِنْدٌ or هِنْدُ - both are correct! But the diptote is more common.		

Non-Arabic names (عَلَمٌ أَعْجَمِيٌّ)		B
Ibrahim (إِبْراهِيمُ), Ramses (رَمْسِيسُ), Iran (إيرانُ)	Words borrowed from foreign languages (more than three letters).	1
Noah (نُوحُ), Hud (هُودُ), Lot (لُوطُ)	Foreign names consisting of **three** letters: the second letter has سُكُونٌ.	2
→ You can choose if you want to add تَنْوِينٌ or not: نُوحٌ or نُوحُ.		

Proper names with three consonants plus Aleph ا and ن = ان		C
Ramadan (رَمَضانُ), Adnan (عَدْنانُ), Marwan (مَرْوانُ)	These words are mostly names.	

Proper names having the pattern of a verb (عَلَى وَزْنِ الْفِعْلِ)	D

'Ahmad (أَحْمَدُ), Yazīd (يَزِيدُ), Yathrib (يَثْرِبُ) - the old name of Medina	These words look like verbs (present or past tense).

Proper names that follow the pattern فُعَلُ (fuʿal)	E

Omar (عُمَرُ), Zahal (زُحَلُ) - the name of the planet Saturn	Words formed of three letters having the vowel pattern "u-a".

Proper names that consist of two names (composite noun)	F

Hadramaut (حَضَرَ مَوْتُ), Bethlehem (بَيْتَ لَحْمُ), Baalbek (بَعْلَبَكُّ)	Two nouns! The second part is declined (= it gets case endings).

Two important exceptions:

- You cannot apply this rule to numbers like *fifteen* (خَمْسَةَ عَشَرَ) which have an entirely indeclinable shape (مَبْنِيٌّ).

- Names ending in وَيْهِ like *Sībawayhi* (سِيبَوَيْهِ) are indeclinable (مَبْنِيٌّ). They are often Persian names or words.

II. Adjectives (صِفةٌ)

In Arabic, there are only three types of words: nouns (اِسْمٌ), verbs (فِعْلٌ), and particles (حَرْفٌ) – and only nouns get case endings! A اِسْمٌ may qualify as an adjective in Arabic if it is located in a suitable position (after a noun; gets agreement).

Adjectives following the pattern فَعْلانُ (fa'lān) Watch out: words of the measure فُعْلانٌ (fu'lān) get تَنْوِينٌ!	A

thirsty (عَطْشانُ), hungry (جَوْعانُ), drunk (سَكْرانُ)	Such adjectives have the feminine form فَعْلى and the plural form فَعالى.

Adjectives of the pattern أَفْعَلُ ('af'al): comparative and colors	B

bigger (أَكْبَرُ), nicer (أَجْمَلُ), more important (أَهَمُّ), smaller (أَصْغَرُ)	These adjectives have the feminine form فُعْلى.	1
Notice the difference between the feminine form of the *noun of preference* (اِسْمُ تَفْضِيلٍ) and the patterns of colors. **Comparative:** أَفْعَلُ – فُعْلى versus **colors:** أَفْعَلُ – فَعْلاءُ		
blind (أَعْمَى - عَمْياءُ), dumb (أَبْكَمُ - بَكْماءُ); deaf (أَصَمُّ - صَمَّاءُ -)	Adjectives denoting disabilities (عُيُوبٌ بِالإِنْسانِ).	2

Adjectives that are used as numbers: the patterns فُعالُ (fu'āl) and مَفْعَلُ (maf'al).	C

one by one; in one row (أُحادُ or مَوْحَدُ)	Both patterns describe how things are arranged. You can choose which form you prefer; they both mean the same. They are **only used with numbers from 1 to 10.** Mainly found in literature.
in pairs (مَثْنَى or ثُناءُ)	
in pairs of ten (مَعْشَرُ or عُشارُ)	

III. Broken plurals (جَمْعُ التَّكْسِيرِ)

Broken plurals can give you a headache and are often accompanied by internal cursing. True, there are dozens of patterns. Yet, they are actually quite tame, if one confines oneself to the main patterns and heeds their inner logic.

The most important pattern is the so-called *secondary* or *ultimate plural* (مُنْتَهَى الْجُمُوعِ). Why is it called *ultimate plural*? The answer is related to the idea of the *plural of a plural*.

Excursus: The plural of a plural and the ultimate plural

In Arabic, you can form the plural of a plural (جَمْعُ الْجَمْعِ). This sounds strange at first and is connected to the several **types** of plurals. In Arabic, we have plurals for **small** and **big** numbers, and we have **collectives**. Furthermore, we can even interpret the *minor plural* (جَمْعُ قِلّةٍ) – for **small** amounts up to ten – as a collective.

So, can we form the plural of a minor plural? **Yes**, this is possible! The idea is to multiply the units it includes. The plural of the plural denotes numbers from nine and up – because it indicates plurals of three and more, from plurals including themselves three units. Some examples:

singular	(minor) plural	plural of the plural
يَدٌّ	أَيْدٍ	أَيَادٍ
hand	several hands; assistance	acts of assistance

فَوْلٌ	أَقْوالٌ	أَقَاوِيلُ
saying; doctrine	doctrines; sayings	groups of (common) sayings and doctrines

مَكانٌ	أَمْكِنةٌ	أَماكِنُ
place	several places	groups of places

So, what's the big deal?

- If you check مَكانٌ in a dictionary, you will find two plural options: أَمْكِنةٌ and أَماكِنُ.

- The minor **plural** أَمْكِنةٌ can be put into a plural form too, resulting (again) in أَماكِنُ. Now comes the crux: This last form, however, **cannot** build any further plural form! (الصِّيغةُ نِهايةُ الْجَمْعِ الَّذِي يُمْكِنُ أَنْ تَصِلَ إِلَيْهِ الْكَلِمةُ)

- That is why a word like أَماكِنُ is called an **ultimate plural**. Why did we mention all this in this chapter? Many ultimate plural forms are **diptotes**!

The *plural of a plural* and the *ultimate plural* are related to each other – but are strictly speaking different concepts.

The *plural of a plural* is used to multiply **units**. Its base is already a plural. The *ultimate plural*, on the other hand, is mainly a morphological concept.

Watch out: You may see that the *plural of a plural* is formed by using sound plural schemes (but only empirical/سَماعِيٌّ): the sound masculine plural (if the singular is masculine human) or, in all other situations, by the sound feminine plural pattern (جَمْعُ الْمُؤَنَّثِ السّالِمُ).

groups of houses	بُيُوتاتٌ	←	houses	بُيُوتٌ

Now let's get back to our main topic. All **ultimate plural patterns** have the following DNA:

part 1		part 2		part 3
two letters	+	Aleph	+	two or three letters

After the first two letters, there is an **extra Aleph,** and after that Aleph, you will have **two or three letters.** There are 19 patterns. **Four patterns** are **diptotes** – we will focus on them!

pattern	plural	singular	meaning	
أَفَاعِلُ	أَصابِعُ	إِصْبَعُ	finger	1
	أَكارِمُ	كَرِيمٌ	generous	
مَفَاعِلُ	مَساجِدُ	مَسْجِدٌ	mosque	2
	مَكانِسُ	مِكْنَسةٌ	broom, sweeper	
	مَنازِلُ	مَنْزِلٌ	house	
	مَدارِسُ	مَدْرَسةٌ	school	
	مَصانِعُ	مَصْنَعٌ	factory	
أَفَاعِيلُ	أَضابِيرُ	إِضبارَةٌ	file, dossier	3
	أَسالِيبُ	أُسْلُوبٌ	style; method	
مَفَاعِيلُ	عَصافِيرُ	عُصْفُورٌ	bird	4
	مَوائِيقُ	مِيثَاقٌ	contract	
	مَصابِيحُ	مِصباحٌ	lamp	
	مَفاتِيحُ	مِفْتاحٌ	key	

You can remember the patterns with the following English sentence: You need a **lamp** (مَصابِحُ) and your **fingers** (أَصابِعُ) to read the **dossier** (أَضابِيرُ) in the **house** (مَنازِلُ).

What are the main takeaways?

- The plural of *men* (رِجالٌ) gets nunation (تَنْوِينٌ) because after the Aleph, there is only **one letter**.

- A doubled letter (شَدّةٌ) counts. Therefore, the plural of the following words don't get تَنْوِينٌ and are diptotes.

toil	مَشاقُّ	مَشَقّةٌ	harm	مَضارُّ	مَضَرّةٌ	material	مَوادُّ	مادّةٌ

IV. Special situations

When we see an Aleph at the end of a word, no matter what form it may take, we should keep our eyes open.

Let's take a look at what that might mean for us regarding the *nunation*. Note that such words are usually **feminine**.

The Aleph ى is additional (اِسْمٌ مَقْصُورةٌ)	A

We get this special situation when the letter ى (أَلِفْ مَقْصُورةٌ or *shortened Aleph*) is preceded by **more than two radicals** (root letters). In other words, the letter ى is additional and not part of the root.

good news	ب-ش-ر	بُشْرَى	pregnant	ح-ب-ل	حُبْلَى
larger; major	ك-ب-ر	كُبْرَى	Salma, f. name	س-ل-م	سَلْمَى

However, if the letter ى is preceded by only two radicals (root letters), it does get nunation! In other words, the **weak letter is part of the root**! See *question #13*.

hospital	ش-ف-ي	مُسْتَشْفًى

meaning	ع-ن-ي	مَعْنًى

The Aleph I and the ء are additional (اِسْمٌ مَمْدُودَةٌ)	B

We have this situation if the *extended Aleph* (أَلِفٌ مَمْدُودَةٌ) is preceded by **more than two radicals** (root letters) and followed by a Hamza (هَمْزَة) → resulting in اءُ.

desert	صَحْرَاءُ
red	حَمْرَاءُ
friends	أَصْدِقَاءُ

beauty	حَسْنَاءُ
scientists	عُلَمَاءُ
arrogance	كِبْرِيَاءُ

Watch out! In the following examples, the ء is either part of the root or was originally و or ي that turned into ء. In other words, Aleph and Hamza are not preceded by more than two radicals. Such words get nunation (تَنْوِينٌ). See *question #12*.

news	نَبَأٌ - أَنْبَاءٌ	ن-ب-ء
sky	سَمَاءٌ	س-م-و
name	اِسْمٌ - أَسْمَاءٌ	س-م-و

building	بِنَاءٌ - أَبْنِيَةٌ	ب-ن-ي
enemy	عَدُوٌّ - أَعْدَاءٌ	ع-د-و
member	عُضْوٌ - أَعْضَاءٌ	ع-ض-و

Excursus: What about sound feminine plurals?

They have only **two case endings** ("*un*" and "*in*"), but they can take nunation (تَنْوِينٌ). They are <u>not</u> diptotes (مَمْنُوعٌ مِن

الصَّرْفِ)! In the accusative (مَنْصُوبٌ) and genitive (مَجْرُورٌ) case, they share the same ending: "-in" → ٍ see also question #34.

Remark: If you are interested in a deeper discussion about the idea behind diptotes in Arabic, see *Arabic for Nerds 2, question #46*.

240. How do you mark cases in diptotes (مَمنُوعٌ مِن الصَّرْفِ)؟

Instead of -un, -in, and -an, you use two vowels: "u" or "a".

A *diptote* is a noun which does not get nunation (تَنْوِينٌ). In order to receive nunation, a word has to be **indefinite** (نَكِرَةٌ). As soon as there is a diptote in a sentence, you'd better check it twice before you place case endings. Let's see the whole story.

1. Indefinite diptote in the **nominative** case (مَرْفُوعٌ)

These are clean streets.	هٰذِهِ شَوارِعُ نَظِيفةٌ.
These are new buildings.	هٰذِهِ مَنازِلُ جَدِيدةٌ.

We have two diptotes (شَوارِعُ and مَنازِلُ). So, we can only mark them with **one** ضَمّة. Now, what about the adjectives which are placed after them? **Adjectives** need agreement (مُطابَقة). Since they refer to an indefinite noun in the nominative case, we have to mark them as such – in other words, they get nunation: "**-un**".

2. Indefinite diptote in the **accusative** case (مَنْصُوبٌ)

I saw clean streets.	شاهَدْتُ شَوارِعَ نَظِيفةً.
The engineers build new houses.	يَبْنِي الْمُهَنْدِسُونَ مَنازِلَ جَدِيدةً.

Same story here. The two diptotes do not get nunation. Instead, we mark them with a simple vowel: "**a**". What about the adjectives? They have to agree with the word they describe – in both examples, with an indefinite noun in the accusative case. Hence, they get nunation. We mark them with "**-an**".

3. Indefinite diptote in the **genitive** case (مَجْرُورٌ) - watch out!

From a visual point of view, this is the most confusing situation. If an indefinite diptote needs the genitive case, we mark it with "**a**" (فَتْحةٌ).

In the examples, only the sentence with the **indefinite** noun marked in gray is behaves out of the norm(مَمْنُوعٌ مِن الصَّرْفِ).

I walked in clean streets.	مَشَيْتُ فِي شَوارِعَ نَظِيفةٍ.	1
I walked in **the** streets of the city.	مَشَيْتُ فِي شَوارِعِ الْمَدِينةِ.	2
I walked in **the** clean streets.	مَشَيْتُ فِي الشَّوارِعِ النَّظِيفةِ.	3

- In the first example, we have an indefinite diptote which is followed by an adjective.

- In the second example, we have a definite diptote since the word serves as the first part of a إِضافةٌ.

- In the third example, we also have a definite diptote (definite article الـ).

→ The **indefinite** diptote gets the vowel "**a**" in the genitive.

→ The **definite** diptote is marked as usual with the vowel "**i**".

241. Is حَسْناءُ the feminine form of أَحْسَنُ (better)?

No, it isn't.

أَحْسَنُ is masculine. It is a *noun of preference* (اِسْمُ تَفْضِيلٍ) and may express a comparative (*better*) or superlative (*best*). If we want to form the feminine form of أَحْسَنُ, we apply the pattern فُعْلَى and eventually get حُسْنَى.

Now, what does حسناء mean then? First of all, we have to set the vowel on the first letter: it is حَسْناءُ ("a"). The pattern فَعْلاءُ is used to create the **feminine** form of words that denote **colors** or **deficiencies**.

What is the nature of أَحْسَنُ and حَسْناءُ? Both words are *quasi participles* (صِفةٌ مُشَبَّهةٌ). The masculine version of such nouns, which are usually placed as adjectives, uses the same pattern as the اِسْمُ تَفْضِيلٍ which is: أَفْعَلُ. That was quite a lot of information, and it's best to process it in a table.

	meaning	feminine		masculine	
1	*red*	حَمْراءُ	فَعْلاءُ	أَحْمَرُ	أَفْعَلُ
2	*bigger/biggest*	كُبْرَى	فُعْلَى	أَكْبَرُ	

But that's not all. Is it true that the **masculine counterpart** of حَسْناءُ is أَحْسَنُ? Yes, it is. But wait a second! If we look at the examples in the table above, we see that this does not fit a comparative! It is a *quasi participle* (صِفةٌ مُشَبَّهةٌ) like in example 1. Regarding the meaning, the difference is huge. It is not *better/best* → it is *beautiful*.

There are some adjectives of beauty that use the same pattern as colors and deficiencies:

- أَفْعَلُ for masculine and فَعْلاءُ for feminine forms.

أَحْسَنُ is rarely applied to a man whereas it is pretty common to use حَسْناءُ to describe a woman as *beautiful*. Instead, you should better use حَسَنٌ for a man which practically means the same as أَحْسَنُ. Let us summarize:

meaning	grammatical form	feminine	masculine	
better; best	إِسْمُ التَّفْضِيلِ	حُسْنَى	أَحْسَنُ	1
beautiful; nice	الصِّفَةُ الْمُشَبَّهَةُ	حَسْناءُ	أَحْسَنُ (not used)	2

A few more examples from this category:

meaning	feminine form	masculine form
smooth	مَلْساءُ	أَمْلَسُ
nice; bright	بَلْحاءُ	أَبْلَجُ
brave; courageous	شَجْعاءُ	أَشْجَعُ

Notice that both forms (masculine & feminine) are diptotes!

242. مَشَيْتُ وَالْبَحْرَ. - How would you translate that?

The meaning is: I walked along the sea.

The *object of accompaniment* (مَفْعُولٌ مَعَهُ), also called *object in connection*, is a rare but quite sophisticated tool. In the sentence مَشَيْتُ وَالْبَحْرَ, the expression وَالْبَحْرَ is the مَفْعُولٌ مَعَهُ.

When you look at the translation of our example (I walked *along* the sea), we see that one can easily get the translation wrong if the مَفْعُولٌ مَعَهُ is not correctly identified. The مَفْعُولٌ

مَعَهُ is a **noun** in the **accusative** case (اِسْمٌ مَنْصُوبٌ) which is directly placed after the device وَ. The وَ in such instances conveys the meaning of (*together*) <u>with</u> (and **not** the coordinating *and*). Hence, you could replace وَ with مَعَ and wouldn't change the meaning – but you would produce a different case ending since the noun after مَعَ would need the genitive case (مَجْرُورٌ).

Interestingly, it is not وَ that induces the accusative. It is the **verb**. The وَ is only there to transport the meaning of the verb.

I walked along the sea.	مَشَيْتُ وَالْبَحْرَ.
	مَشَيْتُ مَعَ الْبَحْرِ.

I work during the night.	أَعْمَلُ وَاللَّيْلَ.
I woke up by the chirping of the birds.	اِسْتَيْقَظْتُ وَتَغْرِيدَ الطُّيُورِ.

Not only the verb may take an *object of accompaniment*.

The father is sitting with his family.	verb (فِعْلٌ)	جَلَسَ الْأَبُ وَالْأُسْرَةَ.
I like that you walk on (along) the pavement.	infinitive (مَصْدَرٌ)	يُعْجِبُنِي سَيْرُكَ وَالرَّصِيفَ.
The man is walking in (along) the gardens.	active participle (اِسْمُ الْفَاعِلِ)	الرَّجُلُ سَائِرٌ وَالْحَدَائِقَ.
The car is left with the driver.	passive participle (اِسْمُ الْمَفْعُولِ)	السَّيَّارَةُ مَتْرُوكَةٌ وَالسَّائِقَ.
Be patient with the angry man!	verbal noun (اِسْمُ الْفِعْلِ)	رُوَيْتَكَ وَالْغَاضِبَ.

243. What is the root of مِينَاءٌ (port; harbor)?

Some say the root is و-ن-ي. But is it derived from a root?

Scholars have suggested that the origin of مِينَاءٌ may go back to ancient Egyptian (where *port* is *mni*; *mena* denotes *to tie up a boat in a port*), from where it entered Greek (*limen*), Hebrew (*namel* – נָמֵל), Syriac (lmênâ) and eventually: Arabic.

There are three common Arabic words for *harbor*:

1. مَرْفَأٌ (plural: مَرَافِئُ). This is the *noun of place* (اِسْمُ الْمَكَانِ) of the I-verb رَفَأَ - يَرْفَأُ (*to drag on shore; to mend; repair*).

2. مَرْسًى (plural: مَرَاسٍ). The only root in the **Qur'an** connected with the sea is I-verb رَسَا - يَرْسُو (*to be at rest; i.e., to anchor*). مَرْسًى is its *noun of place* (اِسْمُ الْمَكَانِ).

3. مِينَاءٌ (plural: مَوَانِئُ or مَوَانٍ). The ending may suggest the feminine gender, but it is masculine! Note that مَوَانٍ is the correct plural, but مَوَانِئُ is quite widespread. If you use مَوَانٍ, don't forget that the ي will show up in a إِضَافَةٌ-construction, for example, مَوَانِي الْمَدِينَةِ (*ports of the city*).

Starting from a very early stage, Classical Arabic scholars have tried to find a root for مِينَاءٌ, and found و-ن-ي. This is kind of far-fetched if we look at its core meaning but it does fit into our morphological framework quite well.

I-verb وَنَى - يَنِي is tricky because it contains two weak letters: R1=و, R3=ي. It expresses **to rest**; *to be weak, to be tired*. Some scholars stated that we should therefore think of the port as a place of refuge for ships when they are "weak" and need to rest and to be supplied with fuel, food, and the like.

Before we examine مِينَاءٌ (assuming that it is based on the root و-ن-ي), let's see how the corresponding I-verb behaves. It is perhaps the most difficult regular verb in Arabic!

subjunctive (مَنْصُوبٌ)	jussive (مَجْزُومٌ)	imperative (الأَمْرُ)	present t. (الْمُضَارِعُ)	past tense (الْمَاضِي)
يَنِيَ	يَنِ	نِ - نِي - نُوا	يَنِي	وَنَى

passive part. (اِسْمُ الْمَفْعُولِ)	active part. (اِسْمُ الْفَاعِلِ)	infinitive (مَصْدَرٌ)	passive present tense	passive past tense
مَوْنِيّ	وانٍ	وَنْي	يُنى	وُنِيَ

So, how did we arrive at مِيناءٌ? The Arabic word for *harbor* was originally مِوْناي following the pattern مِفْعالٌ. This pattern is used to create a **noun of instrument** (اِسْمُ آلَةٍ). Like the Arabic word for *minaret* (#176), it was originally intended to denote a tool rather than a place. However, مِوْناي would be difficult to pronounce. Hence, the more handy مِيناءٌ was created.

What kind of operations had to be done to get مِيناءٌ?

- The و was converted into ي to facilitate that the initial م can carry كَسْرةٌ.

- The final ي became Hamza which always happens in such circumstances. For example, بِناءٌ (*building*), سَماءٌ (*sky*).

- Why do we use مَ in the plural although we have مِ in the singular form? This is typical for the مِفْعالٌ-pattern of *nouns of instruments*. Some examples: مَقاييسُ ← مِقْياسٌ (*scale*) or مَوازينُ ← ميزانٌ (*scale*) or مَفاتيحُ ← مِفْتاحٌ (*key*).

Remark: Depending on the function in the sentence (= case ending!), the spelling of the final Hamza in مِيناءٌ may change!

nominative (مَرْفُوعٌ)	genitive (مَجْرُورٌ)	accusative (مَنْصُوبٌ)	
مِيناؤُنا	مِينائِنا	مِيناءَنا	*our harbor*

244. How do you express *whereas* or *while* in Arabic?

Basically, you have three options.

- In English, *whereas* indicates a contrast between two facts or ideas: *in contrast or comparison with the fact that.*

- *While* can be used in two ways. It may express *during the time that something else happens.* Or: *in contrast with something else.* We will only focus on the latter.

	1
The construction with أَمَّا plus فَ	

I liked the mountains **whereas** my friends hated them.	أَلْجِبالُ أَعْجَبَتْني أَمَّا أَصْدِقائي فَقَدْ كَرِهُوها.

	2
The construction with بَيْنَما	

بَيْنَما is an *adverb of time* (ظَرْفُ زَمانٍ - مَفْعُولٌ فِيهِ). Therefore, it is located in the position of an accusative case.

I asked her to come to the party, **whereas** she wants to stay at home.	طَلَبْتُها بِحُضُورِ الْحَفْلَةِ, بَيْنَما هِيَ تُرِيدُ الْبَقاءَ فِي الْبَيْتِ.

بَيْنَما is often used to join two actions or events which simultaneously happen. Then it expresses the meaning of عِنْدَما or حِينَما. In such application, بَيْنَما is followed by either a nominal (جُمْلَةٌ إِسْمِيَّةٌ) or verbal sentence (جُمْلَةٌ فِعْلِيَّةٌ). The verb may be used in the past or present tense → don't forget that the tense (for the translation) is marked by the **main clause**.

I read a book while (during the time that) you watched a soap	قَرَأْتُ كِتابًا بَيْنَما أَنْتَ كُنْتَ تُشاهِدُ مُسَلْسَلًا.

opera.	
While she was reading, she fell asleep.	بَيْنَما كانَتْ تَقْرَأُ غَلَبَها النَّعاسُ.
Could you get some bread while you're about it (shopping)?	هَلْ يُمْكِنُكَ أَنْ تَشْتَرِيَ خُبْزًا بَيْنَما تَتَسَوَّقُ؟

The expression فِي/ عَلَى حِينِ أَنَّ	3

He is generous whereas she is not.	هُوَ كَرِيمٌ فِي حِينٍ أَنَّها لَيْسَتْ كَذلِكَ.

245. How do you express *his brother came laughing?*

It is best to use a so-called circumstantial description (حال).

In English, if you want to explain the circumstances of a complete sentence, you can use *while, when, although, that is*. Another option are participles (*smiling, crying*) which work as modifiers.

In Arabic, we use a *circumstantial description*, also called *circumstantial qualifier* or *status* (حال). It is added to an already complete sentence as a kind of supplement. The حال expresses the **state or condition of the subject** (or object) **while the action takes place**. The صاحِبُ الْحالِ (*concerned by the status*) is the entity (subject and/or object) whose circumstances are described, qualified by the حال.

In Arabic, if you ask *how are you?*, you can say: كَيْفَ الْحالُ؟

Some people may jokingly answer: الْحالُ مَنْصُوبٌ

This is a reference to the حال which gets the accusative case (مَنْصُوبٌ). In order to identify a حال, you ask كَيْفَ؟ (how?). In our ex.: *How did his brother come? Answer: smiling* (ضاحِكًا).

The حال can consist of a word (e.g., an active participle) or even an entire sentence! There are several candidates for a حال.

OPTION A: The حال is a single word.

The man drank the coffee smiling.	شَرِبَ الرَّجُلُ الْقَهْوةَ مُبْتَسِمًا.

Question: How did he drink the coffee?

Subject (فاعِلٌ) of the verbal sentence (جُمْلةٌ فِعْلِيّةٌ). It is the صاحِبُ الْحالِ.	الرَّجُلُ
Direct object (مَفْعُولٌ بِهِ), accusative case (مَنْصُوبٌ)	الْقَهْوةَ
Circumstantial description (حال)	مُبْتَسِمًا

If the حال is not expressed by a single word (مُفْرَدٌ), it will need a **connector** (رابِطٌ). There are three possibilities to connect the حال with the preceding sentence:

The device وَ, a so-called واوُ الْحالِ.	وَ	1
A pronoun at the end of a verb, for example the ضَمّة (meaning *he*) in the verb: يَتَحَدَّثُ	pronoun only	2
و plus pronoun (ضَمِيرٌ)	وَهُوَ	3

Notice that you don't translate the connector. Therefore, don't say, for example, *and* or *and he*, etc.

OPTION B: The حال is a full sentence.

- If you use a nominal sentence (جُمْلَةٌ إِسْمِيّةٌ), you need a connector (رابِط) to link the حال with the preceding sentence.
- The verbal sentence (جُمْلَةٌ فِعْلِيّةٌ) doesn't need a رابِط. The hidden, concealed pronoun (ضَمِيرٌ مُسْتَتِرٌ), which is included in the verb, is enough to link both parts.

I repeated my lessons while the people were sleeping.	راجَعْتُ دُرُوسِي وَالنَّاسُ نائِمونَ.	1

The subject (فاعِلٌ) is a hidden, concealed pronoun ex-pressing *you* (أَنْتَ) which is also the صاحِبُ الْحالِ.	راجَعْتُ

The entire nominal sentence (جُمْلَةٌ إِسْمِيّةٌ) is lo-cated in the position of a حالٌ.	وَالنَّاسُ نائِمونَ

The whole second sentence is placed in the location of an accusative case (فِي مَحَلِ نَصْبٍ) since it occupies the location of a حالٌ ← but you can't see that.

I left the house with open doors (and left the door open).	تَرَكْتُ الْبَيْتَ وَالْبابُ مَفْتُوحٌ.	2

The direct object (مَفْعُولٌ بِهِ) is the صاحِبُ الْحالِ.	الْبَيْتَ

This entire nominal sentence (جُمْلَةٌ إِسْمِيّةٌ) is lo-cated in the position of a حالٌ.	وَالْبابُ مَفْتُوحٌ

The director sat down talking.	جَلَسَ الْمُدِيرُ يَتَحَدَّثُ.	3

The verbal sentence (جُمْلَةٌ فِعْلِيّة) is the حالٌ for الْمُدِيرُ (= the صاحِبُ الْحالِ). Since it is a verbal sentence, there is no need for a connector.

The same is true in the following sentences:

The director came driving his car.	أَتَى الْمُدِيرُ يَقُودُ سَيَّارتَهُ.	4
I started sleeping when the sun rose.	بَدَأْتُ النَّوْمَ وَقَدْ طَلَعَت الشَّمْسُ.	5

Option C: The حَالٌ is expressed by a prepositional or adverbial phrase (شِبْهُ الْجُمْلةِ).

The شِبْهُ الْجُمْلةِ may be an adverb of time, and adverb of, or a prepositional phrase.

I received the prize with joy (joyfully).	إِسْتَلَمْتُ الْجَائِزَةَ فِي فَرَحٍ.
The prepositional phrase (جَارٌّ وَمَجْرُورٌ) works as a حَالٌ for the subject (the concealed, hidden pronoun أنا) which is also the صَاحِبُ الْحالِ.	

I left the car in the parking lot.	تَرَكْتُ السَّيَّارَةَ عِنْدَ الْمَوْقِفِ.
The adverbial phrase (ظَرْفُ مَكَانٍ) works as the حَالٌ. What about the صَاحِبُ الْحالِ؟ It is the word السَّيَّارةِ.	

Watch out: All three options (A, B, C) express the same meaning. For example: *He greeted me saying...*

participle	verbal sentence	nominal sentence
سَلَّمَ عَلَيَّ قَائِلًا...	سَلَّمَ عَلَيَّ يَقُولُ...	سَلَّمَ عَلَيَّ وَهُوَ قَائِلٌ...

Let us summarize the main conditions for a حالٌ:

- The حالٌ has to be <u>indefinite</u> (نَكِرةٌ) and in the <u>accusative</u> case (مَنْصوبٌ).
- The صاحِبُ الْحالِ has to be <u>definite</u> (مَعْرِفةٌ). It can be either the subject (فاعِلٌ) or the object (مَفْعولٌ بِه).

246. Why are نَعْتٌ and حالٌ often confused?

They can have the same form - but serve in different functions.

نَعْتٌ and صِفةٌ both mean *description* in Arabic. In grammar, both are used to denote *attribute* or *adjective*.

The نَعْتٌ is a **derived noun** (إِسْمٌ مُشْتَقٌّ) from a root. There are several types. The most common are:

صيغةُ الْمُبالَغةِ	الصِّفةُ الْمُشَبَّهةُ	إِسْمُ الْمَفْعولِ	إِسْمُ الْفاعِلِ
form of exaggeration	adjectives similar to active (and passive) participles	passive participle	active participle

Let's look at this in one sentence.

I bought a new car.	إِشْتَرَيْتُ سَيَّارةً جَديدةً.

The object that is **described** (مَنْعوتٌ).	سَيَّارةٌ
The **description** (نَعْتٌ). It needs agreement (مُطابَقةٌ) and takes the same grammatical features as the object which it describes.	جَديدةٌ

The نَعْت has to agree with the مَنْعُوت in four things:

1	Determination (def. or indefinite)	نَكِرَةٌ • مَعْرِفةٌ
2	Case marker	مَرْفُوعٌ • مَجْرُورٌ • مَنْصُوبٌ
3	Gender (نَوْعٌ - جِنْسٌ)	مُذَكَّرٌ • مُؤَنَّثٌ
4	Number (عَدَدٌ)	مُفْرَدٌ • مُثَنَّى • جَمْعٌ

Now we actually have everything together to answer our question. The نَعْتٌ is different from the حالٌ – and here is why:

- A sentence following a **definite** word is a حالٌ. It describes the subject or object while the action takes place.

- A word (or sentence) following an **indefinite** word is a نَعْتٌ → a description that is not connected to the action which the subject/object is doing.

I don't want to see **a crying child**.	لا أُحِبُّ أَنْ أُشاهِدَ طِفْلًا باكِيًا.

باكِيًا is an **adjective** (نَعْتٌ) and not a حالٌ! The حالٌ can only refer to a definite word! Here, the نَعْتٌ is a **general statement**.

I don't want to see **the child crying**.	لا أُحِبُّ أَنْ أُشاهِدَ الطِّفْلَ باكِيًا.

Now باكِيًا is not an adjective anymore. It is a **circumstantial description** (حالٌ) for الطِّفْلَ which is the صاحِبُ الحالِ. It describes the condition of a **certain child** while I am watching the child.

Another example:

I live in a house close to the beach.	أَسْكُنُ فِي بَيْتٍ بِحَيِّ الشَّاطِئ.

Indefinite (نَكِرَة) → it can't be a حالٌ. It is the مَنْعوتٌ.	بَيْتٍ
It is possible to use a full or semi sentence (= prepositional phrase) to function as an adjective (النَّعْتُ وَالْجُمْلَةُ). In our example, it is a prepositional phrase.	بِحَيِّ الشَّاطِئِ

The following two sentences can't work as a حالٌ because the word which is described is <u>indefinite</u> → they are adjectives.

I live in a house with big rooms.	أَسْكُنُ فِي بَيْتٍ غُرَفُهُ واسِعةٌ.
I live in a house opposite the beach.	أَسْكُنُ فِي بَيْتٍ أَمامَ الْبَحْرِ.

247. Why should you pay attention when you see مَهْما?

مَهْما induces the jussive mood (مَجْزُومٌ) in verbs. If you translate such sentences, you should use the present tense.

مَهْما looks harmless, but that shouldn't fool you. It is a conditional noun (اِسْمُ شَرْطٍ) which expresses the meaning of *despite; although; whatever; whatever the case... no matter what/how.* مَهْما induces the jussive mood (مَجْزُومٌ) in verbs.

How and when can we use مَهْما?

- If مَهْما **starts** the sentence, you normally use a verb in the **jussive** mood (مَجْزُومٌ). → The verb ends in سُكونٌ or you need to delete a weak letter (حَرْفُ عِلّةٍ).

- If مَهْما is placed in the **second part** of a sentence, you normally use a verb in the **past tense**. However, the verb conveys the **meaning of the present** or future tense!

| Whatever effort you do, you will find a result. | مَهْما تَجْتَهِدْ تَلْقَ. |
| I will be the same person whatever people say. | سَأَظَلُّ بِهذا الشَّكْلِ مَهْما قالَ النَّاسُ. |

In the last example notice that we use the past tense of *to say* to express a present tense meaning!

Some more examples.

Whatever the case…	مَهْما يَكُنْ مِنْ الْأَمْرِ...
No matter how I try, I can't.	مَهْما حاوَلْتُ لا أَسْتَطِيعُ.
As long as you do good, we shall not dismiss you.	مَهْما تَصْلُحْ فَلَنْ تَعْزِلَكَ.
They said, "We will not believe in you, no matter what signs you produce to cast a spell on us." *(Sura 7:132)*	وَقَالُوا مَهْمَا تَأْتِنَا بِهِ مِنْ آيَةٍ لِتَسْحَرَنَا بِهَا فَمَا نَحْنُ لَكَ بِمُؤْمِنِينَ.

If you don't want to use مَهْما, you have some options:

> مَهْما = حَتَّى لَوْ = إذا حَدَثَ

All three expressions introduce an **indefinite conditional clause**. This is different to لَوْ or إِذا which limit the number of possible conditions in the *if*-part, whereas words like *whatever, whoever, wherever* leave it open to almost any situation.

- Indefinite conditional clause: *Whatever the weather will be, we will go*. In indefinite conditional sentences, the verbs are almost always in the **jussive** mood (مَجْزُومٌ).

- *If the weather is nice, we will go*. In conditional constructions with لَوْ or إِذا, you **don't use** the jussive mood.

248. فَتْحةٌ ("a")? لا إلٰهَ إلّا اللّٰهُ - Why does God have a

The sentence means: There is no God but God.

The long vowel "ā" in God (إلٰه) and *Allah* (اللّٰه) is written with a vertical dash: a *dagger Aleph* (أَلِفٌ خَنْجَرِيّةٌ); see #22.

But this is not our main concern here. If we want to understand the idea of the vowel on the last letter of إلٰه ("la 'ilāha..."), the single form of God, we have to enter the field of the *generic* or *absolute negation* (لا النَّافِيةُ لِلْجِنْسِ).

Let us first check the different forms of the device لا.

	type	translation	example
1	Negation of a verb (حَرْفُ نَفْيٍ)	The boy doesn't play football in the street.	الْوَلَدُ لا يَلْعَبُ الْكُرَة فِي الشّارِع.
	The verb *to play* has ضَمّة at the end which is the marker for the standard, indicative mood (مَرْفُوعٌ). This type of لا does not induce any mood or case.		
2	Interdiction, prohibition (لا النَّاهِيةُ)	Don't play soccer in the street!	لا تَلْعَبْ بِالْكُرة فِي الشّارِع.
	This type of لا conveys the meaning of *don't* (negated imperative). It does influence other words in the sentence. The verb after لا needs the jussive mood (مَجْزُومٌ). Notice the سُكُونْ at the end of the negated imperative تَلْعَبْ.		
3	conjunction (عَطْفٌ)	Nagīb Mahfūz is a writer, not a poet.	نَجِيب مَحْفُوظ كاتِبٌ لا شاعِرٌ.
	The word after a conjunction takes the same case as the preceding word. Thus, both words (*writer*; *poet*) take the same case.		

4	generic, absolute nega-tion (لا النّافِيةُ لِلْجِنْسِ)	There is no student in the room.	لا طالِبَ فِي الْغُرْفِةِ.

Type 4 is what we need to look at. This negation is called *generic* or *absolute negation* because it denies the existence of the entire genus. Therefore, it expresses the meaning of *there is no... (at all)*. Or: *there is not a...* Or: *none at all*.

- Such لا intervenes in a nominal sentence (جُمْلةٌ اِسْميّةٌ). There is no verb involved!

- The noun after لا must be **indefinite** (نَكِرةٌ) and never gets nunation (تَنْوينٌ).

- The noun has to follow the لا immediately.

- The predicate is in the nominative case (مَرْفوعٌ) and gets nunation.

- Such لا works like the particle إِنَّ. It is a حَرْفٌ ناسِخٌ, so it abrogates rules. The "**subject**" (اِسْمُ لا النّافِيةِ لِلْجِنْسِ) is in the **accusative** (نَصْبُ الْمُبْتَدَإِ) and the predicate (خَبَرُ لا) takes the **nominative** case (رَفْعُ الْخَبَرِ).

- The underlying grammar is profound. The noun after لا gets fixed on the open vowel "*a*" (مَبْنِيٌّ عَلَى الْفَتْحِ) which explains why we only see one فَتْحةٌ. But this "*a*" is not the case marker! We use this sound to cement a noun in such position and make it indeclinable. Hence, we can only assign a place value and say that the اِسْمُ لا النّافِيةِ لِلْجِنْسِ is found in the spot of an accusative case (فِي مَحَلِّ نَصْبٍ).

- **Watch out:** If you are referring to a specific person or thing, you negate the nominal sentence with لَيْسَ.

Now, we should focus our eyes on the information after لا.

| A | We have a **single noun** (مُفْرَدٌ). |

The underlying grammar is pretty theoretical. You don't have to worry to much about it because even if you just remember to use the accusative case (without nunation), the result will be fine.

So, what's going on? Although you don't see it, we fix the word after لا on a vowel or letter and thus make it indeclinable (مَبْنِيٌّ). It may look like the regular marker of the accusative, but it is not. We can only apply place values. See also *Arabic for Nerds 2, q. #278*

There is no popular liar. (Lit. meaning: No liar is popular.) Notice the **فَتْحَةٌ** on *liar*.	لا كاذِبَ مَحْبُوبٌ. 1
There are no popular liars. Notice that و turns into ي here!	لا كاذِبِينَ مَحْبُوبُونَ. 2
There are no (female) popular liars.	لا كاذِباتِ مَحْبُوباتٌ. 3

Watch out: Feminine sound plurals and duals have two case markers only: one for the nominative (مَرْفُوعٌ) and another one for the so-called *oblique* (مَنْصُوبٌ and مَجْرُورٌ). However, they do not belong to diptotes (مَمْنُوعٌ مِن الصَّرْفِ). Sound feminine plurals get nunation (تَنْوِينٌ) whenever they are indefinite!

| B | We use a إِضافةٌ-construction and **regular case markers**. |

- The 1st part of the إِضافةٌ is in the <u>accusative</u> case (مَنْصُوبٌ).
- The 2nd part is indefinite (نَكِرةٌ) and in the <u>genitive</u> case (مَجْرُورٌ).

There is no professional who loses his wage. (Lit. meaning: No professional loses his wage.)	لا مُتْقِنَ عَمَلٍ يَضيعُ أَجْرُهُ. 1
There are no professionals who	لا مُتْقِني عَمَلٍ يَضيعُ أَجْرُهُم. 2

lose their wages.	
Notice: In sound plurals, the و turns into ي in the accusative case (مَنْصُوبٌ). Furthermore, the ن disappears in a إِضَافَةٌ.	
There are no (female) professionals who lose their wages.	لَا مُتْقِنَاتِ عَمَلٍ تَضِيعُ أَجْرُهُنَّ. 3
Why do we use the كَسْرَةٌ ("i") here although it is مَنْصُوبٌ? Because we have a feminine sound plural! See *question #34*.	

C	We opt for an expression that resembles a إِضَافَةٌ-construction (شَبِيهٌ بِالْمُضَافِ); grammatically, however, it isn't.

- The 1st part takes **nunation** (تَنْوِينٌ) → the accusative (مَنْصُوبٌ). Use "-an" if you have a singular noun, or change و into ي if you have a sound masculine plural.
- The 2nd part is a **direct object** (مَفْعُولٌ بِهِ) and therefore takes the accusative case (مَنْصُوبٌ).

There is no professional who loses his wage.	لَا مُتْقِنًا عَمَلًا يَضِيعُ أَجْرُهُ.
Note that عَمَلًا is a مَفْعُولٌ بِهِ. The part after the object is the predicate (خَبَرٌ) in form of a verbal sentence (جُمْلَةٌ فِعْلِيَّةٌ).	
There are no professionals who lose their wages.	لَا مُتْقِنِينَ عَمَلًا يَضِيعُ أَجْرُهُم.
There are no (female) professionals who lose their wages.	لَا مُتْقِنَاتٍ عَمَلًا تَضِيعُ أَجْرُهُنَّ.

Watch out:

Neither the students nor the pro-	لَا الطُّلَّابُ حَاضِرُونَ وَلَا الْأُسْتَاذُ.

fessor are present.

The subject (مُبْتَدَأٌ) is in the nominative case (مَرْفُوعٌ) and is pronounced *"at-tullābu"* because the first word is <u>definite</u>! This sentence is **not a general statement.**

It is addressing a specific situation/certain people. Grammatically speaking, we negate a regular nominal sentence (جُمْلةٌ اِسْمِيّةٌ) with لا, which is possible (see *question #133*). So we have a normal negation (لا النَّافِيةُ) which means that after لا, we need a subject (مُبْتَدَأٌ) in the nominative case.

There is no peace nor justice in the world.	لا فِي الْعالَم سَلَامٌ وَلا عَدْلٌ.

We have our main ingredient for a generic negation (لا النَّافِيةُ للْجِنْسِ): the **indefinite** noun (نَكِرةٌ). But there is an issue. You are not allowed to separate لا and the denied thing (here: سَلام). Thus, we have a normal negation (لا النّافِيَةُ).

You are clever without doubt.	أَنْتَ ذَكِيٌّ بِلا شَكٍّ.

The preposition بـ turns the sentence into a regular negation (لا النّافِيَةُ), and a standard لا does not change the case (except in a special application, see *question #133*). For the correct case endings, just treat the sentence as it would be written without لا.

No doubt.	بِلا رَيْبٍ = لا رَيْبَ فِي ذَلِكَ.

No doubt in that.	لا شَكَّ فِي ذَلِكَ.

This sentence fulfills all requirements for an absolute negation (لا النَّافِيةُ للْجِنْسِ): indefinite, nothing in between, no preposition!

249. Why are Arabic if-clauses difficult to translate?

The translation depends on the context – not on tenses or moods.

In most languages, if-clauses are pretty abstract constructions. I was teaching German in Egypt. In one lesson, I talked about New York and said a sentence which in English means: *If I had money, I would fly to New York.*

After the lesson a student came to me and said: *Congratulations! When are you going to New York? We will miss you!* The sentence I used conveys, in fact, a complex and abstract idea. So I asked my listeners to do two things: (1) **imagine** that I am rich and (2) **imagine** what I would to do as a rich person.

In English, we love to speak in *would-*, *could-* and *should-*sentences. But in Arabic, there is no easy way to express this idea. The Arabic verb lacks tenses and moods and specific rules for if-clauses. Instead, it all depends on the context!

Some hints:

- Verbs in conditional sentences have no real temporal significance. The actual tense is determined by the context.

- The verb in the **first part** of the if-sentence is typically in the **past tense** – regardless of whether a reference to a past, present, or future situation is intended.

- The verb in the **second or main clause** is usually in the past tense too – but other tenses are possible as well.

- The actual meaning (of the verbs) corresponds to a number of English tenses depending on the idea of the condition and the context.

250. What does the jussive mood (مَجْزُومٌ) express?

A condition, a prohibition, or an imperative.

The term *jussive* is based on the Latin word *jubeō*: to order, to command. The corresponding Arabic term, مَجْزُومٌ, literally means *cut short; clipped*. In grammar, it denotes *with deleted ending*. So where is the conceptual bridge between the Western and Arabic term?

Let's start with the technical part. Elision (جَزْمٌ) describes a grammatical situation that requires to **cut the end of the present tense verb** (الْمُضارِعُ). We achieve that by using سُكُونٌ. If there is a weak letter involved (حَرْفُ عِلّةٍ), we drop و or ي to mark this mood.

Now let's look at the practical application. When do we use the jussive mood (مَجْزُومٌ)? When you see a مَجْزُومٌ-ending,

- probably there is a connection to the meaning of *should;*

- maybe there is a command involved (*imperative*);

- maybe the sentence has a conditional meaning;

Important to know: The jussive mood (مَجْزُومٌ) **does not occur by itself**. It has to be induced by certain devices, so-called *particles of elision* (حَرْفُ جَزْمٍ). They may even have enough power to influence two verbs (often conditional sentences).

cutting **two** *verbs*		*cutting* **one** *verb*	
if; even if	إِنْ	negation (past tense)	لَمْ
whenever	إِذْما	prohibition (لا النَّاهِيَةُ)	لا
who	مَنْ	(even) if	إِنْ
that which	ما	since	لَمَّا

whatever	مَهْما
what a	أَيُّ
in whatever way	كَيْفَما
when	مَتَى
wherever	أَيْنَما
in what time	أَيّانَ
whence	أَنَّى
wherever	حَيْثُما

Lām of the imperative (لامُ الْأَمْرِ); It conveys the meaning of: *let's...; to*	لِ

Don't play with fire!	لا تَلْعَبْ بِالنَّارِ!	cutting one verb
Be a responsible man!	لِتَكُنْ مَسْؤُولًا!	
He did not go.	لَم يَذْهَبْ.	

If you are lazy, you will be a loser.	إِنْ تَكْسَلْ تَخْسَرْ.	cutting two verbs
Wherever you sit, I sit.	أَيْنَما تَجْلِسْ أَجْلِسْ.	

251. When do you need the jussive (مَجْزُومٌ) in if-clauses?

When the condition is initiated by a device of elision (حَرْفُ جَزْمٍ).

Several words can start a conditional sentence (*if...*), but not every device initiates the jussive mood (مَجْزُومٌ). Most of them, however, do. Let's go through them carefully.

إِنْ	*if*; used for time or place

If you put an effort in your work, you will succeed in your life.	إِنْ تَجْتَهِدْ فِي عَمَلِكَ تَنْجَحْ فِي حَيَاتِكَ.

مَتَى	*when*

If/when you come to Egypt, you will find beautiful weather.	مَتَى تَأْتِ إِلَى مِصْرَ تَجِدْ جَوَّهَا جَمِيلًا.
The weak letter of يَأْتِي (present t. of I-verb أَتَى; *to come*) is dropped.	

مَنْ	*who*; for persons

مَا	*who; whoever; which* – for animals, trees; non-human objects

Whoever travels a lot will see different people.	مَنْ يُسَافِرْ كَثِيرًا يَرَ شُعُوبًا مُخْتَلِفَةٍ.
The weak letter in يَرَى (present tense of the I-verb رَأَى; *to see*; also: *to think*) is deleted. **Remark:** رَأَى is one of the few extremely irregular verbs. You can't conjugate it according to the standard rules. The Hamza disappears in the present tense and the imperative looks totally weird: رَ (masculine – only one letter!) and رَيْ (feminine) for the singular and رَوْا (masculine) and رَيْنَ (feminine) for the plural.	

مَهْما	*what; which; whatever*

What you do for the good of the people will make you happy.	مَهْما تُقَدِّمُوا مِن خَيْرٍ لِلنَّاسِ تُصْبِحُوا سُعْدَاءَ.

أَيْنَما	*where*; for places

Wherever you travel, you will find friends.	أَيْنَما تُسافِرْ تَجِدْ أَصْدِقاءَ.

كَيْفَما	*how*

The way you treat friends, the way they will treat you.	كَيْفَما تُعامِلْ زُمَلاءَكَ يُعامِلُوكَ.

أَيٌّ	*every; whoever*. For people, places, time. Notice that you need to put a noun (اِسْمٌ) after أَيٌّ and never a verb because أَيّ is used in a إِضافَة-construction.

Every worker who works diligently will find the fruits of his work.	أَيُّ عامِلٍ يَعْمَلْ بِجِدٍّ يَلْقَ ثَمَرَةَ عَمَلِهِ.
The weak letter of يَلْقَى (present t. of I-verb لَقِيَ; *to find*) is elided.	

252. Do you always need the مَجْزُومٌ - mood in if-clauses?

No, you don't.

Conditional sentences are quite unmanageable and confusing in Arabic because there are so many words with which they are introduced. What complicates the whole thing: Several words may start a conditional sentence without interfering in the mood of verbs. In fact, two of the most prominent words for conditional sentences are of that nature: إذا and لَوْ.

إذا | *if; when*

The condition expressed by إذا is a **situation which is likely or expected** – thus, it is usually translated as *when*. The only uncertainty is often just the time of the event.

The verb after إذا has to be in the **past tense** although it has a **future** meaning.

If morning comes, people will go to their work.	إذا طَلَعَ الصَّباحُ ذَهَبَ النّاسُ إلَى أعْمالِهِم.

لَوْ | *if; whether*

- لو is used for **hypothetical** situations, for things that are **improbable** or **contrary to fact**. We talk about something that has already occurred or we know that the scenario we are introducing doesn't match reality.

- Similar to إذا, the temporal meaning of the verb is not determined by its form, but by the meaning of the condition.

- Regarding the use of ف in the main clause, see *qu. #253*.

How do we use لَوْ?

- If the first part of the if-clause **cannot be achieved** anymore, logically, the second part (or answer) is also not going to happen. In English, we call such sentences *imagined conditions* or *third conditional*. In Arabic, we call it إمْتِناعُ الشَّرْطِ. The word إمْتِناعٌ means *impossibility; refraining*.

- That's why you need the **(emphatic) particle** لِ ("*la*") to **connect** the second sentence and underline the hypothetical meaning. Such لِ is called *Lām of the complement* (لامُ

الْجَواب). It is used in the second part of a conditional sentence with لَو or لَوْلا and in oaths.

If I had known (it), I would have walked.	لَو عَرَفْتُ لَمَشَيْتُ.

Had you put effort into your work, you would have won the prize.	لَو اِجْتَهَدْتَ فِي عَمَلِكَ لَحَصَلْتَ عَلَى الْجائِزَةِ.

Watch out: The normal interpretation of this sentence would be as a **counterfactual**. So don't get confused! The sentence does not mean: *If you put an effort in your work, you will earn the prize.*

لَوْلا	**if not**; *if it were not for; if it had not been for; if there was no*

لَوْلا precedes a single noun or noun phrase and **hypothetically denies** it.

- You have to place a **noun** in the nominative case (اِسْمٌ مَرْفُوعٌ) immediately after لَوْلا.
- In the second part of the sentence, you use the particle لِ. It conveys emphasis and serves as a binder. See *quest. #126*.

If there was no Nile, Egypt would be a desert.	لَوْلا النَّيْلُ لَأَصْبَحَتْ مِصْرُ صَحْراءَ.

The word مَوْجُودٌ (*found; existing*) is implicitly understood after the word *Nile* – but never written. See *Arabic for Nerds 2, quest. #224.*

كُلَّما	*every time; whenever*

Every time I walked in the streets of Cairo, I found a crowd.	كُلَّما سِرْتُ فِي شَوارِع الْقاهِرة وَجَدْتُ ازْدِحامًا.

Notice: In the second part of the sentence, you have to use the past tense! Such sentences are also often translated with the past tense!

253. When do you use فَ in conditional sentences?

It depends on how you start the second part.

In most conditional sentences with لَوْ or مَنْ or إِذا, you will find the letter فَ in the second part.

فَ is used to connect the first sentence (*protasis*) with the main clause (*apodosis*). So it is no coincide that we call it *Fā' of sanction* (فاءُ الْجَزاءِ). Practically speaking, فَ is a conjunction and expresses *then; thus; hence; therefore.*

ANALYSIS 1: When do you have to use فَ?

> If the **second** part (main clause) does **not** start with the **verb** directly, you should add فَ.

Generally speaking, فَ is found <u>before</u>:

هُوَ	إِنَّ	قَدْ	سَـ سَوْفَ	لـ	لَنْ	لَمْ	ما	لا
or any other pronoun to emphasize and start a nominal sentence (جُمْلة إِسْمِيّة)	to stress the main clause	to emphasize the meaning of the past tense	future indicator	negation				

| Whoever enters the room is safe. | مَنْ دَخَلَ الْغُرْفَةَ فَهُوَ آمِنٌ. |
| If you get married, you won't marry me. | إذا تَزَوَّجْتَ فَلَنْ تَتَزَوَّجَنِي. |

Some remarks about the character of فَ:

- فَ **emphasizes** the time or sequential aspect (*then, hence*) and therefore can work as a rhetorical element.

- فَ offers us **greater flexibility** since فَ can be followed by the future, a negation, etc.

- فَ often indicates that the second part/ main clause (*apodosis*) is **not the logical result** of the conditional clause.

If you start the second part (main clause) directly with a verb, you don't need فَ – but instead maybe the device لَ, which is an amplifier and underlines one idea: The situation, which is described in the second part, will only be true if the first part happens.

In other words, if the first part doesn't happen, the second part won't either. The لَ is normally used for if-clauses type II (*if I was...*) and III (*if I had been...*). Notice the difference to لِ with كَسْرَة which expresses *in order to*. An example of لَ:

| If I had known (it), I would have walked. | لَوْ عَرَفْتُ لَمَشَيْتُ. |

ANALYSIS 2: What is the grammatical impact of such فَ?

If the **second** part starts with فَ,
the **jussive** mood (مَجْزُومٌ) is **prohibited**.

The verb gets the regular indicative mood (مَرْفُوعٌ) and ends in "*u*".

Despite the different tenses, the following examples mean more or less the same: *Whoever works hard, will succeed.*

1	We only use the verb → we don't need فَ.	مَنْ يَعْمَلْ بِجِدٍّ يَنْجَحْ.

2	Here, we need فَ!	مَنْ يَعْمَلْ بِجِدٍّ فَنَجاحُهُ مُؤَكَّدٌ.

The second and main clause is a nominal sentence (جُمْلةٌ اسْمِيّةٌ). Subject (= فَنَجاحُهُ) and predicate (= مُؤَكَّدٌ) are in the nominative case (مَرْفُوعٌ).

3	The future tense needs فَ.	مَنْ يَعْمَلْ بِجِدٍّ فَسَيَنْجَحُ.
		مَنْ يَعْمَلْ بِجِدٍّ فَسَوْفَ يَنْجَحُ.

Note that the second verb ends in ضَمّة (yanjah**u**). Don't get confused. Grammatically speaking, the verb is nevertheless located in the position of a jussive mood (فِي مَحَلِّ جَزْمٍ).

How can we justify and explain that we don't use the jussive mood after فَ? Or, to confuse you even more, is it even true that we don't use the jussive? We will see.

If you are lazy, you will be sorry.	إِنْ تَكْسَلْ فَسَتَنْدَمُ.
→ The virtual, estimated meaning of the second (main) clause: *you (yourself) will be sorry.*	فَأَنْتَ تَنْدَمُ.

Think of فَ as a kind of breakwater. After فَ, we now have a nominal sentence (جُمْلةٌ اسْمِيّةٌ).

- The **verb** itself functions as the predicate (خَبَرٌ).
- What about the subject (مُبْتَدَأٌ)? → It was deleted.

Now, it becomes theoretical. The nominal sentence, consisting of the predicate and the deleted subject, is located in the **position** of a **jussive mood** (الْجُمْلةُ مِن الْمُبْتَدَإِ الْمَحْذُوفِ وَالْخَبَرِ تَكُونُ في مَحَلِّ جَزْمٍ). ▷ So YES, we do have the jussive mood, but it is not visible!

We say that predicate (خَبَرٌ = سَـتَنْدَمُ) is in place of the deleted second (main) clause of the sentence.

→ If you want to dig deeper, see *Arabic for Nerds 2, #389, about* فَ.

254. What is the difference between إذا and إنْ؟

It's similar to the difference between if and when.

Let's take a quick look at the English language. *If* is used to introduce a possible or unreal situation or condition. *When* is used to refer to the time of a future situation or condition that we are certain of.

In Arabic, the difference between *if* and *when* is often fluid. Theoretically, you can use both words to express *if* or *when* – but there is a difference.

This word implies a positive or negative meaning; something may happen – or not! Closer to *if*.	إنْ
This particle indicates that **something is going to happen.** Closer to *when*.	إذا

Here is an example:

When morning comes (and it will definitely come)...	إذا طَلَعَ الصَّباحُ

Important: It doesn't matter which tense you use! All three sentences in the table have more or less the same meaning:

If you strive (make an effort) in your work, you will be successful in your life.

1	past tense	إِنْ اِجْتَهَدْتَ فِي عَمَلِكَ نَجَحْتَ فِي حَياتِكَ.

You can't mark the jussive mood (مَجْزُومٌ) in a past tense verb. Although the verb is in the past, it conveys the meaning of the future.

2	present tense	إِنْ تَجْتَهِدْ فِي عَمَلِكَ تَنْجَحْ.

You have to use the jussive mood (مَجْزُومٌ).

3	imperative	اِجْتَهِدْ فِي عَمَلِكَ تَنْجَحْ.

You use the jussive mood (مَجْزُومٌ). Don't forget to write سُكُونٌ in both verbs: the imperative (اِجْتَهِدْ) and the jussive mood (تَنْجَحْ).

255. What are the essential rules for writing numbers?

There are five essential rules.

Numbers are among the most difficult things in Arabic grammar. There are many rules that do not always follow normal logic. Let's dig through this mess.

The number 1

In early times, the Arabs had not distinguished between one or two. They used the dual for two. Otherwise, it was only one. So, don't use *one* or *two* in إِضافةٌ-constructions. For emphasis, you use an adjective which must follow the word it describes.

A man came.	جاءَ وَاحِدُ رَجُلٍ.	incorrect
	جاءَ رَجُلٌ.	correct

Two men came.	جاءَ إِثْنا رَجُلٍ.	incorrect
	جاءَ رَجُلانِ.	correct

#	feminine	masculine
1	واحِدةٌ	واحِدٌ
1ˢᵗ	الأُولَى	الأَوَّلُ
11	إِحْدَى عَشْرةَ	أَحَدَ عَشَرَ
11ᵗʰ	الْحادِيةَ عَشْرةَ	الْحادِيَ عَشَرَ
21	إِحْدَى وَعِشْرُونَ or واحِدةٌ وَعِشْرُونَ	واحِدٌ وَعِشْرُونَ

What is the difference between واحِدٌ and أَحَدٌ؟

واحِدٌ	In English, this would be the **adjective** one. In Arabic too, it is used as a صِفةٌ/نَعْتٌ which means it **always comes after the word it describes** and never before! For example: one word (a single word): كَلِمةٌ واحِدةٌ

أَحَدٌ	In English, this would be the **noun** one. • Normally, this word is used as the first part of a إِضافةٌ. Meaning: one of. • It is often used independently and functions as an indefinite pronoun (anyone, someone). It is usually part of a negated sentence! See question #115.

The number 2

2	إِثْنَتَانِ - إِثْنَتَيْنِ	إِثْنَانِ - إِثْنَيْنِ
2nd	ثانِيَةٌ	ثانٍ
12	إِثْنَتا عَشْرةَ - إِثْنَتَيْ عَشْرةَ	إِثْنا عَشَرَ - إِثْنَيْ عَشَرَ

The numbers from 3 to 10
The numbers 30, 40, 50, …

- The numbers from 3 to 10 are **regular**. The feminine form is built by adding **ة**.

- The numbers 30, 40, 50, … have only one form, so there is **no feminine form**. For example: 40 (أَرْبَعُونَ).

- Watch out if you have *ten* (عَشر). The vowel in the middle varies depending on the gender – see *question #257*.

The numbers 100, 1000, and 1 million

They are nouns which have either a masculine or feminine form – but never both.

	feminine	masculine	plural
100	مِائَةٌ (also مِئَةٌ)	---	مِئَاتٌ
1000	---	أَلْفٌ	أُلُوفٌ or آلَافٌ
1 million	---	مِلْيُونٌ	مَلَايِينُ
1 billion	---	مِلْيَارٌ	مِلْيَاراتٌ

Remark: Why does *thousand* have two plural forms? → See *question #127*. If you want to know more about the spelling of مِائَة, see *Arabic for Nerds 2, question #198.*

Now, let's see how we can use numbers (عَدَد) with nouns (e.g., *14 apples, 300 pens, 7 houses*, etc.). The *counted* or *numbered noun* (مَعْدُود) has a decisive influence! The مَعْدُود is responsible for the **gender of the number**. We need two steps.

FIRST STEP
> check the **singular form** of the مَعْدُود

Some examples:

meaning	masc. singular	fem. singular	plural
pen	قَلَم	---	أَقْلَامٌ
tree	---	شَجَرَةٌ	أَشجَارٌ
Gineh; EGP	جَنَيْهٌ or جِنَيْهٌ	---	جُنَيْهاتٌ

Gineh is the Arabic name of the Egyptian currency, the *Egyptian pound (EGP)*. The *guinea* was a gold coin used in Great Britain between 1663 and 1814. The origin of the word relates to the Guinea region in West Africa, from where much of the gold used to make the coins was sourced and shipped to Britain.

Most currencies called *pound* in English are known as جِنَيْهٌ in Arabic (including the *pound sterling* - الْجُنَيْهُ الْإِسْتِرْلِينِيُّ); however, the Lebanese pound and Syrian pound are called لِيرَةٌ (līra) in Arabic.

SECOND STEP
> find the correct form + agreement for the number

Our **five important rules** mentioned at the beginning now play an important role.

| RULE 1 | The number has to <u>agree</u> with the مَعْدُودٌ, and the مَعْدُودٌ has to be <u>singular</u>. |

This rule is applied to:

- the numbers 1 and 2
- 11 and 12
- 21, 31, 41, …

I bought (only) one pen.	اِشْتَرَيْتُ قَلَمًا واحِدًا.
I bought (only) two pens.	اِشْتَرَيْتُ قَلَمَيْنِ اِثْنَيْنِ.
I read (only) one page.	قَرَأْتُ صَفْحَةً واحِدَةً.
I read (only) two pages.	قَرَأْتُ صَفْحَتَيْنِ اثْنَتَيْنِ.
11 days have passed.	مَرَّ أَحَدَ عَشَرَ يَوْمًا.
12 days have passed.	مَرَّ اثْنا عَشَرَ يَوْمًا.
I read 11 pages.	قَرَأْتُ إِحْدَى عَشْرَةَ صَفْحةً.
I read 12 pages.	قَرَأْتُ اثْنَتَيْ عَشْرَةَ صَفْحةً.
21 days have passed.	مَرَّ واحِدٌ وَعِشْرُونَ يَوْمًا.
22 days have passed.	مَرَّ إِثْنانِ وَعِشْرُونَ يَوْمًا.
I read 21 pages.	قَرَأْتُ إِحْدَى وَعِشْرِينَ صَفْحةً.
I read 22 pages.	فَرَأْتُ اِثْنَتَيْنِ وَعِشْرِينَ صَفْحةً.

| RULE 2 | The number has to <u>disagree</u> with the مَعْدُودٌ, and the مَعْدُودٌ has to be in <u>plural</u>. |

This rule is applied to:

- the numbers from 3 to 10

| I bought 10 books. | اِشْتَرَيْتُ عَشَرَةَ كُتُبٍ. |
| I read 10 pages. | قَرَأْتُ عَشْرَ صَفْحاتٍ. |

Note that the Arabic word for ten in our examples has different vowels → see question # 257.

| RULE 3 | The number has to <u>disagree</u> with the مَعْدُودٌ, and the مَعْدُودٌ has to be <u>singular</u>. |

This rule is applied to:

- 13, 14, … 19, and so on

Some examples where the rules (2 and 3) are applied:

I bought 3 books.	اِشْتَرَيْتُ ثَلاثَةَ كُتُبٍ.
I read 3 pages.	قَرَأْتُ ثَلاثَ صَفْحاتٍ.
14 days have passed.	مَرَّ أَرْبَعةَ عَشَرَ يَوْمًا.
14 years have passed.	مَرَّتْ أَرْبَعَ عَشْرة سَنةً.
I have 26 books.	عِنْدي سِتّةٌ وَعِشْرُونَ كِتابًا.
I read 26 pages.	قَرَأْتُ سِتًّا وَعِشْرينَ صَفْحةً.

Remark: Theoretically (although rarely used) you could also place the number after the noun. If you do so, you can use the masculine or feminine form. For example:

Three men came.	جاءَ رِجالٌ ثَلاثةٌ or ثَلاثٌ.

RULE 4	Numbers which <u>never change</u> their form. → no agreement

This rule is applied to:

- 20, 30, 40, ...
- 100 (for the spelling of *hundred* – see *question #196* and *Arabic for Nerds 2, question #199*)
- 1000
- 1 million

RULE 5	How to combine numbers with *hundred* and *thousand*.

In English, you don't have to worry about the grammar when you say *300 men* and want to correct it to *3000 men*. It is the same. In Arabic, it is a different story.

- In most situations, you use the word for **hundred** in the <u>singular</u> form and the word for **thousand** in the <u>plural</u>.
- The number (e.g., *three*) and the word for **hundred** or **thousand** form a إِضافةٌ-construction.
- In our examples (300; 3000), this would mean: ثَلاث is the first part and مِئة or آلاف is the second part of the إِضافةٌ.

Let's now apply rules 4 and 5.

In the room are 20 (masc.) students.	فِي الْغُرْفَةِ عِشْرُونَ طالِبًا.
In the room are 20 (fem.) students.	فِي الْغُرْفَةِ عِشْرُونَ طالِبَةً.
A century has 100 years.	الْقَرْنُ مِئَةُ عامٍ.
I read 100 pages.	قَرَأْتُ مِئَةَ صَفْحَةٍ.
In the faculty are 100 (m.) students.	فِي الْكُلِّيَّةِ مِئَةُ طالِبٍ.
In the faculty are 100 (f.) students.	فِي الْكُلِّيَّةِ مِئَةُ طالِبَةٍ.
In the faculty are 300 (m.) students.	فِي الْكُلِّيَّةِ ثَلاثُمِئَةِ طالِبٍ.
In the faculty are 300 (f.) students.	فِي الْكُلِّيَّةِ ثَلاثُمِئَةِ طالِبَةٍ.
In the faculty are 3000 (m.) students.	فِي الْكُلِّيَّةِ ثَلاثَةُ آلافِ طالِبٍ.
In the faculty are 3000 (f.) students.	فِي الْكُلِّيَّةِ ثَلاثَةُ آلافِ طالِبَةٍ.

256. Are numbers in Arabic nouns (إِسْمٌ)?

Yes, they are.

In English, we use the term *numeral* for numbers. They are a part of speech and have a special behavior. When a numeral modifies a noun, it may replace the article: *the* kids played in the room → *four* kids played in the room. That is why we call them determiners. Only when they do not come before a noun, numerals are a subclass of nouns (*the three* of us).

Arabic follows a different logic. Numbers are **nouns** (إِسْمٌ) which has serious consequences for our analysis. In principle, numbers (عَدَدٌ) are treated like any other إِسْمٌ which means that a number can serve, for example, as a subject or object and most importantly, numbers **get cases!** So it's not just difficult to create numbers. There is still something left to think about: the correct case marker. Let us check some examples.

1	مَضَتْ ثَلاثَةُ أَيَّامٍ مِن الشَّهْرِ.	**Three** days of the month passed.
2	قَرَأْتُ ثَلاثَةَ فُصُولٍ مِن الْكِتابِ.	I read **three** chapters of the book.
3	يَشْتَمِلُ الْكِتابُ عَلَى ثَلاثَةِ فُصُولٍ.	The book consists of **three** chapters.

1	ثَلاثَةُ	**Subject** (فاعِلٌ) of the verbal sentence; thus, it is in the nominative case (مَرْفُوعٌ).
2	ثَلاثَةَ	**Direct object** (مَفْعُولٌ بِهِ); therefore, it gets the accusative case (مَنْصُوبٌ).
3	ثَلاثَةِ	This noun **follows a preposition** which drags it into the genitive case (إِسْمٌ مَجْرُورٌ).

Since numbers can have very different forms in Arabic, it is not that easy to mark the case. We can derive three rules.

RULE 1	The numbers 20, 30, 40, … → you mark the case by a letter: و or ي. You need to apply either ونَ or ينَ.

1	تَدْرُسُ بِالْمَرْكَزِ عِشْرُونَ طالِبَةً.	**Twenty** (fem.) students study in the center.
2	اِسْتَقْبَلَ الْمَرْكَزُ عِشْرِينَ طالِبَةً.	The center receives **twenty** (fem.) students.
3	رَحَّبَ الْمَرْكَزُ بِعِشْرِينَ طالِبَةً.	The center welcomes **twenty** (fem.) students.

In the center are **twenty five** (masc.) students.	فِي الْمَرْكَزِ خَمْسَةٌ وَعِشْرُونَ طالِبًا.	4

Subject (فاعِلٌ), nominative case (مَرْفُوعٌ).	عِشْرُونَ	1
Direct object (مَفْعُولٌ بِهِ), accusative case (مَنْصُوبٌ).	عِشْرِينَ	2
After a **preposition**; genitive case (اِسْمٌ مَجْرُورٌ).	عِشْرِينَ	3
This is a so-called *follower* (تابِعٌ) in Arabic. A follower takes the same case as the preceding word. The conjunction وَ (عَطْفٌ) is responsible for this. So, عِشْرُونَ gets the same case as خَمْسَةٌ: the nominative (مَرْفُوعٌ).	عِشْرُونَ	4

RULE 2	Numbers **between 11 and 19** always end in فَتْحَةٌ. They are compound nouns. Both parts are **cemented** on the vowel "*a*". → They are **indeclinable** (مَبْنِيٌّ عَلَى الْفَتْحِ).

11 (male) students came.	حَضَرَ أَحَدَ عَشَرَ طالِبًا.
I met 11 (male) students.	قابَلْتُ أَحَدَ عَشَرَ طالِبًا.
I met 11 (male) students.	اِلْتَقَيْتُ بِأَحَدَ عَشَرَ طالِبًا.

RULE 3	A special situation – the **dual**: Numbers which are combinations of the number *two* are treated like a **dual**.
	If you want to emphasize the number *two*, add the number as an **adjective** – after the main word. As always, adjectives need agreement (مُطابَقَةٌ) → the same case!

Two (masc.) students came.	حَضَرَ طالِبانِ اثْنانِ.	1

Two (fem.) students came.	حَضَرَتْ طَالِبَتَانِ اثْنَتَانِ.	
I met two (masc.) students.	قَابَلْتُ طَالِبَيْنِ اثْنَيْنِ.	2
I met two (fem.) students.	قَابَلْتُ طَالِبَتَيْنِ اثْنَتَيْنِ.	
I met two (masc.) students.	الْتَقَيْتُ بِطَالِبَيْنِ اثْنَيْنِ.	3
I met two (fem.) students.	الْتَقَيْتُ بِطَالِبَتَيْنِ اثْنَتَيْنِ.	
In the department are two hundred (fem.) students.	فِي الْقِسْمِ مِئَتَا طَالِبَةٍ	4
In the faculty there are two thousand (fem.) students.	فِي الْكُلِّيَّةِ أَلْفَا طَالِبَةٍ.	

Adjective (نَعْتٌ); nominative case (مَرْفُوعٌ).	اِثْنَانِ , اِثْنَتَانِ	1
Adjective (نَعْتٌ); accusative case (مَنْصُوبٌ).	اِثْنَيْنِ , اِثْنَتَيْنِ	2
Adjective (نَعْتٌ); genitive case (مَجْرُورٌ).	اِثْنَيْنِ , اِثْنَتَيْنِ	3
Delayed subject (مُبْتَدَأٌ مُؤَخَّرٌ) of the nominal sentence (جُمْلَةٌ اِسْمِيّةٌ); nominative case (مَرْفُوعٌ).	مِئَتَا , أَلْفَا	4

257. Why can it be difficult to pronounce *ten* (عشر)?

The pronunciation depends on the word that comes after it.

You may have noticed that the number *ten* (عشر) doesn't always get the same vowels. It is pronounced differently.

There's a reason for that. To find the correct vowel of the **letter ش**, you need to check the gender of the noun it is referring to, i.e., the word that comes after عشر.

RULE 1	If عشر points to a **masculine** word, you need to put فَتْحَةٌ on the letter ش.

I bought 10 pens.	إِشْتَرَيْتُ عَشَرَةَ أَقْلَامٍ.
I bought 13 pens.	إِشْتَرَيْتُ ثَلاثَةَ عَشَرَ قَلَمًا.
ten days	عَشَرَةَ أَيَّامٍ
ten men	عَشَرَةَ رِجالٍ
ten thousand	عَشَرَةَ آلافٍ

The Prophet said: "Had only ten Jews (among their chiefs) believe me, all the Jews would definitely have believed me." *(Saḥīḥ al-Bukhārī 3941)*	قَالَ: لَوْ آمَنَ بِي عَشَرَةٌ مِنَ الْيَهُودِ لآمَنَ بِي الْيَهُودُ.

RULE 2	If عشر points to a **feminine** word, you have to put سُكُونٌ on the letter ش.

I read 10 pages.	قرأتُ عَشْرَ صَفْحاتٍ.
I read 13 pages.	قرأتُ ثَلاثَ عَشْرَةَ صَفْحَةً.
ten degrees	عَشْرُ دَرَجاتٍ
ten women	عَشْرُ فَتَياتٍ

The Prophet remained in Mecca for ten years. *(Saḥīḥ al-Bukhārī 4978)*	لَبِثَ النَّبِيُّ بِمَكَّةَ عَشْرَ سِنِينَ.

What about the numbers 13 to 19? We need the word *ten* to form these because they are compound nouns. It is no coincidence that we are using rules 1 and 2 mentioned above to determine the vowels in the second part (*ten*). The decisive factor is the gender of the word which comes after the number.

fifteen years	خَمْسَ عَشْرَةَ سَنَةً	numbered thing is **feminine** (مُؤَنَّثٌ)
fifteen nights	خَمْسَ عَشْرَةَ لَيْلَةً	

fifteen dinar	بِخَمْسَةَ عَشَرَ دِينَارًا	numbered thing is **masculine** (مُذَكَّرٌ)
fifteen days	خَمْسَةَ عَشَرَ يَوْمًا	

258. Does *few* (بِضْعٌ) sometimes change its shape?

Yes, it does.

بِضْعٌ is a noun that virtually includes a certain magnitude: a number from **three to nine**. It therefore denotes *some, a few, several*. For example, *for a few days; a few hundred*.

The nasty thing about بِضْعٌ is that it changes its **gender** depending on the word it refers to. Not surprisingly, بِضْع behaves similarly to the numbers from 3 to 10 and can stand in for them. You need the **opposite gender** of the numbered word (مَعْدُودٌ). ▷ If it is masculine: بِضْعَةٌ; if it is feminine: بِضْع.

for a few days	You have to use the feminine form of *few* since *day* (يَوْمٌ) is masculine.	لِبِضْعَةِ أَيَّامٍ.
a few years	You use the masculine form of *few* since *year* (سَنَةٌ) is feminine.	بِضْعُ سَنَوَاتٍ.

There were a few hundreds.	You use the masculine form of *few* since *hundred* (مِئة) is feminine.	كانَ بِضْعُ مِئاتٍ.

some men	بِضعةُ رِجالٍ
some women	بِضعُ نِساءٍ
ten- and-something men	بِضعةَ عَشَرَ رَجُلًا
after a few hundred years	بَعْدَ بِضعِ مِئاتِ السِّنينِ
twenty and a few dinars	بِضعةٌ وَعِشْرونَ دينارًا
a few tens	بِضعةَ عَشَرَ

259. What is a logical subject?

*It is the topic of the debate whether you should say: many **are**... or many **is**...*

Let's start our discussion with the following sentence: *Many (a lot of) devices support the operating system.*

What is the subject of this sentence? Is it *many* or *devices*? In Arabic, this has far-reaching consequences for the verb.

	verb refers to	example
1	*many* (الْعَديد)	يُدَعِّمُ الْعَديدُ مِن الْأَجْهِزَة نِظامَ التَّشْغيلِ.
2	*devices* (الْأَجْهِزَة)	تُدَعِّمُ الْعَديدُ مِن الْأَجْهِزَة نِظامَ التَّشْغيلِ.

If we assume that the verb refers to the **masculine الْعَديد**, it needs the **masculine** form (3rd person, singular): يُدَعِّمُ.

If we say, that it is linked to the **feminine** الْأَجْهِزةُ, it needs the **feminine** form: تُدَعَّمُ. But can a verb refer to a word as an agent that is, grammatically speaking, not the subject? In Arabic, a subject needs the nominative case. So, theoretically, only one answer is correct: Only الْعَدِيدُ can be the subject (فَاعِلٌ).

Our topic has to do with what linguists call the **logical subject**. The problem with **quantifiers** is whether they should be treated like real (masculine singular) nouns or ignored in verbal agreement. In English, you ignore quantifiers: You say *some/a lot of people are* here – and not: *is* here.

In Arabic, however, words working as quantifiers are **true nouns** (اِسْمٌ) and form compound إِضافةٌ-constructions with the following اِسْمٌ, so they should be treated as the main اِسْمٌ. But since semantically they are not the salient part, people often make the verb agree with the following word.

What is the solution?

- If you want to be on the **safe side**, you should use يُدَعَّمُ, since عَدِيدٌ is a masculine noun (اِسْمٌ) and is placed as the subject (فَاعِلٌ). It gets the nominative case (مَرْفُوعٌ) and thus marked by a ضَمّةٌ ("*u*").

- However, you can use the **logical subject** (الْأَجْهِزَة) as well for agreement and use تُدَعَّمُ. Although it is grammatically semi-correct, you will encounter it occasionally.

A more striking example of this problem is كُلٌّ. The word كُلٌّ is a masculine singular noun; therefore, verbs and adjectives may (should) agree in the masculine singular.

However, it is also common for the verb (فِعْلٌ) or the adjective (نَعْتٌ) to agree with the gender and number of the word governed by كُلّ (= the *logical subject*). So let's take كُلّ and look at both options.

Option 1	Verbs and adjectives agree in the masculine singular since كُلّ is a masculine singular اِسْم.

They are all silent.	كُلُّهُمْ صامِتٌ.

Option 2	The adjective or verb agrees with the gender and number of the logical subject (= second part of the إضافةٌ).

We all will go.	كُلُّنا سَنَذْهَبُ.

The same applies to جَميعٌ (*all*; *everybody*). When it is the first part of a إضافةٌ, the agreement is **usually** with the number and gender of the **logical subject** (= second part of the إضافةٌ).

→ You will find more examples in *Arabic for Nerds 2, question #148*.

260. How do you express: emphasis?

Arabic offers an arsenal of possibilities to emphasize something (التَّأْكيدُ). By the way, did you know that *arsenal* is perhaps of Arabic origin? It may go back to the expression دار الصِّناعة which means *house of manufacture*.

Arabic grammar alone offers you many tools to emphasize a word. For example: أَنَّ • إِنَّ • the energetic ن in verbs • additional prepositions (بِ and مِنْ) • لِ.

The traditional method is to emphasize with phrases and expressions. You can use the following examples to underline what you are saying when expressing your opinion, dissatisfaction, annoyance, or suggestion.

generally; in general	عَامَّةً or عُمُومًا or فِي الْعُمُومِ or بِشَكْلٍ عَامٍّ
particularly	بِخَاصَّةٍ or عَلَى وَجْهِ الْخُصُوصِ or خُصُوصًا or خَاصَّةً وَأَنَّ
surely; undoubtedly; no doubt; definitely; certainly	بِلَا شَكٍّ or بِلَا رَيْبَ or بِالتَّأْكِيدِ or دُونَ أَدْنَى شَكٍّ or قَطْعًا or بِشَكْلٍ قَطْعِيٍّ or طَبْعًا or بِالطَّبْعِ
in fact; matter of fact; indeed	فِعْلًا or بِالْفِعْلِ or فِي الْوَاقِعِ or وَفِي وَاقِعِ الْأَمْرِ or وَحَقِيقَةُ الْأَمْرِ or فِي الْحَقِيقَةِ or حَقًّا
boundless; infinite; unlimited	لا حُدُودَ لَهُ or غَيْرُ مَحْدُودٍ or بِلا حُدُودٍ or لا حَدَّ لَهُ or بِلا حَدٍّ or إِلَى حَدٍّ بَعِيدٍ or لا نِهَايَةَ لَهُ
to a certain degree; to a certain extent; somewhat; more or less	إِلَى حَدٍّ مَا
There is no doubt that	وَلا شَكَّ فِي أَنَّ
It is certain that	وَمِمَّا لا شَكَّ فِيهِ أَنَّ
I (indeed; certainly) think that	وَأَظُنُّ ظَنًّا أَنَّ or وَأَغْلَبُ الظَّنِّ أَنَّ or وُجْهَةُ نَظَرِي أَنَّ
Things being as they are	الْحَالُ عَلَى مَا هُوَ عَلَيْهِ or سَيَبْقَى الْحَالُ عَلَى مَا هُوَ عَلَيْهِ
at first; in the beginning	فِي أَوَّلِ الْأَمْرِ or فِي بَادِئِ الْأَمْرِ or فِي الْبِدَايَةِ
First of all, I'd like to mention	بِدَايَةً وَقَبْلَ أَيِّ شَيْءٍ، أَوَدُّ أَنْ أَذْكُرَ أَنَّ

There are two reasons: first	هُناكَ سَبَبانِ: أَوَّلًا
It goes without saying	أَنَّهُ أَمْرٌ مَفْرُوغٌ مِنْهُ
I totally agree with you.	أَتَّفِقُ مَعَكَ تَمَامًا.
The scientists/academics all agree	وَالْعُلَمَاءُ كُلُّهُمْ مُتَّفِقُونَ عَلَى
I totally disagree with you.	لَا أَتَّفِقُ مَعَكَ عَلَى الْإِطْلَاقِ.
I am supporting (accepting) this opinion.	إِنِّي أَرْتَضِي هٰذا الرَّأْيَ. or أُشَارِكُكَ الرَّأْيَ.
Indeed, I respect your point, but I can't agree with it.	أَحْتَرِمُ رَأْيَكَ، إِلَّا أَنَّنِي أُعَارِضُكَ بِشِدَّةٍ.
I totally reject this opinion.	وَإِنِّي أَرْفُضُ هٰذا الرَّأْيَ بِرُمَّتِهِ لَا حَاجَةَ لِإِضَافةٍ or أَرْفُضُ هٰذا الرَّأْيَ بِرُمَّتِهِ.
This opinion is not acceptable from my point of view.	هٰذا الرَّأْيُ غَيْرُ مَقْبُولٍ مِنْ وِجْهَةِ نَظَرِي.
He himself preferred / supported this opinion.	قَدْ ذَهَبَ هُوَ نَفْسُهُ إِلَى هٰذا الرَّأْيِ. or هُوَ نَفْسُهُ قَدْ أَيَّدَ هٰذَا الرَّأْيَ.
This matter is nothing but	وَلَيْسَ هٰذا الْأَمْرُ إِلَّا...
Without limitation, we could say	وَما مِنْ أَحَدٍ يَسْتَطِيعُ الْقَوْلَ إِنَّ
In the same book	وَفِي هٰذا الْكِتابِ نَفْسِهِ
And the Arabs in general and the Egyptians in particular	وَالْعَرَبُ بِعامَّةٍ وَالْمِصْرِيُّونَ بِخاصّةٍ
Though it clearly seems that	وَإِنَّ الْأَمْرَ لَيَبْدُو واضِحًا إذًا or مِنْ

	الْوَاضِحِ جِدًّا أَنَّ
And one should never think that	وَلَا يَحْسَبَنَّ أَحَدٌ أَنَّ
It is an opinion that is worth mentioning.	وَهُوَ رَأْيٌ جَدِيرٌ بِالْقَوْلِ حَقًّا.

261. How do you express: amplification or likeness?

Amplification (التَّوْسِعةُ or التَّشابُهُ) is a rhetorical tool writers use to embellish a sentence or statement by adding further information. You use such phrases if you want to highlight the importance of an idea.

likewise; similarly	وَعَلَى نَحْوٍ مُمَاثِلٍ or وَعَلَى نَحْوٍ مُشَابِهٍ or بِشَكْلٍ مُتَشابِهٍ
and also	وَأَيْضًا
as well as	وَكَذلِكَ
moreover; besides; furthermore	عِلاوةً عَلَى ذلِكَ or بِالإِضافةِ إِلَى ذلِكَ or وَفَضْلًا عَن ذلِكَ
moreover; and again and once more	ثُمَّ إِنَّ
moreover; just as; quite as; as on the other hand	كَما أَنَّ
as to, as for, as far as... is concerned; but; yet, however; on the other hand	أَمَّا... فَ...
and that's all; and no more; only	فَحَسْبُ or فَقَظ
regarding; concerning	فِيما يَتَعَلَّقُ بِـ... فَ...

Perhaps it would be useful to say that	وَلَعَلَّ مِن الْمُفِيدِ الْقَوْلَ إِنَّ
Perhaps it is clear that	وَلَعَلَّ مِن الْوَاضِحِ أَنَّ
It is known that	وَمِنْ الْمَعْلُومِ أَنَّ
Notably; it is noticeable that	وَمِن الْمُلَاحَظِ or بِصورةٍ مَلحوظةٍ
A question arises here, which is	وَيَبْرُزُ هُنَا سُؤَالٌ مُهِمٌّ وَهُوَ
It should be noted here	وَتَجْدُرُ الْإِشَارَةُ هُنَا إِلَى
It is worth mentioning that	وَجَدِيرٌ بِالذِّكْرِ أَنَّ or وَالْجَدِيرُ بِالذِّكْرِ أَنَّ
In the same manner; likewise	عَلَى حَدٍّ سَوَاءٍ or عَلَى السَّوَاء
It seems that	وَيَبْدُو أَنَّ
It is strange that	وَمِن الْغَرِيبِ أَنَّ
The strange thing is that	وَالْغَرِيبُ فِي الْأَمْرِ أَنَّ
Not only this, but	لَيْسَ هذا فَحَسْبُ وَلْكِنْ
That was just the beginning.	كانَ هذا الْبِدايةَ وَحَسْبُ.

262. How do you express: contrast or concession?

If you want to show opposing ideas, you need the right words and expressions – tools that express contrast or concession. In English, you use *but, although, however, despite.*

contrast (الْمُقابَلةُ)	I used to live in Alexandria, **but** now I live in Tunis.
concession (التَّسليمُ)	**Even though** I live in Alexandria, I work in Cairo.

but	وَلٰكِنَّ	وَلٰكِنْ
however	بَيْدَ أَنَّ	إلَّا أَنَّ
but; except (for)		غَيْرَ أَنَّ
nevertheless		وَمَعَ ذٰلِكَ or وَمَعَ أَنَّ
although		وَعَلَى الرَّغْمِ مِن... فَـ...
whilst		عَلَى \ في حينِ أَنَّ
probably; most likely		وَالْأَرْجَحُ أَنْ or عَلَى الْأَرْجَحِ
most likely		وَفي أَغْلَبِ الظَّنِّ
It is likely that; in all probability		وَمِن الْمُرَجِّحِ أَنَّ
If it was not for		وَلَوْلا أَنَّ
In contrast to		وَعَلَى النَّقيضِ مِن ذٰلِك
In contrast to this view		وَفي مُقابِلِ هٰذا الرَّأْي or في المُقابِلِ،
The other opinion is that...		وَيَذْهَبُ رَأْيٌ آخَرُ إلَى
On the other hand		وَمِنْ ناحِيةٍ أُخْرَى وَمِنْ جِهةٍ أُخْرَى
One could say that		وَقَدْ يُقالُ إنَّ

If we compare this view to	وَإِذا قارَنَّا هذا الرَّأْيَ بِ
After examining this view/opinion, it looks to me that	وَعِنْدَ تَمْحِيصِ هذا الرَّأْي يَبْدُو لِي أَنَّ
And if we challenged this	وَإِذا وَضَعْنا هذا بِإِزاءِ...
It is acknowledged that; it is agreed upon that	مِن الْمُسَلَّم بِهِ أَنَّ
It can't be denied	وَمِمَّا لا يُمْكِنُ إِنْكارُهُ
Whatever the case/matter is	وَمَهْما يَكُنْ مِن أَمْرٍ or مَهْما كانَ الْأَمْرُ
I agree with this opinion.	وَإِنِّي أَتَّفِقُ مَعَ هذا الرَّأْي.
I accept this opinion.	وَإِنِّي أَرْتَضِي هذا الرَّأْيَ.
I tend to agree with this opinion.	وَإِنِّي أَمِيلُ إِلَى الْأَخْذِ بِهذا الرَّأْي.

263. How do you express: to give an example?

Try to count how many times you say *for example* in English in just 15 minutes?

It is indeed one of the most important expressions. In Arabic, there are sophisticated ways to show that you want to explain something or give an example (الْمِثالُ).

like this; similar to this	وَشَبِيهَة بِهذا or عَلَى هذا النَّحْوِ
This is similar to; this is like	وَيُشْبِهُ هذا بِ or وَهذا شَبِيهَة بِ
This is like	وَهذا مِثْلُ

for example; as an example	فَمَثَلًا or فَعَلَى سَبِيلِ الْمِثالِ
An example of this is	وَمِنَ الْأَمْثِلةِ عَلَى هذا
The clearest example of this	وَأَوْضَحُ مِثالٍ عَلَى هذا
The closest (most tangible) example of this	وَأَقْرَبُ مِثالٍ عَلَى هذا
What shows/illustrates this	وَمِمَّا يُوَضِّحُ هذا
What makes this idea clearer	وَمِمَّا يَزِيدُ هذِهِ الْفِكْرةَ وُضوحًا
An example that illustrates my opinion	وَمِن الْأَمْثِلةِ الَّتِي تُوَضِّحُ رَأْيِي
One example cited/given by the author	وَمِن الْأَمْثِلةِ الَّتِي ذَكَرَهَا الْمُؤَلِّفُ
A counterpart to this	وَنَظِيرُ هذا

264. How do you express: proof?

People always have doubts. If you want to convince people, you need to show them that there is evidence or proof (الدَّلِيلُ) of what you are saying or writing.

the proof	الدَّلِيلُ = الْحُجَّةُ = الْبُرْهَانُ = الْبَيِّنَةُ
The evidence of this	والدَّلِيلُ عَلَى هذا
The evidence that supports this view	والدَّلِيلُ الَّذِي يَدْعَمُ هذا الرَّأْيَ

According to his statement; as he asserts; in his own words	عَلَى حَدِّ قَوْلِهِ or حَسَبَ قَوْلِهِ
As far as I know	حَسَبَ ما أَعْرِفُ
According to what they say	حَسَبَ ما يُقالُ
I quote what I am saying from	وَأَسْتَدِلُّ عَلَى ما أَذْهَبُ إِلَيْهِ بِ or أَسْتَنِدُ فِي رَأْيِهِ عَلَى مَا يَلِي
What supports my opinion	وَمِمّا يَدْعَمُ رَأْيِي
I support my opinion with some evidence.	وَأَدْعَمُ رَأْيِي بِعِدَّةِ أَدِلَّةٍ.
This is conclusive evidence of	وَهذا دَلِيلٌ قاطِعٌ عَلَى
This is a clear proof of	وَهذا بُرْهانٌ ساطِعٌ عَلَى
Real life evidence of this is	وَالدَّلِيلُ عَلَى هذا مِنْ واقِعِ الْحَياةِ هُوَ أَنَّ
What confirms this opinion and supports it are the words of... (name of a person)	وَمِمّا يُؤَكِّدُ هذا الرَّأْيَ وَيَدْعَمُهُ قَوْلُ (فُلانٌ)
Perhaps the best evidence of what (name of a person) said	وَلَعَلَّ خَيْرَ دَلِيلٍ عَلَى هذا ما قالَ (فُلانٌ)
And (name of a person) agrees with me in this opinion	وَيَتَّفِقُ مَعِي فِي هذا الرَّأْيِ (فُلانٌ)
I don't agree with this opinion because it seems to me that	وَلَسْتُ أَتَّفِقُ مَعَ هذا الرَّأْيِ إِذْ يَبْدُو لِي أَنَّ
The clearest evidence of my opinion are the words of (name of a person) in his book "xy" in	وَأَوْضَحُ دَلِيلٍ عَلَى ما أَذْهَبُ إِلَيْهِ قَوْلُ (فُلانٌ) فِي كِتابِهِ xy حَيْثُ يَقُولُ: zzz

which he says: "zzz"	وَقَوْلُ (فُلانٌ) فِي كِتابِهِ xy خَيْرُ دَلِيلٍ، حَيْثُ يَقُولُ: zzz

265. How do you express: cause and effect?

Cause and effect is a common method of organizing and discussing ideas. To determine **causes** (السَّبَبُ), you ask: *Why did this happen?* To identify **effects** (النَّتِيجةُ): *What happened because of this?* Let's see some examples in Arabic.

It is evident that; it is clear that	وَمِنْ هُنا يَتَّضِحُ أَنَّ
Thus, we conclude that	وَمِنْ ثَمَّ نَسْتَنْتِجُ أَنَّ
Hence, it is evident (clear) that	وَهٰكَذا يَتَّضِحُ أَنَّ
It is true to say that	وَعَلَى هٰذا يَصِحُّ أَنْ يُقالَ إِنَّ
It necessarily follows from this	وَيَنْتِجُ مِنْ هٰذا بِالضَّرُورةِ
This necessarily requires	وَيَقْتَضِي هٰذا بِالضَّرُورةِ
As a result of this	وَنَتِيجَةٌ لِهٰذا
For some reason or other	لِأَمْرٍ مَا or لِسَبَبٍ مَا or شَيْءٍ مَا or وَرَاءَ مَا يَحْدُثُ or شَيْءٌ مَا أَدَّى إِلَى
Though; although; even though	وَإِنْ (see below)
Accordingly, we can say that	وَعَلَى هٰذا يَصِحُّ القَوْلُ إِنَّ
We can conclude from this	وَيُمْكِنُ أَنْ يُسْتَنْتَجَ مِنْ هٰذا

so...	لِذا or لِهٰذا or لِذٰلِكَ
For this reason we can say that	وَلِهٰذا السَّبَبِ يُمْكِنُ الْقَوْلُ إِنَّ
And to explain it...	وَتَعْلِيلُ ذٰلِكَ
This goes back to	وَهٰذا راجِعٌ إِلَى or وَهٰذا عائِدٌ إِلَى
Perhaps the reason for this is that	وَلَعَلَّ السَّبَبَ فِي هٰذا أَنَّ

Excursus: How do you use وَإِنْ?

If it denotes *although*, it needs to be preceded by وَ. We call this device إِنْ الْوَصْلِيَّةُ. After وَإِنْ you use either (1) a **past tense verb** or (2) لَمْ **plus** verb in the jussive mood (مَجْزُومٌ) The same is true for وَلَوْ which also conveys the meaning of *although*.

Zayd, although he is rich, is stingy.	زَيْدٌ وَإِنْ كَثُرَ مالُهُ بَخِيلٌ.
He has guided you, although before, you were of those astray. *(Sura 2:198)*	هَداكُمْ وَإِنْ كُنتُم مِّن قَبْلِهِ لَمِنَ الضَّالِّينَ.
So invoke Allah [...], although the disbelievers dislike it. *(Sura 40:14)*	فَادْعُوا اللّٰهَ..وَلَوْ كَرِهَ الْكافِرُونَ.

266. How do you express: restatement?

Once you have presented your ideas in a paragraph, it is often useful to summarize or restate the main thought (إِعادَةُ تَقْرِيرِ الْفِكْرَةِ). Here are some expressions that might help.

in short	وَبِعِبارَةٍ مُوجَزَةٍ or وَبِعِبارَةٍ مُخْتَصَرَةٍ

briefly; concisely	وَبِإِيجَازٍ
Briefly, this means	وَيَعْنِي هٰذا فِي إِيجَازٍ or بِإِيجَازٍ هٰذا يَعْنِي or بِاخْتِصَارٍ
In other words	وَبِعِبارَةٍ أُخْرَى
It can be summarized as	وَيُمْكِنُ إِجْمالُ هٰذا فِي
To summarize this we can say that	وَإِيجازًا لِهٰذا يُمْكِنُ الْقَوْلُ إِنَّ
And the bottom line is that; all in all	وَخُلاصَةُ الْقَوْلِ أَنَّ
This means	وَمَعْنَى هٰذا or هٰذا يَعْنِي أَنَّ
To explain this idea I say that	وَإِيضاحًا لِهٰذِهِ الْفِكْرَةِ أَوَدُّ أَنْ أَقولَ إِنَّ

267. How do you express: conclusion?

If you have to write an article, these expressions might be useful to express a conclusion (الْخاتِمَةُ) and end it.

finally	وَخِتامًا or فِي الْخِتامِ or وَأَخِيرًا
in short; in sum; in conclusion; in essence	وَجُمْلةُ الْقَوْلِ إِنَّ or وَخُلاصةُ الْأَمْرِ أَنَّ
all in all; in a summary of the aforementioned	وَإِجْمالًا لِمَا سَبَقَ
So,	وَإِذَنْ or وَمِنْ ثَمَّ

To sum it up, I say that	وَعَلَى سَبِيلِ الْإِجْمَالِ أَقُولُ إِنَّ
In conclusion, I say that	وَفِي الْخِتَامِ أَقُولُ إِنَّ or أَوَدُّ أَنْ أَخْتِمَ بِالْقَوْلِ إِنَّ
I conclude by saying that this topic	وَأَخْتِمُ هذا الْمَوْضُوعَ بِقَوْلِي إِنَّ
And so we can say in conclusion	وَهكَذا يُمْكِنُ الْقَوْلُ فِي الْخِتَامِ إِنَّ
To conclude this article I say that	وَخِتَامًا لِهذا الْمَقَالِ أَقُولُ إِنَّ
At the end, and to summarize what's above, I say that	وَأُوثِرُ فِي الْخِتَامِ أَنْ أُوجِزَ مَا سَبَقَ فَأَقُولُ بِالْقَوْلِ إِنَّ

268. How do you express: time or place?

Oftentimes, you need to go back in time or jump virtually into the future to express ideas. If you want to make that clear, you need an indicator of time (الزَّمَانُ).

then; at the time (see question #228)	وَجِينَئِذٍ or وَعِنْدَئِذٍ or وَفِي ذلِكَ الْحِينِ
and then; subsequently	وَبَعْدَئِذٍ
at that time	وَوَقْتَئِذٍ or وَفِي ذلِكَ الْحِينِ
from then on; since (then)	مِنْ \ مُنْذُ ذلِكَ الْحِينِ
previously, formerly, earlier, before that	مِنْ قَبْلُ

afterwards; later (on)	فِيما بَعْدُ
following that; (immediately) after that	وَعَقِبَ ذٰلِكَ
what follows	ما يَلِي or وَهُوَ مَا تَبِعَهُ
in what follows	فِيما يَلِي
as follows	كَما يَلِي
immediately; right away	وَعَلَى الْفَوْرِ or فَوْرًا
since then	وَمُنْذُ ذٰلِكَ الْحِينِ or مُنْذُ ذٰلِكَ الْوَقْتِ
later in; at a later stage	وَفِي مَرْحَلَةٍ مُتَأَخِّرَةٍ
until	إِلَى أَنْ
until; up to	وَحَتَّى
(at the time) when	وَعِنْدَما
when; as; while	لَمّا
at the turn of the century	فِي مَطْلَعِ الْقَرْنِ or مَعَ إِطْلَالَةِ الْقَرْنِ

Sometimes you need to change the perspective of the narrator and switch positions and places (الْمَكانُ).

From a distance it looks like that	وَيَظْهَرُ عَلَى الْبُعْدِ وَكَأَنَّهُ or وَعَلَى مَسافَةٍ أَبْعَدَ يَظْهَرُ
up close/far; at a short/long distance (from a distance)	وَعَلَى مَسافَةٍ قَرِيبَةٍ / بَعِيدَةٍ

	عَنْ بُعْدٍ / قُرْبٍ
Taking a closer look at, it seems	وَيَبْدُو عَنْ قُرْبٍ
If we look closer/close enough	وَإِذَا دَقَّقْنَا النَّظَرَ
At first glance xy seems...	مِنْ خِلالِ النَّظْرَةِ الأُوْلَى يَبْدُو xy
And after a careful look, it appears (it appears through a closer look)	وَيَبْدُو مِنْ خِلالِ النَّظْرَةِ الْفاحِصةِ

269. How do you start emails and formal letters in Arabic?

Writing letters or emails in Arabic is not that difficult. Once you have started writing letters or emails, you will get used to the standard phrases pretty quickly. Never forget the most important rule: **try to be polite**!

The salutation (الْمُخاطَبةُ)

The key word is *mister* (سَيِّدٌ) and its plural forms.

plural	sing.	meaning	plural	sing.	meaning
سَيِّدَاتٌ	سَيِّدَةٌ	Miss	سادةٌ	سَيِّدٌ	Mister, Sir

Ladies and gentlemen!	(أَيُّها) السَّادَةُ وَالسَّيِّداتُ!

Phrases to start the letter

Thank you very much for your	جَزِيلُ الشُّكْرِ لِخِطابِكَ الرَّقِيقِ or

kind letter/message.	شُكْرًا جَزِيلًا عَلَى كَلِمَاتِكُمُ الرَّقِيقَةِ or أَلْفُ شُكْرٍ عَلَى رِسَالَتِكَ الرَّقِيقَةِ.
Thank you very much for your quick response, which I was very pleased to receive.	تَلَقَّيْتُ بِبَالِغِ السَّعَادَةِ رَدَّكَ الفَوْرِيُّ.
We thank you for your information which we found interesting.	نَحْنُ نَشْكُرُكُمْ عَلَى المَعْلُوماتِ الَّتِي نَهْتَمُّ بِمَعْرِفَتِها.
We thank you for your order.	نَحْنُ نَشْكُرُكُمْ عَلَى طَلَبِكُمْ.
Thank you very much for your offer dated 7th August.	شُكْرًا جَزِيلًا عَلَى العَرْضِ الَّذِي قَدَّمْتُمُوهُ يَوْمَ 7 أُغُسْطُس.
We thank you for your call.	نَحْنُ نَتَقَدَّم بِالشُّكْرِ الجَزِيلِ عَلَى مُكَالَمَتِكُمْ.
In response to your letter I hereby send...	رَدًّا عَلَى خِطابِكُمْ، أُرْسِلُ لَكُمْ...
We are happy to respond to your inquiry regarding...	نَوَدُّ أَنْ نَجِيبَ عَنْ إِسْتِفْسارِكُمْ بِشَأْنِ
In the absence of a contact address, I turn to you with a request to forward this letter to the right place.	نَظَرًا لِعَدَمِ وُجُودِ عُنْوانٍ لِلْاِتِّصال بِالمَكانِ المَطْلُوبِ، فَإِنِّي أَرْجُوكُمْ أَنْ تَبْعَثُوا بِهذا الخِطابِ إِلَى الجِهَةِ المُخْتَصَّةِ.
I would like to make the following reservation:	أَوَدُّ أَنْ أَحْجِزَ لَدَيْكُمْ كَما يَلِي:
Please tell us the rate for 3 double rooms with bathroom/WC, breakfast included, for the period of 5th to 8th August.	بِرَجاء إِبْلاغِنا بِسِعْرِ 3 غُرَفٍ مُزْدَوِجَةٍ بِالحَمامِ/التَّوالِيتِ وَبِالفَطُورِ فِي الفَتْرَةِ مِن 5-8 أُغُسْطُس.
Concerning your letter dated 4th	بِالإِشارَةِ إِلَى خِطابِكُمُ المُؤَرَّخ 4

August 2018, we are very sorry to inform you that we are not able to…	أُغُسْطُس لِهذا الْعامِ يُؤْسِفُنا أَنْ نُبْلِغَ حَضْرَتَكَ أَنَّنا لا نَسْتَطيعُ أَنْ...
Unfortunately, I have to complain about the poor service of your hotel during my last stay.	إِنَّهُ يُؤْسِفُني أَنْ أَشْكُو لِسِيادَتِكُمْ سُوءَ الْخِدْمَةِ في فُنْدُقِكُمْ وَالَّذي تَعَرَّضْتُ لَهُ خِلالَ فَتْرَةِ إِقامَتي الْأَخيرَةِ لِدَيْكُمْ.

270. How do you end emails and formal letters in Arabic?

The conventional ending (الْخِتامُ) in Arabic letters or emails is usually a very polite expression. In the last part of your message, you may use some of the following examples.

Could you inform me about the formalities and provide me with the necessary forms?	هَلْ يُمْكِنُ أَنْ تُمِدُّوني بِمَعْلُوماتٍ عَنْ شَكْلِيّاتٍ مُحْتَمَلَةٍ, وَأَنْ تُرْسِلُوا لي الْإِسْتِماراتِ الْمَطْلُوبَةَ كَذلِكَ؟
We would be very grateful for your information concerning that matter.	سَنَكُونُ في غايَةِ الْإِمْتِنانِ لِسِيادَتِكُمْ لِلْمَعْلُوماتِ الْخاصَّةِ بِهذا الشَّأْنِ.
Attached you will find a photocopy of...	مُرْفَقٌ بِهذا الْخِطابِ صُورَةٌ لِ
I once again apologize for the inconvenience caused to you and promise you that such mistakes will not happen again.	أَنا أَعْتَذِرُ مَرَّةً أُخْرَى عَنِ الْمُضايَقاتِ النّاجِمَةِ عَنْ ذلِكَ, وَأَعِدُكُمْ بِأَنَّ هذِهِ الْأَخْطاءَ لَنْ تَتَكَرَّرَ مَرَّةً أُخْرَى.
The deadline has now expired, and we expect the immediate settlement of the above men-	وَلَقَدْ إِنْتَهَتْ هذِهِ الْمُدَّةُ, وَنَحْنُ نَنْتَظِرُ السَّدادَ الْفَوْرِيَّ لِلْفاتُورَةِ

tioned invoice/bill.	الْمَذْكُورَةِ أَعْلَاهُ.
We are looking forward to your answer.	نَحْنُ نَنْتَظِرُ رَدَّكُمْ بِشَغَفٍ.
If you have any questions about these changes, please do not hesitate to contact us.	إِذَا كَانَ لَدَيْكُمْ أَيُّ اِسْتِفْسَارَاتٍ عَنْ هَذِهِ التَّغْيِيرَاتِ فَلَا تَتَرَدَّدُوا أَنْ تَلْجَأُوا إِلَيْنَا.
You can reach us by phone (1234). I will be in your area next week and could talk to you on this occasion.	يُمْكِنُكُمُ الِاتِّصَالُ بِنَا فِي رَقَمِ التِّلِيفُونِ 1234, إِذْ إِنِّي سَأَكُونَ فِي الْأُسْبُوعِ الْمُقْبِلِ فِي مِنْطَقَتِكُمْ, وَبِإِمْكَانِي التَّحَدُّثُ مَعَكُمْ.
Therefore, we would like to ask you to clarify the matter in the interest of our future business relationships.	وَلِذَلِكَ نَوَدُّ مِنْ سِيَادَتِكُمْ تَوْضِيحًا لِهَذِهِ الظَّاهِرَةِ لِمَصْلَحَةِ عَلَاقَاتِنَا التِّجَارِيَّةِ الْمُسْتَقْبَلِيَّةِ.
We'd like to ask you to correct the matter as soon as possible.	وَنَوَدُّ إِصْلَاحَ مَوْقِفِكُمْ بِأَسْرَعِ وَقْتٍ مُمْكِنٍ.

Conventional ending

With kind regards; yours sincerely and respectfully	مَعَ فَائِقِ التَّقْدِيرِ وَالِاحْتِرَامِ or تَفَضَّلُوا بِقُبُولِ فَائِقِ الِاحْتِرَامِ or صَدِيقَتُكَ الْمُخْلِصُ
With infinite gratitude	وَلَكُمْ مِنِّي جَزِيلُ الشُّكْرِ وَالِامْتِنَانِ
With the most sincere expressions of gratitude and consideration	مَعَ أَخْلَصِ عِبَارَاتِ الشُّكْرِ وَالتَّقْدِيرِ

GLOSSARY OF ENGLISH GRAMMAR TERMS

adjective; attribute	الصِّفةُ، النَّعْتُ	Words that describe. For example: a *nice* girl, the *big* house.
adverb	الظَّرْفُ	Any word, phrase, or clause that tells you how, when, where, or why: he drove *quickly*; he came *after the appointment*; he entered *smiling*.
		What we call in English an adverb could be in Arabic a: مَفْعُولٌ فِيهِ, مَفْعُولٌ لَهُ, حالٌ, etc.
apposition	الْبَدَلُ	Two noun phrases next to each other, and they refer to the same person or thing. Usually we can reverse the order of the phrases. For example: Michael, their oldest child, is... Their oldest child, Michael, is...
agreement	الْمُطابَقةُ	Shows that a word hangs together with a particular noun – in English, a word may agree in number and gender (sometimes in person) with another noun. In Arabic, you have to pay attention to "harmonize" the case and determination as well.
clause	الْجُمْلةُ	There are basically two types: main clauses and subordinate clauses, which are sentences nested inside the larger sentence and joined by certain grammatical devices such as conjunctions: He said (that) *you are beautiful*. A clause is a group of words that consists of a subject and a verb. A phrase is a collection of words without having a subject.

		What in English would be a clause could be in Arabic a phrase and vice versa.
comparative; superlative; elative	إسْمُ التَّفْضِيلِ	Denotes *more, most; better, best, etc.* Note: The elative is a stage of gradation that can be used to express comparatives or superlatives.
construct phrase; possessive construction	الإِضافةُ	Two Arabic words side by side, like English *the teacher's house.* In order to convert an English construction into Arabic, use this formula: English *B's A* = Arabic *A of B.* (teacher's house = house of the teacher = بَيْتُ الْمُدَرِّس).
declension (inflection); declinable; indeclinable	الإِعْرابُ, التَّصْريفُ	A process which involves changing the form of a word: of nouns, pronouns, adjectives, adverbs, numerals, and articles to indicate number (singular and plural), case or mood (nominative, genitive, accusative case; indicative, subjunctive, jussive mood), and/or gender. Usually achieved by adding prefixes, suffixes, case markers (not in English).
definite article	أَداةُ التَّعْريفِ	Simply said, it is the word *the* in English.
demonstrative	إسْمُ الإِشارة	They single out: *this* book, *that* girl (demonstrative determiners); tell me *this,* what's *that?* (demonstrative pronouns).
ellipsis; supposition; assumption	التَّقْديرُ تَقْديرُ الْحَذْفِ	In a way that is not directly expressed; tacitly. It means that a part of the sentence has been omitted because it is implied. In Arabic, we often use this concept to explain cases, missing words, etc. But it is

		also found in English? Yes. For example: Question: *Why did you go to Egypt?* Answer: *To study Arabic.* Here, the implied part is: *Because I wanted to study Arabic.* This element is implicitly understood, so we can leave it out and use the infinitive on its own.
imperative	الْأَمْرُ	A verb form expressing a request or demand: *Stop* that car! *Drink!*
masculine (feminine)	الْمُذَكَّرُ الْمُؤَنَّثُ	Arabic nouns have a gender, either masculine or feminine. The gender is not necessarily connected with male or female.
mood	صِيغةُ الْأَفْعالِ	The mood or purpose of a sentence is related to its *form*. Tense is a form as well an idea. The past tense, e.g., can express time or an idea (conditional mood). When a sentence makes a statement, it is in the indicative mood (فَعْلٌ مَرْفُوعٌ). Possible Arabic moods are *indicative* (مَرْفُوعٌ), *subjunctive* (مَنْصُوبٌ), *jussive* (مَجْزُومٌ).
object	الْمَفْعُولُ	The object of a verb is the person or thing undergoing the action. For ex., I wrote *the book.* Arabic knows various types of objects which function as *dependent nouns* (الْمَنْصُوباتُ) and get the accusative case (مَنْصُوبٌ).
ordinal number	الْعَدَدُ التَّرْتِيبِيُّ	Indicate order by number: *first, forth.*
participle (active and	إسْمُ الفاعِلِ	They are called participle because they "participate" the properties of both a verb and an adjective. Usually you identify

passive)	إسم الْمِفْعُولِ	them by the ending: -*ing* or -*ed*. The participles of *to write* are *writing* (active = present participle) and *written* (passive = past participle). In English, a participle plays a role similar to an adjective or adverb (a *written* letter). In Arabic, participles can do many jobs in a sentence.
		The whole concept is different in English. The *past* participle is often what we would call the *passive* participle in Arabic: The food was *eaten*.
passive voice	صِيغَةُ الْمَبْنِيِّ لِلْمَجْهُولِ	The passive is used to show interest in the person (or thing) that *experiences* an action rather than the person/thing that *performs* the action (active voice). E.g.: My car *was stolen*.
plural	الْجَمْعُ	Indicates more than one: book vs. *books*
possessive pronoun	ضَمِيرُ الْمِلْكِيّةِ	Indicates to whom or what something belongs or relates. For example, *my* book.
prefix	السّابِقةُ	Bits or devices added before a word – future tense prefixes, noun prefixes, ...
preposition	حَرْفُ الْجَرِّ	Short words (in Arabic sometimes just letters) indicating an object or when, where, how, etc. For ex.: *to* John, *for* you, *with* Sarah, *under* the tree, *after* that. What we call in English a preposition might be in Arabic an adverb.
pronoun	الضَّمِيرُ	They stand in for a specific noun: *they, them, this, someone, who, what*. Personal pronouns denote *I, you, he, she*, ...

regent governor; operator	الْعَامِلُ	Government in grammar is the control by words over other words. It defines the relationship between words (agent and patient). A regent/operator has the power to govern other words and triggers a case or state/mood to describe that relationship.
reflexive verb	فِعْلُ الْمُطَاوَعةِ	Such verbs denote doing something to oneself: he killed *himself*.
relative clause	صِلةُ الْمَوْصُولِ	They add information about a noun: the book *that I wrote* has 770 pages.
root	الْجِذْرُ	Arabic words are based on skeletons of consonants (usually three) from which Arabic words are built.
singular	الْمُفْرَدُ	Indicates one: *book* vs. books.
subject	الْفَاعِلُ الْمُبْتَدَأُ	Subject of sentences are the nouns doing the action (nouns with which the verbs agree). *The dog* bites the post man.
suffix	اللَّاحِقةُ	Bits or devices attached as word endings: dog*s*, mov*able*.
tense	الزَّمَنُ	They determine the form of a verb expressing past, present, and future **time**.
verbs	الْفِعْلُ	Verbs indicate actions (rarely states): to eat, to talk, to love.
vocative	النّداءُ	A form of direct address to indicate the person or thing addressed. For example, *Have mercy, O Lord!*

ISLAMIC SALUTATIONS AFTER CERTAIN NAMES

After mentioning Allah, Muhammad, Islamic prophets or companions of Muhammad, Muslims are supposed to praise them by uttering specific expressions. I don't use these expressions in the book, however, Muslims are supposed to say them. Here is a list of phrases that are used after certain names:

ALLAH (اللّٰهُ): After mentioning Allah, Muslims say *subhānahu wa taʿālā* (سُبْحانَهُ وَتَعالَى) which means: *Glorious and exalted is He (Allah)*. This is exclusively used with Allah. Abbreviation in English texts: SWT.

MUHAMMAD (مُحَمَّدٌ): After mentioning the Prophet's name, Muslims say *sallā Allāhu ʿalayhi wa sallam(a)* (صَلَّى اللّٰهُ عَلَيْهِ وَسَلَّمَ). It means: *Allah bless him and grant him peace*.

You may also hear: *(May) Allah pray for him and save him!* The abbreviation is, SAAS or SAAW or in its English translation: *peace be upon him* (PBUH).

MESSENGERS, PROPHETS and ARCHANGELS: After their names, Muslims say: *ʿalayhi al-Salām* (عَلَيْهِ السَّلامُ) which means: *Peace be upon him*. It is said after mentioning, e.g. Noah (نُوحٌ) or Gabriel (جِبْرِيلُ). Abbreviation in English: AS.

COMPANIONS (الصَّحابةُ) of the Prophet Muhammad: After mentioning one of Muhammad's companions, Muslims say the wish *radiya Allāhu ʿanhu* (رَضِيَ اللّٰهُ عَنْهُ).

It means: *May Allah be pleased with them*. This is said, for example, after Muhammad's father-in-law ʾAbū Bakr (أَبُو بَكْرٍ) or Muhammad's wife ʿĀʾisha (عائِشةُ بِنْتُ أَبِي بَكْرٍ). Abbreviation in English: RA.

INDEX

Printed in the USA
CPSIA information can be obtained
at www.ICGtesting.com
LVHW020138161123
764024LV00015B/83/J

CPSIA information can be obtained
at www.ICGtesting.com
Printed in the USA
BVHW03*1654310518
517795BV00009BA/74/P

9 781118 487570